915.46
ROWELL

Rowell, Galen A
     In the throne room of the mountain
gods / by Galen Rowell. -- San
Francisco : Sierra Club Books,
[1977]
          p.   cm.

     Includes index.
     ISBN 0-87156-184-0

          EUREKA-HUMBOLDT LIBRARY

     1. Karakorum Range--Description
and travel. 2. Mountaineering. I.
Title.

DS485.K2R68   915.4'6

                                          76-21248
                                              CIP
Library of Congress
07535   n(815296   © THE BAKER & TAYLOR CO.   7187

IN THE THRONE ROOM OF THE MOUNTAIN GODS

In the
Throne Room
of the Mountain
Gods

Galen Rowell

SIERRA CLUB BOOKS

San Francisco   1977

In memory of LEIF-NORMAN PATTERSON,
the best of us,
who died in an avalanche in his home mountains
just as this book was going to press

The Sierra Club, founded in 1892 by John Muir, has devoted itself to the study and protection of the nation's scenic and ecological resources—mountains, wetlands, woodlands, wild shores and rivers. All club publications are part of the nonprofit effort the club carries on as a public trust. There are some 50 chapters coast to coast, in Canada, Hawaii and Alaska. Participation is invited in the club's program to enjoy and preserve wilderness everywhere. Address: 530 Bush Street, San Francisco, California 94108.

Library of Congress Cataloging in Publication Data

Rowell, Galen A
   In the throne room of the mountain gods.

   Includes index.
   1. Karakoram Range—Description and travel.
2. Mountaineering. I. Title.
DS485.K2R68 915.4'6 76-21248
ISBN 0-87156-184-0

Book design by Anita Walker Scott

Production by David Charlsen & Others

Printed in the United States of America

Contents

Acknowledgments

Without the assistance of many people, this book would have been just another expedition narrative. I am deeply indebted to the following members of the 1975 American K2 Expedition team whose diaries provided broad perspectives on every event: Leif-Norman Patterson, Dianne Roberts, Rob Schaller, Fred Stanley, Jim Whittaker, Lou Whittaker, and especially Jim Wickwire, who recorded 280 pages of detailed information on every facet of the journey. Steve Marts, our cinematographer, did not keep a diary, but his many tape recordings of conversations proved invaluable. The broader story of the year 1975 in the Karakoram could not have been written without input, through conversation or correspondence, from those who were there: Mo Anthoine, Simone Badier, Will Barker, Martin Boysen, Joe Brown, Linda Burdet, Yvon Chouinard, Michael Covington, Peter Habeler, Peter Hackett, Dennis Hennek, Eduard Koblmuller, George Lowe, Ian McNaught-Davis, Reinhold Messner, Dave Potts, Doug Scott, Allen Steck, Giacomo Stefani, Lito Tejada-Flores, John Thune, and Jack Turner. More information on that Karakoram season came from H. Adams Carter, editor of the *American Alpine Journal;* Uschi Messner, Reinhold Messner's wife; and Ken Wilson, editor of *Mountain* magazine. Many important documents concerning past American Karakoram expeditions were located by Frank de la Vega of the American Alpine Club, and those yellowing pages later came to life during discussions with the people who had lived the events: Bob Bates, Nick Clinch, Bob Craig, Charlie Houston, Dee Molenaar, and Fritz Wiessner. I am especially indebted to Charlie Houston for the loan of a tape recording made at K2 base camp in 1953, during which each team member described his impressions of the tragedy on the mountain. I am no less indebted to Fritz Wiessner for use of his 1939 diary.

Most photographs in this book have been selected from 15,000 taken by our 1975 K2 team. Due credit goes beyond the individuals who clicked the shutters to the fairy godmother of our photography, *National Geographic* magazine. They graciously provided not only film and processing, but also assistance, advice, and a tenth of the expedition's cost. When we returned without a success story, they promptly gave us back our material with full rights. In every way they managed to consider our interests in front of their own. Without their efforts we would not have achieved either the quantity or the quality of our results.

Last, but certainly not least, I wish to thank those who helped give the drafted manuscript direction: Jon Beckmann, my editor at Sierra Club Books, who saved the reader from more pages and excessive philosophizing; Margaret Rowell, my mother, whose eye for continuity is as sharp for language as is her ear for music; and Carol Rowell, my wife, who was not only my most patient critic throughout fifteen months of writing, but also my single protector from the well-meant but ruinous onslaughts of friends, telephones, dogs, and children.

G.R.

Albany, California
October 1976

viii

Preface

This book was originally conceived as an account of one of the largest mountaineering endeavors in recent decades. In the time-honored tradition it was planned to proceed from organization, personnel, and approach march toward the summit of a single mountain in a single year. That concept changed when the 1975 American K2 Expedition failed in its attempt to make a new route up K2, the world's second highest mountain, located in the Karakoram Himalaya of Pakistan.

We began the expedition with two convictions—that we would climb K2, and that we would tell the whole story. We would not allow the summit to make storybook heroes out of complex personalities. The entire team agreed to "tell it like it was," and to keep diaries that could be used by the writer of the expedition book. Yet we realized that this very agreement might color what was to be set down in those diaries. Thoughts to be read by others would naturally be less intimate than those generally recorded in diaries. To preserve spontaneity, we arranged that each writer could submit a copy of only selected parts of his journal to the author of the book, keeping private what he or she saw fit.

This approach to the diaries worked admirably. Words that we hid from each other as we wrote in stormbound tents seemed less private when the expedition was over, and more than 99 percent of the diary contents were submitted. Here was a great body of information on a group of climbers interacting with each other under conditions of unusual stress in the shadow of the highest cluster of peaks on earth. But there was no single meaning to tie it together. That problem bothered me as I read the dozens of books about previous Karakoram expeditions and accounts of the nineteen expeditions that visited the K2 region in 1975. Each had a unique story, but something was lacking.

If we were not to chronicle a summit conquest, a more unusual opportunity soon became apparent: could I use our expedition to pull together threads of mountaineering history? For this task, the year 1975 in the Karakoram was ideally suited. For the first time in fifteen years, major expeditions traveled to the great group of peaks surrounding K2. The end of a political closure brought a flood of climbers from different countries. Some succeeded, and many failed. More than a decade of technical advancements and social change were introduced to the region in a single season.

Mountains are frontiers without civilization or permanent social order. As Bernard DeVoto wrote, "A historian does not speak of the frontier's tastes and preferences. The historian sees the frontier as many different places in many different stages of development, inhabited by many people with many different kinds and degrees of culture, intelligence, racial tradition, family training, and individual capacity." Yet each expedition book showed the Karakoram through the narrow frame of its particular experience. Success vindicated a wide variety of methods. The reader had no context in which to judge a single expedition's experiences.

There is no one right way to climb a mountain. The best methods are those closely matched to the styles and abilities of individual teams, and the structure of this book provides a means of comparing mountain adventures. Chapters narrating the American K2 attempt are alternated with chapters describing other people's experiences in the same region or on the same mountain. Our expedition becomes a focus for the larger story of a decisive year in the history of a mountain, a land, and the sport of high-altitude climbing.

Reading the book, you will see an obvious paradox. Large expeditions offer better odds for both success and for the possibility for interpersonal conflict. Small expeditions trade security for spontaneity. Financial backers favor big expeditions for their higher probability of victory, while the great majority of Himalayan climbers, given a choice, would prefer to go with a small group of friends.

The day-to-day life of our expedition may seem dangerous and fearful, but fear comes to climbers only when the team or the man is temporarily out of control. When a person drives an auto on a two-lane highway, he is seldom gripped by the fear that a slight motion of the steering wheel to the left will result in instant death in a head-on collision; nor do climbers live in constant fear that a misstep will end their lives. Through knowledge and understanding of the mountain environment and their personal limits, climbers find a sense of freedom and joy where the uninitiated might find only terror.

Most expedition books at some point begin to sound alike. This book and the mode of its writing attempt a new route by showing the vastly different experiences of many who found themselves in the same place, during the same eventful span of time. The spectacle of mountaineering on the Karakoram's great peaks will gradually grow through native peoples and creatures, pioneering explorers, and various climbs on K2, culminating in the wildest year in the history of the range.

My task as author was to distill the most significant, most revealing impressions from a wide range of sources on Karakoram expeditions. Each writer of a book, article, or diary has his own point of view; thus, in the historical sections of this work I have reflected the opinions of my sources, while, although other voices are strong, the narrative of the 1975 K2 effort inevitably reflects my own point of view.

Section I

Discovery

It may be wondered why so high a peak has no name. The reason is that, though high, it is not visible from any inhabited place. It is hidden away in a remote mountain region behind other peaks of almost as great magnitude. . . . There is no village within six days' travel of K2 on either side, and, consequently, until it was fixed by observation of the Survey, it was unknown.

—SIR FRANCIS YOUNGHUSBAND

Chiring *Glacier*

Changtok
23260

76° 15'

Moni
Brangsa

SINKIANG CHINA

20000

Nera
▲ 20800

SARPO

LAGGO

GLACIER

19880

20480

16600

20310

21400

Approximate
international
boundary

Mustagh La
17800

Pyramid
22100

Moni La

Mustagh
Tower
23860

35°
50'

Sarpo Laggo
Pass
18520

Moni

Glacier

Biange (Younghusband)

▲ 22080

KASHMIR   PAKISTAN

Lobsang
20420

Mustagh

Chagaran

Glacier

Glacier

21070

Surgus Glacier

Dunge

Glacier

Biale

Glacier

Borum Glacier

Trango
Tower

Nameless
Tower
20530

18720

Choricho Glacier

Trango

Glacier

18870

BALTORO

Biange
14500

22160 ▲

19260

Uli Biaho
Tower
19957

Urdukas
13000

Uli Biaho

Glacier

Paiyu
21658

Liliwa
12000

Yermanendu

Glacier

Biarchedi
22180

11000

Paiyu

Liliwa

Glacier

Urdukas
20890

Mundi

Glacier

35°
40'

Bardomal

Biaho

River

Masherbrum
25660

Masherbrum La
17600

Liliwa
20510

Serac
22000

Aling

Glacier

Masherbrum

Glacier

Chundogero

Glacier

©1977 by Dee Molenaar. Not to
be reproduced in whole or in part
without written permission.

76° 15'

76° 30'
76° 45'

22500

K2
NORTH GLACIER

Skyang Kangri
(Staircase)
24750

hongtar
4050

Savoia
Pass
20400

North Ridge

2

Windy Gap
21300

Skyang Liangpa Glacier

SHAKSGAM RIVER

21380

23160

1
19000

Northwest Ridge

East Ridge

K2
28741
Shoulder

Abruzzi Ridge

21970

17110

nma-ri
329

Southwest Ridge
South Ridge

De Filippi Glacier

GODWIN - AUSTEN GLACIER

Krarut Glacier

Sella Pass
20207

Base
Camp
17600

Negrotto Glacier

The Angelus
22490

Savoia Glacier

Gilkey-Solda
Memorial

26017

North Gasherbrum Glacier

Gasherbrum Glacier

SINKIANG CHINA

35° 50'

24110

20500

Broad Pk
26400

22740

18400

20250

Khalkhal Glacier

Crystal
20460

Marble
20088

17160

Chagbartung

Urdok Glacier

21300

22720

Sgan Glacier

20800

shoro

IV 26180

III 26090

II 26360

Concordia
15000

West Gasherbrum Glacier

V 24013

22560

South Gasherbrum Glacier

East Gasherbrum Gl

GASHERBRUM

Gasherbrum La
21326

GROUP

Gasherbrum I
(Hidden Pk)
26470

GLACIER

Biarchedi Glacier

Mitre
19700

Naurling Glacier

18980

UPPER

BALTORO

VI 22976

Duke of Abruzzi Glacier

Urdok
23950

Vigne Glacier

22800

GLACIER

16380

20500

Baltoro Kangri
(Golden Throne)
23983

Pioneer Pk
22867

Indira Col
18950

Sia Kangri
(Queen Mary Pk)
24350

Conway
Saddle
20670

Kondus Glacier

35° 40'

22480

KASHMIR PAKISTAN

Kondus
Saddle
21000

Chogolisa
(Bride Pk)
25110

Chogolisa
Saddle
19300

Kaberi Glacier

Chogolisa Glacier

76° 30'

76° 45'

THE BALTORO REGION Karakoram Himalaya
Kashmir Pakistan and Sinkiang China

Shown are routes and camps of 1975 American K2 Expedition

Map drawn for Sierra Club Books, from AMS 1:250,000 quadrangles
MUNDIK and CHULUNG (1962), with modifications from ERTS
photographs and from interpretation of ground-level photographs.

0   1   2   3   4   5 MILES
0   1   2   3   4   5   6   7   8 KILOMETERS
To convert feet to meters, multiply by 0.3048

1 The Herdsman

The herdsman turned around for a last look at his home village. The stone huts were barely visible against the brown landscape. Summer was months away but the hillsides were already bare of snow. A brown cloud hovered over the goat herd and new circles of dust rose from every moving hoof. He had never seen a spring so early or so dry.

Others in the village had talked of such years in the past. They said that the fruit and wheat would still grow because water never stopped flowing from the ice-streams-that-were-always-there. But the seasonal snow that watered many of the high meadows would have already melted, and grazing would be sparse. The herdsman would have to search for new pastures.

The man blended well with his herd. Like the goats, he walked with a short, lively gait. His loose garments were made from their hair; his moccasins from their hide. He drank their milk and ate their meat. The herdsman and his animals moved as one body, walking and living together for months on end. When he talked to his goat friends he addressed them each as "Sir," but in his village he always addressed his human friends as "you."

Village on the Braldu River

Askole, the herdsman's village, was perched on a terrace above the Braldu, a river that pushed forth from an ugly black hole at the end of an ice stream. Other villages dotted the banks of the Braldu below Askole, but none lay above. The elders talked of the ancient times when the ice stream lay just around the bend from the village.

To the herdsman ice streams seemed like sleeping bears. Mostly they lay still, but sometimes they moved with deep rumbling sounds. Sometimes they went away altogether and a high pasture would dry up. The elders in the village knew how to make new ice streams. In the fall they carried up parts of a *man* ice stream and a *woman* ice stream to the barren rock cradle where the other had disappeared. There they placed the *man* and the *woman* parts together. Under the white blanket of winter a new ice stream would come to life.

The herdsman began his search for better pastures by following a well-worn trail into the mountains. Beyond the tilled fields the path swung toward sheer cliffs, forced inward by the wide arc of the Braldu. At the narrowest point he passed a stone tower built as a

Peaks of the lower Baltoro during storm

defense against men from Hunza, who periodically raided the villages of the Braldu. Beyond the tower the trail was etched into the cliff above the swirling river, sometimes overhanging the river on a carpet of rock slabs held in place with sticks.

He descended to a wide plain near the river's edge. Only a few clumps of sagebrush broke the barren monotony of the sandy plateau. During most springs the land was alive with grass and wildflowers and his animals normally fed here for a month. But now he found only a few days' worth of grazing.

At the end of the plateau an ice stream flowed from a side canyon, nearly damming the Braldu. It was named Biafo, or chicken's wing, because the campsites along its edge were located under overhanging rocks that gave one the impression of being sheltered by a giant wing. The ice itself was covered with heaps of loose rock. The herdsman looked at the Biafo with foreboding, not because he feared traveling on it, but because it was the route of his enemies. For centuries, tall raiders from Hunza and Nagar had traveled more than seventy miles over ice to attack the meek people of the Braldu. The herdsman had no intention of walking the Biafo in search of greener pastures.

The man and his herd slept near the Biafo, and another day's walking brought them to the junction of the Braldu and the Panmah, a river which led toward a pass named Mustagh La. The

The Herdsman 5

herdsman decided not to follow the Panmah because it too was a known route of the raiders. His people traveled it rarely and only in small groups without animals.

For two more days the herdsman marched his goats up the valley of the Braldu. Then, rounding a corner he saw the river's source. Instead of beginning as a trickle of water running down a hillside, the river leapt full blown out of a grotesque black hole in the snout of an ice stream which his people called Baltoro Gang. On the left bank was a grazing ground long known to his people. His trained eye saw far less vegetation than normal. Already, wild sheep and goats had devoured the best forage. What was left would not last long.

The grazing ground was called Paiyu Brangsa, the "camping place of the salt." Much of the earth was coated with a white salt deposited from mineral springs. The animals were attracted by the natural salt-lick, and the herdsman found peace in the shade of cottonwood trees that followed the stream. For many days the man and his goats languished at Paiyu.

One day the herdsman pursued wild sheep up a steep hillside but he was unsuccessful. Only by working in a team with other men could he hope to kill one of the elusive creatures. His supply of *atta*, or wheat flour, was running low. Soon he might have to kill one of his goats for food. He wondered how many of his goats would have to be slaughtered before the next snows. The thinner the goats became, the more he would have to kill.

The herdsman had never been on the ice of the Baltoro, but he had heard old men in his village talk about it. Once there had been a trade route through here to China across the pass known as old Mustagh La. But an ice stream had moved, blocking the pass, and new Mustagh La, up the Panmah, was no good for animals. The herdsman wondered if there was another way across the mountains. What was on the other side? Perhaps there was better forage for his animals.

He did not know the meaning of the word Baltoro. It may have had the same lost root as the names of his land and his people. His homeland was called Baltistan and his people were called Baltis. They had no written language and no recorded history. Their deeds were no more than memories: clear for a week, fading in a year, and all but gone in a decade. Still, the past, neither understood nor questioned, acted as an unseen keel for lives that would otherwise drift aimlessly.

The herdsman could not have known that his Balti language was a distant Tibetan dialect, unintelligible to modern Tibetans but retaining many ancient sounds of that language. And although his features were basically Caucasian, the hints of Oriental folds above his eyes were similar to those of the people of Tibet whom he had never seen.

At Paiyu Brangsa the herdsman slept inside a stone hut. One night he was awakened by the loud bleating of his goats. He rushed out into the darkness but could find nothing wrong. Soon his animals were calm again. In the morning one goat was missing from the herd. The tracks of a snow leopard came within a few feet of his door. The herdsman spent all day building a stone fence around the front of the hut. He fashioned a gate from juniper branches. That night he moved his animals into this makeshift corral and slept near the gate with a wooden club in his hands. The night was peaceful and clear. His animals were undisturbed.

Several nights passed without incident, but the herdsman worried. Every morning he found fresh tracks of the snow leopard and once, by the stream, he saw the man-like footprints of a brown bear. "Paiyu Brangsa is no good this year," he thought. "It must be Allah's will that I find new pastures."

The herdsman drove his animals toward the edge of the Baltoro Glacier, pausing for a prayer before setting foot on the ice. His Muslim faith raised conflicting emotions about his decision to leave the traditional grazing lands and travel on the ice stream. On the one hand he believed that life was *inshallah*, the will of Allah. Only *He* could alter the world. Human effort could not change things. On the other hand, perhaps *He* had already chosen to alter the world. There was no snow. The pastoral lands were no longer supporting livestock. Perhaps it was Allah's will that he search for new pastures. The older men of his village would have helped him decide how best to follow the divine pleasure. But they were not there. He was alone with his animals.

For miles he marched over ice which had been pressured into swells and folds. Nowhere was there a level stretch to ease walking. Loose rocks moved at every step. The herdsman and his goats were tiny creatures caught in a giant ice maze. The seemingly simplest passages often dead-ended abruptly against an ice cliff or a raging

Balti herdsman

torrent, and the herd would have to retreat and start anew. By evening they had made little progress. Across the glacier, only a few miles away, the brown hillsides of Paiyu Brangsa were still close.

He slept by a stream at the edge of the glacier while his animals fed on the few sparse plants. The next day was similar to the first. All day he marched on the icy labyrinth, slipping and sliding on loose stones. That evening he reached Urdukas, an old camping place on the abandoned Mustagh La trade route. In contrast to Paiyu Brangsa, the hillsides were green. Flowers and bushes clung to steep, gravelly slopes left behind by an ancient retreat of the ice stream. The place was littered with granite boulders. Under the largest was a cave where the herdsman spent the night.

In the morning it was raining. Clouds hung low in the canyon of the Baltoro, forming a white blanket that enveloped the dark, debris-covered glacier. The herdsman did not know that he was being given a vision of the past. Long before his people had walked the Baltoro on the ancient route to China, ice had filled the canyon in much the same fashion as the lowering clouds did now. As he ascended the glacier with his herd, the air grew colder, the sky grew darker, and the ice from the side canyons grew whiter with every mile. He was entering a realm as foreign to humans as the oceans and the skies. No men lived there. It was the domain of the snow leopard, the ibex, and the bear.

The clouds disappeared and morning sunlight shone on the snow-plastered cliffs across the Baltoro. The herdsman did not know that these were among the largest granite towers in the world. His world was small indeed; it encompassed only the Braldu River and its tributaries. He was dimly aware that other worlds existed beyond his own, but he had not given much thought to them.

The herdsman and his animals headed across the ice toward Mustagh La, not to cross the pass, but to camp at Sharagan, an old stopping place for caravans traveling to Chinese Turkestan. They crossed the wide Baltoro, traveled upward a few miles, and turned into a side canyon. There, perched on a grassy slope, were the ruins of more than twenty huts. Nearby was a large flat area where polo matches on foot had once been held between his people and the Yarkandis from across the mountains. Above was Mustagh La, blocked by a steep and broken ice wall. The herdsman stayed at Sharagan for several days. He rested while his animals renewed themselves on the luxuriant grasses. But the forage was limited; it covered only a small area. They could not stay indefinitely. He wondered how many days it would take to cross the mountains by traveling up the Baltoro. "Inshallah," he told himself. "It is the will of Allah that a route will be provided. Why else would Allah have led me into these mountains?"

The next day the herdsman and his goats headed for the end of the Baltoro ice stream. They could see it in the distance. The ice stopped against a giant mountain called Gasherbrum, the beautiful peak. All day they traveled, but like a rainbow, Gasherbrum seemed to recede with each step. At night the herdsman camped on the ice, shivering with his bleating goats. In the morning they set off again.

Balti at Urdukas

The glacier widened as they walked, and Gasherbrum slowly dropped from view behind a ridge. Random bumps and swells in the ice gave way to parallel, rockstrewn ridges. He felt as if he were walking the ribs of a giant monster. He saw that the Baltoro did not end against Gasherbrum. It just split in two directions.

Eagerly he pressed on, hoping to round a corner and find that the icy carpet plunged into a green paradise below. When he finally could see around the corner, he was deeply disappointed. Ice climbed ever higher in both directions, and a mountain, larger than any he had ever seen, rose into the sky in a single thrust. For the first time he felt fear. Had Allah failed him? Or had he failed Allah? His journey had been inspired by a forlorn hope; now he could see that it was a godforsaken venture. Would his family forgive him for trying such a thing? Perhaps he should not tell them.

He rested in a wide amphitheater. It was rimmed by giant peaks and surrounded by ice streams descending from every massif. Each stream contributed another leg to the monster body of the Baltoro. He could see other Gasherbrums behind the one that had nearly disappeared from view. The two major ice streams that divided at the base of that mountain each headed toward separate big peaks.

Trail above Askole

For several hours the herdsman sat quietly in the amphitheater, opening his senses to Allah's command. When it failed to come, he watched the great mountain that blocked his progress. At first sight it had risen in a shimmering pyramid, etched sharply against an indigo sky. Now grayness crept in slowly and the highlights disappeared. Soon the summit was hidden under a bulging dirty-white cloud the shape and color of the goat-hair cap on the herdsman's head. The sky moved toward the mountain, gathering woolly wisps of clouds as if to weave a blanket for the giant eminence. Clouds clung to its summit, stuck to its flanks, and hung in its lee. Only the great mountain itself remained still.

Gradually the blanket of cloud became whole and only the barest outlines of the mountain remained visible. "*Chogori*," the herdsman muttered. The word was not a name but merely a description. It meant simply "a great peak." But the sound of the word in his ears triggered other thoughts. Somewhere in the depths of his memory he remembered something about this very scene. Lost words from his childhood, idle conversations by old men around smoky fires— all came together in a flash. He realized that he had made the same mistake others in his village had made.

He turned toward yet another great peak, lesser than the Chogori, but still a giant. The herdsman thought not in words or ideas, but in shapes and forms of things. This other peak was long, broad, and bold, like the backbone of a yak. He had seen that profile before, sketched years earlier in the sands of Paiyu by an old herdsman, who called the mountain Chogolisa, "the great hunting ground," for its summit seemed to be a level plain elevated miles in the air.

There was no question about it now. The herdsman had made a grave mistake. At some point he had misunderstood Allah's will. Now Chogori was obscured by the clouds; Chogolisa would soon follow. The man gathered his animals and turned around to return

The Herdsman   9

humbly along the same route. He would lose some animals and eat others. Only a few would survive the trip home. His mistake had been foolish and he would try to hide it. His ill-fated journey would not become a part of the lore of his people. Only he would remember the supreme disappointment of his first sight of the great peak that blocked his progress, his fortune, and his pursuit of Allah's will.

K2 seen from Concordia

2 Explorers

The valley of the Braldu, like most of the high-mountain valleys of Baltistan, was unknown to the outside world until the mid-nineteenth century. The first European to reach its villages was probably H. Falconer, who crossed a 16,000-foot pass from the wide Shigar Valley. Falconer walked a few miles beyond Askole where he discovered the Biafo Glacier, an ancient route used by men from Hunza who raided Baltistan. He returned home unaware of the great mountain at the head of the watershed. So did Rudolph Schlagintweit, who attempted, but failed, to cross New Mustagh Pass in 1856 by traveling up the Panmah Glacier.

Also in 1856, Captain T. G. Montgomerie of the Great Trigonometric Survey of India sighted a cluster of high peaks from a survey point 137 miles away. He took measurements and entered them in his log book as K1, K2, K3, K4, and so on—the "K" standing for Karakoram Range and the numbers for his somewhat random order of listing them. Montgomerie recognized K2 as the highest. Two years later, after triangulating it from several points, he computed its height to be 28,278 feet.

The authors of the Great Survey tried to use native names for mountains wherever possible. The peak labeled K1 was visible from several villages and was called Masherbrum. The peaks labeled K3, K4, and K5 were collectively called Gasherbrum. But no established native name was found for K2, and the mountain continued to be known by its survey symbol.

In 1861 another captain in the same survey traveled toward the high peak. Like Schlagintweit, Captain Henry Haversham Godwin-Austen tried to cross New Mustagh Pass but storms stopped him. He did encounter four Baltis who had just crossed the pass, who told him that horses and yaks were commonly taken over the route. (A later explorer, Sir Francis Younghusband, learned that ropes were used to haul the animals up the steepest sections.) Godwin-Austen continued beyond the base of Mustagh Pass to the Baltoro Glacier. After walking on the ice for twenty miles, he scrambled onto a ridge of Masherbrum and saw K2 from a distance of seventeen miles. Then he turned around and returned to India. Generations of geographers wrongly attached his name to the mountain; neither he nor the Great Survey ever approved a name other than K2.

Efforts to find a native name for K2 have been inconclusive. The only native name in use at the time of discovery was Chogori, which means "great mountain." Many pundits believed that the name was used by the Baltis only after Europeans pointed out the existence and size of the peak. Other native names such as Lobsang, Dopsang, and Akbar were proposed but rejected because they had no current usage. Although the Great Survey immortalized its superintendent, Sir George Everest, by naming the world's highest mountain after him, they steadfastly refused to consider naming K2 after any of their staff. Eventually, K2 became the mountain's only official name. Later surveys remeasured its height as 28,250 feet, confirming it as the second highest mountain in the world. This figure was used for a century until, in 1974, the Survey of Pakistan remeasured the peak at 28,741 feet, less than two rope lengths lower than Mount Everest.

Because K2 is not visible from any inhabited places, many historians have assumed that before Captain Montgomerie's sighting, humans had never seen it. This is definitely not true. The mountain is visible from the slopes of Paiyu, a camping spot frequently visited by Balti herdsmen long before the first explorers came. K2 was also visible from the old Mustagh Pass route which connected Baltistan with China until it was blocked by advancing ice in the nineteenth century.

Masherbrum from the Baltoro Glacier

Unnamed towers near Mitre Peak

K2, 50 miles distant,
through the Cathedral group

In 1887 Sir Francis Younghusband made a remarkable crossing of Mustagh Pass from the Chinese side. His guide was a former resident of Askole who had been living on the other side of the mountains for twenty-five years. In Askole, Younghusband was treated with awe and respect, but his guide met with hostile stares. Later, he told Younghusband that his life had been in danger on the visit. Since ice had blocked the pass some years earlier, Askole had not been raided by neighboring peoples. Instead of being welcomed home as a long-lost son, the guide was regarded as a dangerous traitor who had shown a foreigner a possible route of invasion. The Baltis had all but forgotten the benefits of the old ties with Tibet and Yarkand. Long after that part of their history had sunk into unrecorded oblivion, the fear of the raiders was still with them.

Old Mustagh Pass must have been heavily used at one time. The discovery of the ruins of the village Sharagan near the Mustagh Glacier in 1903 by A. C. F. Ferber confirmed this hypothesis. The village, complete with its 160 by 800-foot polo ground, could not have existed above timberline without heavy commerce. When the pass became blocked, both the village and the image of the great mountain faded quickly from the short memory of the Balti culture.

The native people of Baltistan have no written language, no recorded history. Their culture places no value on discovery, especially of something as useless as a mountain. The story of the herdsman who wandered up the Baltoro Glacier in a drought year is imaginary, but that such a journey might have been undertaken is suggested by an incident that occurred in 1892. Oscar Eckenstein, a member of the first expedition to explore the upper Baltoro, asked the men of Askole about the route to Mustagh Pass, which had fallen into disuse because of advancing ice. One man responded and drew a sketch in the sand, showing the positions of both the Mustagh Passes, the Baltoro Glacier, Mustagh Tower, Masherbrum, Gasherbrum, and K2 itself. The expedition's leader, Martin Conway, failed to record the incident in a seven-hundred-page book about his explorations, but later confirmed Eckenstein's account in a personal letter to the Royal Geographical Society.

The question of whether K2 had been seen or named by native peoples was quite important in the early days of Karakoram exploration. Why did an explorer of Conway's renown fail to publish Eckenstein's Askole incident in his voluminous book on that first Karakoram mountaineering expedition? Part of the answer lies in the nature of the nineteenth-century explorers. To admit that natives might have been to K2 would have robbed Conway of some of his glory.

Before the nineteenth century, explorers searched primarily for riches in distant lands. But by 1850 exploration had become an end in itself. The names of explorers were often better known to the general public than the names of the places they visited. Often the two became synonymous: places were named for those who explored them, thus granting a bit of immortality to the discoverer. Unlike the poor Balti herdsman, the returning explorer was a hero. His discoveries became his assets, and they were entered into a ledger of adventures that upheld his social status in society as surely as a banker's bags of gold affirmed his station.

During the latter half of the nineteenth century, adventurers from various nations competed in a frenzied search for the last unexplored places. As undiscovered habitable lands grew scarce, explorers began to look to the mountains. They were not mountain climbers in the modern sense of the word. They climbed mountains for the same reasons that they crossed deserts and oceans.

The typical explorer of this golden age was a highly territorial animal. The hand that lifted a pen to write notes for publication performed a function similar to the lifted leg of an animal marking territorial boundaries. And just as an animal marks the land mainly for the benefit of his own species, the explorer's pen operated only for the Western world, claiming discoveries long known to other humans.

A century ago, the word "discovery" sounded major chords in perfect harmony. Today, dissonance has interfered with the old melodies, and "discovery" is at best a fuzzy word. The clear historical tune of Columbus discovering America must now be keyed with Vikings crossing the North Atlantic, Indians crossing the Bering Strait, and islanders crossing the seas.

Conway's Golden Throne

Still, it would be unfair to think of the majority of Karakoram explorers as only glory-hungry competitors. Most of the early explorers were genuinely enamored of the mountains. They returned repeatedly, as impressed with the grandeur of the scenes as with geographical conquest.

Even Martin Conway, who actively conspired for more than his due share of exploratory credit, was at heart a man with a deep artistic appreciation for the mountains. A British art professor,

Conway came from a Victorian academic world where art and nature were regarded as near opposites, one purposeful, the other random. In the Karakoram he traveled into the Neolithic past, where art was in his mind as he looked at the contours of nature. He could feel the preliminary stages of experience that had once led people to scrawl on cave walls and now set them to work on modern canvases. For him, art and nature merged in the Karakoram.

Most modern mountaineers see the peaks of the Karakoram as the grandest of nature's art forms, thrust into place by the collision of land masses, then sculpted by eternal winds and snows. These mountains have a certain look that is missing in most other ranges of the Himalaya. Much of the region is hewn out of granites and gneisses that favor bold, continuous contours instead of hackly, crumbling ridges. Fracturing in long, vertical flaws, exfoliating in huge parabolic arcs, these rocks give strength and permanence to natural design. All over the world the most prized climbing areas contain such rock: Chamonix, Patagonia, Baffin Island, and Yosemite. Many of the world's great peaks are almost completely blanketed with snow and ice. The Karakoram is an exception. Bold rock outlines shine in the sun, and only weaknesses are hidden beneath the snowy blanket.

The mountaineer's eye seeks latent forms in the chaotic jumble. It favors bold, simple lines. In the mind mountains become pyramids, obelisks, trapezoids, horns, wedges, or needles. Names become symbols of form rather than geographical location. Those of us conditioned to the classic Matterhorn view have a hard time accepting a different view of the same mountain as really being the Matterhorn. Similarly, the Sherpas of Nepal, whose minds have not been confused by geography lessons, assign different names to the same mountains seen from different sides.

The names of the important peaks in the Baltoro region have superseded mere identity and gained an aura of mystique. K2, Hidden Peak, Broad Peak, Gasherbrum II, Gasherbrum III, Gasherbrum IV, Masherbrum, and Chogolisa are the eight highest. The very words evoke images in the minds of mountaineers who have never seen them. The ultimate mystique is in the name of the highest granite tower of the Trango group, which some consider to be the finest rock pinnacle in the world. It is called Nameless Tower, a name that overtly denies the possibility of symbolizing the tower in a word. The tower remains above names—it is too grand to be compared with a lesser form, too unique to be defined by language, too everlasting to be affixed with the name of a mere mortal.

Nameless Tower,
highest of the Trango group

Section II

The Baltoro
Opens Up

I had this fantastic sense of certainty about the climb at the meeting in Los Angeles in 1973. I had the feeling that nothing was going to stop us; that we would overcome all the problems; that we would get permission; and that we would climb K2 in 1975.

—JIM WICKWIRE

1 The Karakoram Closure

The era of the lone Balti herdsman is not altogether past. Through a quirk of international politics, foreign visitors were banned from the Baltoro region of the Karakoram between 1961 and 1974. Mountaineering ceased and ancient rhythms were renewed. The Baltoro region became a real-life Shangri-la, held back in time and saved from the clashes with modern culture that were rapidly altering other high-mountain areas of the world.

The similarity of James Hilton's fictional Shangri-la to the region is far from coincidental. Before writing his famous novel *Lost Horizon*, Hilton visited high Karakoram valleys not far from the Baltoro region and was fascinated by the quiet beauty and giant scale of the landscape, as well as the ordered lives and longevity of some of the people. Only parts of his Shangri-la were imagined.

In other parts of the Himalaya, the hourglass has turned. Grains of mystery, bred by centuries of isolation, are now dropping out of sight rather than accumulating. More foreigners have visited the Himalaya since 1965 than in all preceding history. Members of early expeditions to Mount Everest walked through wild country and villages that few foreign eyes had ever seen. Today the same path has become a trade route for tourism, and the lives of villagers have begun to revolve not around the ways of their elders, but around visiting multitudes who unknowingly reshape the economy, social life, and even the face of the land. At first glance scenes on the Everest trek appear to be little changed from photographs in explorers' books, but the differences are not always visible. It is like the memory of a person who thinks he saw a wolf in the wilds but never learns that it was only someone's pet German shepherd.

Mount Everest straddles the Nepalese-Tibetan border at the eastern end of the Himalaya. K2 sits on the Chinese-Kashmiri border, a thousand miles to the northwest in the Karakoram sub-range. The entire Baltoro region of the Karakoram escaped the tourism onslaught of the eastern Himalaya because the Pakistani government, in an action that had nothing to do with the preservation of village life, closed the area to all foreign visitors during the decade when mountaineering activity was expanding most rapidly.

Explorers of the last century crossed international boundaries with comparative ease. Much of the Karakoram region was then divided into small kingdoms with indefinite boundaries—Hunza, Swat, Baltistan, and Kashmir. When the British left the subcontinent in 1947, Kashmir became disputed territory. According to an agreement, lands that were contiguous with the new country of Pakistan and that had Muslim majorities were to go to Pakistan, while other lands were to remain part of India. Thus, Pakistan became a unique nation composed of geographically separate eastern and western parts. Both Pakistan and India claimed Kashmir and all the tiny mountain kingdoms. Pakistan claimed not only that a Muslim majority existed in Kashmir, but also that it had closer cultural, social, economic, and geographical ties with Kashmir's people than India did. Technically, the ruler had the right to decide the fate of his region. The Maharajah of Kashmir was a Hindu who acceded to India even though more than three-fourths of his population was Muslim.

The Pakistani government took no immediate action on the Kashmir problem because it was too preoccupied with setting up a brand new nation in the chaos following the departure of the British. But thousands of Pathans, fierce nomadic tribesmen from Pakistan's Northwest Frontier along the Afghan border, took it upon themselves to liberate their fellow Muslims in Kashmir. For weeks they marched through the mountains, neither supported nor opposed by their government. The Maharajah first became aware of

The lower Baltoro Glacier, Concordia at extreme left,
Masherbrum right of center

them when the lights went out in his palace in Srinagar. Thirty miles away, the Pathans had captured his powerplant.

The Pathans made the fatal error of stopping to loot and plunder for a few days before attacking Srinagar. By that time Indian troops had been flown in, and the city was successfully defended. Still, the Pakistani government refused to recognize India's claim to Kashmir, and by mid-1948 Pakistani troops were inside Kashmir, defending it against Indian troops. On New Year's Day, 1949, a cease-fire line was finally established. Part of Kashmir was held by India and the rest by Pakistan.

A quarter of a century later the cease-fire line is still not a real boundary. Several wars have broken out between India and Pakistan, and Kashmir is always the most bitter issue. The United Nations has refused to call either country an aggressor, but they have appointed a commission to monitor the cease-fire line. The fabled Vale of Kashmir is on the Indian side, while most of the Karakoram giants are in the Pakistani sector. The prewar overland routes into the Karakoram crossed the cease-fire line and are now closed to most forms of travel. Mountain villagers suffer greatly because their age-old commerce with Srinagar has been halted. A Karakoram highway, which will connect Rawalpindi with Pakistan's sector of Kashmir and China, is now under construction. The only remaining access to Pakistan-held Kashmir is by airplane from Rawalpindi across the high Western Himalaya. Daily scheduled flights are sometimes delayed for weeks because of weather, since planes must fly directly over the spine of the range rather than follow an easier route over Indian territory.

Pakistan has had trouble legitimizing its claim to Kashmir. Many current maps show all of Kashmir as part of India. Major nations

Pathan tribesmen aiming a loaded rifle, Northwest Frontier Province

have been reluctant to take sides in the dispute. However, in 1963 Pakistan signed an agreement with China defining the border between Sinkiang Province and Pakistan-held Kashmir. This was a clever move on the part of Pakistan, because by signing the agreement China tacitly accepted Pakistan's claim to the land. In trade for this agreement Pakistan gave China a strip of land along the border, in some places as wide as thirty miles. Suddenly, by virtue of this gift, K2 and several other giant peaks sat astride the Chinese border.

Many foreign-policy experts believe that the Kashmir situation is too touchy to be solved by an outsider such as the United Nations. One American observer had this to say when asked about Kashmir: "If I were in charge of the Foreign Service, I would have an examination for prospective diplomats. It would have only one question: 'How would you solve the Kashmir question? Explain your solution in detail.' Anyone who answered the question would flunk the test."

Young Pakistani girl and old man

Pakistani government control of Kashmir is somewhat similar to federal government control of the American west in the nineteenth century. Laws are enforced occasionally and selectively, usually by the military. Native people do not necessarily feel a sense of allegiance to the controlling regime. The most distant native villages have had almost no contact with the government and feel loyalty only to themselves. They have lived under various conquerors for hundreds of years. As the Italian anthropologist Fosco Maraini wrote, "Their fear of authority goes hand in hand with the irresistible urge to outwit it."

All these complex political problems contributed to Pakistan's decision to ban visitors to the Baltoro region between 1961 and 1974. During this period the United States, by steadily increasing aid to India, did not earn much diplomatic favor with Pakistan. Also, the revelation of Francis Gary Powers' U-2 flight, which originated in Peshawar, Pakistan, did not make it easy for Pakistan to be publicly friendly with the United States, especially after Khrushchev threatened to draw "a red ring around Peshawar." The chances of an American expedition traveling through Pakistan to a peak directly on the Chinese border seemed very remote.

2 Invitation to the Karakoram

Early in 1974 I was invited to join the American Trango Towers Expedition, which was applying for permission to attempt a colossal granite spire about thirty miles from K2. The Trango expedition was a typical exercise in dream planning. Before the Baltoro was closed American rockclimbing had been confined almost wholly to easily accessible cliffs. The great rock walls in Canada and Alaska were nearly untouched. The giant walls of the Baltoro were considered the province of another generation, perhaps even another century.

During the fourteen years since the Karakoram was closed, rockclimbing had grown fantastically popular in America. Not only had the number of climbers increased manyfold, but their techniques and skill had developed at an equally rapid rate. Americans became unexcelled at scaling huge rock walls. By 1970 the last of Yosemite's unclimbed walls succumbed. A few new routes were still left to be done on the overcrowded cliffs, but many top climbers began setting their sights on the great granite ranges of the world. Bold climbs were made in the Alps, Patagonia, and Alaska. The Karakoram remained forbidden fruit. For many, climbing there became the ultimate dream.

The Trango expedition plans were rooted in such dreams. The expedition had no government permission and no financing. The only real bond among team members was their overwhelming common desire to make the climb. My only misgiving was the possibility that they might not take things seriously enough. They were fun-loving people who might spend two days languishing in a meadow, or an extra night in an unplanned bivouac for the sheer joy of it. I enjoyed such things in my home mountains in California, but I thought the Karakoram would demand far more precise tactics. Luckily, the Trango Tower was barely 20,000 feet high and would not require oxygen or great lengths of fixed rope. Perhaps it could be climbed by a small, happy-go-lucky but competent expedition.

I prepared myself for the expedition by reading as much as possible about the Karakoram. Whenever I had visited a new mountain area in the past, I had been struck by how little it resembled descriptions in books. "So this is Fairy Meadow," I would say to myself. "It's so different than I imagined." Everyone creates a different imaginary picture of an unseen place. Photographs and maps help a bit, but the mystery remains until the spot is actually seen with one's own eyes.

After reading numerous texts and talking to people who had visited the Karakoram before the closure, I realized I would have a better overall feeling for the region if I could relate it to an area with which I was familiar. I couldn't gain a really intimate feeling for individual peaks and glaciers without seeing them, but in an overall sense I could understand the Karakoram far better by comparing it to known terrain in the United States.

After considerable deduction, I chose a most unlikely place for my imaginary Karakoram—Nevada. The more I thought about it, the better the analogy worked. The Karakoram is a convoluted desert, with conditions very similar to what might be expected if a steep mountain range with 28,000-foot peaks suddenly appeared in the middle of Nevada. Both regions occupy similar latitudes, and Nevada is protected from coastal weather by the Sierra Nevada in the same way that the Karakoram is protected by the Western Himalaya.

Whenever I drove U.S. 395 just east of the Sierra, I was always

Lobsang Towers

impressed by the contrasts on either side of my vehicle. On one side of the road were high snowy peaks; on the other, a rolling wasteland of sagebrush and barren ground. The difference was striking, especially when I considered the improbability of giant snowy peaks rising not on the moist, snow-laden Sierra side of the highway, but out of the dry desert to the east.

In Pakistan the upper Indus River and its tributaries form the same sort of geographical boundary that U.S. 395 followed. To the south of the Indus is the formidable wall of the Western Himalaya, capped by 26,660-foot Nanga Parbat and moistened by the annual monsoons. Like the Sierra Nevada, their lower slopes are forested. Meadows fill valley floors and old lake beds. To the north of the Indus is the Karakoram, protected from ocean-born monsoons by the Himalayan wall. In climate and vegetation, the lower elevations of the Karakoram are remarkably similar to large areas of Nevada.

I imagined what Nevada would be like with a range of 28,000-foot peaks running through it. The three-hundred-mile-long Karakoram Range could easily fit into the state. The desert floor would remain dry and waterless except along the immediate banks of streams flowing from the mountains. A radical change would be the incredible view on a clear day. Middle elevations of eight to ten thousand feet would still be barren in summer. A few alpine trees, meadows, and wildflowers would crowd the spring snowline between ten and fifteen thousand feet. The summits would remain forever draped in snow. Glaciers on the heights would seem strangely out of place when viewed from the floor of hot valleys. Somewhere above eighteen thousand feet the landscape would gradually shift into eternal winter. Ice and snow would rule every month of the year, and a mountaineer would feel at home among cornices, ridges, couloirs, and summits.

Invitation to the Karakoram 21

My image of the Karakoram in Nevada was climatically accurate but in other ways crude. In the United States we are spoiled by too many textbook examples of geography. Hydrographic boundaries of water drainage nearly always correspond with orographic boundaries of mountain crests. Every schoolchild learns how the Continental Divide follows the crest of the Rocky Mountains, causing drops of water only inches apart to flow into different oceans. Similarly, the Sierra crest I saw from Highway 395 formed a sharp boundary between drainage to the Pacific Ocean and the Great Basin. To understand Himalayan geography a person must unlearn these oversimplified ideas.

Two of the major rivers draining the Himalaya, the Indus and the Brahmaputra, begin within a few hundred miles of each other in the Tibetan highlands, far to the north of the Himalayan crest. From their sources they actually flow northward for many miles before arcing south through the Himalaya on their way to outlets fifteen hundred miles apart on the Indian Ocean. Their courses seem illogical until we understand that they began well before the Himalayan uplift and continued to cut as the mountains rose.

The Karakoram is a trans-Himalayan range. Geographers still disagree as to whether it is a sub-range of the Himalaya or a separate entity. The deep valleys of the upper Indus River and its tributaries separate the Karakoram from the Western Himalaya. Both ranges had their birth at the dawn of the age of mammals, about fifty million years ago. The rising of the mountains was caused by a collision of continents. India began to slide underneath Eurasia. Geologists theorize that part of India has underthrust the whole of Tibet, causing the famous high Tibetan plateau.

In considering the Mount Everest region it is convenient to think

Arid lands at the foot of the Baltoro Glacier

of the Himalaya as forming the relatively straight rim of the Asian subcontinent, bounded on the south by the plains of India and on the north by the Tibetan plateau. The Karakoram does not fit this pattern. The range is nearly six hundred miles north of Everest, and it is also north of most of the Tibetan plateau. This northerly latitude, combined with the highest mean elevations in the world, has helped to create the largest glaciers outside the subpolar regions. Near K2, the basins of the Baltoro and Biafo glaciers are filled with over five hundred square miles of ice. The tongues of these glaciers extend into arid lands, lapping the sparse sagebrush of dusty, treeless valleys.

I remembered a spring day when I had descended from a 13,000-foot crest into a Nevada valley. At first I had been on skis, cruising effortlessly down faces and bowls to the snowline. Then, with skis tied to my pack, I had walked downhill and felt the air grow hotter. Green meadows gave way to sagebrush. No forests broke the view of the valley or of the seemingly endless row of desert ranges on the horizon. Finally I was on nearly level ground, following the paths of domestic cattle and goats.

I looked back into a temporary alpine world. The snowline was rising. By midsummer it would reach the very crest of the peaks, leaving them dry and barren. In the Karakoram things would be different. The snowline would never reach the crests, and in that zone of eternal winter, where ice carved a landscape far grander than any I had ever seen, I hoped to find the land of my dreams.

Storm over Skardu Valley

③ Beginnings

In North America the conditions most closely resembling Himalayan climbing are found in Alaska on 20,320-foot Mount McKinley. Only in absolute elevation is McKinley a lesser climb than many Himalayan giants, for it rises from lowlands only a thousand feet above sea level, forming one of the greatest overall reliefs on earth. Average temperatures are colder than on any other major mountain. Even altitude sickness is more common on McKinley, since climbers there ascend abruptly rather than traveling for weeks at moderate elevations to reach the base of the climb.

Traditionally, Mount McKinley is climbed by expeditions logistically similar to those in the Himalaya. Fixed camps, fixed ropes, food caches, multiple-load transfers between camps, and weeks or months of time are the usual order of the climb. In the spring of 1972, however, a party of six Americans climbed McKinley in a very different manner. They ascended a previously unclimbed variation near the western rib of the south face in three and a half days, and they carried no tents, fixed ropes, or major expeditionary encumbrances. Nights were spent in snow caves or crevasses. Half the

The author walking in the Braldu Gorge

The 1972 McKinley South Face Expedition: back row: *Patterson, Stewart, Bertulis, Schaller;* front row: *Raymond, Wickwire*

party even forsook full-length sleeping bags, spending the nights in parkas and half-sacks.

Four members of the McKinley South Face Expedition formed the nucleus of the prospective 1975 American K2 Expedition: James Wickwire, Alex Bertulis, Robert Schaller, and Leif-Norman Patterson. On McKinley they talked a great deal about climbing other giant peaks in this simplified, "alpine" style, a method quite different from that of a large expedition with hundreds of native porters.

In 1970 Wickwire had applied to the Nepalese government for permission to climb Chobutse and Dongiragutao, two unclimbed 21- to 22,000-foot peaks not far from Mount Everest. He never received an answer or even a formal acknowledgment. A lawyer and a former legislative assistant, Wickwire began to realize that politics played a major role in obtaining mountain-climbing permissions. Shortly before the McKinley climb, Wickwire, Bertulis, and Schaller met with Pete Schoening, a veteran of two Karakoram expeditions, to discuss the possibility of a small, lightweight expedition to K2 from the Chinese side. As it turned out, Schoening was already one step ahead of them. On his own, he had written to then President Nixon and to John Ehrlichman seeking government support for just such an expedition. Schoening was interested in joining forces and, at Bertulis's request, agreed to be leader of the prospective trip.

Schoening was an ideal expedition leader for such a climb. He had been to 25,000 feet on K2 in 1953 with an unsuccessful American expedition. On 26,470-foot Hidden Peak, only a few miles from K2, he had made the highest first ascent of a mountain ever made by an American. Since all peaks higher than Hidden Peak had been climbed, it was a record that would always stand, but Schoening never flaunted it. Those who had climbed with him on Hidden Peak considered him not only the strongest of the group physically, but also the most modest and patient.

Irrespective of the successful meeting with Schoening, K2 was a distant dream. The McKinley climbers talked of many other peaks, for the odds were heavily stacked against the K2 venture. They were torn between the desire for a very light expedition on a 21- to 23,000-foot peak, or a moderately heavy endeavor on a true Himalayan giant such as K2 with a six-man party supported by an able crew of high-altitude porters.

Leif Patterson was very interested in the K2 plans, but he lived in a remote cabin in British Columbia, whereas Wickwire, Bertulis, and Schaller all lived in Seattle. Patterson was considered by the others to be a strong candidate for the expedition, but he was not part of the early plans. When he climbed with the others on McKinley, political wheels were already grinding for K2 permission.

Wickwire had previously contacted Dave Parker, an old friend from his Washington years who was an assistant to President Nixon, working under H. R. Haldeman in the White House. Parker had checked out the prospects of approaching K2 from Pakistan and had concluded that the area might open to climbers sometime in the next few years. After meeting with Schoening, Wickwire again wrote Parker to ask about approaching the mountain through China. After inquiring through Henry Kissinger's office, Parker reported back that there was nothing in principle that stood in the way of obtaining permission. The main problem seemed to be that of priority. Would Americans be allowed to climb in China before mountaineers from other nations were? Wickwire sent Parker an attractively packaged proposal for the expedition. For nearly a year the group waited for an answer.

After McKinley, Wickwire began to wonder privately about the makeup of the prospective expedition. While their McKinley climb was outwardly a giant success, it had disturbing implications. As happens so often in the mountains, the line between success and failure was razor thin. They had set out from 16,800 feet for the 20,320-foot summit, intending to make the top in one day. At 18,000 feet they had left packs, survival gear, food, and water. The radio had forecasted a storm, and they had tried to rush the summit before it hit. As luck had it, the storm had been slow in arriving. When it came it killed three Japanese women, Himalayan veterans, who were also trying to reach the summit. The stress conditions of such a summit push resembled very strongly what might happen on a summit day in the Himalaya.

Wickwire was not happy with Bertulis's performance. Bertulis had considerable back pain and moved very slowly on the upper part of the mountain. During rest stops he withdrew into himself and did not communicate well with other members of the party. Wickwire thought that he could climb well enough with Bertulis in small groups on lower mountains, but he wondered how Bertulis would get along on a large, cooperative effort. In his journal Wickwire wrote the following about the McKinley climb:

Pete Schoening

A supposedly short jaunt up the final slope resulted in a minor epic. Alex's back pain resulted in a crisis, as for a time we thought a rescue effort might be necessary. Leif and I were able to tension-belay him down the 1600-foot slope after considerable cajoling to get him across the summit plateau to the top of the face. On the whole, however, the expedition was a success. The only friction to speak of took place when we debated whether to push for the summit or put in one more camp at 18,000 feet. Additionally, there were a couple of flareups by Alex. . . . Each time, he temporarily lost control for no substantial reason. I could understand such outbursts if he were provoked, but not in the circumstances under which they occurred. Despite my misgivings about this, Alex and I continue to plan for a Himalayan trip.

Bertulis had different memories of the McKinley climb. He recalled a sleepless night in an upright position before the summit day, which resulted in the aggravation of his old back injury. He felt that he was never in danger and he purposely withdrew into himself on the summit in order to conserve energy. He did not remember being rescued and was quite sure that he descended the mountain under his own power. Patterson and Schaller, however, agreed with Wickwire that Bertulis had been tension-belayed down much of the upper slopes. The conflict was never resolved, and it later had a profound effect on Bertulis's relationship with the prospective K2 team.

Meanwhile, the State Department told Dave Parker that it did not intend to pursue the K2 proposal. Parker continued to push the idea and eventually the proposal traveled to China with Henry Kissinger. Parker reported that the Chinese were not interested. Sinkiang and Tibet were still off limits to mountaineers.

The Russians, however, had exactly the opposite attitude. They extended an invitation to the American Alpine Club for an expedition to the Pamir Range. Wickwire was on the club's Board of Directors, and both he and the club's president were contacted by Bertulis, who strongly urged that Pete Schoening be chosen leader of the Pamir expedition. Schoening became leader, but Bertulis was quite disappointed when he himself was not chosen as an expedition member.

Schoening had made it very clear that he was only interested in climbing K2 from the Chinese side. Especially with his new responsibility as leader of the Russian trip, he had no desire to repeat the same journey toward K2 from the Pakistani side that he had already made twice before. As the odds of getting permission from China dropped to zero, the McKinley climbers once again found themselves on their own, searching for a leader.

Wickwire, Bertulis, and Schaller decided to pursue the idea of an expedition to K2 from the Pakistani side. Seven previous expeditions had attempted K2, but only one had succeeded. In 1954 an Italian team reached the summit by the Abruzzi Ridge on the southeast side. All other serious attempts had been made by this route, which—although much more difficult than the standard route on Everest—appeared to be the easiest way up K2. Several unattempted ridges on the west side of the mountain looked enticing in photographs made by Vittorio Sella in 1909, and the trio tentatively decided to organize a group to climb one of them.

Who could lead a K2 expedition? [Jim Wickwire wrote in his journal]. Although either I or Alex could do it, neither of us had the time or the kind of stature a Schoening has. Alex, who has always been high on Jim Whittaker, suggested him. I was receptive to the point of agreeing that we should see Whittaker. We should have talked to Rob beforehand, but proceeded anyway. I was in Alaska and could not attend the luncheon at which Alex proposed to Jim his leadership of the K2 trip. Jim had come on the American Alpine Club Board that spring and I had gotten to know him, like him, and respect him. Because of the Everest publicity, I think he was probably not taken seriously by most of the better climbers in the country during the intervening period. Although the world knew Jim Whittaker was the first American to climb Everest, climbers thought only of Hornbein and Unsoeld's magnificent climb of the West Ridge in the best of style on the same expedition. I was among them. But in fairness to Jim I should have recalled the circumstances under which he went to the summit with Gombu: in absolutely atrocious weather. He must have wanted very badly to make the top.

Following their lunch, Alex reported that Jim was instantly agreeable. Nick Clinch, who led the 1958 Hidden Peak and 1960 Masherbrum expeditions, was slating an expedition to Paiyu Peak, an unclimbed 22,000-foot peak about thirty miles from K2, in the summer of 1974. Prospects for K2 permission looked good. Although I can't be sure whether Alex mentioned it in our initial conversation following lunch, the one condition Jim Whittaker laid down was that his wife, Dianne Roberts, accompany us to base camp. This could lead to problems later. But as Dianne and Jim were newlyweds, his desire to have her with him was not unreasonable. A professional photographer, Dianne could also take charge of that part of the organizational tasks. Twenty-six years old, she had done little climbing.

Both Whittaker and Wickwire thought that there was no great hurry in drafting an application for K2. First, the application had to be approved by the American Alpine Club. Since both were directors, this hardly seemed to be a stumbling block. But at the December 1973 annual meeting of the club, Nick Clinch got up and announced to a room full of active climbers that the Baltoro region of the Karakoram was opening up to mountaineering after fourteen years of closure. Wickwire and Whittaker realized that many other climbers would suddenly be interested in K2. Unless their application was approved at that meeting, they would have to wait four long months for the next meeting before the club could take action.

Since it was impossible to produce all the signed and notarized application forms, Wickwire and Whittaker arranged to speed up the process. They drafted a letter in a hotel room and obtained a positive recommendation from the Expeditions Committee chairman. Normally, the entire board of directors votes on each completed application during the course of regular meetings. Wickwire, the secretary of the club, realized that the four-man Executive Committee had the power to act on such issues, and he darted about the convention room during cocktail hour seeking a majority who

The Baltoro Glacier and porters

would agree to approve the application immediately when it was submitted the following week. The vice president agreed, and since Wickwire himself was on the Executive Committee, he needed only one more vote. He located the president, William L. Putnam, who read the proposal and said that he would approve if one condition were met: that a friend of his be included in the expedition. Wickwire stared and did not reply. "Well," Putnam said, "will you at least put him at the top of your list of candidates?"

"Sure, Bill," Wickwire muttered under his breath.

When Wickwire and Whittaker returned to Seattle they immediately began preparing the application. Whittaker said there was one more person who had to be included: his twin brother, Lou, who had missed out on the 1963 Everest expedition. The others agreed immediately. Lou's strength and endurance were legendary in the Northwest. Once, Wickwire had worked on a rescue with Lou and he felt a close bond with him. Only Rob Schaller had reservations about three members of the same family going on the same expedition.

Bertulis, Wickwire, and Schaller proposed Leif Patterson as an expedition member. Patterson was teaching mathematics in Tromso, Norway, at the time, so they telephoned him. He accepted immediately. Now the expedition had a basic team of six climbers with Dianne as a photographer. The application was completed, approved by the American Alpine Club, and rushed to the Pakistani Embassy. After an agonizing three-month wait, the coveted permission arrived—it was all on for 1975!

The prospective 1975 K2 Team on Mt. Rainier: left to right: *Dunham, Patterson, L. Whittaker, Bertulis, Schaller, Roberts, J. Whittaker, Wickwire, Rowell*

4 Meeting the Team

My plans for the Trango Towers ended abruptly one spring morning in 1974 when a phone call interrupted my breakfast. Jim Whittaker asked me to join the 1975 American K2 Expedition. He already had permission from Pakistan, and efforts to finance the venture were well under way. As he outlined the plans, I compared them to the unrealized dreams of the Trango expedition, which as yet had no permission and no financing. I immediately answered, "Count me in!"

After the initial pleasure of the invitation wore off, I wondered how I fitted into the team. All the other members lived in the Pacific Northwest. I lived in California. I had never climbed with any of them. Why had I been chosen over others who were superior either in technical ability or high-altitude experience?

Several reasons came to mind. I knew Jim Whittaker, Jim Wickwire, and Alex Bertulis because I had served with them on the Board of Directors of the American Alpine Club. Most other climbers who shared my qualifications did not know the others personally. Also, I had done photo assignments for *National Geographic*, which had purchased first magazine rights to the expedition's story. Although Dianne Roberts was a professional photographer, it was highly probable that the *Geographic* would want more than one professional on such a major venture. If the team did not include a climber-photographer, the magazine would want to send one of their own, thus increasing the expedition's size.

Galen Rowell

Soon a list of the expedition members arrived in the mail. The formal statistics of names, addresses, occupations, and climbing experience gave me no more insight into their real identities than captions in a high-school yearbook. Only two months later, when I joined my teammates for a three-day climbing and planning session on Mount Rainier, did the names and facts come alive.

Alex Bertulis

Alex Bertulis, age 34, Seattle architect. Climbing since 1948. Major ascents: Mt. McKinley south face (Alaska, 1972); Mt. Foraker, first ascent of south ridge (Alaska, 1968); Ruwenzori Traverse (Africa, 1966); Mts. Robson and Sir Donald, first winter ascents (Canada, 1965); Squamish Chief, first ascent of Northwest Passage route (Canada, 1965); Mt. Rainier, first winter ascent of Willis Wall (United States, 1970).

On Rainier I viewed another side of this serious, well-dressed fellow whose Lithuanian accent gave him an air of dignity at Alpine Club meetings. The Alex I now saw wore an old leather vest and dark glasses and held a can of beer in one hand. He laughed, joked, and seemed far more at home in the mountains than I had ever seen him in the city. There was a sense of raw power in his slender, 6 foot 2 inch frame that had previously been hidden beneath a business suit.

Fred Dunham

Leif Patterson

Dianne Roberts

Fred Dunham, age 34, a ski-area assistant foreman from Ellensburg, Washington. Climbing since 1960. Numerous ascents of Mt. Rainier including several new routes; Juneau Icefield Research Project (Alaska, 1962, 1966).

A red-haired Northwestern Okie who poked fun at science, seriousness, and complicated living, Fred wore black denim trousers and suspenders in contrast to the imported woolens of the others. His 185-pound, 5 foot 8 inch body resembled the build of a longshoreman more than that of a mountaineer. He claimed to have greater love for motorcycles than ideas, but belied this boast with a biting wit based on a clear understanding of a wide range of subjects. He had been a high-school classmate of Jim Wickwire's in a small eastern Washington town where the two had played football and learned to climb together.

Leif-Norman Patterson, age 39, math professor from Golden, British Columbia. Climbing since 1957. Major ascents: Mt. Logan east ridge (Yukon, 1961); Tulparaju, first ascent (Peru, 1962); Jirishanca Norte, first ascent (Peru, 1964); Squamish Chief, first ascent of Northwest Passage route (Canada, 1965); Troll Wall, first ascent (Norway, 1965); Mt. Robson, first winter ascent (Canada, 1965); Yerupaja, first ascent west face (Peru, 1966); Huagaruncho, first traverse (Peru, 1970); Mt. McKinley south face (Alaska, 1972).

Leif looked as if someone had pasted a man's head on the 5 foot 7 inch body of a teenager. His tanned face and short graying hair would have seemed right in place behind an executive's desk, but from the neck down his build and supple movements were those of a youngster. He also combined an inward Scandinavian stubbornness with great outward modesty. At first he seemed to be timid, but one glimpse of him climbing confidently up a steep ice serac dispelled that notion. Leif had the greatest record of bold high-altitude climbs of any team member.

L. Dianne Roberts, age 26, Seattle photographer. Climbing since 1973. Three ascents of Mt. Rainier.

Dianne was a slender blonde possessed of great energy and vitality. Although not a member of the climbing team, she was eager to show that she could pull her own weight. Already, she had done far more than her share of administrative chores, and on Rainier she matched paces and packloads with everyone else. She wanted to be an equal partner in the K2 venture, just as she desired to be an equal partner in her marriage to Jim Whittaker. A Canadian citizen, she had gone to court and won against a law that forced foreign women to take the last names of their American husbands.

Robert T. Schaller, Jr., M.D., age 39, Seattle surgeon. Climbing since 1957. Major ascents: Mt. Rainier by several routes, including winter climbs (United States, 1961–1973); several climbs of peaks over 20,000 feet (Himalaya, 1965–1967); several climbs on Mt. McKinley including west buttress and south face (Alaska, 1965–1972).

Tall, gaunt, and handsome, Rob had been one of the nation's top milers (4:01 minutes) during the fifties and he still participated in marathons. As a boy he had been kept out of athletics because of a heart murmur. When doctors judged his heart safe at sixteen, he took up running because it didn't demand the acquired skill that other sports required. Within a few years he was a top competitor. His running, medical training, and expedition preparations were all activities that held greatly delayed gratifications. His approach to our K2 effort seemed stoical, but it was powered by the same underlying passion that had made him a great success in other fields.

James W. Whittaker, age 45, Seattle equipment business manager. Climbing since 1943. Major ascents: Mt. McKinley west buttress (Alaska, 1960); Mt. Everest south col (Nepal, 1963); Mt. Kennedy, first ascent (Yukon, 1965).

"Big Jim" stood 6 feet 5 inches and weighed 210 pounds. He had a weightlifter's upper body perched on a pair of slender runner's legs. His lungs were of legendary size, beyond the scale of many devices for measuring vital capacity. A great advantage at high altitude, this anomaly once caused him considerable trouble in the city when an unbelieving doctor, despite Jim's warnings, punctured his lung by administering an anesthetic near his collarbone. Like Rob, Jim had a habit of setting distant, difficult goals and reaching them. He had made the summit of Everest on his first Himalayan expedition, and he had started as the manager of what was to become the world's largest mountain equipment business at a time when it was little more than a hole-in-the-wall mail-order house. He had a rare ability not only to control things himself, but to transmit his confidence and enthusiasm to others.

Louis W. Whittaker, age 45, operator of guide service on Mt. Rainier and manufacturer's consultant. Climbing since 1943. Major ascents: over 120 climbs of Mt. Rainier by various routes (United States, 1944–74); Mt. McKinley west buttress (Alaska, 1960).

Lou was Jim's identical twin. The two had begun climbing together, gone to Seattle University on basketball scholarships together, managed the guides' concession on Mount Rainier together, and climbed Mount McKinley together, but they had *not* gone to Mount Everest together in 1963. Lou had stayed home to manage the small sporting goods business he owned while his twin reached the summit and became internationally famous. In the years that followed, their careers became totally separate. Lou built a life in the mountains around a successful guiding business. To most of the public, he was "the other Whittaker," but ironically it was he more than Jim who lived the lifestyle of a climber.

Now, more than a decade after Everest, both twins still looked like advertisements for a health salon, though Lou had a slight edge in muscle tone. There were other subtle differences. Jim was generally soft-spoken and genteel, but Lou was constantly joking and making puns. The easiest way to tell them apart was to watch them walk. Jim moved slowly with a natural grace of movement, while

Rob Schaller

Jim Whittaker

Lou Whittaker

Meeting the Team　31

Lou's arms, legs, and hips moved about in a loose, rambling manner. On steep and rough terrain, however, they moved almost as one, and it was this harmony of motion and purpose that they hoped to regain on K2.

James F. Wickwire, age 33, partner in Seattle law firm. Climbing since 1960. Major ascents: Many new routes on Mt. Rainier, including Willis Wall (United States, 1963–1974); Mt. McKinley south face (Alaska, 1972); Mts. Fairweather and Quincy Adams, double traverse (Alaska, 1973).

Jim Wickwire

Sharing a tent with Jim on Mt. Rainier, I almost felt as if I had found a long lost twin myself. Both of us stood between 5 feet 8 and 9, both weighed almost exactly 170 pounds, both were born in the summer of 1940, both began serious climbing in 1960, both were married shortly thereafter, and most remarkable of all, both were still married and still climbing. I jotted down a few notes about our Rainier meeting for possible use in a future article or book, while Jim wrote page after page in his diary.

Although we were both Alpine Club directors, I had not gotten to know Jim very well during those long meetings. Both of us had done the majority of our climbing in our home states. Bred in the Northwest, he specialized in snow-and-ice climbing. His forte was not precise technique on short extreme climbs, but rather the planning and execution of long, serious routes in the mountains. Similarly, my California origins had led me to specialize in rockclimbing, and I had made dozens of new routes on the long mountain walls of the High Sierra crest.

During our conversations we discovered that we both collected old mountain books, loved odd-numbered Beethoven symphonies, and especially appreciated the writings of Aleister Crowley, a mountaineer and mystic whom many found offensive. But there were distinct differences in the way we evaluated life. Jim tended toward tight, analytical judgments, whereas I was inclined toward sweeping generalizations. He was more the inquisitor; I was the intellectualizer. His dreams had precise steps; mine were cryptic intuitions. These differences affected the way we each viewed the K2 expedition. I had jumped into the enterprise totally unsure of the outcome. Jim had logically convinced himself that his drive and skill would put him on the summit.

During our Rainier meeting there was some confusion over names. We had two Jims and two Whittakers. If we called our leader by either his first or last name, someone else was liable to answer. We solved the dilemma by nicknaming Jim Wickwire "Wick" and calling the twins Jim and Lou.

After two days spent discussing equipment and logistics at a camp on Rainier's Nisqually Glacier at 7,000 feet, we decided to climb Rainier by a route through the glacier's icefall. For most of us it was great fun, a relief from the strains of talking about equipment for all too long. For Dianne, however, it was a test. We would be going for the summit from 7,000 feet in deep, soft snow. If she was not able to keep up, then her chances of going above base camp on K2 would be greatly reduced. Our route was harder than the normal way she had previously climbed. But Dianne kept up well, even on the steepest terrain, and reached the summit about an hour behind the fastest rope team.

The next morning we packed up camp and walked out. Everyone seemed much more relaxed and open than at the beginning of the trip. No longer were we just familiar names. By meeting, talking, and climbing with each other, we had become friends.

I rode back to Seattle with Jim and Dianne. Both seemed happy about the results of our days together on the mountain. Dianne especially had the warm, post-fatigue radiance that follows long physical exertions. Often after a hard trip in the mountains followed by a shower and change into clean clothes, I've felt as if I were walking on air. Freed of boots, pack, heavy clothing, and the effects of altitude, my body seemed to be floating as if I were on some strange planet with reduced gravity. The feeling was both physical and mental. In the mountains I was freed of my lowland worries, and upon return to civilization there seemed to be a lull, a pleasant emptiness, while I shifted gears again. Dianne seemed to be caught in the euphoria of the lull, completely fulfilled after an excellent performance.

As we rode from the cool mountain air of Rainier toward the summer warmth of Seattle, our thoughts took a similar course. At first we talked of the great promise, the inevitable success of our climbing team. Gradually we began discussing specific realities necessary to that success, most of all money. We had a budget of $200,000 for food, equipment, oxygen, transportation, and other necessities—all to be completed in less than a year. A few large chunks would be obtained by selling magazine and book rights, but this would not cover more than a fifth of the budget. The rest would have to come from private donations, induced by promises of product endorsements or by such things as autographed postcards.

Jim said that we were already one step ahead of the 1963 American Everest Expedition. They, too, had met on Rainier, but had failed to climb the mountain due to bad weather. Then, out of the blue, Jim turned to me and said, "What did you think of Alex?"

I was unsure of what to say. I didn't know Alex. I had an innate trust of other climbers that had rarely gotten me into trouble. I had thought of Alex in terms of a new friend I would have to get to know better. I realized that I would be spending four months of my life with him, and all I really thought about was sitting down with him sometime and finding out what we had in common.

I answered, "Well, I thought he did fine. I don't know him very well."

Jim asked, "Did you have any trouble communicating with him?"

I said, "No, not that I can remember."

"Even on the summit?"

"He was quiet, but I don't remember any problem."

Later that evening I was to lie awake for several hours before going to sleep. I was both worried and entranced by the size and scope of our project. We planned to form a corporation to handle expedition finances so that each of us would be responsible for the management of the budget. In order to assemble, pack, and ship twelve tons of food and equipment, we would need to rent a warehouse in Seattle. Any doubts I might have had were greatly outweighed by a growing sense of self-importance. It was such a grand enterprise, and I felt proud to be a part of it.

Karakoram and Western Himalaya, Kashmir Pakistan and Sinkiang China

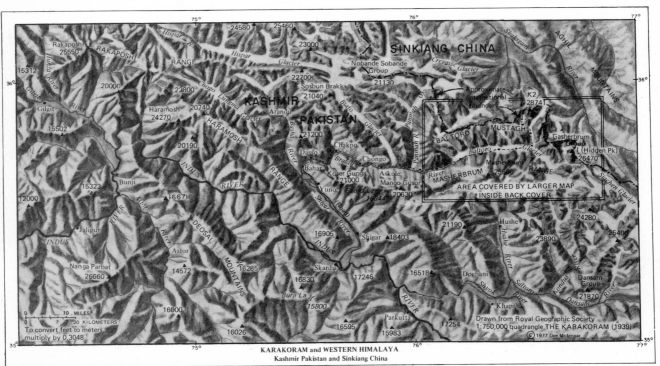

KARAKORAM and WESTERN HIMALAYA
Kashmir Pakistan and Sinkiang China

Section III

Dawnings

From one of our stations we saw more of this Karakoram country. . . . As far as we could see there was a turbulent ocean of peaks without so much as a glimpse of earth in repose. It hardly seemed possible that there should be so much of a disturbed landscape.

—MICHAEL SPENDER

1 Conway and Eckenstein

The first mountaineering expedition to visit the heart of the Baltoro region was in 1892: a British group led by Martin Conway, the art professor/explorer who had a long record of climbing and exploration in the Alps, Greenland, and South America. Personnel included Charles G. Bruce, who later led two Everest expeditions; Mattias Zurbriggen, an Alpine guide who later made the first ascent of Aconcagua; A. D. McCormick, the team's official artist (this was shortly before the dawn of expedition photography); Oscar Eckenstein, inventor of the modern crampon; J. H. Roudebush; Colonel Lloyd-Dickin; plus four Indian Gurkhas who were the forerunners of the Everest Sherpas. For the first time trained natives were used not only as porters but also as high-altitude climbing companions, thus marking the beginning of a tradition.

The expedition left England by ship on February 5. They arrived in the Vale of Kashmir in late April, after crossing India by rail and on foot, and having traveled across the Western Himalaya by the 13,775-foot Burzil Pass. In May and June they explored the region around Rakaposhi, a 25,500-foot giant near Gilgit, a hundred miles from the Baltoro region. In July they traveled up the Braldu River toward the Baltoro Glacier, following in the footsteps of Captain H. H. Godwin-Austen, who had discovered the Baltoro approach to K2 in 1861.

In August, Conway explored the Vigne and Upper Baltoro glaciers for the first time. He made the first ascents of Crystal Peak, about 19,400 feet, and Pioneer Peak, 22,600 feet. He carried out a topographical survey of the upper Baltoro region and discovered Hidden Peak, the second highest peak in the Karakoram at 26,470 feet. He also named Concordia, the amphitheater where the two main tributaries of the Baltoro Glacier join before plunging down the wildest canyon in the world.

Conway on the summit of Pioneer Peak

Conway returned to London in late December, nearly a year after his expedition began. He received a royal welcome and his ascent of Pioneer Peak caused a sensation. The expedition was regarded as a total success. Not only had they explored uncharted territory, but on Pioneer Peak they had reached the highest summit ever climbed. History books cite Conway's venture as a model for all future Himalayan expeditions. Conway was knighted, became president of the prestigious Alpine Club, and in later years became Lord Conway of Allington.

Polite history books never recorded the irreconcilable differences between Conway and Oscar Eckenstein. Eckenstein "thoroughly disliked" the Alpine Club; Conway was a club officer, destined to become president. Eckenstein believed in guideless climbing; Conway normally climbed with a guide. Eckenstein designed his own equipment, including a revolutionary type of crampon and an ice axe only 85 centimeters long, unusually short for that time. Conway scoffed and used an axe as long as a Biblical staff. Eckenstein was fascinated by climbing for its own sake, and was one of the originators of modern "bouldering" on tiny holds; Conway valued exploration over stylish climbing.

After nearly six months with the expedition, Eckenstein was discouraged. The team had failed to make any ascents of importance, and Conway had ordered Eckenstein not to attempt any peaks without his permission. Eckenstein later wrote that he and Conway "had a sort of general meeting at which it was arranged that I should leave the expedition. There had been a good deal of friction." Conway, however, recorded that Eckenstein had been unwell and "it was evidently useless for him to come further with us, so I decided that he had better return to England. The winding up of my arrangements with him delayed us an extra day."

Both men wrote books about the expedition. Conway titled his *Climbing in the Himalaya*. Eckenstein's opinion of the climbing that took place is obvious from the subtitle of his own book, *The Karakorams and Kashmir: An Account of a Journey*. While it is true that the expedition climbed Crystal and Pioneer peaks after Eckenstein left, these ascents were not as important as Conway claimed. Crystal Peak was a very minor summit nearly 9,000 feet lower than neighboring K2; Pioneer Peak, although higher than Crystal, is not actually the summit of a mountain. It is the top of a subsidiary ridge on 23,390-foot Golden Throne, which Conway attempted and failed to climb. The expedition's highly touted height record of 22,600 feet was only about 600 feet above that reached by the Atacama Indians in the Andes before 1550 A.D. A later expedition surveyed Conway's high point as only 21,332 feet, well below the record of the ancient Atacamas.

The petty problems between Conway and Eckenstein would not have much historical meaning were it not for the fact that Eckenstein became the leader of the first expedition to K2 in 1902, the same year that Conway became president of the Alpine Club. When the expedition reached the interior of India, Eckenstein was placed in custody of British authorities and refused entrance into Kashmir. The rest of the group went on without him, and he spent three weeks trying to straighten things out before he finally gained entry and rejoined his group. Eckenstein was bewildered by the incident and could think of no reason for it.

Lord Conway died a famous man; Eckenstein passed on unnoticed in 1921. Many years later, David Dean, a librarian at the Royal Commonwealth Society, became interested in Eckenstein be-

Conway's descent of Hispar La

cause of a literary collection that was donated to the library. Nobody seemed to know who Oscar Eckenstein was, so Dean conducted his own investigation.

Besides Eckenstein's few obscure writings, the main published source of information on his life is Aleister Crowley, his best friend and long-time climbing companion in England, the Alps, Mexico, and on K2. In 1905 Crowley led the first expedition to Kanchenjunga, the world's third highest mountain. The climb ended in an avalanche disaster. A year later he and his wife walked across the Gobi Desert and mainland China. However, Crowley was most famous not as a mountaineer and explorer but as the self-proclaimed "Great Beast 666," a notorious black-magician and master of the occult. He gained most of his notoriety during the 1920s, when, as the author of books on drugs, sex, and black magic, he was subjected to an unprecedented campaign of vilification by the London press. He was accused of "obscene attacks on the King, pagan orgies, blasphemy, obscenity, indecency, stealing, cannibalism, kidnapping, blackmail, murder, and unspeakable crimes." Even after his death in 1947, his obituary labeled him "the wickedest man in Britain."

Crowley's books are mild by modern standards. They employ neither four-letter words nor long passages of prurient prose for their effect. They merely speak openly about drugs, sex, black magic, and the canon of Crowley's own cult, "Do what thou wilt shall be the whole of the law." One of his later works was a 1,058-page autobiography in which several chapters were devoted to mountaineering.

David Dean, the Royal Commonwealth librarian, did not believe Crowley's published version of why Eckenstein had been placed in custody on the way to K2 until he interviewed Guy Knowles, a distinguished British gentleman who had also been a member of the 1902 expedition. Knowles's view "inclined towards that of Crowley, in other words that Conway, by this time Alpine Club President, interposed to put obstacles in Eckenstein's way," and the authorities "did not relent until faced with a threat to expose the whole story to the *Daily Telegraph*." That Knowles should support Crowley on this was especially meaningful, since at 20,000 feet on K2, Crowley had threatened Knowles "with a huge revolver." Knowles had forcibly disarmed him, and he still kept Crowley's old pistol on display in his living room, along with a Degas bronze, two Rodins, ten Whistlers, and a Guardi sketch.

Eckenstein was a humble, practical scientist who constantly tried to persuade Crowley to stop wasting his time on the occult. He told Crowley that the latter's troubles in life were due to his inability to control his own thoughts. "Give up your magick," he said, "with all its romantic fascinations and deceitful delights. Promise to do this for a time and I will teach you how to master your mind."

Crowley tried, and credited Eckenstein with teaching him principles of concentration that helped him achieve the occult power to move objects with his thoughts. At the time of the K2 expedition Crowley was a dedicated mountaineer and only a beginning mystic.

*Balti porter with a goiter
from lack of iodine*

It is highly possible that the conflicts on his two Himalayan expeditions were pivotal in his decision to pursue magic instead of mountains. Today, his inability to get along with gentlemen mountaineers would not be unusual. Many of the top modern climbers are just as radical as Crowley was in his youth. Had the Great Beast 666 been born three-quarters of a century later, he might have gone completely unnoticed on Telegraph Avenue in Berkeley.

Eckenstein's dislike of the Alpine Club was quite well known in his day. Most Britons employed Alpine guides when climbing abroad. Eckenstein and Crowley climbed without guides all over the world and were roundly criticized for it. Crowley accused the Alpine Club of "virulent, dishonest, envious intrigues against guideless climbing and climbers." Both men considered the guide routes on most peaks in the Alps to be little more than scrambles. Eckenstein joked that he could take a cow up the Matterhorn if he were allowed to tie its legs. When someone else repeated this, an ex-president of the Alpine Club began to reply that he himself had climbed the Matterhorn. An Eckenstein sympathizer interrupted, "Did they tie your legs?"

Crowley's notoriety and Eckenstein's hatred of the Alpine Club led Himalayan historians to downplay the first K2 expedition. Crowley's name, and sometimes Eckenstein's, were purposely deleted from texts. When Sir Francis Younghusband chronicled the attempts on high Himalayan peaks, his total description of the 1902 K2 effort was as follows: "The Swiss, Dr. Jacot Guillarmod, explored in the same region." Guillarmod had been the doctor on Eckenstein's trip.

Expeditions such as Conway's, on the other hand, etched their

Conway and Eckenstein 39

way into recorded history not so much by what they accomplished in the field as by their public relations at home. Gentlemen did not discuss personality conflicts, and therefore expeditions composed of gentlemen had no such conflicts. In books of their own they became knights in shining armor; some of the more famous British climbers, such as Conway, actually were knighted.

The fictional world created by the majority of expedition literature is not unlike the environment created by Tolkien in his *Lord of the Rings* trilogy. Vocabularies and emotions are reduced to pleasant simplicities. All life's goals are focused in pursuit of a single distant objective. Petty squabbles are absent. The violence that takes place is of the clean, cartoon variety. Like children's dolls, all the characters have a noticeable absence of genitalia. Tainted heroes are nowhere to be found; only the very good and the very evil exist.

2 Portents from Wick's Journal

"26 June. The full ramifications of the summit episode on Mount McKinley in 1972 [when Alex slowed down and stopped communication with the group due to back pain] did not emerge until a meeting at the Whittaker-Roberts's in mid-March. Although Alex and I had climbed together only on Willis Wall and McKinley, we saw a great deal of each other, mostly talking of tentative Himalayan plans. It wasn't until K2 permission was given that reality came winging home. The feeling I had in Los Angeles that I would stand on top of K2 became stronger. The granting of permission was consistent with the certainty I felt from the beginning.

"But the reality of K2 also forced a reconsideration. Now Alex would be a real rope companion, not a dream one. Would I feel comfortable with him high on the northwest ridge of K2 when the going got tough? I had serious doubts. I expressed these doubts to Jim Whittaker in a telephone conversation. He, in turn, had been substantially concerned about Alex.

"Jim, Lou, and I met for lunch. Hearing about McKinley, Lou wanted to ax Alex from the team immediately. Jim and I were in agreement, but because of what had gone on before when the expedition was being put together we were more reluctant to do anything about it.

"Dianne thought that we should raise our concerns directly with Alex. So one night in the week of March 25, we all met at Jim and Dianne's. Almost immediately after everyone had secured a beer, Jim said to Alex that he had some concerns about him, particularly with reference to back problems on McKinley. Jim also mentioned the Pamir expedition; Alex had not been selected and had been very bitter about it, creating a deep split in his relationship with Pete Schoening. This opening shot, of course, put Alex immediately on the defensive.

"Alex then related a story of the last hours of our 1972 climb on McKinley. Rob and I were dumbfounded. We listened in utter disbelief as Alex related that he had not been in trouble and that we had all overreacted to his back problem. Instead of being in such pain that the necessity of rescue became paramount in at least the minds of Rob, Leif, and me at 19,700 feet, Alex contended that he had merely withdrawn within himself to conserve energy. He denied having been tension-belayed down the steep 1,600-foot slope below the summit ridge. He argued that he must been all right and causing no delay as the other rope team took the same amount of time to descend the slope. Talk of descending toward Denali Pass for a helicopter rescue astounded him, Alex said. The point is that a total lack of communication existed between Alex and the rest of us concerning his real condition. If Alex is correct that we overreacted to his difficulty (which I believe we did not), then the far more serious problem is that Alex failed to communicate such fact to us.

"Throughout the Jim-Alex dialogue, Alex gave many nonresponsive answers, almost as though he had not heard what Jim had asked or said. Later that same evening, at my house, Rob said that the depth of his concern about Alex had not been fully realized until that evening.

"If he is to remain on the team, there absolutely must be a clear understanding with him that he will not withdraw into himself to conserve energy. There must be communication if the rest of us are to rope with him high on K2. As of this moment, I don't know whether this is possible. I feel that I must be the one to raise this issue with Alex. It will be exceedingly difficult but it must be done.

"18 July [actually the 19th—12:45 A.M.]. Just returned from a K2 meeting at Whittaker's. Good session as we got a lot done. Adopted by-laws for the corporation, elected officers (Jim is president, Rob is vice-president, me as secretary, Dianne as acting-treasurer until we elect a permanent one). We are all concerned about raising funds and will make a real effort between now and our next meeting on August 20. The postcard of K2 with inset photos of the team members should be a source of substantial funds. Will print 5,000. They will be signed by us and carried out from the mountain by runner and mailed from Skardu. A card will be sent to each contributor who gives us $10 or more.

"Other items: Lou suggested the possibility of arranging, at no cost to us, a charter flight to Pakistan and back which would take us, all of our equipment and gear (conceivably twenty tons), and charter passengers whom we would humor at a dinner after arrival in Pakistan and again, with a different group, on the way out. A wild idea. Lou will pursue. Are we prostituting ourselves when we even consider schemes like this?

"Pakistan has turned down an aerial reconnaissance this summer, but there's still a possibility this fall of a flight to the mountain just for a look-see. On the way home both Rob and Alex expressed disgruntlement about Dianne's role in this whole affair. I hadn't realized it at the time, but Dianne requested Rob to measure her for an oxygen mask. This means she expects to get to 23,500 feet or better. Oddly enough, I don't see Dianne as the problem Rob and Alex apparently do.

"Interestingly, Alex tonight conceded that it was he who agreed to Jim's sole condition for accepting the leadership, i.e., that Dianne accompany him. Alex said he told Jim it would be okay, but that he would check with me and Rob. Rob recalls that it was a *fait accompli* when he learned of her participation. I don't recall I had much choice when Alex mentioned it to me, but I didn't really see it as a problem then or now. Otherwise, things are on track and K2 became a little more of a reality tonight.

"22 July. Before dropping off to sleep last night imagined myself walking up onto the summit of K2 with Lou Whittaker. Don't know why it was Lou, but there we were, very tired and happy. The only problem was how to get off.

"3 August. To stand on top of K2 (to use Whittaker's turn of phrase), I must be ready for the effort of my life. Running and clean living won't do it either. There must be several strenuous climbs between now and next May.

"5 August. Re K2, Rob is very much concerned about Dianne's role on the expedition. Originally just going along to base camp, she is evidencing every sign of wanting to go much higher, e.g., getting measured for an oxygen mask and taking a crash climbing course in one of Lou's seminars on Rainier. No matter how much she learns about climbing in the next ten months, she will not be in our league. What's more, the condition that Jim laid down to accept the leadership does not require Dianne going high on the mountain. She is not a member of the climbing team but is making all possible efforts to become one—with Jim's acquiescence or encouragement, I know not which. This must be discussed, probably at our next meeting later this month. With this small a group an issue of this kind just has to be laid out on the table—like the concerns about Alex.

"Rob's other chief concern was about Jim's apparent lack of commitment to the proposition that we get as many people to the summit as possible. Rob fears that when the first two get to the top there will be enormous pressure to halt the expedition, mainly because we will have been successful—the *sine qua non* for Jim.

"6 August. Coming out of a deep sleep this morning, I had the conviction we would be very fortunate to put more than two climbers on the summit. Do we really have enough people to carry sufficient food, fuel, oxygen, etc., high on the mountain to assure more than one successful summit climb? I'll continue to support this concept strongly, but we certainly can't expect the two who have come back from the summit to jump back into carrying loads. All of this weighty thinking came hard on the heels of a dream in which several of us went to the top of some incredibly high mountain.

"23 August. On the 20th Fred, Lou, Rob, Alex, Jim, Dianne, and I met again at the Whittakers. *National Geographic* has confirmed $25,000 for the right of first refusal on photographs. Spent some time on oxygen and food. Alex had prepared a multipage food memo for approach, base camp, mountain assault, and summit assault. He wanted to go through it item by item. As it was late by that time and none of us had reviewed the document, we all felt the need to have an opportunity to review the menus and to comment back to Alex. He, however, was insistent that we do it his way. This led to a heated exchange between Alex and Jim.

"At home later I had a sinking feeling about Alex. If these kinds of arguments take place at sea level, what will happen at 25,000 feet? All the old doubts about Alex have again surfaced.

"The next day Jim called to say that both he and Lou were disturbed about the food discussions the previous evening. Again, the principal problem was one of communication with Alex. He seems unable to respond to and accept the views of the overwhelming majority. It has to be his way. Lou feels so strongly that he doesn't trust Alex (not in an honesty sense, but in a tight-spot situation), that he suggests looking for a replacement. With a strong sense of how we got to where we are, Jim and I can't just cast Alex loose without a great deal of agonizing soul-searching. We agreed to meet in a week or so to discuss the matter.

"I thought Rob ought to be involved in such discussions and Jim agreed. Leif's views should also be sought, and Rob and I will talk to him on a conference call before we meet with Lou and Jim.

"A hard decision lies ahead: what to do about Alex. Defend him or cut him loose? It is no easy matter to decide. What it all boils down to may be the weighing of a friendship against placing one's life in greater jeopardy than it will already be in on K2 absent Alex's involvement.

"27 August. Fred Dunham called yesterday to say he concurred in whatever was decided about Alex. He regards Alex as by far the weakest climber. His first choice on replacement is Fred Stanley. Whatever we decide, it will not be easy. If Alex stays on, I'm going to argue for an additional member to give us the strength we desperately need if we are to climb the mountain with a small team.

"30 August. Called Lou Whittaker last night. Surprisingly, he was as critical as either Rob or Alex about Dianne's efforts to be treated as a climber rather than strictly photographer. It is clear to Lou that both Jim and Dianne anticipate her going high on the mountain. Lou, like the rest of us, thinks this is a major problem which must be resolved as soon as possible. He sees Dianne as totally neutralizing Jim, leaving us with seven climbers. He also commented that Jim has exhibited a tendency of late to blow up easily as though a great deal of pressure is on him. Lou will strongly support our contention that Dianne (or any other *person* with her mountaineering experience) is not a climbing member of the expedition. It appears as though the fireworks commence next Tuesday.

"4 September. It is done. Alex is no longer a member of the team. A great weight of anxiety has been lifted from us; maybe now the harmony that I had anticipated, hoped for, and expected will revive. The question of Alex's continued participation in the expedition has been the most perplexing and difficult problem we have faced thus far.

"Today, Rob, Jim, Lou, Fred, and I met to discuss the matter. Our heads told us that Alex had to be dropped; our hearts resisted. How does one sever a friend and climbing companion from the mountain experience of a lifetime, a trip this friend had taken a leading role in initiating and conceiving? Perhaps the central issue was the apprehension we all felt about the possibility of some kind of disaster with Alex, high on the mountain. K2 is risky enough as it is. With Alex the risks seemed to be appreciably higher.

"After nearly two and a half hours it was clear that the only alternative was to drop Alex from the expedition. The two grounds for this could be described as lack of compatibility and communication. Once that Rubicon was crossed, the question then became how to tell Alex. Finally, it was decided that Jim, Rob, and I should meet with him as soon as possible. Why prolong it? The way to carry out a difficult decision is to do it quickly.

"Back at my office, I called Alex. He wasn't there, but I asked his assistant to relay a message that the three of us wanted to meet with him at 5:30 P.M. on an expedition matter. Alex called later to say he had dinner guests coming at 6:00. I suggested 4:50. He wanted to know what it was all about—food? I just said it concerned the expedition.

"Shortly after five, Jim, Rob, and I went up to Alex's office, then across the street to a tavern. After the beer was poured and we all took a sip, Jim straight away told Alex that he had some bad news: that all the team members had reached a decision that Alex was no longer a member of the expedition. Alex's first response was, "Who?" Jim: "Everyone." Without reciting everything that had been said, Rob and I both indicated how difficult the decision had been for us. I talked of the McKinley episode and Alex's recollection of what had occurred being at such sharp variance with Rob's, Leif's, and mine.

"He declined to accept our offer that other reasons be given to the world concerning his departure from the expedition. He wanted the truth laid on the table for everyone to see. We had irreconcilable differences on communication and compatibility and so be it.

"With not much more to say, Alex departed shortly after 6:00. For Rob, Jim, and me it was a great sense of relief. Maybe now we are back on the track. So much energy was expended in concern about Alex. I know that the whole affair has had a definite souring effect on me. Now I feel we will have the compatibility and commonality

K2 from Concordia

of effort that we have lacked. Also laid to rest today at lunch was any notion that Dianne was a climbing member of the expedition. Lou raised the question, and Jim made it absolutely clear that Dianne was not a climber on this expedition, but a photographer.

"5 September (9:20 P.M.). Several times today the pang of Alex's departure from the team hit me. To do that to a friend is about the hardest thing I've had to do. I'm convinced it's the right decision despite the sadness I feel. Alex is a good and decent man; it was his misfortune to be different from the rest of us. In most cases differences can be lived with and accepted; in this situation there was no alternative if we were to avoid going to K2 with great foreboding.

"K2 is already assuming an importance in my life that threatens to shove everything else aside. When I return from K2, will I be able to set aside this drive? I think not. But maybe having experienced the challenge of the mountain, I will be able to gain some peace. That is too goddamn philosophical. How else to explain it other than the attraction of a great peak and the joy of tackling it with the best of companions?

"To close out this part of the K2 journal, an assessment of my companions (including the latest addition, Fred Stanley, Alex's replacement):

"*Jim*. An awesome drive to reach the top. Strong, a bit short on temper, but one senses he would be the ideal mountain companion if he could (or would) set aside his own fame and what it will mean to him to lead the first successful American expedition to K2. I find myself liking and respecting him more as we move closer to the trip.

"*Lou*. The mirror twin. Consumed also by an overriding drive to reach the top of K2. When I dream of standing on the summit, I am with Lou. He has a large heart, and one would go with him anywhere. Just one short, intense time together on a Curtis Ridge rescue established a bond that will stand much straining. Lou and Jim will be the oldest men ever to stand so high on a point of the earth's surface. Of this I am sure.

"*Fred D*. What can one say about one's first climbing partner and, further, closest friend? Fred is technically my equal (if not superior) on rock and ice, yet there lingers doubt about his drive to get to the top of the mountain. He has all that is necessary to do it, but will he exercise that ability? Will he be knocked down by an ear ailment or otherwise? Still, a damn good man to be with in the mountains, and, most significant of all, we will be going together—two small-town lads from Grant County—to the world's second highest mountain.

"*Rob*. Most enigmatic of all. No one can question his drive, especially high on a big mountain. He's the least able of all of us when it comes to leading up difficult terrain. Yet he has sacrificed more than any of us to make this trip. Career repercussions will be sure to follow. Rob is also something of a downer, although that attribute will diminish on the mountain. On our climbs together I quite frankly have dominated: in conception and execution. But Rob is another damn good man with whom I've been through much in the mountains. If his knee holds up, I would rate him as having as good a chance as any of us to get up the mountain.

"*Galen*. No climbing experience with him to speak of—the Rainier romp; nothing else. His record is staggering, but it must be noted no climbing at high altitude—nothing above 14,000 feet. Galen is undeniably an incredibly strong climber; how he will perform on K2 is open to question. My hunch is that he will do well.

"*Leif*. A superb climber on rock and ice. A remarkable man, always putting the interests of others ahead of himself. As I stomped up the final 700 feet of McKinley, my most vivid memory is Leif hard on my heels. His mountaineering judgment is perhaps better than that of any of us. He also has as good a chance as any of us to climb K2. I look forward to being with Leif next year.

"*Fred S*. The most recent member of the team, replacing Alex. He was not my first choice, not because of ability or compatibility, but because of a question as to his commitment to going for the summit. A good trait is his caution, more than I possess. But it might mean, 'Let's stay in camp' when 'Let's go for it' is the only choice if we are to make the top. Don't get me wrong; like Fred D., this man is close to me—all through climbs from 1962 on.

"These assessments are necessarily superficial, not totally fair to each man. But one thing is clear: we have a very strong team, not in the sense of sheer technical climbing prowess but with the experience, resolve, stamina, and push to get up the west side of K2, either via the northwest ridge from Savoia Pass or the west-southwest ridge splitting the west face."

③ 1974 in the Baltoro

The news in late 1973 that the Karakoram had reopened caused a ripple throughout the world of mountaineering, but the floodgates opened too late for a rush of expeditions to appear in 1974. It took a long time to organize, finance, outfit, and transport such major efforts, especially since expedition organizers first had to spend months trading paperwork with the bureaucracy of the host country to obtain climbing permission.

Therefore, the summer of 1974 was unexpectedly quiet in the Baltoro area. Only a few groups were in the field, and no major peaks were climbed. One Japanese expedition marched up the Baltoro Glacier toward 26,400-foot Broad Peak, but not by original plan. The group had applied for K12, an unclimbed 24,000-foot peak in another part of the Karakoram. The Pakistani Ministry of Tourism had subsequently given permission for K12 to another Japanese team, notifying the first group at the last minute that their permit had been issued for the higher and more difficult Broad Peak. Most of the porters quit at Concordia, and the team was unable to get enough equipment to the base of Broad Peak to make an attempt. They gave up and climbed a minor 20,000-foot peak nearby.

Meanwhile, the team that had obtained permission for K12 was not so lucky. Shinichi Takagi and Tsutomu Ito reached the summit on August 30. On the descent one of them fell, and the other made a desperate radio call hanging from a single ice piton. Rescuers were unable to find any trace of the pair.

A joint American-Pakistani expedition was also on the Baltoro that summer, led by Nick Clinch of California. This group was after one of the world's prize unclimbed mountains—21,654-foot Paiyu Peak, which rose in a wildly spectacular snow-draped pyramid of granite directly above the Baltoro's snout. Clinch was America's most successful Himalayan expedition leader and a firm believer in making the native people of a country equal partners on his climbing teams. His two previous Karakoram efforts had resulted in the two highest first ascents ever made by Americans. In 1958 his team had climbed 26,470-foot Hidden Peak, second in height only to K2 among the Karakoram giants. Pete Schoening and Andy Kauffman had made the summit. In 1960 he had made the Pakistani Army a full partner in a joint expedition to 25,660-foot Masherbrum, where Willi Unsoeld and George Bell were the first summit team. Clinch himself had reached the summit a few days later with Captain Jawed Akhter. It was the first time a Pakistani had trodden the summit of a major peak.

On his joint Pakistani-American undertaking to Masherbrum, Clinch had seen the expected Asian red tape part before him as never before. The overall experience had been wonderfully harmonious. He sought to repeat that smooth operation in 1974 on Paiyu, where he once again offered to put Pakistanis on his climbing team. Unfortunately, the wheels of Pakistan's bureaucracy moved slowly, and when the deadline came to ship expedition goods overseas in time for the summer, no permission had arrived. Clinch took a bold gamble and shipped anyway. He was ecstatic when their permission finally came, just before their date of departure.

Paiyu was a lower mountain than those of his earlier climbs, and Clinch planned this venture far more casually. The American contingent was composed of three middle-aged Masherbrum veterans, their wives, and their children. The idea was that the women and children would have a happy wilderness vacation while the men amused themselves making the first ascent of a highly coveted peak. Unfortunately, Clinch's plans came to a halt not far above base camp when one of the Pakistani climbers, Momin Hamid, took an unroped fall down a snowslope and was killed.

The expedition gave up the attempt but decided to settle a long-standing historical dispute by trying to cross from the middle of the Baltoro Glacier to the populated Hushe Valley. They crossed Masherbrum La, a 17,600-foot ice-bound pass that previous explorers had considered impassable. Although Clinch's team used ropes and ice screws to descend a broken icefall, it is possible that long ago, when the configuration of the glacier was different, the native people used the pass as a trade route.

On the Baltoro Glacier near Concordia

A French climber, Jean Fréhel, had also hoped to climb Paiyu in 1974, but his six-man expedition was denied permission because of the American-Pakistani effort. Instead, Fréhel was given permission for Uli Biaho Tower, a 19,957-foot granite spire between Paiyu and the Trango Towers that presented a sheer face of more than 3,500 feet toward the Baltoro Glacier. Fréhel's party attempted the steep but easier back side and reached a point only 135 feet from the summit when a severe storm drove them back. They did not have the resources to make another try.

The highest point reached in the Baltoro region during the 1974 season was just under 24,000 feet, attained by four Austrians on a subsidiary summit of the 24,350-foot Sia Kangri. This mountain was first climbed in 1934 by an expedition led by G. O. Dyhrenfurth, the father of Norman Dyhrenfurth who led the American Everest Expedition. As with other 1974 expeditions, the Austrians' climb was not straightforward. They had intended to make the first ascent of 23,950-foot Urdok I but were turned back by storms. Sia Kangri was a consolation prize.

Two elder statesmen of American Himalayan efforts also visited the Baltoro. Bob Bates had been on K2 in both 1938 and 1953. Ad Carter had been with the expedition that made the first ascent of Nanda Devi in 1936. Both over sixty, they and their wives walked over two hundred miles and reconnoitered the west side of K2 for

Paiyu Peak, left, *and Uli Biaho Tower,* right

the 1975 expedition. They reached 18,000 feet on the Savoia Glacier during a period of poor weather. Their few photographs of the cloudy peak added little to the scanty information on K2's west side, published in accounts of the Italian Duke of Abruzzi's expedition of 1909. Their opinion was that the greatest difficulties lay between 24,000 and 27,000 feet. From the col of Savoia Pass the climb looked continuously difficult to them, but they thought it would be possible with modern techniques and equipment.

With the Bates's and the Carters on their journey was Major Manzoor Hussain, a young Pakistani liaison officer. He was captivated by K2 and applied to be chosen again the following year to accompany the American attempt. His commanding officer, General G. S. Butt, was in complete sympathy with him. As a young captain, twenty years before, Butt had accompanied the Italian team that made the first ascent of K2.

4 The Journey Begins

On the night of April 15, 1975, I met the members of the expedition in Seattle, as I had done several times before. But this time was different. Our year of planning for K2 suddenly gained meaning as our plane took off into the midnight sky, bound first over the North Pole to Copenhagen and ultimately for Pakistan.

Two days later we landed at Karachi, the world's twelfth largest city, with an estimated population of four million. Outside the airterminal door was Asia. In the hour before dawn, people were everywhere. Our senses were bombarded with new languages, mannerisms, and especially smells. Unexpectedly, the dominant sound was of birds chirping from every tree. We entered a waiting bus for a ride through town to a sumptuous breakfast at an American diplomat's home. The ride was quiet and eerie, punctuated only by the ancient vehicle's grinding brakes, howling gears, and creaky springs. In America the bus would have been junked years earlier, but in Pakistan it was better than the average vehicle.

After breakfast we returned to the airport through streets that had suddenly come alive. People and noise were everywhere. I was reminded of the main street of a small town getting ready for a parade. In Karachi every road was bustling with activity all the time.

After holding a press conference we boarded a Pakistan International Airlines flight to Rawalpindi, in northern Pakistan. The Boeing 707, like the Karachi bus, had most of the characteristics of a worn-out taxicab. Windows were cracked, upholstery was torn, outside panels were bent, and even some rivets were missing. A man who spoke English told us that the airline's initials, PIA, stood for "Perhaps I Arrive" or "Please Inform Allah."

From the air our view of Pakistan was in direct contrast to what we had seen of Karachi. The province of Sind appeared to be mostly uninhabited desert until we crossed the mighty Indus River, which drains much of the Western Himalaya and the Karakoram. Flood-plains, deltas, and sandbars were on a grand scale here. The path of the river was tortuous and braided. From the air it resembled a schematic of the human circulatory system, scrawled in gray by the water-borne sediments of the Indus. Both sides of the river showed signs of cultivation, but the overall impression, unlike that of Alberta wheat fields, was that men did not control things here. The river reigned supreme.

We landed in Rawalpindi, a major town of half a million people and the last place where we could buy many needed supplies. We intended to stay for about two days before taking our final flight to the village of Skardu in Kashmir. As it turned out, we waited in Rawalpindi for eleven frustrating days.

Our home was the Flashman's Hotel, a sprawling, single-story remnant of British-controlled India. We could have stayed in the Rawalpindi counterpart of a Holiday Inn, the Intercontinental Hotel, but it was far too expensive and isolated from the world we had come to see.

No one was in a hurry in Pakistan unless he was inside a vehicle. Walkers moved slowly, talking, bickering, but never running. In contrast, the same people became manic when they took control of anything with an engine. Vehicles careened toward each other, passing on blind curves, going through red lights, swerving to avoid buffalo, horse carts, women, and children. No one was willing to give up an inch of roadway. When it came to aircraft, however, the Pakistanis turned out to be far more cautious.

Day after day we were told that we couldn't fly because of the weather. If there were any clouds at all over the mountains, the daily scheduled flight from Rawalpindi to Skardu was cancelled. Only later did we learn that during some months the plane flew on less than five days. PIA is a semi-government airline which often uses planes and pilots from the Pakistani Air Force for the Skardu flight. The pilots get paid whether or not they fly. They themselves decide whether or not the flight goes.

Our expedition now had ten members—eight climbers plus Steve Marts, a cinematographer, and Dianne Roberts, the still photographer. Steve was an experienced climber whose expenses were being paid by the expedition for the sole task of making a commercial film. Replacing Alex Bertulis was Fred Stanley, a long-time climbing companion of Wick's and Dunham's. He was fresh from an ascent of 23,406-foot Peak Lenin in the Soviet Pamirs. Quiet and unassuming, Fred had a reputation for great stamina and determination in the mountains. He and Fred Dunham became such an inseparable pair that we usually referred to them as "the Freds."

Accepting a room key at the Imperial Hotel in Copenhagen after we flew across the Pole from Seattle had seemed insignificant at the time. Each key unlocked the door of a hotel room for two. Five keys were passed out to the ten of us, creating five pairs: Jim and Dianne; Lou and Wick; Rob and Leif; the two Freds; Steve Marts and myself.

Rawalpindi street

Rawalpindi

Except for the married couple, Dianne and Jim, the pairings appeared to be transient. I assumed that as the expedition progressed our associations would change. I was wrong. They remained unbroken, creating three basic forms of expedition experiences: that of the individual, the pair, and the team.

During our idle days in Rawalpindi we all had time to assess each other and the relationships we shared. Leif Patterson was favorably impressed with the way things were going, and he saw in Jim Whittaker the same combination of generosity, stinginess, and egocentricity that he found in himself. He thought that Jim carefully considered his actions and had a good way of delegating responsibility. "Only occasionally do I feel like knowing a bit more about what decisions are made," Leif wrote. Fred Stanley did not agree. In his diary, he wrote,

I'd like to enjoy the company of the Big Four—Lou, Wick, Jim, and Dianne—but they seem very content to exclude the rest from their twosomes, threesomes, or foursomes. I'm getting pretty tired of their ego thrusts, of trying to fend them off while searching for something significant in the conversation. My problem is one of detached longing to be included, yet not wanting to lower myself. The best associations I've had here have been with one or two of the others at a time. I'm not at all sure whether the feeling was mutual, but I was satisfied and felt very satisfied with the time I've spent with Galen and Rob. When with the Big Four I've the impression that everything is all elbows, each man for himself.

At the same time, Lou wrote brief appraisals of the team, excluding the Big Four:

I've just finished tea and juice at a table with Galen. I've never heard a guy talk so much about everything and nothing. . . . He is even worse than Dianne. . . . I hope Galen is a good climber and not just a lot of talk. He's the only unknown at present. Fred Stanley and Fred Dunham are fitting in real well and I see Rob able to laugh more and relax. Leif—a very nice person and no ego trip. Steve is still unsure of himself and I should draw him out more.

Lou was highly critical of Dianne's role on the expedition, especially after learning that press coverage of the expedition's departure from the United States had stressed Dianne as the first American woman to attempt an 8,000-meter peak. In September, Jim had confirmed to Lou, Rob, and Wick that Dianne was not a climbing member of the expedition. But the *Los Angeles Times* had later quoted Jim as saying, "Dianne has proved herself. She is part of the climbing team now." The *Christian Science Monitor* had said, "Neither she nor her husband will rule her out for that final climb." And the *San Francisco Examiner* had quoted Dianne, "I'll go as high on the mountain as I can, the same as everybody else. I don't have any fear."

Steve Marts

The *Pakistan Times* ran a news story that referred to eight members of our climbing team. Since there were ten of us, a wire-service correspondent asked Jim about the discrepancy. Jim said that Steve Marts was not part of the climbing team but that Dianne had earned her place since the expedition was formed. Lou overheard this and did not agree. He decided to confront Jim. Lou described that meeting in his diary:

Told Jim this morning in front of Wick I was afraid Dianne was again aspiring to go high on K2. She has been telling same to press and at parties I've attended. I suggested a meeting last night on her image as a climbing team member and reminded our team that last fall I had a similar meeting. Jim then had said Dianne was only going to base camp. Dianne has now been telling everyone she is going as high as she can go. I gave her a five-day climbing school on Rainier and she still cannot tie her own knot on a rope. She is *not* a climber!! All agreed a real problem exists. She is a bossy, aggressive girl who is using us all to get her credibility as a climber. I refuse and I'm not on K2 to try and get a nonclimber up it. Therefore the meeting. We all agreed to figure how to tell Dianne and Jim we are not going to have her on the upper mountain. This morn I, with Wick beside me, told my brother that Dianne is telling people she is going high. Jim said there would be no time for her up there but he may take her to Camp I or II if he was taking a load himself. The rest of the team has all agreed not to take her up the mountain. Jim said he would talk to her so she wouldn't give the false impression that she is a climbing team member; but it's too late now as far as the press is concerned.

Jim also described the meeting:

Wick and Lou express concern that Dianne might try to go all the way. I told them she would do the best she could for the *whole* expedition. Told her, and she got depressed—naturally. I hope we will be able to break down that foolish type of communication and have everyone tell everyone else how they feel. Direct, on a one-to-one.

Dianne didn't write about the incident for two days. Then she let go:

Two days ago Jim said that Wick and Lou were "concerned" about what I may do on the mountain—to interfere, I guess. Of course I sensed that such talk was passing around. I seem to have some special sort of radar that picks up such vibes, but instead of reacting forthrightly on my suspicions, my intuitions, I allow them to slip inside, to reappear at later, inappropriate moments. So when Jim told me what Wick and Lou had said, my eyes filled with tears and my throat choked with emotion. Partly it was the release I so badly needed of the accumulated tensions of the last few weeks and the leaving. But it was also the realization that I am not, in the sense that the others are, a part of this group. It is as hard for the others to be frank with me as it is for me to speak openly to them. And the sadness of the realization that I've worked so hard—so goddamned hard—to gain such little ground really stunned me when it came. . . . But enough! Suffice it to say that somehow I've got to let the idea out that I'm *not* here to threaten fragile egos or in any other way impede the progress of the expedition. I hope my initial fear of having bitten off more than I can chew has worked itself out—perhaps now I can relax and enjoy myself.

Dianne Roberts

Dianne gained membership into the climbing team wholly within one of the expedition's rigid pairs: Dianne and Jim. None of the rest of us really understood how she had transformed her original role as a trekker and photographer into that of a climber. Ironically, Steve Marts supplied the answer. (Steve's position, by the way, was exactly the opposite of Dianne's. He had joined the expedition strictly as a cinematographer with no intention of going to the summit, although his mountaineering background was equal to that of the rest of the team.) Before the expedition left the States, Steve had recorded interviews with the team for possible use in the soundtrack of his film, during which Dianne had explained her role: "At the beginning I felt a little bit like I was peripherally involved in it. I was on the team because I was married to Jim and that was the only reason. But now I don't feel that way at all because I feel I've contributed as much as anyone else to the planning and I can do as much on the mountain as anybody else. I feel I've earned my place on the team. I've paid my dues."

Dianne and I developed a strong antagonism for each other. Both of us resolved in our diaries to talk to one another as little as possible, yet neither of us could resist challenging things that the other said. Each of us felt the other was overly competitive. We each yearned to be in the center of things, to always be there when something important happened. Dianne considered me a hopeless chauvinist, and I thought of her as a rabid feminist. Fred Stanley accurately perceived our relationship:

The conversations between Galen and Dianne are just the same as ever, neither one is willing to let the other have the last word. Galen will continue with a, "Well . . ." and Dianne with a "Yes, but . . ." and so on. I finally had to go take a dump and never heard the end of it.

It might have been natural for me to enjoy watching Dianne get put in her place as a trekker, not a climber, but I didn't. Both Wick and I were among the moderates who felt that the mountain would sort out Dianne's aspirations to go high. What was printed in the news media would have no direct effect on our activities on the mountain, whereas a confrontation could damage what unity our team still had. For better or worse, we were all married to one another for the duration of the expedition.

One basic factor that differentiated the Big Four from the rest was the way in which they viewed the expedition. They saw strictly a planned assault on K2. For them, any experience or event not directly related to attaining the summit had the potential to subvert the primary goal. The others viewed the expedition as an overall experience that would be meaningful whether we reached the summit or not. They did not share the Big Four's stated belief that the expedition stood a 90 to 95 percent chance of success. When I mentioned fifty-fifty odds to Jim, he said that he was sure all the others would guess much higher. Leif, however, had written, "How easy it is to get carried away with thoughts of success; the facts and odds are otherwise." Rob commented that the team seemed "remarkably optimistic about success. . . . Our aerial fly-by of K2 may revise a few of those optimistic smiles."

In Rawalpindi we met our Pakistani liaison officer, Major Manzoor Hussain. A few months earlier we had paid his way to the United States in the hope that a personal meeting might motivate him to take extra care in preparing for our arrival. The gamble had paid off. Manzoor had worked so hard for us in Pakistan that even his own government took notice. Intelligence men had asked him why he was showing so much interest in American affairs, since he was a Pakistani government official and not, in their eyes, an agent for our expedition.

Manzoor had arranged for us to hire over six hundred porters once we arrived in Kashmir. And, when the scheduled flights continued to fail, he chartered a military C-130 through PIA. At first he thought it could take all of us and our fourteen tons of gear to Skardu. We planned to land, unload the plane, then take off again for an aerial survey of K2. Unfortunately, the charter flight operated under the same flying restrictions as the scheduled flights. It would not fly except in perfect weather.

After eleven days of waiting we finally took off on April 29. The rolling hills above Rawalpindi passed rapidly under the wings as we headed northward. At first the Himalayas were indistinguishable from a distant cloud bank on the horizon. The formless white mass slowly crystallized into individual peaks, valleys, and ridges. Soon everything below us was white. The crest of 26,660-foot Nanga Parbat hovered to our right; the land dropped more than 23,000 feet into the gorge of the Indus River, the largest land escarpment on earth.

Nanga Parbat reminded each of us of Herman Buhl, who had soloed the first ascent of the peak from a high camp in 1953. He had seen the mountain again four years later from an airplane, just as we did now, enroute to the Baltoro. There he triumphed alpine-style on

A Rawalpindi merchant

The Skardu wireless operator

A family in the Chongo fields

Porters pray to Allah, and roll chapatties, by the Braldu River

People of the Braldu

Baltis sawing lumber near Shagarthang

A woman of the Braldu fields

An Askole boy

Balti faces reflect a heritage blending the Orient with the Middle East

Tilling the fields of Chongo

A child in a window, Chongo

A herdsman of the Shigar Valley

Broad Peak, and died soon afterwards on Chogolisa. Although no one on our expedition had been on Nanga Parbat, the peak seemed linked to our destiny; it was a giant landmark that we shared with others who had attempted Karakoram peaks before us.

On the other side of the Indus the terrain differed sharply. The forests of the Western Himalayan foothills gave way to brown barren ground in the Karakoram. Snow cover was definitely thinner, but major glaciers were incongruously larger and longer. We crossed the Biafo Glacier, part of the longest glacier system outside the subpolar latitudes. The barren earth was gone now, and the Biafo gorge seemed like the yawning depths of some imaginary beast's mouth, lined on either side by teeth of red granite capped with snowy white.

In the distance, one mountain stood out. K2 rose alone as a perfect pyramid, each of its ridges ascending at a similar angle. The surrounding 26,000-foot peaks seemed like children in the presence of a giant. The northwest ridge was dead ahead of us, rising for a mile over the top of Mustagh Tower. We approached K2 in the manner of a speeding car heading for an embankment, turning at the last moment to avoid illegally crossing the Chinese border. Those of us in the cockpit were glued to the window, as wide-eyed as children on Christmas morning. We did not agree about what we saw in those moments.

K2 from the air, Northwest Ridge on left skyline

My impressions of that first view of the ridge were clouded by vindictive emotions. Because of a misunderstanding with Jim, I failed to get a single good photograph of any of the major peaks at the head of the Baltoro Glacier. I was in the cockpit for most of the flight, but I had stayed back from the windows for most of the 120 miles between Nanga Parbat and K2. Other team members alternated at the windows while I sat on a bench and set up three different cameras with the proper lenses and filters to photograph the great peaks at close range. As we neared the Baltoro Glacier, I moved to the windows. Just then, Jim entered the cockpit from the fuselage. He saw me at the window, assumed that I had been there for the whole flight, and ordered me back while Dianne stayed in the prime position for photographing during the entire passage over the high peaks. She took exquisite aerials; I felt as if someone had robbed me of a priceless possession.

I knew from past experience that my mental attitude greatly influenced how I judged an unclimbed route. When confident, I usually underestimated difficulties; when apprehensive, I tended to overestimate them. I was consumed by bitterness and jealousy as we flew by K2. The northwest ridge looked wildly difficult to me during those angry moments, but I hoped things would prove easier than they seemed.

As we neared the mountain, I heard voices above the noise of the engines. Wick's and Lou's dominated; they talked excitedly about altitudes, ridges, hanging glaciers, and a snow ramp that easily bypassed the rock towers above Savoia Pass. Standing behind them, I was unable to see the features they described. I regretted not having studied photographs more carefully beforehand. Wick and

Lou had spent considerable time looking at close-ups of K2 taken by the Pakistani Air Force. Rob and Leif were also talking in a far less optimistic vein, while Steve Marts recorded their reactions to our first view of K2 for possible use in the soundtrack of the movie. Months later I heard a playback of his tape:

Rob: You know, it doesn't look nearly as broken up as it did in those picture shots. It just goes up and up and up and up. It's incredible! On all sides! It's just steep.

Leif: I think it's going to be extreme difficulty. We've got our hands full, man!

Lou: At least it's good up on the mountain; at least it's right up higher on that peak. What's that pass at Savoia?

Wick: Twenty-one eight hundred something.

Lou: Yeah, and it's a pretty good walk right to the base of that wall that goes into the pass.

Wick: Did you notice the way you can slip by those gendarmes on the north side?

Lou: Yeah! It goes there; I know it.

Wick: There's a snowslope; there's a hanging glacier.

Lou: There's a whole, god . . . it's a ramp. Yeah, leads right along.

Wick: It's a hanging glacier on the other side of the pass.

Lou: Yeah.

Steve: On the other side of Savoia Pass?

Lou: Yeah.

Wick: Yeah.

Lou: That was our problem—how to get around those gendarmes! There's a ramp that leads . . . (blurred voices)

Leif: (blurred voices) . . . some difficulty.

Rob: Plus we have altitude.

Leif: Yeah, right. People don't take altitude into account. You can just compare the top of K2 to the top of Nanga Parbat. Nanga Parbat was practically flat with a little point on it. K2 is just up and up and up and up. No flat part. No snow.

Rob: Incredible! Incredible mountain!

Leif: Incredibly difficult, we're going to be . . . I wouldn't be surprised if we get into trouble.

Skardu

At Skardu we stepped from the dark interior of the plane into a valley of blinding white sand. It was, simply, the most beautiful valley I had ever seen. The others seemed equally impressed, although I'm sure the superlatives in my thoughts resulted from my years of exploring the desert ranges of the American West. I love arid lands and feel somewhat claustrophobic in places where one life form, such as trees or humans, overwhelm the natural contours of the landscape. Here in Skardu the flat valley, perhaps twenty miles long, was ringed with snow-capped peaks rising 5- to 8,000 feet above the valley floor. This was no single wall of peaks, or series of cliffs lining both sides of a canyon; rather it was a full 360-degree circle of mountains.

Jeeps took us eight miles to the main part of Skardu, a sprawling village of ten thousand people. We drove through blossoming or-

The expedition team and flight crew at Skardu

chards of fruit trees and on wide gravel streets lined with tall Lombardy poplars. The people here looked stronger, healthier, and hardier than their lowland counterparts. We arrived at a rest house overlooking the Indus River; in the background rose snowy summits.

Later in the day we discovered that PIA had let us down. The two tons of gear that we had personally seen loaded on the first plane bound for Skardu did not arrive. It had been off-loaded after we left in favor of passengers.

At first we busied ourselves with various necessary tasks. We met our sirdar, Ghulam Rasul, who would be in charge of our six hundred porters. We hired fourteen additional high-altitude porters, selected earlier by Manzoor and Ghulam, and outfitted them with the same clothing and equipment that we would use on the mountain. They strutted happily through town wearing wool pants, long underwear, down parkas, and double boots on an eighty-degree afternoon.

On May 1 the *Seattle Post-Intelligencer* carried a news story based on a phone call we placed from Skardu. It began with a quote from Jim: "We've seen our mountain and we think the ridge will go. It's an incredible peak and it will be a very, very difficult climb with great exposure, but we're confident a route can be found."

On the same day, the expedition moved by jeep to the village of Dasso, leaving Leif, Rob, and me to wait for the remaining air shipment of equipment. The three of us each felt that we had been left behind as punishment for having created the expedition's first major incident the previous afternoon. Seven of us recorded different perceptions of that event in our diaries:

Truck decor

The Journey Begins   65

Jim Whittaker:

May 1st. Twelve years since the summit of Everest. Found out they won't fly today—May Day. After some discussion convincing Manzoor, we decided to move on anyway. This means getting all our supplies together and loading the jeeps and tractors. Galen and Rob took off this afternoon and caught hell when they came back. The rest of us busted ass working, and they hiked up to a lake and loafed. We paced until dark and crawled into bed all bushed. . . . We had to split the party because all our loads have not yet arrived. I left the three that didn't help yesterday afternoon, Rob, Leif, and Galen.

Lou Whittaker:

Rob, Galen, and Leif took off today and did no work. I told Galen yesterday to stay in camp when he took off then and now he's in a second offense role. I'm beginning to think the guy just doesn't know how to work. Rob apologized and so did Leif. They have (the three) been appointed to stay in Skardu.

Fred Stanley:

Leif, Rob, and Galen were singled out by Jim to wait for the remaining gear to come in by plane and to supervise Skardu closing details as their punishment for not being around yesterday afternoon when things busied up. . . . Jim and Lou came down pretty hard on Galen, not as hard on Leif, for not being around for the afternoon work—especially Galen since he had been gone all day before, saying he'd be back by noon. But they were awfully heavy-handed. I think I would've turned around and walked off.

Leif Patterson:

Rob and Galen are invited on a tour to a lake with local prominents, so in the afternoon I trot down to the river with camera and wash-gear to bathe in the Indus. But where no wind blows the water seems unclean. I detect a path under the fortress and decide to explore it. A true Himalayan path, 200 feet above the water, built in hair-raising style. . . . I scramble up scree slopes to some slabs, in good view from the fortress. Not quite sure if I am wanted here. . . . No sign of life. . . .

I feel quite happy on return between six and seven, but the sensation is soon dispelled as Lou Whittaker gives me a hell of an overhaul for going off while the rest have "busted their asses" loading jeeps and tractors for early departure to Dasso next morning. It is useless to try to explain that there seemed to be nothing to do and that I wasn't trying to escape duties. To underscore his sentiments, Lou hands me a bucket of water to pour in the messy toilets. Well, like a naughty boy, I promised not to do it again. Shortly afterwards, Jim gives the same lecture again. I don't argue because I see their point. Every man must contribute to the physical progress of the expedition. But I feel that tempers got a little too hot, that a little more advance planning or information to the rest of us would help. If in the mornings we discussed and laid out the work to be done, we could do it and then be free. Also Steve Marts and I carried a lot of boxes the other day when the rest of the crew ran to swim in the Indus. . . . Feel rather bad about this incident. Galen and Rob separately get same or worse scolding. The evening ends by us three culprits being ordered to wait in Skardu for rest of loads while main part of expedition moves on to Dasso. This is fine with me. I was going to volunteer for it anyway. But a bad feeling; a wedge has been created. Galen was even told he would not be allowed up the mountain if this kept up. Well, he did go off photographing ibex yesterday, but in truth there has not been that much to do except right now for this "big leap," a sudden surge forward.

Galen Rowell:

After lunch, I joined Rob and we walked to the center of town. The wireless supervisor, the postmaster, and the meteorologist offered to take us on a hike to Satpara Lake, ten miles roundtrip. We returned to the rest house where everyone was sitting around. I told Jim and Dianne that we had been invited on the hike and Jim made no comment one way or the other.

The walk was delightful, next to a stream in a narrow gorge. The wireless supervisor has had two years college plus special training in telecommunications and electronic engineering. After twenty-five years of government service, he makes 830 rupees per month ($85)—less than we are paying our porters! The young weatherman has a degree in physics. He wants to know all about sex in America. He is married and wants to use family planning but has had unsatisfactory results with what is offered in Pakistan. He claims that women are scared of IUD's because of pain and supposed cancer. He says the pill is so strong that women complain bitterly about side effects and most refuse to use them. I wonder who has been handling family planning in Pakistan? If the weatherman speaks for the majority, then the program appears to be a dud.

After tea in a rest house on the shores of Satpara Lake, we hike back to Skardu, arriving at 6:30 P.M. In the congested courtyard of our rest house, Jim Whittaker explodes at me for being away all afternoon. Lou joins in with equal vehemence. I now understand all those rumors I've heard about their violent tempers. The situation is also perfect confirmation of what I wrote this morning—the fact that Jim and Dianne answer with finality all the time, offering no contingency plans and making it nearly impossible to guess the surety of a situation in advance. Early in the morning I asked Jim about the day's plans. I suggested moving ahead with the gear we had. He said no, we would wait at least two days more for the gear to arrive before considering moving. Rob asked if he could help with the radios and found the situation well in hand. Others sat around writing in diaries or doing wash. There was absolutely no forewarning that the afternoon would turn into a hard work session to repack boxes and load them for a move the very next morning. Leif was also caught by surprise. He used the afternoon to climb the fortress hill above Skardu and was scolded on his return. It is hardly coincidence that Jim chose Leif, Rob, and me to stay in Skardu while the others moved on. Truants staying after school.

From 6:30 P.M. to 10:30 P.M. I packed boxes and worked in the kitchen. Jim and I finally met harsh glances and apologized to each other. I am truly sorry I was gone when I was needed, but I also remember my one-man stand to get the boxes from Lou and Wick's room in Rawalpindi when the truck came while they had gone to the Intercontinental Hotel.

In the morning I find that the events have definitely left their mark. I feel guilty taking pictures of others working, especially in the presence of Jim and Lou. I am too scared to photograph their departure from Skardu on jeeps. This is not a healthy attitude for a photojournalist. I think some of Jim's anger must come from a lack of comprehension of how much work photography and writing really is. A week ago he asked me if I considered that I was working hard, and I said yes. I explained that I felt a weight over my head to research text and compile a photographic record just as if I was on a commercial assignment. I think Jim must have taken my answer the wrong way, without understanding how much work, especially mental work, is really involved. He would not comprehend Doug Robinson's statement that he would rather shovel snow for a living than write, because shoveling was so much easier. And Doug is a damned good writer.

It would be all too easy for me to drop the ball on the photojournalist end and concentrate on proving myself as a mountain man, or a mountain warehouseman. Strangely, I have no regrets for joining the expedition or being here. I look forward to each day with eagerness.

Rob Schaller:

Much has happened since yesterday morning. I am detached, saddened, and more lonely than ever—and seemingly not a part of this K2 expedition. Expectations are not reality, and my pen is heavy and does not want to write my heart. I want so much for optimism to prevail and not have to write a sad, morose diary. One might say that the delays and frustrations and lack of communication produced the first "incident" of our expedition. Yesterday, after piddling around all morning trying to find things to do, I accepted an invitation from the local telegraph operator and his assistants to walk to Satpara Lake, five miles and 2,000 feet vertical distance. Previously, I had tried to become involved in the radio testing, but was ignored as the others officiously went about their work. Galen joined me and we experienced a remarkable afternoon together. Perhaps we learned more about Pakistan than in all our time previously spent in the country. Our new friends were animated, intelligent, and remarkably well informed about life, particularly about America, to my surprise. These chaps have all the raw material to become "chiefs" in their own right, reaping the same rewards available to us. All they lack is opportunity. The younger one has a degree in physics. The older one is supervisor of the telegraph office.

Galen and I trade off, hiking in turn with each one and their friends, to and from the lake. Conversation covers most of the "important" subjects: politics, religion, sex, health and disease, morality, race, etc. . . . It is a long and stimulating afternoon and my mind is opened up to the world community of man, again learning that people in other parts of the world are kindred in many ways. . . .

Our return to Skardu is a shock. For the first time in my life, I am bluntly, rudely told that I have let down "the others," goofed off, and disappointed "them." It seems that during our absence the decision was made to move out. I return to the scene of jeeps loading and people milling about in the semidarkness of 7 P.M. First an angry Wickwire tells me "everyone has been working his ass off getting ready to leave!" Then Jim and Lou grind me up and spit me out, although my chastisement is gentler than Galen's. Certainly neither of us intentionally avoided work, it's just that nothing was happening when we departed for the afternoon. Despite the superb organization of this expedition, communications between members have been poor. The "in" group has been running things without discussion or consultation with the "outs." It is almost as if we were along to do their bidding. . . . Now there seems to be a schism. Hopefully the mountain will end our frustrations and bridge the gap between us.

Jim Wickwire:

First big blowup of expedition about two hours ago when Galen walked in after being gone for over seven hours. He, Rob, and Leif had taken off about noon, apparently thinking there was no work to be done. Two Freds, Lou, and I busy setting up base station radio and antenna all morning so didn't see them go. Yesterday, after Galen returned from being gone with George Schaller most of the day looking for ibex, Lou had asked him to stay close and to pitch in with the work. This afternoon we decided to move out to Dasso in the morning with what loads we have here and let the remaining sixty-two loads plus porter supplies follow as soon as possible. This meant a hell of a lot of work all afternoon. . . .

Leif returned first, having hiked to the top of Skardu Rock—clearly illegal, but he didn't realize it. Then Galen walked into a verbal onslaught from both Whittakers, who were mad as hell. Both castigated him for shirking work and not doing his share. Suffice to say it was not the smartest thing Galen has ever done to be gone most of two days in a row. Problem is he fails to see how expedition work gets done, i.e., everyone pitches in. Lou was so worked up, he took it out on Fred D. and me in a short wrestling match. After bouncing me down the hall, I finally grabbed him and pinned him to the inner wall, breaking a window in the process. It was just his way of letting off steam, as he really wanted to punch Galen out. Rob got a milder tongue-lashing and had all sorts of excuses, as I expected he would.

Dunham wants to heal this breach. . . . [He] thought Jim and Lou had come on too strong with Galen, but also that maybe it was necessary. Lou said Jim told Galen that his chances for going to the summit had been hurt. If so, the question of who is determining who the summit climbers are is raised. Is it Jim or the entire team?

Lou Whittaker wrestling Dunham

Fred Dunham didn't keep a diary, but he expressed his feelings by his actions immediately after the "incident." Leif described them:

Fred D. puts his arm around me, clearly trying to offer me some comfort. He is, of course, the one who has done the most physical work for the expedition. Fred is a good guy, solid, quite eager to help, and from what I have observed, trying to tie people together and never commenting adversely in someone's absence.

And I recorded this entry:

Dunham was the only one to offer help and kind words after the dynamic duo's explosion. He said they had been too hard and I shouldn't take it too seriously.

Dianne did not mention the incident in her diary.

Left alone in Skardu, Rob, Leif, and I talked openly about our feelings for the first time. We admitted that we all felt bewilderment at the total-success orientation of the trip and the lack of any contingency plans. We discovered that we shared many ideas and had had many similar life experiences. We reminisced about our childhoods, our climbing, and our jobs. The stories we told each other became parables, evoking different memories in each of us. For the first time in years I remembered a neighbor's treehouse, and a scene from my parent's car window glimpsed when I was very young, preserved, for no apparent reason, as sharply as the day I first saw it.

Rob told us how his earliest climbs introduced him to a new world. "It was like being reborn," he said. "I was in my late twenties, but I felt like a child running free through a candy store. The feel of the trail under my feet, the smell of the wilderness, watching the ever-changing cloud patterns—I could hold onto the real world and see it coming. Everything suddenly had more meaning. I realized that life would go on no matter what I did. It gave me an anchor in life."

These conversations with Rob and Leif had an element I had searched for without success in other conversations on the trip. Both men expressed *how* they thought rather than just *what* they thought. It had been impossible to ever discuss the *how* with any one of the Big Four. My probings were either regarded as challenges, or, more often, they landed with a hollow thud. I suspected that among themselves the Big Four were much more open, but to us they were distant and cold. Each of us singled out Wick as being especially closed about his feelings. When conversation is not based on mutually compatible interpretations of experience, it inevitably builds toward antagonism, especially when the people involved have lived through the same events. It is always delightful to find a shared interest in a conversation with a stranger, and, conversely, it is intimidating not to find shared interests in conversations with supposed friends.

Unknown to us, Dianne was having similar feelings in Dasso. She expressed her discontent in her journal:

I can't sit down and talk to any of the team members because no matter what I say, if it's the least bit negative it will be "I told you so," with the implication that if I wasn't here that would be one less thing to worry about. I don't feel close to anyone—hardly even Jim. Having to be careful about what I say in front of the team members is really a drag. Never in my life have I felt like I was in such a vacuum.

Early one morning in Skardu I was awakened by the sound of Islamic chants blaring through a worn loudspeaker. Unable to go back to sleep, I dressed and walked through town. Gone were the hordes of people that had lined the streets during the day. The green of the poplars was muted in the dim light of early dawn. A few soldiers with modern rifles were on a hillock, silhouetted against the first light, incongruous amidst the primitive huts and flowering orchards. Modern padlocks clashed with handcarved wood on the closed, windowless doors of the bazaar. In a few hours the bustle of human activity would draw attention away from the essential contrasts of the scene. My eyes would then follow only movement.

I walked through the quiet town and thought about the shape the expedition had taken. The bright, flying colors under which the team had left America three weeks earlier seemed as muted as those of Skardu in the twilight. The framework of the expedition, like the artifacts of the town, stood out in bold relief when people stopped moving in the foreground. The Big Four seemed as distant and intimidating now as the soldiers on the hillock. As I approached the rest house and saw Rob and Leif, the sense of isolation that had been with me as I walked through the town disappeared. Here were friends with whom I could be candid. I looked forward to climbing with them on the mountain.

Section IV

Something Hidden

He thought of the time when he would leave Shangri-La. . . . He pictured the long, arduous journey, and that eventual moment of arrival at some planter's bungalow in Sikkim or Baltistan—a moment which ought, he felt, to be deliriously cheerful, but which would probably be slightly disappointing.

—JAMES HILTON

1 Akbar's Village

Akbar Ali hurried up the Basha Valley toward his home in the highest village. It had been unusual for a man of Baltistan to make a journey in winter, but Akbar was not a common man. Most Balti men were dark-skinned and not much over five feet tall. Akbar was a full six feet and looked more like a southern European than a native of the Karakoram. Thirty-two years old, he walked with a long, proud stride. He wore an army officer's jacket, purchased in the bazaar at Skardu with money he earned from a mountaineering expedition.

His village, Arandu, was nestled at nearly 10,000 feet, just below the snout of the twenty-seven-mile-long Chogo Lungma Glacier. Another glacier, the Tippuri, descended a side canyon and almost reached the village. A third, the Kero Lungma, occupied a hanging valley opposite the Tippuri. At the head of the Kero Lungma was Nushik La, a 16,400-foot pass that connected Baltistan with the tiny mountain kingdoms of Hunza and Nagar. Over this route, now blocked by advancing ice, Akbar's parents had emigrated from Hunza.

The people of Arandu wintered like bears, staying under the snows and rarely venturing outside their windowless stone huts. They huddled around tiny fires of animal dung, and ate only wheat and dried apricots.

The last winter had been unusually snowy and long. Akbar had decided to leave when food stores grew low. Most of the villagers feared walking in the snow, but after working for several expeditions Akbar had learned not to be afraid. He had marched for five days from the heights of Arandu to the arid valley of Skardu. Now, months later, he was returning.

Spring had come to the village. Every watercourse was full. Yaks drew wooden plows across the fields. Women followed closely behind, bent low, sowing wheat. Some men worked with the yaks, but most sat on their haunches on the town path, engaged in idle conversation. They were dressed in native wool, undyed and the color of the brown earth.

Akbar walked through the village, greeting his friends with tears and hugs. They commented on his new clothes, for Akbar was wearing a cotton *kurta* blouse and loose-fitting *shalwar* trousers,

Akbar Ali

purchased in the city. Only the tax collector from Shigar ever wore such clothes in the village. And the military coat! And the pure white cap! Akbar must have many tales to tell. He acted so happy and important. No one pestered him for answers, because Akbar was a man of the village and would tell them in due time. Now he had other business. His pace quickened as he neared a two-story hut.

At the doorway to his home he was greeted warmly by his mother. Behind her, his wife waited quietly and expectantly along with several other women. All were Akbar's relatives. More than a dozen people lived in the tiny hut. Until the birth of her child, Akbar's wife had had the lowest status in the family. By Islamic tradition she could participate in her husband's family only through her children. If she failed to bear him a son to carry on the family line, he had the right to take a second wife. Now she nursed their only child, a daughter just over a year old. The woman had been trained to be modest, docile, and unassertive; she was not disturbed that Akbar greeted his mother first. Someday, if she bore him a son, she too might become such a powerful woman. The other women often chided her about her husband, saying he was a good-for-nothing because he was always gone. But now he hugged her, showing far more affection than the other husbands in the house. He opened a goatskin that he had been carrying over his shoulder and pulled out the wonderful things he had bought for her in Skardu—jewelry, bright cotton cloth, halva, and several kinds of tea.

Balti woman

Perhaps, she thought nervously, he will live up to his name. He is different than the others and his name is different, too. The names of the others—Hassan, Ismail, Mohammed—are from the Koran, given in the hope that they will live within the faith. But Akbar is a name of distant power; a Mogul emperor who ruled wisely and powerfully far and wide, bearing gifts to his friends and death to his enemies. Akbar the Great was always traveling, always searching. She didn't want her husband to bear this trait. Arandu was her world, and even though Akbar told her of faraway places such as Skardu, she had no intention of leaving home.

Soon the snowy outlines of the village would disappear with the melt. The landscape would be swept with green, and pink blossoms would burst forth on the apricot trees. New leaves on the poplars and sycamores would bring shade from the summer sun. The pace of life in Arandu was slow and muted. Summer and winter were like transparent curtains—through each a tantalizing image of the other showed. During the dry heat of summer eternal winter was always in sight on the high peaks, breeding the ice streams that flowed to the outskirts of the village. Winter snows were rarely heavy; they never quite hid the contours of the land.

Balti praying, near Dasso

On the morning after his return to Arandu, Akbar awoke and rubbed his eyes. Smoke filled the chimneyless hut, and he could barely see the outlines of the several women gathered around the fire, although he was nearly close enough to touch them. His wife handed him a hot *chapatti*, a flat wheat cake fried in animal fat. He downed it quickly and asked for another. Lately, his appetite had been unusually hearty. He never used to have more than one chapatti in the morning.

His wife wore the jewelry and the brightly colored scarf that he had brought the day before. As she prepared to go outside, she took them off and covered herself with a plain black shawl. Akbar felt himself flinch in a way that he had never done before. Most of the women in Skardu wore their jewelry and bright colors openly, but Islamic customs were far more strict in Arandu. When Akbar was a small boy, religious leaders from Persia had trained people of the village to rigidly respect the custom of *purdah*, which called for women to cover their faces in the presence of men outside the family. In Skardu, many women were lax about purdah. Akbar was puzzled by the difference. Both villages claimed to be believers in the same sect of Islam, yet they lived in different modes.

Akbar was unaware of earlier trends and transitions in his village. When an American couple, Fanny and Hunter Workman, visited Arandu in 1902, they had both been greeted by unveiled women bearing gifts. But later, after receiving Persian training in strict religious ways, the *Mullah* of Arandu forbade the villagers to allow "unbelievers" from mountaineering expeditions into their homes, regardless of whether the women were veiled. The customs had been relaxing slowly since then, but to Akbar, having visited Skardu, they seemed unchanging.

He walked out of the hut toward the central path of the village. The sun had not yet risen, but already a dozen men sat on their haunches, talking aimlessly. Sometimes they would sit there all day, leaving briefly to check the irrigation ditches or their wives' progress in the fields. One of the men, a short, swarthy fellow

Three Balti villagers

named Mahdi, approached Akbar eagerly. "Did you bring your scissors today?" he asked.

"I have them."

"Then cut my hair. I have been waiting long for you to return. You are the best barber in the Basha Valley."

"I will cut it today, but you will have to find someone else to cut it next time. I will soon be leaving on a long journey and I will not be back until after the apricots are ripe."

"Where do you go, Akbar?"

"To Skardu, to be hired by Americans who are coming to climb Kechu, the great mountain beyond the villages of the Braldu."

Mahdi laughed. "You can cut my hair next time, too. I will be a coolie for the Americans. A man named Ghulam came from Skardu while you were gone. He asked many of us to work for the Americans. We are to meet some of them at Dasso. Why do you go all the way to Skardu?"

Akbar was surprised. No one had hired Arandu men to carry on the Baltoro before. Mahdi continued, "Ghulam wrote our names and said only those on his list would be hired. Are you on his list?"

"No. I did not know about the list. Besides, I do not want to be a coolie. I want to be a high porter."

"But Ghulam told us that he had already selected the high porters. They were all men from Satpura and the Braldu."

"I will tell the Americans that I have been a high porter on Malubiting, Leila, and Spantik, with the Polish, Austrians, and Japanese. They will see that I am big and strong and that I know the mountains."

Skardu

"But those are mountains of our Chogo Lungma. Kechu is up the Baltoro. I think you had better cut my hair very short."

Akbar finished Mahdi's hair without further conversation. He thought about what he should do. If he went to Skardu, he might not get hired. But if he waited for the Americans at Dasso with the others from his village, he would lose face. He would look foolish for having gone to Skardu in the winter. And if he was not hired, he would have to return alone to his village. Even the women would laugh at him then.

When Mahdi stood up after the haircut, Akbar told him, "Your hair is not cut short because I will see you in Dasso. I will go first to Skardu and meet the Americans' airplane. I will help them with their loads, and if they do not hire me I will travel to Dasso and meet you. We can tell them that I am not on the coolie list because I am a group leader for the village."

The other men had been listening to the conversation. They talked among themselves. Akbar looked impressive in his military jacket and blue cotton *shalwar*—more impressive, in fact, than Ghulam Rasul, who controlled all the coolies for the Americans. "Yes, Akbar," they finally said. "If you are not a high porter when you come to Dasso, you will be our group leader."

2 To Askole

On May 4th, Leif, Rob, Manzoor, and I left Skardu in two jeeps bound for Dasso, where the rest of the expedition was waiting for us to bring the remaining sixty-two boxes of gear. The boxes had failed to arrive, and after sending telegrams to PIA, the American Embassy, and the Ministry of Tourism, we decided to rejoin the others and inform them of the situation. The eleven-day wait in Rawalpindi had been bad enough, but with the five extra days in Skardu our rate of travel was beginning to match that of the nineteenth-century explorers who had walked every inch of the route from central India.

I rode with Rob in an American jeep of indeterminate age. The doors didn't latch, the radiator leaked, and we had a better view of the road through holes in the floor than through the broken windshield. At first our driver seemed to possess the usual Asian patience; then the roar of the car's engine dropped a starter's flag somewhere in his brain. We hurtled through town, racing against some unseen competitor and creating a wake of dust and gravel. The driver seemed lost in a world of his own, a faint smile on his lips. He negotiated the rough road at full throttle, and we had the combined sensations of being in a sports-car race and riding down rapids inside a barrel. Later we learned that during one six-week period twenty-three people had been killed in jeep accidents in the Skardu region.

We crossed the Indus River on a suspension bridge with a narrow wooden roadbed. On the other side was a desert—a lifeless landscape of exposed rocks and blowing sand, broken only by a few low plants and an occasional herdsman with a flock of sheep or goats. As we approached the sprawling fields of Shigar, a sandstorm began to blow. Veiled women were silhouetted in the fields as they braced themselves against the wind. We were traveling a convoluted Sahara, and far above our valley were glaciers that fed their meltwater into streams that poured out of the dirty skies. At each point where a stream reached the valley, a village utilized the water for agriculture.

Leif, riding in the other jeep, was greatly impressed by what he saw in the village of Shigar. In his diary he wrote,

I would love to just stroll leisurely among the neatly kept fields. Everything bears witness to the lack of machinery. No wires, no bulldozer scars, no waste of any sort. Every stick, every branch, every bit of bark of a felled tree is carefully used. It is such a delightful experience to see what neatness and pleasure the unassisted human hand alone can produce. Life could be good and stable here, yet I know that the hard work and toil would look less romantic after awhile. It is never possible to judge life from a car window.

A woman of Baltistan

We drove through the Shigar Valley for many miles until a large tributary joined it from a deep canyon. This was the Braldu River, which the expedition would follow for sixty miles to its source, the Baltoro Glacier. The Braldu Valley was flat and wide near the river's mouth. Large boulders dotted the sandy plains, looking as if they had just tumbled from the hillsides that very afternoon. Immediately beyond the boulders were several tents and a large mob.

As we approached the camp, I felt apprehensive. I had not seen the rest of the team since the morning after the incident in Skardu. I wondered how we would be accepted by the others. Would all be forgotten? Or would we remain outcasts, a cut below the rest? Rob shared my apprehensions. Even before the incident he had had the feeling that he was an extra appendage of the expedition, merely fulfilling the need for a medical professional. He was never sure of his place on the team. After Alex had been dropped, Rob had expected to receive his own invitation to the tavern from Jim and Wick. "I don't feel included in what is happening," he confided to me.

We were therefore overjoyed and somewhat surprised to be greeted warmly by the rest of the group as if nothing had happened. When we suggested that one or two of us could remain behind until the extra gear arrived, the problem was discussed more openly than anything had been since the expedition began. The consensus was that it would be a mistake to advance without the remainder of our gear. We would wait while Leif and Manzoor returned to Skardu, perhaps even to Rawalpindi if necessary, to break the logjam.

The only damper on the team feeling came when we asked about setting up a tent. Rob, Leif, Steve, and I were advised to sleep in the cook tent even though a brand new tent had just been issued to four policemen who were to accompany us to the glacier. The policemen got their tent by loud demands. We were afraid to risk breaking the renewed but fragile web of camaraderie by pursuing our request for a tent. While the others laid out their personal gear in clean, private tents, we slept in the cook tent, sweeping the dirty floor after everyone left in the evening and packing our things out of the way each morning.

During much of our first night in camp the policemen held some sort of loud celebration in their tent, only a few feet away from our own. Unable to sleep, I thought about the concept of a big expedition and wondered what effect it had on the personalities of those involved. Supposedly, team members had been selected for their compatibility as well as for their technical ability. Yet now we were having more personal difficulties than I had ever experienced in all my years of climbing. Had we really misjudged each other? Or had we changed since leaving America?

I was especially concerned about the pettiness, the tendency to make major issues out of minor things. All of us were guilty of this fault to some extent. The trivial matters we had argued about would have been passed over gently on a climb in the States. But we weren't in our home mountains. And we weren't out purely for enjoyment, using climbing as an escape from the stress of normal life. The expedition had become our life. It had all the seriousness and stark reality of an eight-to-five job. The expedition had become the totality of our existence—our family, our home, our transportation, our job, our entertainment, our hopes, and our fears. For some it had even become a religion. All of us had thought of ourselves as individualists and viewed our prior successes in climbing as self-directed. Now we were suddenly thrust together into a situation more socialized than a Chinese commune. Most of our equipment was community property. We shared money, food, lodgings, and labor. Our venture was a prophecy based on a vision. Did we really share the same vision? I thought not.

On the surface we had a common goal: to place someone from the expedition on the summit of K2. Underneath we each favored different methods of attaining that goal. In a Seattle living room we had found it easy to agree on changing our individual lifestyles to fit the group's needs. After all, we were people who regularly sought a sense of control over our destinies by pursuing wilderness adventures. We were, however, accustomed to only a certain measure of unpredictability in our lives. When the scales tipped toward general uncertainty, each sought to gain control in the way he or she knew best. We each looked backward to the normal order of our lives rather than forward to working together toward a common goal.

In its simplest form, our trouble was only homesickness. Each of us tried to view the experience through a familiar frame. I sought out stories of the land and its people as if I were on a comfortable commercial assignment in the States. Collecting this material was only part of my role on the expedition, but as uncertainties mounted in other areas I began to overemphasize it. Lou and Jim, as business managers, had increasing needs to control what went on around them. In addition, Jim tended to amplify his comparisons of our expedition to his climb of Everest as time went by. Rob looked forward to becoming involved in medical work in the villages. Wick, the lawyer, planned his personal brief as if the mountain were a judge who would render an absolute decision of success or failure. Even Leif, the most flexible of us all, saw an image of his Canadian mountain home in the quiet order of the Balti villages. Some of us viewed the new road from Skardu to Dasso as a wonderful thing that cut two days' march from our journey. To Leif it was a wedge of destruction moving in on the simple lifestyle he worshipped. He had only to close his eyes, and the roar of the jeeps through the villages became the sound of logging trucks plundering the landscape near his home.

The mountain was our common bond. Like the threat of war or disaster, it had the potential to hold us together through troubled times. But our mutual drive was already fragmented. I had been told that my own chance for the summit was hurt by the incident in Skardu. Wick, on the other hand, was nearly certain that he would reach the summit. The two Freds were sure that they had been brought along to carry loads, not to climb the mountain. Both Rob and Leif held onto the image of climbing high, but they felt more distant from that goal than they had in America.

Now, three weeks out from America, we were just on the verge of beginning the 110-mile trek to the base of K2. For the first three days we would travel through villages, but after that we would be in uninhabited land for the duration of the expedition. If all went according to plan, we would be on the mountain in two weeks.

Bridge at Dasso

Manzoor Hussain

Jeep road through Shigar

In the morning it was snowing. The harsh landscape was suddenly softened. Rugged peaks were molded by the thick mists. Apricot blossoms seemed to be floating above green pastures. The once roaring river murmured in tones muted by the laden air. Distant voices of hundreds of prospective porters seemed as gentle as the cool breezes.

I could hardly believe it when the others said it had been 110 degrees the day before I arrived. They had gone barefoot and shirtless, but now we all wore boots, woolens, and parkas. The Baltis had not changed their clothes. They wore the same heavy but loose-fitting woolens in heat, cold, rain, sun, or snow. Hundreds of these men sat quietly on their haunches, together forming concentric arcs around our camp. Today they were as motionless statues, fringed in snowflakes like the trees and the rocks. There seemed to be more porters than loads, and I learned that they had been gathered here for weeks, waiting in suspended animation for us to arrive and hoping to be hired.

Near noon the clouds began to lift and I took a walk with Manzoor Hussain. He told me that the porters would soon become very animated. There were 850 men here and only 600 loads to carry. Two hundred men from the village of Askole had traveled for three days to Dasso, against Manzoor's orders. He had instructed them to remain in Askole so they could be hired for carrying the porter food that was already stored in their village for use on the remote glaciers beyond. If we didn't hire the Askole men now, they would cause trouble, but if we hired them to carry regular loads, we would not have enough men to carry the food stored for us in Askole.

Manzoor was twenty-seven years old. He had joined the Pakistani Army at seventeen and had become a captain at twenty, and a major at twenty-four. During that time he had also completed two years of college-level training in civil engineering and was assigned to the Corps of Engineers. As liaison officer between the government and our expedition, he was enjoying a break from his work in Hunza on the Karakoram Highway, which will soon connect Pakistan with Sinkiang Province in China. Manzoor was a mixture of boyishness and discipline. He conducted official matters with serious deliberation but was full of spontaneity at other times. Anyone could make him double over with laughter by telling an off-color joke. But the next moment, as if nothing had happened, he would resume the role of a boy-king, old before his time, with slightly exaggerated authoritarian mannerisms. A thick mustache added dignity to his elfin appearance, but he still made me think of a child prodigy giving a performance when he would rather have been outside playing.

On our walk, Manzoor emphasized that the Baltis were simple folk. The task of supervising over five hundred porters was formidable, but he didn't anticipate having many problems as long as we observed the ground rules. He thought we should move on now, and let the rest of our goods catch up. He hoped to be considered a real member of the team, rather than just a liaison officer. He too wanted to be a K2 summit climber.

Rob Schaller with 68-year-old patient

When we returned from our walk, Manzoor and Leif left for Skardu in a jeep. The rest of us spread to the winds, some staying in camp reading, others practicing climbing on nearby boulders, and still others hunting crystals of quartz, topaz, and aquamarine on the hillsides.

The next day was cloudy. We were quite surprised when Leif and Manzoor arrived in the evening with our remaining loads. The weather seemed much worse than on many days when the cloud-shy pilots had refused to fly. Perhaps our telegrams had brought some action.

The following morning, May 7, was hiring day. The name of each man we hired was to be recorded along with that of his village and his father. The prospective porters sat in long rows; each group of thirty to fifty was accompanied by a group leader. The men appeared generally strong, and even though the winter had been hard they showed no signs of malnutrition. Years of mountain walking had developed their thighs to nearly the size of their waists. They wore tattered woolens, varying in pattern only slightly from group to group. The greatest diversity was in footgear. Some sported leather mukluks that came well above the ankles. Others wore only open sandals, and still others had cheap plastic oxfords, usually without laces and always without socks. We wondered what would happen to those with unprotected feet when we reached the snow and ice. Our government contract stipulated that porters were to supply their own clothing and footgear. Could these men walk on glaciers for days on end in plastic shoes? When we queried Ghulam and Manzoor, we were told that we were very lucky to have them at all. We were the first expedition of the year; the eighteen expeditions behind us would have great trouble hiring anyone to carry for them.

I walked among the rows of waiting men. I could not casually judge their fitness as I might have done with a group of Americans. They had few external signs of strength or weakness. These men did seem more vibrant and healthy than the men in the lower cities of Pakistan. It was easy to hold a romantic image of only the strong surviving the harsh winters, and to forget the high incidence of chronic diseases such as tuberculosis, amoebic dysentery, and pneumonia among the mountain population. The porters had been preselected by Ghulam Rasul, and it was not possible for us to give each of them a medical exam, or make more than a cursory check of their clothing and footgear before moving on the trail.

The faces in this crowd of men were as varied as the four corners of the earth. I imagined myself as a casting director in Hollywood and I found a face to fit every role. One was a perfect pirate. Another looked like an American Indian. I spotted sheiks, Napoleons, bushmen, and Vikings. A group from one village looked Chinese, yet another looked Greek. Never had I seen such ethnic diversity. Still, it was not hard to "describe" the "average" Balti. He stood about five-foot-four, had straight black hair and hints of the Middle East and the Orient in his basically European features. But I wouldn't find him sitting there on his haunches, waiting to be hired. I wouldn't find him anywhere. The "average" Balti was as unreal as an "average" American hastily sketched in a clothing advertisement.

As the hiring progressed, the Baltis became painfully aware that there were more of them than there were loads to carry. Restlessness rippled their ranks like a breeze blowing through one of their wheat fields, though no one moved out of place. Jim and Lou realized something was happening and tried to lighten up the mood of the group. Jim, a foot taller than most of the Baltis, grabbed a *matu*, or resting stick, from one of the men and took his place in line to be hired, matching his posture to that of the others. Waves of laughter spread through the group, but the undercurrent of discontent remained. Lou attached a pair of yak horns to his head and stood on top of some boxes, bellowing in mock rage toward the crowd. Once again, the laughter passed quickly.

I busied myself by walking through the orderly rows taking portraits of the Baltis. Awareness of the camera usually spoiled the men's natural expressions, so when I chose a subject I would stop at least twenty feet away and pretend to take pictures of groups near me. When the novelty of the camera on the tripod wore off, I would change to a powerful 500mm lens. For several more minutes I would peer through it, laughing and joking with the men nearby, sometimes even allowing them to push the shutter release. By this time my subject would usually have tired of the game and lost interest in me. Twenty feet away, he would be on the fringe of the activity, unaware that my camera was focused on his face alone.

At one point I went back to camp to get more film, and when I returned the orderly rows were gone. A human whirlwind was

Dianne photographing a Balti woman and child

advancing on Ghulam Rasul, who was no larger than the average Balti. Ghulam stood his ground, shouting and gesticulating wildly with a heavy stick. The men from Askole were demanding that they be hired as regular porters in Dasso instead of as food porters above their village.

I couldn't understand how the disturbance had come about. A moment earlier I had been inside the group with no inkling that it had the potential to turn into an angry mob. But the men had moved suddenly and in unison like a flock of birds following a leader. The mob was not in fact as out of control as it had first seemed. It could have easily overpowered Ghulam, for instance, but it did not. I watched our fourteen high-altitude porters join in the melee, running back and forth like sheepdogs at the flanks of the crowd. Their intent was certainly to protect us, but they did little to stop the actual disturbance. The Baltis were responding only to their village group leaders. Some of these were yelling rabidly, inciting the others to riot. A few seemed to be forming a blockade around Ghulam, defending him and shouting down those who stepped forward. Among Ghulam's defenders I recognized three men who had helped us more around camp than our specially chosen high-altitude porters did. To me they were the heroes of the skirmish, and I sought to fix their faces in my memory. It was of little use to refer to them by name, for there were dozens of Hussains, Ghulams, and Alis. As the disturbance died down, I returned to my mind-game and tried to cast them in imaginary roles.

The first was easy. He had a broad face with wide-set blue eyes. He walked and spoke with great flair and confidence. I named him Marlon Brando. The next was an older man with a cruelly lined face and long yellow teeth—a perfect Wolfman Jack. The third was different from the others, almost a Balti superman possessed with an abundance of energy. He had high cheekbones, a light complexion, and a quick smile. He stood a head taller than the average and wore an old military jacket. He wasn't a movie star but a mountain man of some sort—a southern European, perhaps an Italian. When he smiled I saw a strong resemblance to a climber who had been the first to climb Gasherbrum IV and who had also reached over 26,000 feet on K2. I would call him Walter Bonatti.

That evening the team discussed the performance of the fourteen "HAPs," the high-altitude porters, during the skirmish. We were all disappointed, especially Jim, who felt that they compared very negatively with the Sherpas of Nepal. None would work unless sternly ordered and supervised. One, in fact, did no work at all and seemed content to strut like a peacock among the regular porters showing off his new clothes and playing his new transistor radio (purchased with the advance money we had given him to support his family) at full volume day and night. We talked about firing him, but Manzoor and Ghulam, who had hired him, did not favor the idea. They claimed he would be a good worker once we got into the mountains.

"I've been watching the regular porters," I told the others," and there are at least three guys who seem much better than our HAPs:

"Marlon Brando"

"Wolfman Jack"

"Walter Bonatti"

To Askole 83

Marlon Brando, Walter Bonatti, and Wolfman Jack." The incredulous looks slowly vanished as I explained whom I meant. The hard work and alertness of these three had impressed others on the team too. We regretted having allowed Manzoor and Ghulam to select the HAPs before our arrival. Like political appointees, the HAPs seemed to have been chosen more out of favoritism than ability. And, like political appointees, they seemed very firmly installed in their posts. Rather than risk dissension from Manzoor and Ghulam, we decided to let the matter rest.

On May 8 we established the daily routine that would characterize the approach march. Each morning from now on the giant caravan would awake before dawn. Porters wearing numbered badges would seek out loads marked with the same symbols. Some would appear at the doorways of tents, complaining loudly until the tents and kitchen were packed into numbered loads. Orderly rows of thirty to fifty porters would march into the cool gray morning, and the sun would rise on an empty campsite.

The porters tied their loads with rope woven from animal hair. Shoulder straps were made from the same narrow ropes; they cut off circulation and limited the carries to only a few minutes before rest was required. Once, when a porter was given a fine American pack to carry, he ignored the padded shoulder straps, tied the pack with his own rope as if it were a box, and slung it over his back with the cord biting into his shoulders.

The porters moved like waves, advancing, resting, advancing, resting, until they swelled over the final rise into camp. The climbers and HAPs moved more continuously, starting behind the porters but gradually working toward the front of the line. Their efforts were hampered by the rigid nature of the porters' movements. Climbers were always addressed as "sahib," which means master or sir, but this appellation seemed to include no deferential behavior on the trail. Porters did not step aside to let climbers pass, and they rested squarely in the middle of the trail, making it impossible for the climbers to move ahead on steep terrain.

During the first part of the trek we ended each day at a village that contrasted sharply with the surrounding arid land. The villages were always located at the base of an alluvial fan, and were composed of blossoming fruit trees, shady sycamores, and a network of mud and stone huts all clinging to the landscape like barnacles. Green fields spread away from the center of each village. Upon our arrival, these villages were always inestimably quiet. Only the breeze through the trees or the murmur of distant voices broke the silence. Gradually the din of arriving porters would overwhelm the peacefulness as six hundred visitors squatted on land that generally supported less than a hundred residents. All work would cease. Villagers, porters, and climbers would gape at each other. Campfires would burn long into the night, and we would fall asleep to the sounds of melodious Balti chants.

On the night we spent in Chongo we camped in a glade of fruit trees as usual, while villagers gaped at us. The caravan had been moving in fine rhythm, and we expected to reach the mountain in two weeks. Our relations with each other had improved with each mile as we moved ahead toward our common goal.

Our youngest HAP, Ibrahim, was from the Chongo district. He was the one who had done no work for us in Dasso and who strutted cockily among the regular porters playing his infernal radio. Near his home his behavior became even worse. Our whole team was of the opinion that we should fire him after he gave his pack of personal gear to a paid porter and walked all day with no load. Ghulam and Manzoor, who had chosen him in the first place, continued to insist that we should keep him because he was popular and influential, and could stir up trouble with other porters if we fired him. We decided on a compromise. We would continue to employ Ibrahim until we reached the foot of the glacier, but we would now hire one of the village group leaders to take his place above. The man we selected had already worked harder for us than any of the HAPs. He was a tall, attentive fellow named Akbar, the man I had earlier nicknamed Walter Bonatti.

Young porter

Our group had conflicting emotions about the Baltis. Rob, Leif, Steve, and I had faith in their innate goodness. We believed that by learning to understand their nature we could resolve most conflicts that might arise. The two Freds felt strongly antagonistic. "The milk of human kindness ran out after I met these lazy, thankless people," Fred Dunham told me. He felt that they were shirkers and thieves who were not to be trusted.

Jim and Dianne expected Western performance for Western rewards; such had been Jim's experiences with the Sherpas of Nepal. Before the expedition left, Jim had said, "I don't see any real problems. We're paying them better than any porters have ever been paid. I think I've done everything I can to get their cooperation. We're dressing our HAPs in exactly the same clothing and they're going to wear the same type of sunglasses, the same everything that we have, so they will feel like a part of us, I hope, and by feeling a part of us they will want to achieve the same goals that we want to achieve."

To those of us outside the Big Four, it appeared that Lou and Wick shared Jim's confidence that our approach march would be trouble-free. Actually, they both had considerable doubts about our control over the porters but kept them more to themselves than the rest of us did. Wick had studied accounts of numerous expeditions that had suffered porter strikes beyond Askole, but the information he picked up was tempered by Jim's infectious confidence.

As the villages rolled by, each left subtle impressions. They were more similar to each other than American cities are because similar geography dictated their locations. Every one was constructed on a terrace or a series of terraces left behind by the retreat of the Baltoro-Biafo ice stream. They were always located where a tributary supplied water for drinking and irrigation. Generally, the larger the side stream the larger the village. Since there was no industry here, the villages were all supported by the same agrarian activities.

However similar the outward form of the communities, the peoples of each village were distinctly different from each other. In this remote valley, the racial melting pot was reversing itself. The once-contiguous breeding population of Baltistan had fragmented several hundred years ago. The wide intermingling of people had ceased and each village had its own inbred characteristics. Now each remnant was a population of its own, evolving in its own direction. The smaller and more backward the village, the more obvious the inbreeding was to the visitor. The people of a large village might not share any more similarities than those we would expect to see at a large family picnic. Similar faces and bone structures, everyone a cousin. But some of the small villages went far beyond this stage. We saw many dwarfs, cretins, mongoloids, and people with six toes. "Too many cold nights with their sisters," as one person put it.

Our first day's hike brought us to a glade in the village of Chakpo, where pink apricot blossoms fell like snowflakes. A crowd of villagers surrounded our camp and curiously watched our every move. As I glanced from face to face I saw an unusual frequency of Tibetan features—broad cheekbones and taut eyefolds. Suddenly I found myself staring at an apparition. One face was disturbingly familiar. The features were identical to those of the ancient Egyptian queen Nefertiti. A sculptor three millenia ago had traced her contours into stone, and a picture of the bust had adorned my father's study. Now that same profile was before me again. A straight and slender nose rose toward bold eyebrows shaped like the wings of a gull in flight. The lips were a slender line above a prominent but narrow chin. The head curved boldly backward like a gourd, yet the neck was as slender as my wrist.

There was no mistaking the face, but I could not imagine how it had come to appear in one of the most woeful of Balti villages. I speculated wildly as I thought about the ancient Nefertiti and I remembered the fact that seven consecutive Egyptian Pharaohs had married their own sisters. Could this be the explanation? Had inbreeding originally produced Nefertiti's captivating features, and was it also responsible for the face I saw before me now?

The image of this face had once been fringed in gold in the tomb of a Pharaoh. Now it adorned a ten-year-old boy, who turned to walk hand-in-hand with his Asian-featured father toward a hut on the hill.

Dwarf, Chongo

③ First to K2

Oscar Eckenstein waited a full decade after his sour experiences with Conway before he and Aleister Crowley organized the first expedition to attempt K2 in 1902. Their small, guideless party was composed of three Britons, one Swiss, and two Austrians.

Eckenstein urged everyone to learn and practice Muslim conduct before going on the trip. He told them that most of the native people did not believe that the moral laws of the Koran applied to unbelievers. Unless they behaved as believers they would not be treated fairly.

Crowley went to India months before the expedition began. He grew a beard and conscientiously taught himself never to touch his face with his left hand. He tried to learn both the Hindustani and Balti languages, but of the latter he was only able to pick up a little basic grammar because it was unwritten dialect. Although he thought Muslim rituals were bunkum, he developed a great respect for the religion of Islam because it emphasized the power of natural forces over human values.

Crowley became the expedition's leader for three weeks when Eckenstein was barred from Kashmir by the British authorities and accused of being a spy. Today, detaining someone like Eckenstein would cause an international incident; accounts would be sprawled across all the front pages and given prime time on television. But in 1902 travelers expected the unexpected in India. Eckenstein's reaction was to calmly ask Crowley to move the expedition ahead into Kashmir, since he realized that a long delay could destroy the expedition's chance to climb K2. Then he traveled to Delhi, where he told the ranking British official that he would expose the whole story of Conway's shenanigans to the London papers unless he was al-

Aleister Crowley

Balti porters, near Dasso

lowed into Kashmir. He eventually rejoined his expedition in Srinagar.

There Eckenstein and Crowley hired a group of Pathan tribesmen to supervise the coolies and act as high-altitude porters on the mountain. It was a poor choice, for the Pathans proved domineering with the other natives and strongly inclined toward thievery.

Historically, this expedition was the first in a series to search in vain for competent high-altitude porters in the Karakoram. Since then, various expeditions have tried Baltis, Hunzas, Brokpas, and Pathans. So far, none of these people have demonstrated the ability or cheerfulness of the Sherpa people of Nepal. Some early expeditions actually imported Sherpas into the Karakoram, but this has not been allowed since the Indo-Pakistani conflicts following World War II.

Still, thanks to their understanding of native ways, Crowley and Eckenstein were able to march their caravan from Srinagar to Baltistan for seventeen continuous days without a halt. Even more impressive was the fact that this was done not by a single body of carefully selected porters, but by people who were hired in local villages and, with few exceptions, were changed every day.

Food was never a problem for porters close to home, but as the expedition neared the mountain it became a major factor in planning. The last village, Askole, is ten days' march from the base of K2. Thus the approach is quite unlike the more populated one to Mount Everest and most of the world's other high peaks. Crowley described a situation that has plagued every expedition to K2: "Our problem was how to get 110 loads deposited at a distance representing [there and back] not less than 20 marches. . . . A man who eats say, two pounds a day and carries sixty pounds can carry nothing except his own food on a journey of 30 marches."

The expedition claimed to have bought every pound of edible goods in the valley and employed every available man. They had to hire three men to carry every load: one for the load itself and two to carry the food of the three.

Crowley was a strict disciplinarian with porters who straggled to test the authority of the expedition. He ignored them until the end of the day, then whipped them publicly in front of their friends. He believed that to avoid putting himself in constant jeopardy, a foreigner had to show both cultural equality and moral superiority over the natives. Crowley found the Balti people to be honest and loyal in many ways but to have unaccountable lapses in morality. Certain expedition items were never touched, while others disappeared as soon as night fell. Crowley was amused that Baltis from remote villages would walk for many days in order to sneak into the daily pay line and attempt to collect what amounted to less than ten cents without working for it.

Crowley's greatest source of control was his ability to administer justice within the native laws. Once he was called to settle a dispute between two porters, a Pathan and a Kashmiri. The Pathan was a notorious bully who claimed that he had won the Kashmiri's ragged topcoat in a fair contest. The poor Kashmiri owned little more than

*Walking through
the Braldu Gorge*

rags while the Pathan pranced about in one of the magnificent new
coats that the expedition had furnished to each of the high-altitude
porters. In front of the assembled crowd, Crowley pronounced that
by the concepts of native justice, the Pathan owned the Kashmiri's
topcoat. The Pathan demanded that his victim be disrobed immediately so that he could bear away his spoils. "But wait," Crowley said. "His coat is yours, but the one you are wearing belongs to
me! Since you now have one of your own, give my coat to the man
who has none at all." To the cheers of the entire caravan, the lowly
porter walked away in well-dressed splendor, while the Pathan
crept off in rags.

At one point on the journey, after the expedition's entire sugar
supply disappeared, all the Pathans were fired. Baltis were hired in
their place.

As the expedition marched up the Braldu Valley, word of the
remarkable healing powers possessed by Jacot Guillarmod, the
team's doctor, traveled ahead of them. Once, when Guillarmod
began to use forceps to pull out a Balti's diseased tooth, the man,
who had walked from a distant village, said, "Oh no! I want to be
cured like the others; put your hand on my head and make me
well!"

In those days few men appreciated the scale of Himalayan geography. Pfannl and Wesseley, the two Austrians on the expedition,
proposed a rushed ascent of K2 from Askole with three days' food.
Crowley was contemptuous of their failure to understand that Askole was still ten marches from the *base* of the peak. But he, too, fell
victim to the same phenomenon of scale. When they finally reached
the base of the peak, Crowley looked up at what would later be

called the Abruzzi Ridge and commented, "There should be no difficulty in walking up the snow slopes on the east-south-east to the snowy shoulder." From this point, which is just over 25,000 feet, Crowley was sure that the summit "could be reached without question, given one fine day."

Crowley was in favor of trying the Abruzzi Ridge, but he was out-voted. Instead, the expedition attempted the Northeast Ridge, where they reached about 21,650 feet before turning back. Their decision was forced by the inability of the Balti high porters, on whom they were dependent, to carry loads up the climb. The Austrian members wanted to climb 24,750-foot Skyang Kangri, but Eckenstein insisted on staying with K2. Compromising, they decided to attempt a col between the Northeast Ridge of K2 and Skyang Kangri.

Pfannl became suddenly ill. Crowley later wrote, "Pfannl was suffering from oedema of both lungs and his mind was gone." They gave up the attempt on K2 and carried Pfannl to Urdukas, where he quickly recovered at the much lower elevation.

Modern mountain doctors have pondered over why Pfannl's ailment was diagnosed as edema instead of pneumonia. Until the 1960s, and even occasionally today, the condition now recognized as high-altitude pulmonary edema (or oedema) was usually diagnosed as pneumonia. High-altitude edema is a physiological malfunction which fills the lungs with fluid, though the germ-caused infection of pneumonia is absent. Edema, which simply means the abnormal accumulation of fluid in parts of the body, accompanies pneumonia but was not generally recognized as occurring spontaneously at high elevations until long after Crowley's expedition. Expedition physicians usually assumed that fluid accumulation was the result of pneumonia and treated the symptom as such. Many climbers died because the drugs used against pneumonia did absolutely nothing for pulmonary edema. By chance, Crowley's group did exactly the right thing by removing Pfannl immediately to lower elevation. The isolation of edema from pneumonia in Crowley's account was long before its time and one of the earliest ever recorded. Was it a fluke? Or did Crowley's genius balk at making the normal assumption from symptom to disease?

Crowley was ahead of his time in another aspect of high-altitude physiology as well. Many climbers believed that they could acclimatize right up to the highest summits. Crowley thought the human limit was well below the top of the highest peaks. Modern physiologists believe that above an elevation of 17- to 19,000 feet, depending on the individual, the body is in a constant state of deterioration. Since no one had ever been near the tops of the highest peaks at the turn of the century, the subject was open to speculation.

Crowley never states an exact altitude of maximum acclimatization, although he doesn't mention exceeding it on climbs of 14,000-foot peaks in the Alps or 18,000-foot peaks in Mexico. He is quite specific, however, about Himalayan climbing. "You cannot live permanently in conditions unsuited to your organism. . . . The only thing to do is to lay in a stock of energy, get rid of all your fat at the exact moment when you have a chance to climb the mountain, and jump back out of its reach . . . before it can take its revenge. To talk of acclimatization is to adopt the psychology of the man who trained his horse gradually to live on a single straw a day and would have revolutionized our system of nutrition, if the balky brute had not been aggravating enough to die on his hands."

As might be expected, the Crowley-Eckenstein expedition was rife with personality conflicts. Dr. Guillarmod thought that Crowley was neurotic. Crowley thought that Guillarmod was incompetent. The Austrians, Pfannl and Wesseley, complained of Eckenstein's rigid discipline. Knowles had been threatened by Crowley with a revolver. There was universal unhappiness over Wesseley's constant pilfering of food and Crowley's insistence on taking along a large library. On the approach march Crowley was told that his personal valise could not exceed forty pounds on the glaciers. He threatened to quit the expedition if he couldn't bring "Milton and the rest." Begrudgingly, he was allowed his overage. Wesseley's manners and food pilfering offended the expedition to such a degree that he was expelled after a vote on the return march. Pfannl decided to go with him, and the two men split from the group.

The vote came immediately after Wesseley had eaten the better part of two whole sheep that had been slaughtered for a celebration of the expedition's return. Sheep in Baltistan are very small, usually not exceeding thirty pounds. Even so, Wesseley must have been a considerable glutton. Crowley called him a perfect pig, saying, "He would bend over his plate and, using his knife and fork like the blades of a paddle wheel, would churn the food into his mouth with a rapid rotary motion. There was always some going up and some going down."

The expedition discovered that Karakoram weather in the arid valleys bore little resemblance to what went on in the Baltoro basin. Of sixty-eight days spent on the Baltoro Glacier or above, only eight were fair, and no three of those eight were consecutive. The season was worse than normal, but Crowley correctly described the average weather as "quite exceptionally abominable."

Throughout the trip the group used many different forms of transportation. For the earlier parts of the journey, between the cities of India and the mouth of the Braldu River, horses and ponies were the most efficient means. Foot travel became necessary through the narrow Braldu Valley, and the expedition traveled with a veritable barnyard of sheep, goats, and chickens in order to reduce the food loads and keep the number of porters to a minimum.

The most exotic form of transport was reserved for the return trip. Between the village of Dasso on the Braldu River and Skardu on the Indus River, the group managed to avoid fifty miles of desert travel by floating down river in five hours on rafts made of inflated goat skins. Five months after they had left the Indian plains, the four remaining members of the expedition floated into Skardu, "youth at the prow, pleasure at the helm," into a world of fresh grapes, potatoes, apricots, and corn.

So ended the first of eight expeditions attempting K2 between 1902 and 1975. All but one failed. For some climbers, it was a once-in-a-lifetime experience. It became a crest on the wave of their memories that colored all other intense experiences. For others it was even more than that. So much more that they returned to the Baltoro again and again, exposing themselves to dangers, fatiguing their bodies into frail shadows, and striving for summits that they rarely achieved. After each journey they went home feeling the indescribable sense of sad-happy serenity that only long adventures far from civilization can bring.

Aleister Crowley never returned to the Karakoram, but he became addicted to the mental state he acquired from the experience. He searched for it again and again during the remaining forty-five years of his life. In religion, magic, and occult rituals he found something of what he had previously experienced from climbing mountains. A statement he wrote years later in his autobiography is a timeless creed for exploration:

I meant to tell mankind about a new state about which I could tell them little or nothing, to teach them to tread a long and lonely path which might or might not lead thither, to bid them dare encounter all possible perils of nature unknown, to abandon all their settled manners of living and cut themselves off from their past and their environment, and to attempt a quixotic adventure with no resources beyond their native strength and sagacity. I had done it myself and found not only that the pearl of great price was worth far more than I possessed, but that the very perils and privations of the quest were themselves my dearest memories. I was certain of this at least: that nothing in the world except this was worth doing.

4 To Paiyu

On the way to Askole, the last village on the approach to K2, we stopped at a hot springs. For more than an hour we soaked in the steaming waters, thinking about how wonderful it would feel to return to the springs after the climb. I remembered a picture in *Life* magazine of the same pool, filled with members of the successful 1954 Italian K2 expedition. The two victors, Lacedelli and Compagnoni, both had frostbite. One stayed completely out of the water, and the other kept a bandaged hand held high. Lying in the same waters, I wondered if all of us would bathe there on the march out. Would there be hands held out of the water? Would everyone return?

Askole was the jumping-off point for K2, still seventy-five miles away. There was no human habitation in between. The village sits at 10,000 feet, only a few miles from the tip of the Biafo Glacier. It is poised on an old morainal terrace hundreds of feet above the Braldu

Plowing fields in Askole

The village of Askole

The Lambardar *of Askole with family*

River. I had read all the geographical facts about the village, I had seen photographs taken by other expeditions, but I was not prepared for the reality. It was, simply, a grand place to live. The natural design of the area was near-perfect. Sheer cliffs stopped abruptly at the edge of level fields, just now being planted. Through a vee in the canyon, we could see the snowcapped pyramid of Bakhor Das, 19,060 feet, rising sharply into the sky. The river carved a giant arc just beyond the village, then descended toward Chongo in gentler curves.

As I walked through the town, almost every man greeted me with a friendly "*Salaam!*" The women did just the opposite. Many stood on top of their houses to get a glimpse of us, but if my eyes met theirs they quickly dropped through holes in the roof like surprised prairie dogs. Those I met on pathways covered their faces and ran. Only Dianne could approach the women without evoking such reactions. In her diary she described her visit with Jim to the house of the village *Lambardar*, who had inherited the rule of the village:

The Lambardar took us first into the oldest part of his house, a dark, low-ceilinged room with a square hole in the roof to admit a little sunlight.

To Paiyu 93

Another square hole in the floor had a ladder leaning against one edge. It led to a dugout basement just below the hole. Below were the two wives of the Lambardar—one a woman of perhaps twenty-five years, the other a girl of fourteen. We descended into the smoky room, shook the hands of the two wives and inspected the workmanship of the wood beams and posts. My eyes watered and I wanted to cough—how can these people live in smoke-filled rooms so much of the time? The two women looked much older than their years. Their faces were covered with soot and their hands were dry and cracked like those of very old women. They were shrouded from the world, down in the basement or up on the rooftops, or working in the fields. I wanted to look into their faces and understand something of what their lives must be—they were so friendly and bright in the darkness of that room. What a pity that we had no universal language. I wished to be able, with a look, to tell who I am, what I feel, what it is to be a woman in North America—and to know the same from them.

For Rob, Leif, Steve, and me, Askole was the place where we made the pleasant move out of the infernal cook tent and into a tent of our own. The team had planned to lay over for one extra day in Askole in order to hire 180 more porters to carry food for the others. I looked forward to the peace and quiet of roaming the village with a camera, but tranquility was one thing Askole did not hold in store for us. In the afternoon, Askole became a very busy place. Our hundreds of loads were neatly stacked in a courtyard, and our porters were wandering through the village, tripling its population. As I strolled through the crowd, pandemonium suddenly erupted. A man started yelling and gesticulating wildly from the top of a stone fence. Soon all 584 porters had gathered below him. Other men spoke out from the crowd, and emotions rose like the swelling of the tide. I was reminded of Sproul Plaza in Berkeley during the Free Speech Movement of the 1960s.

I pushed my way through the crowd to a cottonwood tree so I could get a better view of what was going on. Though the expedition was clearly under verbal attack and the porters were rallying, those nearby showed no antagonism toward me. They gave me a boost into the branches of the tree so that I could photograph the scene. These people were able to separate us as individuals from our cultural trappings, and that, literally, is exactly what they were planning to do.

According to government regulations, we were paying the porters the maximum rate of 30 rupees per day plus food. If they procured their own food they received an extra 10 rupees a day. A year before, the going daily rate had been 15 rupees. Now the porters were demanding even more than the 30 plus 10. Not only did they ask for an increase in basic wages, but also for half pay on layover days and extra pay for the days they would spend walking back to their villages after they left the expedition.

A rupee is worth about ten cents. Four dollars per day may not sound like much for arduous load-carrying in the mountains, but by Asian standards it matches the pay scale of Americans working on the Alaska pipeline. In both instances, relatively unskilled laborers are hired to live and work in nomadic camps for wages that are

Morning on the Baltoro Glacier

Aerial of the Biafo Glacier and the Ogre group

Paiyu Peak

Deceptively sheer Mustagh Tower

Camp below the Biarchedi Towers

*The free-standing shaft of Nameless Tower
culminates the Trango group*

Sunrise on a lenticular cloud gives K2 a golden helmet

Uli Biaho Tower

Alpenglow on Masherbrum

much higher than those received by most college-educated people in their own countries.

Why, then, were the porters striking? They certainly had no pressing need for the money, since they lived in a relatively stable cashless economy. Slowly, I began to realize that their demands were not based on need. They lived in a thought world without our abstract concepts of justice. We believed that our government contract was a closed concept. If no provisions were made for payment other than 40 rupees per day, then we owed no extra payments. The Baltis had an entirely different view. They believed that everything not defined in the contract was now negotiable, and, further, that the very wage agreed upon was merely a starting point for negotiations to be conducted on their home ground.

Jim was shocked by the many expenses not in our budget. "In our regulations there was nothing said about paying the twelve village heads," he said, "and they don't carry any loads. There are four paid policemen, and they don't carry loads. The fourteen HAPs carry only their personal gear. Manzoor doesn't carry a load. That's thirty-one people that have to have eleven porters hired just to carry their food. We're getting ripped off. There sure was no mention of any of this by Manzoor, the Pakistani Embassy in Washington, or by the Pakistani Ministry of Tourism. I know one thing. We will be over budget by at least $15,000 by the time we reach base camp."

Dianne did not agree. Reluctant to tell the others of her feelings, she recorded them in her diary:

Team members talking about how we're getting ripped off. What shit! They sit (some of them) huddled in tent city, unwilling to share any of themselves with the people here. So we're paying them high wages. So what? We'll still leave this country with far more than we've given the people here. Does it occur to anyone that perhaps, just perhaps, some of the people here are just simple, friendly, honest mountain people? Of course they're just as anxious about us as we are about them. Why shouldn't they be? We invade their land, their culture, and expect everything to run the way it goes in America. Christ, we need some humility—both towards the people and the mountain. What arrogant, cold bastards we can be.

Jim and Dianne

The sahibs won the first round. The porters agreed to continue for the same rate. We would not pay them for a layover in Askole. The "going-back pay" was left in the air.

Manzoor's prediction at Dasso came true: we were not able to hire 180 food porters in Askole as planned. Many of the men had already been hired as regular porters, leaving men from other villages unhired. Now the villagers of Askole were reluctant to part with the rest of their manpower, especially since the winter had been late and the fields were still being tilled. After much discussion, we succeeded in hiring seventy men. We would have to send other porters back to Askole for more food during the trek. This development was actually not as serious as it seemed at first, since each day the caravan consumed more than a dozen food loads. The porters thereby liberated could return to Askole and bring back additional food.

Meanwhile, Rob had been fighting a battle of his own. That evening, he wrote a description of his attempts to provide medical treatment to the villagers:

I am overwhelmed by village and porter patients—76 in five-and-a-half hours. How evident it was that modern medicine has become dependent on diagnostic laboratory tests. Here it is like veterinary medicine: a poor history at best through two interpreters from English to Urdu to Balti back through Urdu and to English again, accompanied by a sketchy, public exam before a village of onlookers. For some patients it was a game—the thing to do. See the doctor for some minor complaint. Be examined and get some medicine. For others, fortunately few in number, the visit was a matter of life and death. One six-year-old (the size of a three-year-old) emaciated, weak, and chronically ill, but had no positive physical signs. I guessed intestinal parasites and out of desperation prescribed *Povan*. Terribly frustrating and depressing to know that he could be diagnosed and probably cured in most American hospitals. Another serious case is probably *myasthenia gravis* [a progressive muscular failure]. Almost too weak to walk, he will surely die unless he can be carried the thirty miles to a jeep and then to Rawalpindi. People here seem very fatalistic about death. Perhaps it comes from the inevitability of watching someone die when no help is available. When asked what happens in Askole when people get really sick, the Lambardar replied, "They die."

"Doctor Sahib" at work

During the night, the head policeman got up in the dark to urinate, fell over a four-foot wall, broke some ribs, and injured a kidney. The other three policemen did not want to continue without him. They demanded to be paid and released from duty. They also wanted extra pay for walking home and three porters to carry their food. After a long argument, Jim gave in just as our porter train was beginning to move out of Askole.

The first camping ground beyond Askole is named Korophon, for a single rounded boulder about twenty feet high that marks the site. The campsite itself is situated on a very flat plain, but to reach it we had to pass the snout of the Biafo Glacier. We didn't know that the usual trail headed up a side valley and crossed the glacier about half a mile back from the river. We started out ahead of the porters and chose our own route, following the faint paths of herdsmen who had not intended to go beyond the glacier.

When I reached the snout of the glacier, I was surprised to see it actually jutting into the river. Only Lou was ahead of me and I could see him a short way in front of me, picking his way along the steep, rock-strewn ice wall. Behind me, several of the others were fording the stream to gain an easier path. The idea of getting wet up to my waist was not appealing, so I followed Lou. The morning sun was loosening many rocks from the steep face of the snout, and some of them came tumbling down nearby. At first it was no problem, because I could easily see where they were coming from and avoid them. But when I walked beneath an ice overhang, I was only able to see a few feet overhead. A large rock became dislodged and suddenly rolled over the brink straight at me. I made a quick leap into the river, expecting the water to be only inches deep where I landed near the edge. The rock missed, but I landed in swirling water up to my chest. My camera was momentarily doused and I quickly climbed out to dry it off.

I checked the possible alternatives. Lou was completely out of sight, and many rocks were now rolling down the face of the snout. The river raged close by the ice cliff for at least another quarter mile. The route looked too dangerous, so I picked a spot that seemed shallow and attempted to ford the river. It was much swifter than I expected. Using my ski poles for support, I made it quite easily to an exposed rock in the middle of the river, but from there I was unable to find a shallow traverse to the opposite bank. With my camera gear wrapped in a parka and stuffed high in my pack, I committed myself to a short section of rapids. The water was probably not over my head, but it was at least chest deep and flowing far too fast for me to stand up. I pushed madly at rocks with my ski poles and tried to arch my back to keep my pack dry while floating wildly for about twenty feet. I finally reached a spot where I could resume walking to shore. I had been in the icy water more than five minutes, and I shook convulsively with chills long after getting out.

For half a mile I walked across a level plain. Suddenly the river cut off further progress. It curved completely across the valley and flowed by a vertical rock wall on the opposite side. I would have to cross again. As I was deciding what to do, Wick, Fred, Leif, and Steve walked up behind me. The four of us tried to cross in one spot for the better part of an hour, but the river was too deep and swift. Finally, we headed downstream and found a long diagonal bed of boulders where we crossed in water not much above our knees.

After the crossing I felt acutely sick and vomited several times while the others went on. A few minutes later I was hit with diarrhea. In a cold sweat, I plodded slowly toward Korophon, reaching camp early in the afternoon. Lying in the sand by the river, I rested for several hours until the porters arrived with our tents. They were in a surly mood, arguing noisily over the distribution of rations and once again demanding "going-back-pay" from base camp. When evening fell I felt suddenly better, and I noticed that the angry sounds from the porters' area were gone. I decided to take a walk through the porters' campground.

Groups of six to ten men sat in circles around the campfires, baking chapatties and drinking tea. One man was singing in a high tenor voice and others were dancing and chanting. I recognized the singer. It was our new HAP, Akbar. He motioned me into his campfire circle and offered me a chapatti. I sat down among the smiling, happy men. What a contrast to the daytime haggling and sullenness of a few hours ago!

In the morning I felt much better. After walking a short distance we came to the Dumordu River, which drained from the Panmah Glacier. It was quite easy to ford, but Manzoor told us that it would be a raging torrent later in the year when the ice began to melt. On our return we would have to walk five miles out of our way to a rope bridge made of twisted vines.

We were nearing the heart of the mountains. Above the Braldu Gorge, uncounted peaks rose in jagged splendor. The blanket of winter still reached down to the snow-covered meadows only a few thousand feet above the river. Large glaciers filled the heads of every high valley we could see.

For many people in the world, the landscape before us would be foreboding. For us, it had been a gradual ascent from the unknown into the familiar. Beyond the last villages we no longer saw strange human alterings of the scene, but rather the workings of nature common to all the world's alpine areas: glaciers, rivers, rounded stream rocks, angular moraine rocks, sagebrush, clouds, granite, blue sky, raindrops, wildlife, and friends who shared our passions. We were home again.

The next camp was Bardomal, "river bank of trouble." The path, often indistinct, followed the river's edge in some places and was etched out of the nearly vertical walls of morainal mud and stone in others. Leif, the two Freds, and many of the porters narrowly escaped death as boulders plunged spontaneously from a thousand feet above.

The Braldu River in a narrow gorge

We were reminded, once again, that geological processes are not always the slow, imperceptible changes we read about in textbooks and superficial travel articles. In the Karakoram the environment is a constant threat to human beings. In America our impressions of natural change are far more subtle; we may argue with friends about possible long-term shifts in the weather without suffering unduly if we make mistakes. But to the Baltis, whether or when a glacier will advance on a village is a critical question, not a casual conjecture. As recently as 1913, for instance, the Tippuri Glacier threatened the village of Arandu and overwhelmed a sawmill on its outskirts. Some anthropologists believe that the ruins of ancient villages are now buried under the lower sections of the Baltoro Glacier. Rockfalls and mudslides are part of a way of life. Almost every expedition to the Baltoro region has either witnessed such catastrophes or come across a broad hillside, barren of living things, where the trail has recently slipped into the river. The tons of suddenly falling earth and rock have the potential to kill hundreds of people, but they land in the torrent like a pinch of dust, diffusing almost instantly with the flowing waters that carry the run-offs of the Karakoram to the sea.

Bardomal lived up to its name—trouble. For Jim problems began to arise shortly after he left Korophon. For the first time he had started out in the morning without Dianne, hoping to hike with Lou and Wick ahead of the porters. About a mile out of camp a HAP came running from behind, sweating profusely and carrying no pack. He said Jim must return to Korophon because several porters wanted to quit and be paid. Manzoor had forgotten to tell Jim the evening before.

Jim, Lou, and Wick returned to the camp, paid off six porters, then sublimated their anger with a rapid hike to Bardomal. Starting behind most of the porters and all the other sahibs, they passed everyone and arrived at camp at 10:30 A.M. Wick was especially pleased when the twins, who had set speed records on both Mounts Rainier and McKinley, told him, "You're a tough S.O.B."

"That satisfies," Wick wrote in his diary, "because they are moving dudes."

The satisfaction was short-lived. As the porters arrived, they began a noisy second act to their Askole performance. They now demanded 7 rupees per day for hiking back without loads from base camp and a guarantee of half-wages for all layover days. Since we were already spending in the neighborhood of $2,500 per day for porters on the move, meeting the latter demand would mean a $1,200 expenditure for each day on which an excuse was found to stay put. We refused. The strikers gave us an ultimatum: accept the terms or they would all quit.

In earlier years the expedition held the trump card on matters of porters' wages. It was usually alone in the region and the only source of wage-paying employment. Only workers who had something to offer could benefit. This year the situation was reversed. With nineteen expeditions scheduled to travel the Braldu, the porters gained bargaining power. They wanted to carry only at low elevations on easy terrain. As they neared the snowline, they sought excuses to quit so they could return to the lowlands and hire on with another expedition. Already, the French Gasherbrum II

Barefoot porters, near Bardomal

expedition had arrived in Dasso and seven other expeditions were stacked up in Rawalpindi waiting long weeks for the daily flight to Skardu. Government regulations meant nothing to these tribal people on their home ground. For generations they had supposedly been under the control of various rulers—the Dogras, the British, and now the Pakistanis—who had never actually invaded their mountain strongholds.

Throughout the afternoon, negotiations went on. The language barrier was severe because everything had to be translated from English to Urdu by Manzoor, then from Urdu to Balti by Ghulam, and then back through Urdu and English again. Manzoor told Ghulam to ask whether the porters would accept 5 rupees per day for return pay before the team had agreed to make the offer. Jim, still angry from the morning's misunderstanding, thought that Manzoor seemed to favor the porters rather than us. Wick wasn't sure whose side Manzoor was on, but thought he lacked the necessary toughness to deal with the recalcitrant porters. Fred Stanley suddenly appeared in the negotiating tent and announced that he and several of the others thought the porters should receive no extra payments. Wick retorted, "Stanley, if you think you can run this expedition any better, you're welcome to try." Jim said something similar and Manzoor reiterated that at least two hundred porters would quit unless an agreement was reached then and there. Finally, it was agreed, most reluctantly, that we would pay the porters 5 rupees per day on the return march, but only those who carried all the way to base camp would benefit. Quitters or troublemakers who were fired would not receive the return pay. The question of layover pay was not resolved, but we hinted that we might pay half-wages for one stopover at Paiyu while the porters cooked chapatties to eat on the glacier.

In the morning we began walking toward Paiyu. A few raindrops fell out of cloudy skies. As we reached the crest of an alluvial fan, the vast panorama of the Baltoro came into view. There, only a few miles ahead of us, lay the dark snout of the Baltoro Glacier. It was at once stupendous and disappointing. In the distance giant rock towers rose into the clouds like tiered cakes of granite frosted with snow. The towers were far more impressive from the ground than they had been from the air. It was the glacier that was disappointing. I had expected a pure white carpet running from the heights, but the Baltoro was totally covered with rounded piles of rock debris. It looked as if God's own construction company had run out of funds and left the scene incomplete.

As I continued toward Paiyu I saw in the distance a tall, slender figure walking toward us quite alone.

Manzoor bargaining with group leader

Section V

The Legacy of Heinrich Harrer

The Eigerwand demands the uttermost of skill, stamina, and courage. . . . To climb it the mountaineer must combine in himself every attribute that marks a true man of the mountains. All climbing techniques must have become second nature to him; yet he must feel in himself the same serene strength exhibited by the first peasant who dared to put up his homestead among the great and savage mountains.

—HEINRICH HARRER

1 Extreme Climbing

Himalayan climbing is not necessarily the ultimate expression of the art. In other parts of the world, the style of an ascent means more than the attainment of a summit. By their nature, Himalayan peaks inhibit the style of a climb. Because of their remoteness many people are usually included in the party to carry food and equipment. Because of their altitude progress is slowed and hence even more people, food, and equipment will be needed. And because of low temperatures and eternal snows, semipermanent camps are normally established within a day's travel of each other, and fixed ropes are placed over difficult sections to aid those who subsequently carry loads.

All this is quite opposite the goal of modern extreme climbers, who challenge difficulty for its own sake with as little equipment as possible. Many mountaineers have returned home from their first Himalayan expedition quite depressed and disappointed because the range in which they sought the ultimate climbing experience had provided only unfamiliar exercises in high-altitude freight handling.

Extreme climbing is just beginning in the Himalaya. In the past this style was so seriously misunderstood that a whole generation of Alpine climbers were harshly discredited by their contemporaries. That unfortunate era, just before World War II, was to have a profound effect on future Himalayan climbing, even influencing the tragic outcome of the 1939 American K2 Expedition, which very nearly reached the summit.

It is important to understand the early history of extreme climbing in the Alps and, even more significant, the motivations of its proponents. If one common thread links all great climbers, past and present, it is not so much a list of impressive ascents as a state of mind in which the act of climbing is enjoyed purely for itself. When an important first ascent is made, publicity always focuses on the attainment of the summit, while the climber's underlying motivations lie hidden from the public eye. On modern difficult routes, many climbers do not even bother going to the summit even though it may be within a few minutes' easy walking from the end of their difficulties.

At the highest levels of difficulty or endurance, climbing demands total concentration of one's senses. All thoughts converge on the task at hand. No room exists for such normal mental activities as time measurement or self-contemplation. Consciousness becomes a smooth, purposeful stream of energy fitted to the task. Feet, eyes, and mind work in total harmony as each receives instantaneous feedback from the actions of the others. No random thoughts block the flow between body and mind. Only by attaining this smooth and tranquil state can climbers do their best. Conversely, climbers intent on doing their best, whether they admit it or not, are seeking this satisfying state of mind, often more directly than the summit itself.

Not surprisingly, the "style" that climbers consider the best is normally that which makes this purity of consciousness possible. A climber is most likely to reach this state when climbing alone or with a few quiet companions, and least likely when being guided, acting as a guide, or consciously trying to follow someone else's description of a climb. Equipment is also a factor. Climbing with a few classic tools that become extensions of the body is quite conducive to the sought-after feeling; using a plethora of gadgets is not. Climbing near one's limit brings on the feeling; staying well within one's margin does not. Viewed in this context, reaching the summit of a mountain is not all it is cracked up to be; it simply marks the end of a highly pleasurable state of mind.

The ecstasy that a climber seeks is not to be found solely in the mountains. The identical feeling is the goal in all sorts of activities that require intense concentration and that do not involve direct rewards such as money or prestige. Chess brings on the self-communication of intense concentration, but lacks the meld of physical and mental action. Most team sports involve too many distractions and only a short-term commitment. Many top climbers feel that climbing is basically useless, but return to the mountains again and again because they cannot experience the same ecstasy in performing the actions our society deems useful. For them, the summit is merely the curtain falling on a grand play. The curtain, like the achievement of the summit, tells nothing about what happened beforehand.

Novice climbers can only experience hints of this emotional reward because their actions are not yet ingrained in the motor nerves, and the feeling cannot be realized when one is outwardly contemplating one's own actions. Similarly, if a climb is either too hard or too easy, then horror or boredom respectively will interfere with the tranquility of this state of mind. When and how a person experiences the shift of consciousness depends on his own personal level of ability. An intermediate climber might reach it on a moderate climb, but an expert would have to do a harder climb or change the style of the moderate climb by using less equipment or climbing solo. The significant point is that the climber must be working at his own top capacity for difficulty, endurance, or both.

In the early days of mountaineering, climbs requiring technical expertise and those requiring great endurance were held to be quite distinct from each other. Expeditionary climbers rarely tackled great

Cliff detail, Trango Towers

technical difficulties, while technical climbers rarely made long climbs requiring great endurance. Each specialist developed a certain contempt for the other. To the technical climber the expeditioner was a clumsy oaf who couldn't compete with the local lads on rock or ice, and therefore sought glory on big, easy peaks. To the expeditioner the technical climber was a talented but misguided fellow who never practiced the *real thing*, but preferred to waste his talents on meaningless small outcrops and ice gullies.

All sorts of things happened when the twain finally met. For one thing, technical standards of short climbs began to be applied in the high mountains. Extremely difficult maneuvers, in the past attempted only on "practice climbs," became part and parcel of modern routes. Previously unexplored frontiers opened up. First in the Alps, then in the Himalaya, men attempted once "impossible" faces and ridges. The media and the general public, conditioned to believe that reaching the summit was all-important, failed to understand what was happening. As a result, history imparted false motives to many of the greatest pioneers of modern mountaineering. There is no better example of this sort of misrepresentation than the events surrounding the first climb of the famous north face of the Eiger in Switzerland.

By the standard route the Eiger is an easy mountain to climb, but because of its north face, the Eigerwand, it has dominated popular ideas of climbing for nearly half a century. Notorious for the number of climbers it has killed, the 6,000-foot face was first climbed successfully in 1938 by a party of two Germans and two Austrians. Prior to that climb, Hitler had announced that he would award Olympic Gold Medals to the first Eigerwand climbers. Afterwards, the climb was sensationalized with worldwide publicity which titillated the public and offended many climbers. Hitler's association with the climb caused the neck hairs of mountaineering pundits around the world to rise. They deplored the climb, believing it to be motivated by political propaganda. They claimed that the climb was an expression of the Nazi philosophy, an acting-out of Hitler's superman concept.

This episode might have remained merely an isolated historical footnote if Nazi associations with the Eiger had not become ingrained in mountaineering literature and lore. Circumstantially, the evidence suggested that Nazi beliefs had a lot to do with motivating people to climb the Eigerwand. Eight climbers lost their lives on the face between 1935 and the 1938 success, and all were from Nazi countries. A year before the 1938 success, the president of the Alpine Club of London, Colonel E. L. Strutt, declared that the climb "continues to be an obsession for the mentally deranged. . . . He who succeeds first may rest assured that he has accomplished the most imbecile variant since mountaineering began."

In 1941 James Ramsey Ullman wrote a widely read history of world mountaineering in which he omitted the names of the first successful climbers of the Eigerwand—probably the most significant Alpine climb in the first half of the twentieth century. Ullman cited the climb as an example of how "perverted nationalism can infect even the most unpolitical of human activities." He described "the jingoistic fervor that developed in the decade before the Second World War," and suggested that it "touched new heights of absurdity." He continued with a verbal bomb raid on the motivations of German and Austrian mountaineers:

Aflame with the hero-philosophy of Nazi-Fascism and egged on by flag-wavers and tub-thumpers at home, brown-and-black-shirted young climbers began vying with one another in what they conceived to be feats of courage and skill. All or nothing was their watchword—victory or death. No risk was too great, no foolhardiness to be condemned, so long as their exploits brought kudos to *Vaterland* or *patria*. . . . [T]here appeared to be an over-growing supply of young men eager to devise still more spectacular and gruesome ways of killing themselves. Since the war a measure of sanity has been restored; the hordes of storm-trooper heroes have disappeared, and the mountains are being given back again to those who understand and love them.

Ullman wrote his book when anti-Nazi feelings were at their height, so the ferocity of his tirade is somewhat understandable. But his theme is commonly expressed even today. A quarter century after the first climb of the Eigerwand, the prestigious journal *Mountain World* published a history of the Eiger written by a Swiss mountaineer, Othmar Gurtner. The article stated that the 1938 climb nevershould have been made because it was dangerous, foolhardy, and attempted for all the wrong reasons. Gurtner cited a 1932 route on the edge of the Eigerwand as the definitive route and argued that, given the existence of that route, no one should have climbed the center of the face. He likened the people who have attempted the center of the Eigerwand to members of the Children's Crusade being led to slaughter.

Again, Gurtner describes the early Eigerwand climbers without naming them:

These wiry fellows, whose skin was at stake, had a clean style; with calf muscles of iron they stood on their twelve-pointed crampons, like artistes they understood every variation of covering or advancing rope technique; they were perfect alpine technicians of the best kind—without counting their endurance, their courage, and their push. But they were no longer complete mountaineers, because what they did, they did in the limelight and in the wrong place. The *ratio legis* had slipped away from their mental equipment; they thought they could make up for denying reason by sanctioning unreason. Before themselves and their "alpine fathers" they were prepared to trust their fate to blind chance, to choose kismet as their gospel and fatalism for spiritual comfort. This, however, would not have mattered had they committed this heresy secretly. But they made it possible for their achievements to stand before growing youths as an absolute scale and a guiding star.

In *History of Mountaineering in the Alps,* Claire Engel quotes Anderl Heckmair, the leader of that first Eigerwand success, as having written, "we the sons of the older Reich, united with our companions from the Eastern Border to march together to victory." Engel cites this quote as proof that the party was motivated solely by Nazi philosophy. Heckmair doesn't read English, so this quote didn't come to his attention for many years. When confronted with it, he said, "We were misquoted. It was a passage from our book, *The Eiger Climb,* which was published in 1938. The exact passage read: 'Isn't it a dispensation of providence? Two men from Munich went to their death with two Austrians [on a 1936 attempt]. Two Austrians now go to victory with two men from Munich.' I have never thought, said, or written the sentence that Claire Engel imputes to me."

Heckmair, like the other successful German and Austrian climbers of his era, was apolitical. He lived in Switzerland during most of the prewar period. Neither he nor his companions were members of the Nazi party. In fact, the closest that Nazis came to climbing the Eigerwand was in 1936, when a pair of climbers deserted the German Army to attempt the route. Heckmair himself, on his return to Germany, became a landscape gardener in Munich. He continued to make outstanding climbs. He came back from the difficult Walker Spur of the Grandes Jorasses without any fanfare. Instead of emphasizing the difficulties of the route, he talked about the natural design of the rocks and wildflowers on the cliff, which terrain appealed to the landscape gardener in him.

In recent years Heckmair was interviewed by *Mountain* magazine, published in London. The editor found his attitudes "still simple and honest, unchanged by the endless controversy that has raged round his greatest climb." When questioned about his supposed quote that the climb's "most splendid reward" was being presented to Hitler, Heckmair replied, "We felt exactly as anyone else would, normal climbers who were suddenly taken out of their anonymous lives and presented to the mightiest man in Germany at that time. This could have happened as well to a dancing bear. The same situation happened to Sir Edmund Hillary when he was honored by Queen Elizabeth for conquering Mount Everest.''

Human beings have an amazing capacity to store contradictory information in separate compartments of their brains, allowing them to simultaneously hold beliefs that seriously conflict with one another. In this manner, many mountaineers are able to believe that, one, somehow the Eiger climbers were wrongly motivated by nationalism and glory, and two, climbs such as the first ascents of Annapurna and Nanga Parbat were great human achievements. The incompatibility of these ideas is underscored by the fact that Louis Lachenal, who was the first to stand on top of Annapurna with Maurice Herzog, had already made the first successful repeat of the vilified Eigerwand. His Annapurna companions, Rébuffat and Terray, were also early repeaters of the Eigerwand. So was Herman Buhl, who climbed 26,660-foot Nanga Parbat solo in 1953. In more recent years a great number of the world's top climbers have climbed the Eigerwand. Most important Himalayan expeditions include an Eigerwand veteran or two.

Another participant in that first Eigerwand climb, Heinrich Harrer, had been a skier in the 1936 Olympics. Two years later, after he had climbed the Eigerwand, he received countless kudos in his country, including awards from Hitler. Harrer could no more be called a Nazi than an American who received a presidential award during the Nixon administration could be labeled a Watergate conspirator. Soon after receiving the award Harrer was invited to join an expedition which planned to climb Nanga Parbat in 1940. In 1939 he accompanied Peter Aufschnaiter, the expedition leader, to the base of the mountain to make a reconnaissance for the next year's climb. As they were returning through India, war broke out between Germany and England. Both climbers were thrown into a British prison near Delhi. Over a period of years, Harrer and Aufschnaiter made several attempts to escape. Once they succeeded briefly but were recaptured. Finally, in 1944 the two men escaped, disguised themselves as peasants, and began to walk across India toward forbidden Tibet. Months later they bluffed their way across the Tibetan border and began a thousand-mile march toward the fabled city of Lhasa. Their motive was pure adventure. They figured that if they were recaptured, at least they would have seen more of the world in the process.

Only a handful of Europeans had ever visited Lhasa, and none had viewed the city's most intimate places. On their arrival, Harrer and Aufschnaiter were quite satisfied just to have reached the end of their journey. Politics were delicate, and a wrong move could quickly land them back in India and prison. But after several years in Tibet both Harrer and Aufschnaiter became confidants of the Dalai Lama, who ruled the Tibetan theocracy by divine right.

This Dalai Lama was only five years old upon his ascendancy in 1940. He proved to be the last Dalai Lama Tibet would have. In 1951 the Chinese Communists overran the country and destroyed most of its culture, and the sixteen-year-old Dalai Lama fled to India to live in exile. Harrer and Aufschnaiter fled at the same time. They could have returned to Germany years earlier, but their spirit of adventure was far stronger than their nationalism.

After leaving Tibet Harrer wrote a best-selling book titled *Seven Years in Tibet*. He continued climbing, traveling to Alaska in 1953 where he made the first ascents of difficult Mounts Hunter and Deborah with Fred Beckey, an outstanding American climber. He visited New Guinea and made the first ascent of the 16,024-foot Carstenz Pyramid, the highest summit on the big island. Later he wrote *The White Spider,* a book about the history of the Eigerwand. It set the old Nazi rumors straight, but many diehards regard the book as a careful whitewashing job, written long after the fact.

One easy way to convince people that false rumors are true is to imbed them in fiction, which is relatively invulnerable to criticism of misrepresentation. Ullman, for example, continued to make his case against the Eigerwand climbers by writing novels about vainglorious Germans in the Alps. In 1972, an author with the pen name of Trevanian wrote a mystery story about an Eiger climb. *The Eiger Sanction* revived all the old clichés, this time in best-seller form. The novel's characters included a number of humorless, sinister Germans, and the plot was a mixture of overt politics and mountain climbing. The hero was an American undercover agent who was trying to kill another foreign undercover agent. Both agents were climbers, and the novelist skillfully placed them together on an international ascent of the Eigerwand. The climb was billed in the novel as the hardest and most dangerous in the world, although in reality it has been exceeded by countless other routes since 1938. The real importance of the Eigerwand was as the first of a genre, not as the ultimate climb.

After film rights to the novel were sold, a crew was sent to location in Switzerland, and Clint Eastwood was cast in the starring role. During the shooting, a pair of South Tyrolean climbers arrived on the scene. Reinhold Messner and Peter Habeler were two of the top alpinists in the world. For them the Eiger was no longer the ultimate climb; it was a practice ground for a greater commitment. Messner and Habeler were more than the top climbers of their generation. Just as the first Eigerwand climbers had accomplished a route far beyond the goals of most other climbers, these two set their sights on climbs that most regarded as dangerous and foolhardy. They were the modern inheritors of the Eiger myth, with all its ramifications.

A playwright would have been hard pressed to invent a more dramatic contrast between generations of mountaineers than the real-life version that occurred on the Eigerwand during the filming. In the thirties the climb had been considered "the last great problem of the Alps." Now *The Eiger Sanction* depicted a classic ascent, setting it in modern times as if it were still the ultimate. The actual death of a cameraman by rockfall reinforced that image. Even the climbers who worked as stuntmen began to believe the old tales. In the midst of this myth-building activity, Messner and Habeler ventured onto the 6,000-foot face one morning and descended late that same day, having climbed the wall in an unprecedented ten hours. Since neither Hitler nor the Queen was about, their pictures were taken with a stone-faced Clint Eastwood and a bevy of movie stars.

The public fame of the pair, however, was as fleeting as their ascent. As Messner said, "A team is admired for the number of bivouacs it makes." That is, the public normally believes that the longer a climb takes, the greater the show of endurance. Often, precisely the opposite is true. For Messner and Habeler, the ten-hour ascent of the Eigerwand was preparation for a much more serious project—an alpine-style climb of a Himalayan peak. If successful, their attempt would revolutionize Himalayan climbing even more drastically than the first Eigerwand climb had revolutionized alpine climbing.

Nevertheless, Messner and Habeler were soon forgotten on the movie location as the crew resumed the job of reviving the old Eiger legends.

2 Two Schallers

As our K2 team approached Paiyu camp, Leif and I saw the distant figure of a lone man approaching. Who would be wandering in this wilderness by himself? As he came closer, we recognized the tall, slender American whom we had met in Rawalpindi nearly three weeks before. At that time, coincidentally, Leif and I had been the first in the group to realize who this man was. I remembered that afternoon clearly.

In an ancient room of the Flashman's Hotel we had been holding a team meeting, discussing such matters as the $2,000 for porter insurance required by the government and the $700 bill for *ghee*, a kind of cooking grease made from butter that was a must for the porters. During that meeting this same slender man had entered the room. He asked whether someone named Dr. Schaller was a member of our expedition. We replied that Robert T. Schaller was our doctor. He said, "My name is Dr. Schaller, too. I've been getting phone calls from a young lady I do not know in the United States. She's on the phone right now, in the hotel lobby." Rob Schaller, the marathon runner, shot out the door as if he had heard a starter's pistol. The new Dr. Schaller turned to leave. Something clicked in my head, but I thought, No, it couldn't be; this man is too young to have done all that.

Leif was one step ahead of me. He asked the new Dr. Schaller if he was by any chance the man who had made field studies of large mammals and had written books on the gorilla, lion, and tiger.

George Schaller, in the village of Kachura

Modestly, he answered "Yes," then ducked out the door nearly as quickly as his namesake had.

What a coincidence, I thought, meeting such a man in a place like Rawalpindi. But the coincidences were just beginning. Dr. George B. Schaller was not at all the type of man I had imagined him to be. He looked about my age—mid-thirties—but was actually in his early forties. Physically, he appeared to be in as good shape as our team members, not what one would expect from a dedicated scientist. He was one of America's most eminent field zoologists as well as a skilled writer and photographer whose work appeared frequently in such magazines as *National Geographic* and *Natural History.* His best-known book, *The Year of the Gorilla,* had the rare distinction of becoming both a best-seller and a National Book Award winner.

Curiosity got the best of me, and I visited George Schaller in his hotel room that evening. I learned to my surprise that he planned to follow our same route, walking two hundred miles round trip up the Baltoro Glacier to Concordia. This was his fourth trip to the Karakoram; he had been working on a long-range survey of large mammals in the Himalaya. Also, he had been asked by the Pakistani government to assess the need for a proposed K2 national park. Because the nineteen scheduled expeditions might disturb his study area, he had hoped to be the first visitor of the season. He too had been held back by flight delays to Skardu.

Looking about the empty room, I asked where all his provisions were. He pointed to a small box on the floor that contained about twenty pounds of nuts and meats. He would be accompanied by only one porter and a Pakistani wildlife enthusiast and photographer, Pervez Khan.

Although other expeditions in 1975 would certainly bring back new aesthetic and topographical information about the high peaks, they would contribute little to such practical concerns as whether to establish a national park. To make that decision the government needed answers to such questions as, How much pristine flora and fauna were left to save? Did human habitation in the valleys make the concept of a park untenable? Who would benefit? Who would lose? Schaller's tiny expedition had a better chance of answering these questions than all the others put together, but as I talked to him I wondered if we each might be wearing our special brand of blinders. I would be marching straight toward K2 in a caravan of six hundred, as insulated from the actual environment as a politician touring a ghetto in a limousine. Meanwhile, Schaller would walk the narrow path of science, rendering unfathomable splendor into a rigid jargon of numbers and words.

I couldn't have been more wrong. At first his thought world seemed closed to me. He answered questions like a computer—just what I expected from a dedicated scientist. Then he began to quiz me:

"What route are you trying on K2?"

"The West Ridge. It's unclimbed, you know."

"Oh. That's on the other side of the mountain from the Italian route. You must be going up the Godwin-Austen Glacier, then up the Savoia very near the Chinese border."

"Exactly. Our route lies directly on the border. How do you know so much about the mountain? You're a zoologist, not a climber."

"I've read a lot about the expeditions. I used to climb some myself."

Schaller went on to describe an experience that really surprised me. In 1954, during his undergraduate days at the University of Alaska, he had attended a lecture by a man who had recently returned from Tibet. Afterwards, the lecturer asked around for a climbing companion. George volunteered and accompanied him on the first ascent of 12,000-foot Mount Drum, a major glacier-laden volcano in Alaska's Wrangell Mountains. The man was none other than Heinrich Harrer, the first Eigerwand climber, who had subsequently walked across the Himalaya disguised as a peasant.

I mentioned that I had done many climbs with another man of German descent, Fred Beckey, who had been Harrer's companion on other Alaskan first ascents that same summer. I was astonished at how two strangers meeting halfway around the world could share such a closely-woven network of experiences. Climbers and other wilderness explorers travel the world through hidden corridors which converge at the most unexpected times and places.

Schaller was shaped from clay that even in middle age had yet to harden. His interests were as diverse as a child's, and his sense of wonder was totally alive. He had yearned to follow Harrer's tracks into Tibet but had been turned down by the Chinese. Eating chapatties in a native village was more natural to him than reclining in a comfortable chair in academia.

What separated Schaller from most adventurers was his chilling intellect and his well-ordered pursuit of specialized knowledge. He accepted nothing from others' research without confirming the findings firsthand. Thus he avoided the all too common pitfall of building a pyramid of logic on a foundation of someone else's misconceptions. However, he was not quick to dismiss a proposition just because it was not backed by data. He would tuck it into his mind to investigate in the future should the chance arise.

Schaller openly held one belief regarded as heretical by many wildlife managers: "It is sometimes necessary for radical protective measures to precede, rather than follow, scientific studies and surveys." Pakistan was a classic example. Wildlife research here was at least forty years behind that in North America. Only two intensive studies on large mammals in Pakistan had ever been published, whereas a single decade produced over three hundred such studies on large East African mammals. Local universities were not ecologically oriented, and Schaller believed that Pakistan's wildlife officials worked practically in an intellectual vacuum. "I met no one who knew details of the wildlife research program in neighboring Iran," he commented. "I work mainly with large mammals not just because they are my specialty, but also because their status and condition normally indicate the concern with which a country treats its natural resources. In Pakistan, a great number of animals are on the threshold of extinction."

The night before I met Schaller I had dined with a Pakistani who seemed most knowledgeable about local wildlife. When I brought

Shapu ram

Village on the Braldu River

up the Abominable Snowman, he laughed in open contempt. Schaller fielded the same question in an entirely different way: "I don't know whether such a creature exists, but if it does it will be found in the forested regions between Nepal and Bhutan rather than in the arid Karakoram. I've studied photographs of the tracks and there are characteristics that have not yet been explained to my satisfaction. Some of them may be melted-out tracks of smaller animals, or of bears, but others have subtle things in common with gorilla tracks—things that no one could fake unless they had spent years studying primates. I'm not saying that the Abominable Snowman is a gorilla—quite to the contrary—but the latent similarities intrigue me. I would not be that surprised if an undiscovered large primate exists in very small numbers."

During the long days of waiting in Rawalpindi, Schaller and I talked at length. Our interests were complementary, since I was an amateur wildlife enthusiast and Schaller an amateur mountaineer. When there happened to be extra space in our chartered plane, Schaller accompanied us on the flight to Skardu. While we waited there for the arrival of additional gear, Schaller set about surveying wildlife in nearby valleys. One day he invited me to join him, and with permission from the team, I accepted. We rode with government wildlife managers to Shagarthang, a nearby valley that was reported to have ibex—large wild goats that inhabit mountains in Europe, North Africa, and Asia. Not far beyond the end of the jeep road, the officials stopped to go fishing. Schaller and I continued, hiring a native boy to help spot wildlife. As Schaller drank from a stream, it occurred to me that his posture was exactly like that of the big cats he had studied for so long, a hint that he was somewhat more than a passive observer.

Shagarthang was a typical Karakoram valley. Except for the planted orchards and shade trees, the terrain was practically treeless, broken only by a few scattered junipers. Insulated from the monsoon by the western Himalaya, it was devoid of lush vegetation. The main wild growth was sagebrush and *Ephedra*, similar to vegetation in some of the high deserts of the American West. Cultivation extended beyond 10,000 feet, and livestock grazed much higher, usurping almost all the available wildlife habitat. During the summer, ibex could graze the steep hanging meadows up to 18,000 feet, but their population was limited by their need to descend into lower valleys in winter for forage. Here they were often shot if they didn't starve. Even with these problems, the ibex were doing better than many other species in the region.

Pakistan's environmental controls were a series of paradoxes. There were large forest departments but few forests; there were no range-management departments although much of the terrain was rangeland. Strict laws against the killing of large mammals did exist but were almost never enforced. One of the Skardu officials openly traveled with a rifle and had recently shot nine ibex and eight mountain sheep.

We ended our day in the environs of Shagarthang without seeing a single large mammal other than domestic yaks, zoes (a yak-cow hybrid), sheep, and goats. But for Schaller the trip had not been a failure. He had questioned villagers carefully and gathered considerable information on wildlife in the valley. To test his informants he had thrown out a few curves about species that were not present. If they passed the quiz, he placed some credence in their reports of sightings.

Now, at Paiyu, as the lone figure approached Leif and me on the trail, I wondered how far Schaller had gone and what he had found. The Baltoro region was reputed to be the finest area in the Karakoram for alpine wildlife. Several early expeditions had hunted wild sheep and goats for food. Even as late as 1960, the famous Italian mountaineer Ricardo Cassin had shot two ibex above the glacier, and his Gasherbrum IV expedition had feasted on what they called wild goat goulash à la Baltoro.

③ The Inheritor

Reinhold Messner was not a born rebel. Like thousands of other boys raised in the Alps, Reinhold was introduced to climbing by his parents. The family lived in the mountains of South Tyrol, culturally part of Austria but politically part of Italy. In the early fifties Reinhold's father took the boy up his first 3,000-meter peak before he was six years old; by the age of thirteen he was climbing technical routes with his two brothers. He had the potential for a career as a top Alpine guide, but there was even then something different about him. He outperformed most of his companions, yet he claimed that he was not competing with them.

Very early, Reinhold began to feel that climbing was spoiled if it was done for outside motives. He intuitively believed that the most important goal was personal satisfaction, not how an achievement might be rated by others. He distinguished what he called noncompetitive climbing from climbing for the sake of a conquest. In noncompetitive climbing a person subjects himself to a personal discipline to fulfill his own idea of style, rather than following someone else's predetermined rules or consciously competing with earlier achievements. Noncompetitive climbing allows some people to reach a high level of enjoyment with a low level of ability. But the discipline allowed the young Reinhold Messner to pursue personal goals that had been only unattainable fantasies for most of the great names in mountaineering history.

Reinhold realized that, rightly or wrongly, Alpine history was based on conquests. Therefore, even after he had made solo climbs and established record times on some of the hardest routes in the Alps, he felt that he deserved no major place in the history of the range, because by the end of the 1950s all the important new ground

Reinhold Messner

had been ascended. For him, climbing virgin terrain in the best possible style was the essence of historically significant mountaineering.

Reinhold did not plan to make his living by climbing. That would have entailed accepting money for sharing personal experiences, and this went against his belief that climbing was only valuable when done for its own sake. He became a certified guide out of a strong desire to introduce others, especially youngsters, to the self-determination he himself had found in the mountain environment, but he also went to college and became a grammar school teacher. Often when he arrived ruffled and puffy-eyed on a Monday morning, the principal would smile and say, "Bivouac again, Reinhold?"

Reinhold the teacher was a polite, charming, average-looking man. Just under six feet and 170 pounds, he lacked the bulging muscles and wild appearance that many people associate with mountain climbers. But before and after school he carried on an unusually demanding regimen of physical training. He developed specific exercises for climbing and often trained four hours a day. He would run uphill on his toes 3,000 feet in less than an hour to develop his calf muscles for cramponing. Then he would hand-traverse back and forth on an old sawmill to strengthen his fingers, often moving nearly two hundred feet without stopping. In winter he ran up and down hills on cross-country skis.

Reinhold did much of his early climbing with his brother, Günther, who attended college with him and took a job in a bank while he taught school. By the late 1960s they had made many outstanding climbs in the best possible style, and the mountaineering world began to take notice. But the name that Reinhold was making for himself was not always favorable. His solo climbs were beginning to earn him the reputation of a crazed daredevil. His critics, though, were rarely aware that his extensive training and incredible ability often made him safer unroped and alone than many roped parties on the same routes. Reinhold had begun solo climbing when he was sixteen and slowly graduated to such difficult ascents in the Alps as the Soldi route on the Sassolungo, the Phillip/Flamm on the Civetta, and the north face of Les Droites. These climbs attracted great attention and comment, much of it negative. After one solo climb he received the following letter: "You're a madman, a real nut case—soon to become a child of death, if you cannot find the strength and courage, combined with reason, to give up such ventures." Reinhold was inheriting the legacy of Heinrich Harrer.

Hoping to dispel this kind of misunderstanding, Reinhold began to write articles and books explaining the philosophy of his style. In the process, he often had to contradict other climbers. He made bold, direct statements which rang true to many experienced climbers but seemed fanatical to many more. The Mohammed Ali of the climbing world, he made rash predictions and harsh judgments, then proceeded to prove them by his own actions.

Reinhold openly deplored the recent trend of climbing faces once

Nanga Parbat

considered impossible by using quantities of bolts, pitons, and fixed ropes in place of skill. In an article titled "The Murder of the Impossible," he wrote, "*Impossible.* The word doesn't exist anymore. The dragon is dead, poisoned, and the hero Siegfried is unemployed." He berated climbers who "carried their courage in their rucksack." Rather than slaying the impossible with an arsenal of equipment, Reinhold spoke for a renewed search for the "limits of the possible."

He did not advocate scrapping equipment entirely—taken to the logical extreme, that would mean climbing naked. He subscribed to the use of a few classic tools—those which enable a climber to use what nature provided rather than ones which alter the existing scene. An expansion bolt drilled into the rock permanently alters the scene, while front-pointing with crampons and ice axe leaves almost no trace. Fixed camps are portable environments; bivouacs mean living with the mountain.

For Reinhold, the greatest climbing experiences occurred in totally wild situations. "Something is absent on a practice climb in a training area," he wrote. "There is the start and the rope run-outs to the top, but the real adventure begins with the solitude; when he has achieved this, the climber finds himself in another world."

In 1970 the inevitable happened: Reinhold and Günther Messner were invited to join a Himalayan expedition. The objective was the highest mountain wall in the world, the Rupal Face of Nanga Parbat in Pakistan, rising 15,000 feet in a single swell. The leader was Dr. Karl Herligkoffer, leader of the first successful expedition to Nanga Parbat in 1953 and stepbrother of Willi Merkl, who had been twice to the mountain in the 1930s and perished on its slopes. The peak had claimed thirty-one lives before Herman Buhl soloed the summit from a high camp in 1953.

Herligkoffer was obsessed by Nanga Parbat. He had led five expeditions to the peak since 1953. As youths, the stepbrothers Herligkoffer and Merkl did not get along well. Merkl was the black sheep of the family, always fooling around in the mountains while Herligkoffer, the good brother, went to medical school. Because of Nanga Parbat, things were suddenly reversed. Merkl became famous; Herligkoffer remained unknown. After Merkl died, Herligkoffer decided to step into his shoes. He began to plan Nanga Parbat expeditions as profitable commercial extravaganzas. As if the journeys were Hollywood films, the stars of the expeditions signed complex contracts; publicity began to flood the media long before the actual climb was under way. Funds were raised by full-time secretaries who wrote letters to rich companies and individuals asking for donations of money or goods. Herligkoffer became an expedition organizer par excellence, but he was never a true mountaineer.

Like Reinhold Messner, Herman Buhl had been invited on his first Himalayan climb by Herligkoffer. Buhl first became aware of Herligkoffer when he was visiting Heinrich Harrer, who was then writing *Seven Years in Tibet*. Harrer showed Buhl an article in a news magazine about a prospective Nanga Parbat expedition to be led by Dr. Karl Herligkoffer. Neither man had ever heard of Herligkoffer, but both were intrigued with the idea. Harrer had reconnoitered Nanga Parbat in 1939, just before he was imprisoned, but had never returned to the mountain.

Herligkoffer invited the cream of German and Austrian mountaineers on his first Nanga Parbat expedition. Both Harrer and Heckmair, veterans of the first Eigerwand climb, refused the invitation after learning how the trip was organized. Buhl accepted and hastily signed a long contract which Herligkoffer assured him was "all a mere formality." Like most of Herligkoffer's climbers, Buhl had no other way to finance an expedition to a major Himalayan peak—Herligkoffer was simply the man who was giving him a chance to go.

Before the expedition left, Buhl saw his name and achievements flaunted almost daily in newspapers and magazines. He did not care for this, and later wrote: "As a mountaineer I found it, to say the least, unusual to start beating the big drum and gathering laurel wreaths in advance."

There is no doubt that the expedition would have failed but for Buhl's persistence. After weeks at high altitude, during which the first monsoon clouds arrived, Herligkoffer ordered the climbers down from the high camps. Buhl and three others refused to descend, claiming that a summit attempt was still possible because the monsoon was so far confined to lower elevations. After days of

Herman Buhl

fierce clashes over the radio, Herligkoffer grudgingly gave the protesters permission to go on. When Buhl couldn't get his tired comrade to go with him on the morning of the planned summit day, he set off alone. Forty-one hours later, after a bivouac in the open at 26,000 feet, Buhl returned to the high camp, having made the highest solo climb in history.

During the previous summer, Buhl had suffered frostbite of the feet while making the eighth ascent of the Eigerwand. Now they were frostbitten even more seriously by the summit ordeal. Though he ripped out his felt boot liners and left off one pair of socks, Buhl was barely able to get the boots on his swollen feet to descend to base camp. The reception Buhl and his three companions got at base camp was decidedly hostile. Herligkoffer did not even congratulate Buhl and, since he had already shipped off his box of medical gear, did little to treat his frostbite. Buhl eventually lost two toes.

Returning to Austria, Buhl found that he was a national hero. Although Edmund Hillary had made the first ascent of Mount Everest during the same season, many mountaineers considered Buhl's climb to be more significant. He was interviewed by the press and gave frank answers to searching questions about his relations with the expedition leader. Herligkoffer produced the contract that Buhl had signed, pointed to fine print dictating that all media contact be approved through him, and promptly initiated a lawsuit against Buhl. The case lingered in the courts for years.

Buhl wrote his autobiography, and in 1957 he returned to Pakistan, this time to climb Broad Peak, a 26,400-foot neighbor of K2. His plans for this expedition contrasted sharply in every way with Herligkoffer-style arrangements. With a four-man party he attempted the first ascent of an 8,000-meter peak using no oxygen and no high-altitude porters. Only fixed campsites and the ferrying of multiple loads distinguished the climb from the purest alpine-style ascent, a venture most considered impossible on the great Himalayan peaks.

All four climbers reached the summit. After they descended, Buhl was in such good condition that he proposed trying a first ascent—with just two climbers—on 25,110-foot Chogolisa, a few miles away. Buhl and Kurt Diemberger found this mountain easier than Broad Peak, and on only the third day they set out for the summit. At 24,000 feet storm clouds suddenly moved in, forcing them to descend. Because they were in a hurry and the terrain was not difficult, they climbed unroped. Without warning, Diemberger heard a cracking noise through the mist; Herman Buhl fell through a cornice into the clouds and disappeared, never to be seen again.

Back in Austria, Herligkoffer proceeded to wrap up his lawsuit against Buhl's estate. Buhl had been his own star witness, and without him Herligkoffer was able to have the fine-print clauses of the contract enforced. Herligkoffer thereby won the right to 25 percent of the royalties from Buhl's autobiography because it mentioned Nanga Parbat. This money would otherwise have gone to Buhl's young wife and three small children, who had no means of support.

Reinhold and Günther Messner knew Herligkoffer's history, but

Porters and Chogolisa

they wanted very badly to go to the Himalaya and could not finance their own trip. The brothers signed a contract similar to the one Buhl signed in 1953, but they were not greatly worried—their purpose was strictly climbing, and they were happy to have someone else handle the media.

History began to repeat itself. After nearly forty days on the Rupal Face, monsoon clouds appeared in the distance, an indication that the climbing season was nearly over. The Messner brothers were in a high camp, within striking distance of the summit. They decided to make the attempt together if the weather held for a few days, but if bad weather seemed imminent Reinhold would go alone. The plan was discussed over the radio with Herligkoffer, who later denied that he approved of Reinhold's suggestion of a solo climb. But five other expedition members later signed a statement affirming that Herligkoffer had in fact answered, "Reinhold, that is what I hoped you would say; you have guessed my own thoughts."

The brothers arranged for Herligkoffer to send them weather reports by firing colored rockets from base camp, since the summit assault would begin from a high camp with no radio to receive the forecasts from Rawalpindi. A blue rocket would mean that good weather was predicted and that the summit could be reached by both brothers (and possibly two other climbers). A red rocket would mean that bad weather was coming and that Reinhold should solo as fast as possible.

At the prescribed time, Herligkoffer mistakenly sent off a red rocket though the weather was clear. He discovered that he had no blue rockets and could not reverse his signal. Reinhold began soloing at 3 A.M. When Günther awoke to clear weather, he decided to follow. Reinhold climbed unroped and Günther followed likewise. They reached the summit together, but Günther had pushed so hard trying to catch up that he felt unable to descend one area without a rope. They decided to descend an unclimbed route on the Diamir Face, which appeared much easier at the higher elevations.

Reinhold had studied all the available information on Nanga Parbat, and he was quite sure the descent would go. After two bivouacs together, the brothers reached the glacier at the base of the face. The terrain was still steep and the ice badly broken up into seracs. Somehow during the crossing the brothers became separated. Reinhold reached a moraine and waited. Günther didn't come.

I wasn't too worried [Reinhold wrote later]. I waited about three hours, thinking he might have gotten off the glacier and just be drinking or having a rest. Then I climbed slowly up onto the glacier again and started searching. By this time the sun had melted any trace of tracks. I went down the other way and found avalanche debris. I searched and searched, but there was no trace of him. Eventually it started to get dark and I had to make another bivouac, my third on the mountain. It was during this bivouac that the frostbite started on my toes. . . . Next morning I searched. . . . I stayed there for another day and night, hoping that someone would come round from base camp. . . . For three days I was without drink and five without food; I spent three nights on the ice without shelter. Finally I crawled down the valley as I could no longer stand on my feet. Climbers all over the world said it was a miracle that I had survived the ordeal, but I do not believe in miracles.

Most of Reinhold's toes were amputated. He felt that he had not received proper medical treatment from Herligkoffer, who remained aloof through all the postexpedition events, and even failed to send his condolences to the Messner family. Reinhold believed that Herligkoffer's strict contract was not only invalid to begin with, but also unenforceable because the expedition had not held up its end of the bargain. Proper medical care had not been provided and a false weather signal had begun the chain of events that killed his brother. Like Buhl, Reinhold began to speak out publicly about the climb, his brother's death, and his personal opinion of the expedition's organization. When another member of the expedition printed a letter critical of the leadership in *Alpinismus,* a prominent German mountain magazine, Herligkoffer's lawyers had the circulation of that issue halted. Every one of Reinhold's contentions was denounced by Herligkoffer in published counterclaims. Reinhold sued Herligkoffer for libel, and Herligkoffer sued Reinhold for breach of contract. *Mountain* magazine investigated both sides of the argument and concluded, "The most damning indictment of the leader is that eight members of the expedition should have felt so outraged by his public account that they felt compelled to break their contract and denounce his version in print."

The legal tangles continued for years. Reinhold wanted only to clear his name and have the freedom to express his opinions in public. Herligkoffer's reputation was beyond salvaging, but he hoped to boost his financial assets by winning a large settlement from Reinhold. On the day of the first major court hearing, Reinhold's wife got up the nerve to talk to Herligkoffer privately, urging him to give up the legal duel. "You are poisoning our lives," she implored. "Please, let us settle this ourselves. Reinhold and I cannot be happy while this drags on for months and years. End it now. Give us our lives."

"Your lives?" Herligkoffer was said to reply, glancing about to make sure no one was overhearing them. "Don't worry, my dear. I just want your money."

But Reinhold had lost a part of his life. During the late 1960s he had practiced an Olympian ritual of training, preparing himself for the hardest climbs. Now he could not continue his training, let alone hope to make the climbs. His amputations were not healing, and sores remained open for over a year. His feet were sensitive to even the slightest cold. He couldn't climb difficult rock without toes, and he couldn't stay on a big mountain with his hypersensitivity to cold. Doctors tried various treatments, but Reinhold made no progress. Finally, against medical advice and with considerable skepticism, he tried a special cream made by a Tyrolean farmer who would not divulge the contents. Within days the sores began to heal, and—most miraculous of all—his sensitivity to cold disappeared. Soon Reinhold was climbing again. Though unable to wear the soft shoes required for the hardest rock climbs, he found himself able to perform nearly as well as ever on ice and snow wearing stiff mountain boots.

In 1972 Reinhold returned to the Himalaya with another big expedition. Once again he found himself in position to attempt the summit with far weaker companions. Once again he set out alone. He reached the summit of 26,870-foot Manaslu by himself and descended successfully. Again, tragedy struck. Two of the climbers in the high camp died during a storm. Some blamed Reinhold, claiming that his single-minded drive for the summit had contributed to the deaths.

Reinhold returned more cynical than ever about large expeditions. His legal tangles with Herligkoffer were still unsettled, but the majority of the mountaineering world sided with him. Walter Bonatti dedicated his autobiography "To Reinhold Messner, the last youthful hope of the great tradition of mountaineering."

In 1973 Messner wrote *The Seventh Grade*, in which he proposed that another rating be added to the usual six used to classify the difficulty of new climbs. Many thought his proposition was incredibly arrogant. "A seventh grade? Might as well add another day to the week or another quart to a gallon."

In the United States the rockclimbing grading system had already been altered. During the thirties, the European grades I through VI had been Americanized into classes 1 through 6, expressed in Arabic instead of Roman numerals. At the upper end, class 5 meant that climbing had to be done with ropes and pitons for safety, and class 6 indicated that artificial aids were necessary to directly support a climber's weight. Class 5 was broken down into decimalized subdivisions of 5.1 through 5.9. When climbs obviously harder than class 5.9 were made, they were given the illogical numeral of 5.10. In recent years 5.11 came into use, and now 5.12 has been proposed.

The American system neatly sidestepped the necessity for Messner's seventh grade. Class 5 meant free-climbing difficulty and class 6 meant using aids. Only novices misunderstood the fact that hard class 5 climbs were much more difficult than most class 6 climbs, since in the latter the climber can rest by holding onto anchors driven into rock or ice.

The European grade VI originally applied to routes on which good climbers had to use direct aids. More and more climbers were able to free-climb VI's without aids, yet the rating stayed the same. In the United States the rating of a climb made a definite shift from, for instance, class 6 to 5.8. Eventually, to make the rating systems even more descriptive, some mountaineering organizations proposed that the letter A be used with numerals to describe increasingly difficult aid climbing (A1, A2, and so on). In the United States, A grades replaced class 6, but class 5 remained untouched. In Europe, the A grades did not take over any previously established numerical classification. Grade VI became unclear. Many still believe that it refers to ultimate climbing, whether it be free climbing, aid climbing, or ice climbing. Thus, Messner's proposal for a seventh grade was scoffed at by many climbers. Who needed a grade beyond the ultimate?

Reinhold Messner did.

What Reinhold advocated was not an extra grade for technical difficulty, but rather an extra grade for style. When he soloed grade VI routes without a rope, he was overcoming exactly the same surface difficulties as those who did use a rope for safety. He said, "If the most difficult routes in the Alps can be climbed solo and often without any form of belay, then it stands to reason that a roped party can cope with greater difficulties than those hitherto encountered." If Reinhold could climb with a companion of equal ability, a whole new realm of ascents would become possible.

In *The Seventh Grade*, Reinhold made an astounding statement, half wish, half prophecy: "Accompanied by a man like Peter Habeler, I would risk trying an 8,000-meter [26,250-foot] peak, having equal chance and less risk than when attached to a great expedition with all its customary ballyhoo."

Peter Habeler was a South Tyrolean guide and ski instructor with whom Reinhold had occasionally climbed. Both of them had always outdone their companions, and they soon discovered that they were extremely well matched. Not only were their levels of endurance and ability nearly identical, but their judgment and temperaments were also perfectly synchronized. They rarely spoke to one another on climbs because they intuitively made the same decisions.

Their first major climb together was the east face of Yerupajá in South America in 1969. Unaware that a highly competent team of American climbers had made the first ascent of the face a year before, Reinhold and Peter began their ascent of the steep 4,000-foot ice wall at 2 A.M. and reached the summit at eleven the same morning. The Americans had taken three days to make the climb.

Reinhold and Peter also climbed the north face of the Matterhorn in eight hours; later they ventured onto the Eigerwand for their ten-hour ascent. One important difference distinguished them. By the spring of 1975 Reinhold had been on four expeditions to peaks over 26,000 feet. Peter had never climbed in the Himalaya, and the odds are against first-time Himalayan climbers on high peaks.

In 1974, just before climbing the Eigerwand with Peter, Reinhold visited the Pakistani Ministry of Tourism in person and applied for permission for a two-man expedition on 26,470-foot Hidden Peak, the second highest summit in the Karakoram. He was no stranger to Pakistan. Besides his first ascent of Nanga Parbat, he had returned with his wife to search for his brother's body and had trekked through Hunza. Even so, he did not get far with Pakistani officials. His application was taken under consideration. They told him that they would rather "sell" the mountain to a large expedition that would employ more porters and bring more money into the country. Reinhold explained that more small groups would come to Pakistan if they were granted permission and that all these groups together might bring in more money than a limited number of large expeditions. The ministry gave no definite answers, but did make it clear that whatever the size of the expedition—two or two hundred—a $1,000 fee would be charged for permission to attempt the peak.

In May 1975 Uschi Messner opened a letter granting her husband permission to attempt Hidden Peak that season. Reinhold was still in Nepal, about to return from an unsuccessful expedition on the difficult south face of Everest's neighbor, Lhotse. Most wives would have been depressed at the prospect of their husbands taking off on yet another expedition. Not Uschi. With a big smile she told Peter that the permission had been granted. She recognized that the very qualities she loved and admired in Reinhold were nurtured by his mountain experiences. And she believed that danger was not necessarily a bad thing. Without life-threatening predators, gazelles would not be fleet of foot, bighorn rams would not stand on cliff tops, and rabbits would not make giant leaps. On the other hand, the domestic animals, isolated from danger, are not particularly interesting to be around. Uschi treasured the time she had with the wild Reinhold more than she would an uninterrupted lifetime with a fully domesticated schoolteacher.

After Reinhold returned home from Nepal, he and Peter prepared to leave for Pakistan in just a few weeks. They sorted out 220 pounds of gear for the climb, far less than had ever been taken to a major Himalayan peak. They were acutely aware that only the barest essentials could be included. They could afford not one match too many nor one too few.

Reinhold and Peter intended to climb the virgin northwest face of Hidden Peak in the purest alpine style. They would use no oxygen, no fixed ropes, no fixed camps on the upper mountain, and no yo-yoing of loads up the peak. Together, unroped if possible, they would move up the giant mountain like snails, carrying their homes on their backs. But unlike snails, they would have to move faster at high altitude than any climbers had before, or they would surely fail. Their entire plan was dependent on a single upward push above 20,000 feet lasting no more than three days.

Reinhold had often been compared with Herman Buhl. Now he was following in Buhl's footsteps. Solo climbing—the Eigerwand—Nanga Parbat—missing toes—tangles with Herligkoffer. Now, finally, a tiny expedition to a Karakoram giant. From a similar venture Buhl had never returned.

4   Ibex

When we met George Schaller on the trail, I expected him to fill us with tales of rare wildlife and overwhelming mountain scenery. His first comment was, "The Baltoro Glacier is probably the ugliest in the world." He told of walking for days over dark heaps of loose rock covering the ice. The weather was consistently poor and the peaks were hidden in clouds. Masherbrum was the only great peak to show itself. High on the glacier, late snows made his progress

Parallel fox and human tracks on the Godwin-Austen Glacier, at 16,000 feet

through the rockfields even more difficult. Schaller turned around before reaching Concordia. Now he was walking ahead of his two Pakistani companions, eager to return to civilization as quickly as possible and apply for a permit to visit northern Hunza, where he hoped wildlife studies would be more productive.

Excitedly I told him about my own experience photographing a band of ibex from several hundred feet away. He asked me for exact details of what I saw, and suddenly I found myself in the same position as a native being subjected to one of his quizzes. I flunked. I had not seen ibex at all, but rather *shapu*, an Asian mountain sheep. There must be a little bit of the trophy hunter in me, for I was disappointed. Even though shapu are rarer animals, ibex have much bigger horns.

As he shouldered his pack to leave, George said, "If you want to try your hand at photographing ibex, there's a large herd above Liliwa camp next to the glacier. They're very hard to approach."

George was very disappointed in the results of his rough wildlife census of the Baltoro region. According to estimates of the Pakistani Forest Department, 4,500 ibex, 2,500 shapu, and 450 musk deer inhabited the area, but no staff member of the department had ever been there. George could not survey all 1,600 square kilometers of the proposed K2 national park, but much of that terrain was ice-bound throughout the year and could not support large mammals anyway. He estimated that only one hundred ibex actually lived in the heart of the region along the vast Baltoro Glacier, moving below Paiyu in winter but ranging as high as Concordia in summer. Even fewer shapu lived along the Baltoro, and he found no evidence of musk deer at all but thought that a few of the animals might possibly inhabit isolated forest patches above the valley and downstream from Askole. Overall, he estimated that the Forest Department statistics were as much as ten times too high.

With the population of prey animals so low, few predators could exist in the region. George found only old, faint signs of wolves and snow leopards. The only fresh predator tracks he saw were from several foxes and one brown bear. George's census did not bode well for the proposed national park. To him, the ideal national park was a well-preserved ecosystem. He seriously questioned whether much would be gained by making the K2 region into a protected wildlife area. He thought that other areas of the Karakoram were better suited "as last refuges for animals and plants, as repositories of genetic stock in the event that some day the species may be needed to revitalize this plundered land."

I was not sure I agreed with Schaller's park concept. I still hold to the old belief that national parks are basically shrines celebrating the grandest works of nature. A well-preserved range of biota might not be so necessary in a region with the grandest mountain scenery in the world. George was aware that the scenery he never saw might alone qualify the region for park status, but he could not hide his disappointment. His vision of an ideal park had glimpses of animals moving against a misty backdrop of peaks, while mine was of the peaks themselves, with wildlife decorating the foreground. These were not opposite viewpoints, but rather subtle shifts of the same basic impressions. We both believed that the essence of what must be preserved by a national park is unstructured wildness where people can imagine their own destinies.

That evening at Paiyu camp, K2 seemed remote, distant, and even more inaccessible than it had from halfway around the world. It was raining, the porters were threatening to strike again, and for the first time several of them were seriously ill. Besides some cases of pneumonia, one fellow had a severe stroke with partial paralysis, and another had all the symptoms of meningitis. We were already short 140 porters for carrying loads and food up the glacier, but now we were faced with sending out not only the sick men, but also other healthy porters to carry them.

The next day was supposed to be a rest day during which the porters would cook chapatties to eat on the glacier. The weather remained poor, and the porters did not cook. Another day and night passed; and another. On the third morning, a dreary one, I was awakened by the nasal voice of a porter calling, "Galen sahib, Galen sahib." It was Ali, an old porter who bore badge number fifty-five, which corresponded to the number on my frame pack. He was asking for my load—not in a few minutes, but immediately. Even though it was drizzling slightly, we were moving on to Liliwa.

I got up hurriedly and stuffed my sleeping bag, foam pad, and personal gear into the pack. Ali grabbed it impatiently and disappeared into the mist. He was old for a porter, perhaps over fifty, and he rarely failed to tell me, in his few words of English, that he had been a porter for the 1954 Italian K2 Expedition. I never thought to ask this smiling little man, who so obviously equated himself with the Italian success on K2, if he had been one of the many porters who deserted that expedition before it reached base camp.

After Ali ran off with my load, Steve, Leif, Rob, and I tried to satisfy other porters who held numbered badges in our faces. One man wanted the tent; another five wanted medical boxes. Three more wanted the kitchen, but we hadn't even eaten yet. Finally all the porters were gone, and the camp was quiet as I packed my day pack with parka, water bottles, and camera gear. I wanted to leave as soon as possible, pass all the porters, and try to be well ahead of them by the time I reached ibex country near Liliwa.

The dark mass of the glacier seemed to be just a few hundred yards beyond Paiyu camp, but it was actually about a mile and a half away. I walked through the drizzle, skipping steps and sometimes running on the brief straight stretches, hoping to overtake the mass of porters on open terrain before they crowded the loose, tortuous path across the boulder-strewn ice.

As I descended from the final hillside, I witnessed a grand scene. A natural amphitheater had been formed between one side of the retreating glacier's snout and a steeply cut, ancient moraine. A steady roar came from the river, which burst forth from a black hole in the ice at the head of the amphitheater. The dark, silt-laden waters shot from the ice like water being released at the base of a giant dam. In the distance hundreds of porters had stopped at the edge of the ice. As I neared I could hear another sound above the roar of water. The porters were singing. The ragged chorus was joining in a melodious prayer to Allah, asking for protection on the

Porters singing before walking on the Baltoro Glacier

Overleaf: Gasherbrum IV dominates the approach to Concordia

Porters at Concordia; left, Gasherbrum IV, right, Mitre Peak

Porters in the Braldu Gorge

A porter rests on the Baltoro Glacier

Porters strike at Askole

Porters gather around a campfire

The K2 team during a porter strike

Unhappy porters stand in a snowstorm at Urdukas

A porter, moments after having a tooth extracted

Lou, Fred Dunham, and Wick
in a hot spring near Askole

The lower Baltoro Glacier

Wick nears Concordia and his first close view of K2

K2 and Concordia camp

ice ahead. Each man sang the same tenor notes in a clear, unselfcon-scious fashion. Some stood, others sat on rocks, on their loads, or in the middle of the trail. Many held hands and looked into each other's faces, but a few gazed up at the glacier as they sang, looking toward the point, not many miles ahead, where the clouds bent to earth and vision was obscured. They would be many days on the ice, and their song lasted a long time.

I slowed my pace as I walked among the porters, enchanted by the spectacle. The emotions of the singers were so powerful that I felt guilty when I stepped hurriedly onto the ice without partaking in some kind of ceremony myself.

On many glaciers it is dangerous to walk alone because crevasses can be hidden by the snow cover. But the lower Baltoro had no snow cover and the few small crevasses were as obvious as cracks in a concrete sidewalk. I walked briskly toward Liliwa and soon found that I was not alone. Lou and Leif had also come through the throng of porters as they sang. We walked, more or less together, until just before 11 A.M., when we reached a level terrace on the south side of the glacier. Windbreaks of piled stones and signs of old campfires indicated that we had reached Liliwa.

Across the glacier, both Paiyu Peak and the camping place at its base were hidden in cloud. The visibility was about half a mile, and as Lou and I gazed up a steep ravine, we saw the same sight simul-taneously. Fifteen hundred feet above us, five ibex bucks were crossing a snowfield. I hurriedly set up a tripod with my longest telephoto lens, a squat 500mm mirror optic shaped like a one-pound coffee can. Even through the strong lens, the animals were distant and unclear. I decided to climb after them for a closer look. Both Lou and Leif preferred to stay at Liliwa, lounging in the great silence before the porters arrived.

Liliwa was at 12,200 feet. As I climbed the hillside, the ibex quickly became aware of my presence and moved higher. Soon I left the rock-strewn gullies and climbed on a granite wall broken by grassy terraces, chimneys, and cliff bands. The wall was not vertical, but it formed a vast maze with countless blind alleys leading to smooth headwalls and sheer drop-offs. Still, route-finding was easy; I had only to follow the fresh tracks and droppings of the ibex, who always chose the best path. As I climbed I caught occasional glimpses of the animals, always above me, always alert. The great bucks roamed haughtily across snowfields, stopping occasionally to paw through the snow and browse on buried grasses. Their heavy horns forced them to move deliberately, slow and regal, as if they were knights wearing suits of armor. The does moved more com-pulsively, sometimes climbing a point of rock to stare at me and pirouette a time or two before returning to the fold.

For the first time on the trip, I really felt the altitude. Every terrace was buried in soft snow and at nearly 15,000 feet, it took consider-able effort to move uphill. I realized that I had no hope of sneaking a close-up photo of the ibex. In every way they were far better suited for travel in the mountains than I was.

I remembered that Conway's 1892 expedition had witnessed the

Siberian ibex, above Liliwa

death of an ibex herd in an avalanche. George Schaller had told me that avalanches were a major cause of ibex mortality. But these animals were not oblivious to that danger. I was amazed at how much their behavior in the snow resembled that of trained mountaineers and cross-country skiers. They minimized the hazard by crossing steep slopes one at a time, and often they moved vertically rather than horizontally on the most slide-prone slopes so that their paths did not bisect the unstable snow. Even their daily activity cycle offset the avalanche hazard: they rested on ledges during the dangerous warm tours of the afternoon.

Not far above me, the terrain changed abruptly. Cliffs became steeper and glacial ice hung in fractured tongues down the few couloirs that would otherwise have been easy ascent routes. The ibex were no longer moving straight up the slope to avoid me, for they too were nearing the upper limit of their habitat. I began to realize that the animals had a precise flight distance. If I moved too close by even a few feet they would retreat, but if I walked back a few steps and pretended to ignore them, they resumed feeding on the dead grasses under the snows.

Finally I saw a way to get a closer view. The ibex had moved onto the floor of a nearly level bowl bound by several sheer walls of rock. If I entered the bowl from the right side, their probable route of escape would be a snow ramp that led back toward me on the left side of the bowl. I was moderately sure that they wouldn't try to scale the nearly vertical walls at the back of the bowl, though I recalled being surprised when a group of mountain goats I was tracking once in North America climbed directly up a cliff that even the most skilled human would have needed ropes and pitons to ascend. Still, I was pretty sure that these walls were too sheer. If the ibex took the ramp, they would be profiled on a ridge top against the vast Baltoro tableau, which was beginning to come out of the clouds. Also, they would have to pass a point nearly twice as close to me as their normal tolerance allowed.

Breathing hard, I climbed as quickly as possible to a vantage point just inside the bowl. I had barely found a perch for my tripod and focused my camera on the ridge when an ibex came into the viewfinder—then another, and yet another. They were doing just what I had hoped they would do. I counted fifteen animals ascending the ramp. They moved one by one to a rock outcrop, then regrouped and started for the next outcrop. Does took the lead, youngsters stayed in the middle, and eight bucks brought up the rear. The first ibex crested the ridge, looked down at me, then disappeared around the corner. Each animal took its turn while I shot a roll of thirty-six photographs in little more than a minute.

Watching the animals' movements, I felt two conflicting emotions. The first was a sense of communion; I saw the animals as counterparts of human mountaineers. Their ancestors had forsaken a more predictable mundane existence in the lower valleys for an active alpine life filled with danger in the harsh world of rock and snow. Life forms shaped by adversity in the rugged mountain environments seem to show recognizable brush strokes of the same grand artist. I saw a hidden sameness in the curl of an ibex horn, the twisting grain of a timberline juniper, the lines in an old Balti's face, and the giant arcs in the path of a living glacier.

My other emotion was less subtle—I was elated by the stalking of the animals. Calculating my moves and theirs gave me great satisfaction, and the urge to pursue them was irresistible. I remembered when, some years earlier, a deer had passed close to me in twilight as I lay resting after a long climb. Startled by my presence, it had made a graceful leap into a boulder field, landing with hooves grating and sparks flashing out of the darkness. Something had come over me in that instant, and I had leapt up and given chase to the creature with no forethought whatever. The deer had been out of its elements among the unfamiliar boulders, and I had come within inches of catching it. If I had succeeded I don't know what I would have done. I had just been chasing it; it had suddenly seemed to be the thing to do. I have often gone over that incident in my mind—the darkness, the sparks from the flashing hooves, my total exhaustion and lack of conscious thought beforehand. Something of the same feeling returned when the ibex crested the ridge.

My urge was simply to stalk and to pursue, a feeling shared by the modern field zoologist, wildlife photographer, and hunter. It was very similar to the emotion I feel when climbing—I experience far more elation just being involved in the process than in the culminating movements of achieving a summit. With the ibex the pursuit took precedence over the goal of getting a photo on the ridgecrest. I knew then that George's days in the field meant far more to him than the recognition he received from the scientific community. Like my experience of the deer, he was just chasing, but in a far more organized fashion than mine. I suspected that the human race's so-called "hunting instinct" is also related more to the chase than to the final act of killing. The chase accounts for a child's joy in playing hide-and-seek as much as for an armed soldier's thrill in stalking an enemy.

It is not surprising that a species which has spent countless generations pursuing wild animals should find pleasure in doing just that. However, primeval man normally culminated the act at close quarters. The squeeze of the trigger by a modern hunter at two hundred yards is certainly not yet implanted in the human psyche, but the overhand throw that once guided rocks and spears toward prey is now expressed in many of man's leisure activities. Some of the joy of climbing mountains may be rooted in these ancient urges as well. When our ancestors wielded their rocks and spears in the hunt for the giant mammals of the Pleistocene, their minds must have been tuned to the pitch of concentration that climbers cultivate today. The need was the same on the hunt as it is on a difficult climb: to keep a cool head while planning delicate maneuvers in life-or-death situations.

My time with the ibex was over. Evening was falling as I descended to Liliwa. I stopped on a knoll about 1,500 feet above the camp. Voices, clatter, and smoke rose from the scene. If I had been an animal, I would have ventured no closer.

The next morning I got a much earlier start than on the previous day, hoping to reach the fabled green hillsides of Urdukas camp before the multitudes. Not far from camp I came across the tracks of two snow leopards running parallel to our route. One set was large and the other small: probably a mother and a cub.

George Schaller is the only person ever to have photographed snow leopards in the wild. Although I never caught a glimpse of one of these beautiful animals, the tracks in the snow, only hours old, made me feel something of their presence. With so few prey species in the wilds, only about 250 of these extremely rare cats exist in all of Pakistan. Some have taken to preying on domestic sheep and goats. They have the Achilles' heel of eating their dinner slowly; many have been killed by villagers while savoring their last supper. Others have been shot for their valuable furs. Importing the hides into the United States is illegal, but probably more snow leopard furs are to be found in Pakistani bazaars than living animals roam the country. As George wrote after one of his Karakoram visits, "The mountains will remain magnificent even without wildlife, but when the last snow leopard disappears from the icy crags, an intangible aura of mystery will vanish too."

Snow leopard

Steve Marts holding snow leopard pelt, Askole

Section VI

The Year of the Baltoro

More than in histories of campaigns or battles, it is essential that, in the history of a climbing day, the actual reactions and feelings of the climbers, in relation to the details of the difficulties they encountered, should be reported. Because, in great mountaineering, the result, the reaching of a summit, is of minor importance; but the pleasure, the discipline, the whole merit of the climb, depend upon the way it was done, *that is the method, behavior and mental attitude of the climbers during the ascent, the descent, and the whole long day. The result of a climb is negligible, the satisfaction in it soon passes; but the process is vitally important, because its human effect will be lasting.*

—GEOFFREY WINTHROP YOUNG

1 Nineteen Expeditions

Austrian, Polish, American, French, Italian, British, Swiss, and Japanese expeditions were all bound for Karakoram peaks in 1975. The roster of climbers read like a *Who's Who* of world mountaineering. It included individuals who had walked the summits of such peaks as Everest, Cerro Torre, Kanchenjunga, Nanda Devi, Mustagh Tower, Fitzroy, Manaslu, Makalu, and Nanga Parbat.

When the Baltoro region was reopened to visitors in 1974, the Pakistani Ministry of Tourism had little appreciation for the dynamics and the aftereffects of several large groups moving through the same area in the same season. Things had changed vastly from the earlier days, when men like Eric Shipton and Bill Tilman crossed numerous international boundaries and made attempts on high peaks with expeditions that they jokingly claimed to have organized "on the back of an envelope in half an hour."

Today even the smallest parties must make complex government applications far in advance and follow rigid, costly procedures that appear to benefit neither visitor nor host. The regulations would be understandable if they protected the mountain environment or controlled the number of expeditions in a region, but such is not the case. The only limiting factor is that no more than one expedition can attempt the same peak in the same season.

For the 1975 season the Ministry of Tourism approved nineteen different applications from expeditions proposing to travel the Braldu Valley toward peaks above the Baltoro and Biafo glaciers. (Aleister Crowley had claimed that in this very region one major expedition seriously strained the available resources!) No one in the ministry had ever actually been to the mountain regions. The officials apparently harbored the misguided hope that Pakistan could match the quantity, if not the quality, of mountain tourism in Nepal.

All expedition members had spent months training for the rigors of high elevations, but few were prepared for the complicated ordeal of the approach march to their chosen peaks. Karakoram approach marches are quite unlike those at the opposite end of the Himalaya in Nepal. The giant peaks of the Baltoro region are clustered near the head of a single drainage; Nepalese giants are spread farther apart and can be approached by a number of different valleys. Expeditions in Nepal can use different sources of porters for different

Porters on the Baltoro Glacier, and K2

approaches, and can rely on several different food resources. Since valley glaciers in the Baltoro region are longer than those in Nepal, villages are much farther away from the peaks and many more access problems exist. The arid hillsides of the Baltoro region do not support crops or animals as well as the moist slopes of Nepal do, so the surplus of men and food available for expeditions passing through is limited.

By June 1975 most of the Karakoram expeditions were in the field. Instead of the boon to the economy envisioned by the Ministry of Tourism, the region began to experience shortages and rampant inflation. Before half the expeditions reached Skardu, gasoline for jeeps and wheat for porters were in short supply. Porters demanded higher and higher wages, and villagers raised prices for the few eggs, goats, and chickens they had left to sell. Many natives ended up with more paper money than they had ever possessed, but they quickly discovered that they could not eat it. Men left their fields untilled to work for the expeditions, thus ensuring that the food shortage would continue long after the expeditions had departed.

Once on the mountain, an expedition's success depended directly on the skill, planning, and cooperation of the team. But success on the approach march was an entirely different matter. All the parties were in competition for the same goods and services, and in this situation the best teams did not always win. And, biblical parables

Nineteen Expeditions 149

Mitre Peak, from Concordia

aside, those who triumphed did not necessarily display a high degree of altruism. Selfishness, cunning, and a few well-placed bribes often guaranteed enough porters and goods for one group, but just as surely spelled doom for another. It was first come, first served at an international banquet with too many guests.

When the American Trango Tower Expedition arrived in Rawalpindi, they found themselves in the company of six other expeditions which had been waiting for up to two weeks for the daily flight to Skardu. The Americans, however, had more serious problems. They had been denied permission for the Trango Towers and instead had been awarded Mitre Peak, a striking 19,700-foot mountain with a Matterhorn-like crook in its neck that rises directly above Concordia. In photographs Mitre looked like a Karakoram gem, but up close it was more in the line of a cheap carnival prize. Mitre was 6,000 feet lower than nearby peaks and composed of crumbly, metamorphic rock plastered with steep snow that frequently avalanched. The Americans were very disappointed—they had not come halfway around the world for dangerous, unesthetic climbing at low altitude. Rather, they had intended to attempt one of the great granite peaks of the lower Baltoro, none of which had been climbed.

In the Ministry of Tourism office the Americans discovered that other expeditions were going not only for six of the eight highest peaks in the Baltoro region, but also for three of the prize granite peaks: Paiyu Peak, the Grand Cathedral, and, of course, the Trango Towers. Headed for Paiyu was a French team led by Jean Fréhel, who had nearly climbed Uli Biaho Tower in 1974. Bound for the Grand Cathedral was an Italian group, which included members of the crack Lecco Spiders Climbing Club. And signed up for the Trango Towers was a British team led by Chris Bonington, a famous British climber who had previously led expeditions to Everest and Annapurna.

The Americans believed that they had applied for the Trangos first and that Bonington must have obtained permission through some sort of political favoritism. They also knew that Bonington had hedged his 1975 bets by applying not only for the Trangos but also for the southwest face of Mount Everest. When Everest permission came through at the last minute, the American team expected Bonington, who knew them personally, to give them the Trango permission. Bonington gave it instead to other members of his prospective party who had a much earlier claim to interest in the Trangos. Joe Brown and Ian McNaught-Davis had wanted to return to the Baltoro granite ever since their first ascent of Mustagh Tower, nineteen years earlier.

The Americans finally obtained permission for the more obscure group of peaks and towers not far from the Trangos called the Lopsangs. Before they left Skardu, they vented their frustrations toward the British in what they thought was a harmless practical joke. They sent a telegram to the British Trango Team which stated, PERMISSION TRANGO TOWERS GRANTED AMERICANS. YOUR EXPEDITION GRANTED MITRE PEAK. As a give-away that the message was a joke, the Americans signed it, MINISTRY OF TURDS.

The telegram arrived in England with an error. The signature read, MINISTRY OF TRUDS, which the British climbers took to be the initials of the tourism department. Immediately, they wired an inquiry to Pakistan. In a typical state of disorganization, the Ministry of Tourism could not locate the paperwork and wired back saying that they were unsure at that time just who had permission for the Trango Towers. The distraught British spent hundreds of dollars on telegrams and telephone calls to discover eventually that their original permission remained unchanged.

The Karakoram expeditions of 1975 did not by and large resemble the classic Himalayan climbs of the past. In size, appearance, and behavior they were as different from one another as are the creatures in a zoo. Our K2 expedition, to the highest Karakoram peak, was perhaps the most conventional. The two-man attempt by Reinhold Messner and Peter Habeler on Hidden Peak, the Karakoram's second highest mountain, was the least orthodox of the nineteen. A fifteen-man Polish attempt to climb Broad Peak, the third highest summit, was another more conventional effort. This group planned a minor variation on Buhl's 1957 route, using far more personnel and equipment than the first ascent had required.

The fourth highest Karakoram summit, 26,360-foot Gasherbrum II, was being attempted by a French expedition that included two top climbers with intriguingly different backgrounds. Louis Audobert was a forty-one-year-old abbot in the Catholic Church; he had a strong record of difficult solo and winter ascents in the Alps, plus a new route on 22,208-foot Huascarán in the Andes. Yannick Seigneur had made the first ascent of the west pillar of 27,825-foot

The Grand Cathedral,
from Urdukas

Makalu in Nepal in 1971, but he later made an illegal climb on a holy mountain and was forbidden to visit Nepal through 1979.

The holy mountain was Taweche, a striking and difficult 21,463-foot peak often photographed by trekkers on the way to the base of Mount Everest. This peak had been attempted a decade earlier by members of an expedition led by Sir Edmund Hillary that had as its primary purpose the building of schools for the Sherpa people. When three members of Hillary's group wanted to attempt the holy mountain, they participated in a ceremony with the Sherpas to appease the god Taweche before setting foot on the peak. One Sherpa accompanied them and the head lama at Thyangboche Monastery gave them a prayer flag to leave on the mountain to placate the spirits. After weeks of fixing ropes over difficult parts of the lower mountain, they gave up only two hundred feet from the top because of rotten snow on a narrow, corniced ridge. The Sherpa climber left the prayer flag in the snow, and the fierce god Taweche did not harm Thyangboche.

Seigneur's group began climbing Taweche without consulting either the government or the Sherpas. They obtained a vague permit allowing them to practice skiing on peaks below 20,000 feet, then quickly established a camp below Taweche and pushed for the summit. Five climbers reached the top. The Nepalese Ministry of Foreign Affairs took a dim view of their mountaineering achievement. The ascent was unauthorized, and the peak was not on the permitted list. Seigneur claimed ignorance of this, saying "*After* our ascent, the mountain was declared taboo." With a keen sense of timing, Seigneur escaped immediate punishment from the ministry by promising them on a Friday that he would give a full explanation on Sunday. He left Nepal on Saturday.

The Nepalese government fined the expedition $600 *in absentia* and banned the members from the country for five years. The prestigious Himalayan Club was outraged because of the possible adverse effect the incident could have on future climbing in Nepal. Nevertheless, since the Nepalese restriction did not apply to Pakistan, Seigneur ignored the whole affair and planned to continue his high-altitude climbing in the Karakoram in 1975.

The fifth highest Karakoram summit, Gasherbrum III, was the world's highest unclimbed peak. A most unusual group, composed of ten women and seven men from Poland, planned to attempt it. One of the women, thirty-three-year-old Alison Chadwick Onyszkiewicz, was a native of England, and in 1974 was one of the first women to be admitted into the exclusively male Alpine Club. From the time of Lord Conway's presidency at the turn of the century into the 1970s, the attitude of the club toward women had remained unchanged.

A typical incident resulting from this old-school-tie attitude occurred during a meeting not many years ago when some young upstart brought up the subject of admitting women. A dignified octogenarian rose feebly from his seat, pointed his finger in accusatory fashion, and in an orator's voice boomed two words: "Rather death!"

In 1974 the Alpine Club reopened discussion of equal rights. Lord Hunt, one of the club's most respected patriarchs and leader of the first successful Everest climb, made a motion to admit women. It carried by a large majority, unhindered by the venerable gentleman of the earlier meeting, who by then had most probably exercised his stated option.

Alison Onyszkiewicz was a natural to be among the first women to join the prestigious organization. She had climbed for more than a decade on British crags before venturing into the higher mountains of the Alps, the Tatras, and the Hindu Kush. In 1971 she married Janusz Onyszkiewicz, a professor of mathematics at Warsaw University. She moved to Poland with him and became a member of an expedition to 24,580-foot Noshaq, the highest peak in the Hindu Kush, near the Karakoram in Afghanistan. Several Polish women climbers reached the summit by the west ridge, while a men's team made an alpine-style ascent of the southwest face. The climb set an altitude record for Polish women.

Porters

After the climb, five of the Noshaq climbers began to lay bigger plans. They started organizing an expedition called "Himalaya '75," with Annapurna as the objective. As chances of permission for Annapurna dwindled, the expedition was renamed "Himalaya-Karakoram '75." The prospective leader was Wanda Rutkiewicz.

Muslims introduce a fervor into their male chauvinism that exceeds even that of the early British climbers. There is hardly anything Muslim women are allowed to do on their own; knowing this, the Polish were hesitant about disclosing to the Pakistanis that their expedition had a majority of women. Applications to climb in Pakistan must be written in English, which is the official government language although it is not in common use by the general population. Fearing Muslim prejudice, Onyszkiewicz, who handled the team's paperwork, played down the female element of the expedition by omitting the designations Mr., Mrs., and Ms., hoping that the vowel-ridden Polish Christian names wouldn't be recognized as feminine. The procedure was reversed in midstream, however, when there seemed to be a chance that Mrs. Begum Bhutto, wife of Pakistan's Prime Minister, would sponsor the expedition as part of International Women's Year. "Then," Alison said, "it became a problem to explain the male presence!"

This effort, popularly referred to as "The Polish Ladies Expedition," was supported by the Polish Ministry of Sports and Tourism; Polish television; the city of Warsaw; Orbis, a national tourist agency; and the Central Trades Union Council. Organization was handled by the Association of Polish Alpine Clubs. Given the strong financial support, plans were flexible and long-ranging. The first climbers were scheduled to leave Poland in late April, and the group had the option to remain in Pakistan until September.

Other 1975 expeditions were headed for Chogolisa, Sia Kangri, Skyang Kangri, and Teram Kangri, all mountains near the head of the Baltoro drainage. Several more expeditions aimed for peaks up the Biafo Glacier. The great silence of the mountains would be the exception rather than the rule in 1975. No one on these expeditions would come close to finding the wild solitude experienced by Godwin-Austen, Conway, Eckenstein, or the Duke of Abruzzi, except for brief periods at higher altitudes. And those groups that did not enter into the lively competition for food and porters were destined to lose out altogether. Some would not even reach the base of their proposed mountains. In this instance the advantages of modern travel had turned inward upon themselves. The odds of an expedition reaching the base of its peak were actually less in 1975 than in the late nineteenth century. Nineteen groups were trying to run their efficient modern machines through the ancient, handmade culture of the Balti people.

Urdukas camp

2 Beethoven at Urdukas

As we walked up the Baltoro Glacier, we had only rare glimpses through the clouds of the wild peaks. The true architecture of the scene was lost to us because we saw only isolated bits and pieces—bricks but not buildings. Like George Schaller, we had been disappointed on our trek so far by the desolate blandness we experienced day after day. We walked on gray rock, peered into gray mist without ever seeing the sun, and hoped that one day would dawn clear.

On May 19 it happened. I awoke before dawn at Urdukas camp,

which was set on a hillside several feet above the glacier. Directly across from our camp, the clouds were lifting to reveal the most breathtaking alpine panorama I had ever seen. On the left was Paiyu Peak; it rose 11,000 feet from the gorge of the Braldu River into a spearhead of red granite tiered with snow. On Paiyu's right was Uli Biaho, a smaller but perfectly formed shaft of rock rising to 19,658 feet. Then came the fabled Trango Towers. They were not the single crest of pinnacles I had expected, but rather a bulky massif, bordered on three sides by large valley glaciers and crested with the most varied array of jagged granitic forms imaginable. Their highest point, called Nameless Tower, was a free-standing perpendicular shaft rising at least 2,500 feet. To its left was a cleanly cleaved 4,000-foot wall with a long vertical crack on its skyline. Then came a ship's prow, rising to a magnificent crest that was connected to the top of the sheer wall by a long arc of corniced ridge. In the midst of these giant forms was a tiny, delicate tower—vertical, flawless, and beaked like a slender bird. From the crest of a bulky dome it rose at least 300 feet into the sky.

There was great mystery and beauty in the utter randomness of the summit rocks in the Trango Group. Smooth walls, fluted walls, slender towers, bulky towers, domes, and square corners melded together into an intriguing chaos. But the granite massif to the right of the towers, the Grand Cathedral, had precisely the opposite effect. The side facing Paiyu Peak was cleaved by perfect master joints, giving it a feeling of purposeful design. Here was an unfinished Gothic cathedral built on a scale never conceived by mortals. Shapes and forms were repeated all across the face. Huge pointed arches rose skyward and flying buttresses hung to the earth. In contrast, the Baltoro face of the Cathedral must have been planned as the back side. The shapes and forms that appeared so striking from Paiyu blended into a single wall, promising a 6,000-foot rock climb. Not one summit in the vast granite panorama from Paiyu to the Cathedral had been reached. Much of this realm would be the challenge of another generation of alpine climbers, perhaps as yet unborn.

As I gazed at the scene, my eyes slowly became attuned to the muted, predawn colors. But suddenly everything changed. A rosy spotlight shone on the summit of Paiyu; the surrounding peaks and valleys seemed to darken. Paiyu stood alone now, singled out on the grand stage—but not for long. A snow peak behind the Trangos began to glow, and a sheet of pink light moved slowly down its latticework, turning the tops of the Trangos into dark silhouettes. Then the Trangos themselves began to come to life. The tips of towers and ridges glowed as orange as a giant's branding iron. Eagerly I waited for light to engulf the whole massif, but as the glow descended the cliffs, it quickly faded from vivid pink to a dull yellow. The sunrise colors were especially brief because the light was traveling from the east at high elevation through hundreds of miles of clear mountain air on its path from the east across the top of the Karakoram Range.

The sunrise was the high point of the day. From then on things

The Trango Towers

proceeded down, down, down to a dark ocean bottom of disappointments. The porters were striking again. Two hundred porters were threatening to quit and go home because fresh snow had fallen on the glacier and their footgear was inadequate. Again, the fact that we had a signed contract did not influence them in the least. Their concept of the future was entirely different from ours, and they based today's decisions on how they felt at the moment, not on some half-forgotten pact made long ago.

Our sirdar, Ghulam Rasul, was a man who had proved over the course of a dozen expeditions that he could negotiate with porters better than anyone else in the Karakoram. But he was still at Liliwa, sick with what seemed to be a bad case of flu, and Manzoor was now our only English-speaking interpreter. He attempted to mend the breach by appealing to the porters' sense of honor, asking them to "do this thing for the good name of our country, Pakistan." But to the porters, Pakistan was merely the latest in a series of remote ruling governments to whom they felt not the slightest allegiance. Needless to say, Manzoor's plea fell on deaf ears.

We went to sleep that night knowing that we would not be moving in the morning. The strike was at an impasse and the deep, fresh snow had not yet settled on the trail. So far on the trek, mornings had been either hectic rushes to break camp or bleak spells spent waiting out bad weather. Tomorrow would be different. For the first time we would wake up in view of the grand peaks with no obligation to get up and move on. I described that idle morning in my diary:

Like clockwork, I awoke before dawn. It was a morning for pure fantasy and I turned on a tape recording of a Beethoven piano concerto while a pink glow lit the summits. I felt far removed from a rugged mountaineering expedition. My body was completely warm. My ears were tuned to Beethoven. My nose sensed the giant cathedral of the Baltoro, not just the Grand Cathedral itself, but the entire scene of towers, buttresses, gables, and altars glowing ever brighter in the morning light. The experience was unmistakably religious. For the moment, all my questions were answered. I certainly felt more at ease with the universe than I ever had on one of those fidgety Sunday mornings in a lesser cathedral built by men. I was not provided with any supernatural answers to the basic questions a person asks about life, but I experienced a shift of perspective whereby the answers were no longer important to me.

Who am I? What is life's purpose? What is my purpose? How great are the limits of the universe? These questions seemed as irrelevant as the medieval problem about how many angels could dance on the head of a pin. For the Baltis, such questions were simply not asked. Their life was understood, not questioned. They build bridges, irrigation ditches, and simple machines without the heavy emphasis on the prestige of symbolic understanding that we Westerners deem so important. Yesterday, after several frustrating hours of negotiations, I overheard Jim Whittaker exclaim, "I don't think they even know that two plus two equals four." Precisely my point! They probably don't know the answer to two plus two because they live without resorting to symbolism—even without written language. But in their own way they perform actions as complex as two hundred and eleven times two hundred and eleven.

Balti porter on strike

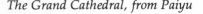

The Grand Cathedral, from Paiyu

Jim Whittaker and Manzoor negotiating with porters at Urdukas

We have also misjudged them because they do not share our concerns about death. Once again, this is related to their lack of emphasis on the future, but even more important, it reflects a failure in our own thinking. Because they are not as impressed by death, we rashly jump to the conclusion that life is not as precious to them. This does not necessarily follow. It is possible to value life without grieving death, and the Baltis exhibit more compassion for one another than we do. In the sick tent I watched a porter rock an ailing companion in his arms with the same warmth a mother would give to a sick child. The best measure of the value people place on life is the happiness they are able to achieve, and in the evenings, after the work of the day is done, laughter and flashing smiles come from the primitive Balti campfire circles just as frequently as from the slick camp of the sahibs.

Most Western people, like dogs chasing their tails, devote their lives to a conscious pursuit of happiness. We run in circles, making a lot of noise and raising considerable dust, chasing the illusion that happiness can be reached through symbolic understanding and material possessions. Those of us hoping to climb K2 have widened the circle of the chase. We are after a tangible goal—the summit of a mountain—which will function in our lives exactly as a material possession would, except that it will be nontransferable, theft-proof, and inflation-proof. Our society will register the achievement on an equal level with other, less abstract rewards of Western living. "I'd like you to meet Mr. Jones, the president of our local bank. And this is Mr. Dunham; he climbed the second highest mountain in the world." No wonder that Balti and Sherpa people have trouble understanding why Westerners want to climb mountains. For them happiness is a life force within, not some elusive quantity to be chased to the ends of the earth.

H.R.H. Prince Luigi Amedeo of Savoy, Duke of the Abruzzi

The Duke of the Abruzzi after an Alaskan expedition

③ The Duke

At sunrise on Good Friday in 1909, a steamer chugged into the Bombay harbor. A strikingly handsome man with genteel manners disembarked along with 13,280 pounds of baggage and an entourage of ten men. He claimed to be of Italian royalty, but some observers must have wondered if he was an impostor. Although he talked and acted like a man of breeding, subtleties belied the Good Life. It was more than just his rugged complexion, for that can come easily to a gentleman who relaxes in the sun. This man's eyes didn't look right. They were the tight ovals of a man who had spent a lifetime gazing into distances, rather than the usual round eyes, outlined by drooping lids, of those who live in the hypercivilized world of royalty. And something else: his hands were as rough as a laborer's, and his hat was held cleverly at his side to hide two missing fingers. His Royal Highness, Prince Luigi Amedeo of Savoy, Duke of the Abruzzi and grandson of King Victor Emmanuel II, was in truth a most unusual potentate.

The duke lost his fingers in 1899, while trying to reach the North Pole. One of his men came within two hundred miles of the pole, setting a record for the farthest north ever reached. Two years earlier the duke had planned to attempt Nanga Parbat, but when an outbreak of bubonic plague swept India he changed his plans and went to Alaska instead. On that journey he made the first ascent of 18,000-foot Mount St. Elias and on the same journey discovered Mount Logan, the highest peak in Canada and the largest single mountain mass on earth.

The duke did not limit his explorations to the North. In 1906 he led the first party to explore the Ruwenzori, the fabled Mountains of the Moon in tropical Africa which the ancient geographer Ptolemy claimed were the source of the Nile. Traveling through a land where rain fell 350 days a year, the duke not only mapped and surveyed the range, but also climbed the main peaks for the first time, reaching nearly 17,000 feet. He proved that the snows of the Ruwenzori did indeed drain into lakes that were the sources of the Nile. His team of naturalists, geographers, photographers, and Alpine guides brought back an important body of information about one of the earth's major unexplored regions.

Many of the men who accompanied the duke in Bombay had participated in his earlier explorations. Filippo de Filippi, a geographer, and Vittorio Sella, a photographer, both had been to Alaska and Africa with him. Joseph Petigax, an Alpine guide from Courmayeur, had accompanied the duke on all his expeditions. Two other guides, the Brocherol brothers, had been with Tom Longstaff on the highest climb in the world at that time, the ascent of 23,406-

foot Trisul. Federico Negrotto, a topographer, and four porters and assistants rounded out the group.

The duke's expedition was not a group of friends out for a good time; it was a superbly planned exploring machine in which each man had a distinct function. The party was headed for K2. The vast number of crates and boxes contained cooking and camping goods, climbing gear, photographic equipment which included glass-plate negatives and a cine camera, and a host of scientific instruments for topographical, meteorological, and photogrammetrical surveys. The equipment was the finest money could buy, but the duke and his companions had not indulged in much luxury for themselves. Conscious of the great distances to be traversed in the Karakoram as well as the problems of transport, the duke wisely left behind the brass bedstead that he had taken onto the Alaskan glaciers. By experience he had learned that such comforts of civilization rarely function well in the wilds. Sleeping on a bed under which cold breezes perpetually blew had often been less comfortable than lying on the ground. For himself and his K2 climbers, he now brought special sleeping bags made of four separate layers. The inner layer was made of camel's hair, the next was eiderdown, followed by goatskin and waterproof canvas. Each layer was a bag in itself and could be used separately or in any combination with the others. The bags could thus span the wide temperature range from 100-degree heat to sub-zero cold.

The duke was setting out on an expedition that would become a model for all future Himalayan exploring ventures. Every detail was planned as carefully as the sleeping bags had been. Although the expedition would travel a thousand miles by rail and horse-cart before requiring native bearers, the 262 loads for the final stage of the trek had been packaged, waterproofed, and equipped with carrying straps before the party left Europe.

The expedition had hired an advance man, who knew India and Kashmir well; he moved a day ahead of the caravan and made arrangements for porters and lodging. Tired from a long day on the road, the duke and his companions would often arrive in a village to find tea waiting at the home of a dignitary or even a polo match about to be played for their benefit. When needed, porters were always waiting at the beginning of each stage, eager to be hired at the princely wages offered—a whole rupee per day. Since the native people did not have much trust in paper money, the duke had begun the trek with 450 pounds of small change.

Filippo di Filippi and Vittorio Sella

The duke did not think it necessary for the caravan to move as one unit. Often the entourage took three days to pass a single point. First would come Baines, the advance man. Next came the duke and his companions, traveling fast with the most important equipment. Bringing up the rear was bulky and replaceable food and equipment, items that could catch up during rest days in major villages.

Moving precisely according to plan, the expedition reached Urdukas in late May. They had nothing but praise for the Balti people, calling them "scrupulously honest, mild of manners, gentle and good-tempered, naturally amenable to discipline, capable of the hardest labour, incredibly temperate, happy with very little, and invariably good-humored." Twenty-two days' march had brought the party nearly three hundred miles without an interruption or a mishap. When necessary, the expedition had hired over five hundred porters, but the usual number was less than three hundred.

Beyond Urdukas, food was a major concern. Crowley and Eckenstein had been stymied by the problem of traveling with porters who consumed their carrying capacity in food every thirty days, but the duke took a different approach. Baines became the Baron of Urdukas. There, in a semipermanent camp, he superintended a supply cache, a flock of sheep and goats, and a group of Balti shepherds and porters. Periodically he would send provisions to the climbers on the heights, keeping them supplied not only with such staples as sugar and flour, but also with fresh milk, mutton, and poultry.

When the expedition first reached Urdukas, snow began to fall. The porters refused to move and the expedition members sympathized. "Even had it been possible to induce the coolies to move," de Filippi later wrote, "we could not have gone far over ground so treacherous, even when uncovered, that you risk a fall with every step." The Baltis did not strike for layover wages or threaten to go home, because nowhere else could they make such grand wages. No expedition had visited the Baltoro for seven years and none was likely to follow for years to come.

The expedition made good use of the two days spent waiting out the bad weather. Sella and Negrotto set up a device to measure movement of the glacier. When the weather cleared one afternoon, Sella climbed far above camp in order to take a panoramic photograph of the lower Baltoro. Meanwhile, the others were busy setting up a meteorological station that was to remain at Urdukas for the duration of the expedition. Exact temperature and barometer measurements at a base altitude would add considerable precision and credibility to high-altitude measurements made on the same days during the actual ascent. One of the expedition's chief objectives was "to contribute to the solution of the problem as to the greatest height to which man may attain in mountain climbing." The duke's solution was simply to stand on a point of the earth's surface higher than that which any human being had ever reached before. Besides preparing the most meticulously designed expedition in history, the duke had brought along as guides the current high-altitude record holders. His goal was more to experience high altitudes than to reach a specific summit. He wanted to climb K2, but if that proved impossible he was prepared to try going high on another Karakoram giant.

The expedition left Urdukas with only a hundred-odd porters. At the end of May the party established a base camp below the southern flanks of K2. A day hike around to the east side convinced them that the Crowley-Eckenstein route on the northeast ridge was not practical. The duke himself investigated the western side of the peak, traveling up what he named the Savoia Glacier. He saw a high pass below the northwest ridge which he judged to be the least steep approach to the peak. The pass itself looked too steep and difficult for the coolies, so the duke decided instead to attempt the southeast rib that rose directly above base camp. The porters balked at the lower part of this route, later known as the Abruzzi Ridge, and after several days of climbing deceptively steep snow and rock slabs, the duke called a halt to the effort at 19,685 feet. It was higher than the duke had ever been, but still almost 9,000 feet short of the summit.

Entranced by his view of the western side of K2, the duke decided to move camp onto the Savoia Glacier and ascend the snow pass at its head to see if a feasible route existed. The pass proved more difficult than he expected because of the hundreds of feet of exposed blue ice. On the third attempt, the duke and his three guides spent twelve hours cutting steps in the ice, finally cresting Savoia Pass at the base of the northwest ridge of K2. After taking altitude readings that fixed the pass at 21,870 feet, the duke looked in vain for a passage to the upper mountain. Rocky towers and pinnacles barred a direct traverse onto the ridge. On the north side of the pass, invisible from the Savoia Glacier, a broad cornice extended toward the ridge and totally blocked his view of the great north face. De Filippi wrote, "As a reward of his labours, the duke thus saw utterly annihilated the hopes with which he had begun. . . . The excursion to the westward side of K2 had not revealed any feasible way of ascent."

While the duke worked at gaining high altitudes, Vittorio Sella set about his life's greatest work: the photographic documentation of the Karakoram. Although he had been to Africa, Alaska, and the Caucasus, and had circled Kanchenjunga, the third highest mountain in the world, Sella had never encountered a subject so grand. He was fifty years old and nearing the end of his active participation in rugged expeditions, but he pursued his subject with the vigor of a man half his years. De Filippi wrote, "Sella was spending whole days of patient waiting, renewing the experience of the Ruwenzori expedition, on the ledge of a crest some 2,000 feet above camp, where, crouched by his machine, he watched for a break in the clouds."

Sella's work expressed a combination of sensibilities. His panoramas demonstrated his skill as a patient technician; his landscapes showed that he had the romantic eye of an artist. In his mountain portraits he used the trained eye of a climber to single out the essential character of each peak. Many years later an emerging virtuoso in mountain photography, Ansel Adams, wrote an essay in appreciation of Sella. At one point he compared Sella to Edward Weston, noting that both men produced images "as concise, factual, and miraculously detailed as could be desired, yet they contain that magical and spiritual potential of vision which transcends analysis." Adams was not an aficionado of high-mountain photography for its own sake. He found most of it dull, merely a factual recording of the scene. But in Sella's work he saw the qualities of greatness which, to him, supported the concept "that intuition is the basic creative fac-

The duke's camp
on Savoia Glacier

The Duke 161

tor rather than a self-conscious awareness of modes and manners."

Sella's intuition for rendering mountains on film did not emerge out of nowhere when he lugged his first camera along on an expedition. He was a great mountaineer in his own right, and had made the first winter traverses of the Matterhorn in 1882, Monte Rosa in 1884, and Mont Blanc in 1888. The whole Sella family was influential and well known for their appreciation of mountains. Quintino Sella, Vittorio's uncle, was the founder of the Italian Alpine Club, and it was said that Vittorio inherited not only his uncle's love of the mountains but also his great thoroughness in whatever he undertook.

Although Sella was the K2 expedition's official photographer, he made no claim to be the only person who could take good pictures. He freely imparted both his technical knowledge and his sense of discipline to others on the trip. Ironically, the outstanding photograph of K2 from the expedition, a view from Staircase Peak with wispy snow plumes, was taken by the duke himself, although it is often credited to Sella.

The expedition was far from over when the duke retreated with his guides from Savoia Pass. The party spent weeks making a detailed survey of the upper Godwin-Austen Glacier. They reached several new passes and made an attempt on 24,750-foot Skyang

Savoia Pass   K2

162   THE YEAR OF THE BALTORO

Kangri, although progress ended abruptly at 21,650 feet, where a cleft blocked the route. After viewing K2 from all approaches except the north, which was known to be a steep wall laden with hanging glaciers, the duke was greatly discouraged. He asserted that the peak would never be climbed—not because of its altitude but because of its remoteness, its unfavorable climate, and the great technical obstacles along every route.

The expedition then moved a considerable distance to the upper Baltoro Glacier, where the duke hoped not only to continue mapping and surveying, but also to find a relatively high peak that he could climb. All those above 26,000 feet seemed out of the question. He narrowed the choice to 23,983-foot Golden Throne and 25,110-foot Bride Peak (now usually known as Chogolisa). He opted for Bride Peak, and Sella accompanied him there with several of the guides. After spending days waiting out a bad storm, Sella descended to finish his photographic tasks while the duke continued with the three guides. After several attempts they set up a camp only 2,600 feet from the summit. The next day they climbed the corniced, low-angle ridge, and just as they were sure the summit was theirs, a dense fog obscured their vision. They waited for it to clear, but it only grew worse and threatened to snow. Unable to see the edge of the cornice, they were forced to descend.

22,490   Bride Peak   20,974

Panorama E: West side of K2 from an ice hummock at the head of the Savoia Glacier.

At 24,600 feet on Bride Peak, the duke had set an altitude record that was to last until the British attempt on Everest in 1922. Although he didn't have a modern understanding of altitude sickness, he rightly disputed the conclusions of several prominent mountaineers who felt that humans could not function above a level well below the summits of the greatest peaks. The duke and his guides had slept at altitudes well above 20,000 feet and had experienced no headaches, unusual breathing difficulties, or rapid pulses. At altitude the duke's own pulse was sixty, much lower than that of any of his guides. He concluded that "rarefaction of the air, under ordinary conditions of the high mountains, to the limits reached by man at the present day, does *not* produce mountain sickness."

The duke arrived home with a great body of information on the Karakoram. The photographic record of the expedition far surpassed that of any prior mountain exploration. By photogrammetry a fine 1:100000 scale map of the main Baltoro peaks was produced. Filippo de Filippi wrote a 470-page book, illustrated with Sella's photographs, which became a classic of mountain literature.

Neither the duke nor Sella ever returned to the Karakoram. When World War I erupted, the Duke of Abruzzi became Chief Admiral of the Italian Fleet in charge of all Allied fleets in the Adriatic Sea. However, two members of his expedition did return. In 1913 Filippo de Filippi, accompanied by a bevy of scientists, led the most comprehensive scientific expedition ever to visit the Karakoram. Joseph Petigax, who had been the duke's guide in 1909, was a member of the party. After wintering in Skardu, the de Filippi expedition spent 1914 studying areas north and east of the Baltoro.

In an abstract sense, however, the duke has returned to the region again and again. The planning of every expedition into the Baltoro region is based on traditions and information generated by his explorations. Sella too has had a tremendous effect on the mountaineering world. His photo of Mustagh Tower was the single motivation for both a British and a French climb of the tower in 1956. And "Panorama E," a fold-out plate that accompanied de Filippi's book, provided the only glimpse of the Northwest Ridge of K2. A book-collecting Seattle attorney named James Wickwire shared it with his climbing friends.

4 Trouble on the Glacier

At Urdukas the sun shone for the better part of two days while the expedition remained in a holding pattern. Every day since we began walking on the glacier had seen some sort of minor strike, but this was a real deadlock.

Korophon camp, between Askole and the Baltoro Glacier

Although most major expeditions traveling up the Baltoro had experienced porter problems at Urdukas, our strike was of a different breed. The glaciers were covered with an unseasonable amount of snow, and we had over five hundred loads to be transported by men whose footgear was totally inadequate. By contract, the men were to have supplied their own shoes. Also, when they were hired the porters had been told that some would be sent home before high altitudes as the loads of food were consumed. The same illusion that leads a man into a game of blackjack thinking that he is "lucky today" caused each porter to believe that he would definitely be among the few to go home early. The wages we paid were much higher than those that had kept porters loyal to expeditions in the past, but one glaring flaw spoiled the system: by government regulation, wages were the same for carrying on low-altitude trails as on high-altitude ice. Therefore, porters could earn the same wages with less effort and risk by quitting when at the snow line and returning down valley to be hired by another expedition.

For these reasons literally every porter wanted to quit at Urdukas, the last camp off the ice at the glacier's edge. Their requests for higher pay, boots, socks, sunglasses, tents, and stoves were heart-rending but peripheral to the issue. The porters were using the bargaining power built into the nondifferentiated wage scale. We became prisoners of our own bold plans, and our only weapon was

Trouble on the Glacier 165

to withhold payment to those who refused to honor their contract to carry us to base camp.

Most of the porters had hopelessly inadequate footgear. Some men actually walked barefoot, and although they had performed well in the lower valleys where their half-inch-thick calluses protected their flesh as surely as shoe leather, they faltered in the higher regions where water froze in the cracks on their soles and created large, bleeding fissures that healed slowly and painfully. As I had noticed with some apprehensiveness on hiring day, those who had shoes usually wore open sandals or cheap plastic oxfords without laces or socks. Only the men from the high villages near Askole had decent footgear, but even their goatskin mukluks were not waterproof.

Balti footgear

We tried to improve their footgear by dipping into our personal supplies of wool socks, cutting out insoles from ensolite pads, and fashioning mukluks from burlap grain sacks and plastic bags. Usually the porters liked the new gear initially, used it for a few hours, and then never wore it again.

Of the five hundred porters still with us, a group of about two hundred made it clear that they would continue to work only on condition that we give full pay to the three hundred others who were quitting, plus extra for layover days and return time. We couldn't accept those terms. Jim was especially adamant, believing that we should not resort to shuttles of a few men, but should try at all costs to continue moving as a group.

Finally, a compromise was struck. About 100 men returned to Liliwa for the last remaining loads and another 130 carried loads partway to the next campsite. We, in turn, agreed to pay off any porters who had legitimate reasons for returning home. Among these were the genuinely sick and those who had been hired at Askole to carry food for their comrades. The porters who carried loads ahead came back complaining bitterly, "Bad road, sahib," and motioning that the snow was up to their thighs.

That evening I walked outside the tent to urinate before going to sleep. After my fly was unzipped, I realized that I was surrounded by staring Baltis, who urinate sitting down while covering themselves modestly with their loose clothing. I stood there . . . and stood there. . . . First one Balti laughed. Then another. Moments later I was laughing too, along with the Baltis, who found my situation immensely funny. The laughter reached a crescendo when I zipped up my pants and walked back to the tent, having failed to produce a single drop.

The next day Jim and Lou decided to check out the route and found the opposite of what the porters had reported: excellent walking, with no more than six inches of snow over a much more even surface than we had encountered on the lower parts of the glacier. Meanwhile, one section of camp began to resemble an emperor's traveling court. Hundreds of porters crowded into the entrance of a large umbrella tent, hoping to be paid and excused from the expedition. Inside, the Emperor (Wick) sat grandly in a folding aluminum

At the door of "the Emperor's tent," Urdukas

lawn chair, flanked by his aides. One by one his ragged subjects were brought before him, pleading illness or hardship. The Adjutant (Manzoor) acted as interpreter and curtly described the problems to the Doctor (Rob), who examined cracked feet, infected eyes, catarrhs, and coughs, and only gave leave easily to the halt and the blind. When salaries were calculated, the subject handed his numbered badge to the Keeper of the Exchequer (Leif), and a sum of money was counted out with purposeful slowness. The Emperor took notes while the money was recounted and passed to the headman of the subject's village, who sat on his haunches just inside the door. After recounting the money again, the headman placed it in the subject's outstretched hand. Often the subject would complain that he was receiving too little, even if he himself was unable to count. Occasionally a real error occurred, whereupon the Emperor, after a request from his aide, would recognize justice and order his Keeper of the Exchequer to hand out more rupees. Forty porters were dismissed with full pay.

Manzoor Hussain had a heavy load on his shoulders. No young major in the Pakistani Army—nor, for that matter a five-star general in the American army—could be expected to control five hundred unruly porters with only the help of ten mountain climbers who did not speak the native language. Technically, Manzoor was only supposed to be our government observer and interpreter, but in fact his task had grown far more involved. He interpreted culture as well as language, advised us on important decisions involving the porters, and increasingly bore the responsibility when things went wrong. Sometimes we did not agree with his suggested methods and other times, especially during negotiations with the porters, we expressed ideas in a way that Manzoor was sure would offend them. As our only translator, Manzoor began to alter the wording of our demands

Trouble on the Glacier 167

for our own good. He thought he was doing the expedition a service by dealing with the porters in a manner more acceptable to them. Unfortunately, his good intentions resulted in chaos. Complex deliberations became hopelessly garbled when we acted on our agreed-upon resolves while porters responded to Manzoor's altered statements.

Manzoor adjusted his behavior to meet the situation in another subtly important way. At the Whittakers' invitation he had visited the United States to get acquainted with the team and assess the expedition's requirements. As any good military man would, he had quickly learned what pleased his superiors. The Whittakers liked concise, positive answers to questions and were irritated by too many ifs, ands, and buts. Consequently, Manzoor learned to give overoptimistic answers to questions, a habit which was further reinforced when he saw team members chided for pessimistic predictions. Thus, at Urdukas Manzoor told us that once the porters began moving, we would be at base camp, thirty-five miles further into the mountains, in four days. He also allayed our fears about running low on porter food due to the strike, assuring us that more food was on the way from Askole and that the store we had on hand was more than enough to reach Concordia. Both predictions proved to be little more than empty reassurances.

During our troubled negotiations, Ghulam Rasul arrived from Liliwa camp, still sick and weak. Ghulam spoke Balti and some English, relieving a considerable part of Manzoor's doubled work load as both liaison officer and temporary sirdar. After more than a dozen expeditions, Ghulam was the most highly regarded sirdar in Baltistan, but even he had great trouble leading men who did not want to be where they were. Ghulam was a thin, small man who handled the porters with great vigor, shouting, waving his arms, threatening violence, and sometimes even hitting those who stood in his way with a stick or ski pole. Manzoor did not deal with the porters in a physical way, and many of us felt that he lacked the toughness necessary to deal effectively with them. But with Ghulam sick, it was Manzoor in the end who persuaded 350 porters to move on to Biano campsite, opposite Masherbrum.

For most of the team the day we hiked to Biano was happy and uneventful. We were glad to be moving again, especially on terrain that was becoming steadily smoother and easier to walk on as the covering of rock debris gave way to exposed snow and ice. But for Rob and Manzoor the beginning of that day had been a nightmare.

In Urdukas we had to distribute 350 loads among 480 porters, since some of the gear had been shuttled ahead. After two hours of haggling, shouting, and negotiating, all the loads were finally on their way. Rob and Manzoor were left quite alone with 130 hungry, angry porters, all from the village of Satpara, who decided that since they had no loads to carry, they would demand immediate payment and food and go home. Jim had taken most of the money with him in order to avoid paying strikers who refused to carry. The theory was that the strikers would have a choice: walk hungry and poor toward their homes, or walk two hours unladen to the next camp, join the expedition again, and receive full payment and food. The Satpara men were not interested in theories, however. Rob and Manzoor found themselves surrounded by an angry mob threatening physical violence. As the porters pressed closer and closer, blocking all chance of flight, Manzoor bravely handed his ice axe to the enraged Satpara leader, telling him, "Here, kill me now. We have no money. Take my life if that is what you want."

The porters suddenly realized the futility of their actions. Standing back, they allowed Manzoor and Rob to shoulder their packs and leave. Later in the day they walked down the glacier toward their homes. It was not the last we would see of them.

The events of that morning strengthened an already warm bond of friendship between Manzoor and Rob. In future disputes with the expedition, Rob would usually side with Manzoor. When an important decision had to be made, Manzoor would usually appear at our tent, expressing his views to Rob more openly than he would to other members of the team. Manzoor's credibility was a favorite topic of conversation among team members, and when Rob argued with someone who claimed that Manzoor withheld information from us, both were often right. Rob would have heard a more complete version in a private conversation than Manzoor gave to the team as a whole.

An equally strong bond of friendship had burgeoned between Wick and Lou, who had become nearly inseparable. In fact, Jim's and Lou's walk above Urdukas to check out the condition of the route had been one of the few occasions on which the two had been separated. The Whittakers had returned from that walk in exceptionally high spirits. Not only had they seen the great peaks at the head of the Baltoro for the first time, but they had been alone together in the mountains, a rare experience for them in recent years. Each reinforced the other's basic optimism about reaching the mountain and climbing it. That evening, Lou confided to Wick that Jim had tentatively picked the first and second summit teams. The first shot would go to Wick and Lou; the second to Jim and another climber, Leif being the most likely candidate.

Before the twins had left for their reconnaissance of the route, Lou had turned to Wick and asked, "Why don't you come?"

Wick responded, "No, you brothers go off together and I'll pay the sick porters."

Lou replied, "You're family. Come along."

Most expeditions choose summit teams when the party is high on the mountain. The choice is made either by a vote of the whole group or by the leader alone, and the criteria for both methods are team members' performance, physical condition, and location when the summit is within reach. All of us by now were aware that the approach march was turning into a contest and that we were being judged in part by our pack weights and hiking times.

Lou and Wick were the hands-down winners for the first team. Every day, carrying sixty- to seventy-pound packs, they arrived at the new campsite before the others. Jim also carried a very heavy

Porter on glacier

load. When he walked with Dianne, who carried about forty-five pounds, they usually arrived somewhere in the middle, but on the few days that Jim walked with Lou or Wick, he showed that he too was able to keep up with the front-runners. Leif carried about fifty-five pounds and never appeared to be in a hurry. Rarely resting, he usually arrived within a few minutes of Lou and Wick. Fred Dunham, carrying a similar pack, was usually not far behind. Last place always went to Rob or Fred Stanley, both of whom usually arrived with the porters hours after the others were in camp. Rob, a very fit marathon runner, could easily have reached camp each day many hours earlier. Apparently, he never heard the starter's pistol.

Similarly, I didn't view myself as taking part in the competition, but I usually arrived in camp very near the front. I thought it would be obvious that with my light load I was in no way engaged in the weight/speed contest. I had several reasons for going light. I had severely sprained my ankle several months before the trip, and it had not yet healed. When the expedition had left Seattle I had been unable to run even a hundred feet without feeling pain, and I made up my mind then not to carry a heavy load on the approach march and risk re-injury. Also, I wanted to walk ahead of the main body of the expedition in order to experience the wildness of the Karakoram before it was interfered with by the passage of our giant caravan. I had plenty of time in the mornings and evenings to observe and photograph the camp and the porters. For a few hours during the day, I hoped to have a different perspective on the region—to pass through villages that were in their normal state before the inhabitants lined the paths to watch our parade, and I wanted to wander up hills and into side valleys to view wildlife and search for vantage points from which to record the caravan's passage from afar.

These habits of mine were sharply criticized by the Big Four. Wick wrote in his diary that by spending afternoons trying to photograph wildlife, I was in his judgment, "neglecting his basic duties of photographing the expedition's progress toward the base of K2." My pack was the object of constant jibes. Everyone else carried a large-capacity frame pack, but I carried a smaller soft pack, which made it easier for me to dart ahead when I saw a good picture or to jog past a line of porters. At lunch stops, my pack was frequently hefted by Jim, Wick, or Lou. One would say, "Wow, that's light. Not over thirty-five pounds." Another would lift it and say, knowingly, "More like thirty."

I'd like to be able to say that I wasn't bothered by these taunts, that I knew what I wanted to do and felt good about it. But that wasn't the case. I thought about explaining that the pack contained thirty-eight pounds of camera gear which had been weighed accurately at home, and that with a parka, water, and the weight of the pack itself the total was certainly forty-five pounds. But what would I have proved? That I carried forty-five pounds to their seventy? By arguing about weight, I would have become part of the load-carrying competition. Other things were more important to me. Or were they? One part of me longed to prove myself, to sack wildness, mobility, and the fear of hurting my ankle before reaching the mountain to show that I, too, could carry a heavy pack quickly over rough terrain. I didn't think I could keep up with Lou, especially if he pushed hard, carrying a seventy-pound load, but I was quite sure that I could hold my own in the expedition.

From Lou and Wick's standpoint, I was definitely trying to participate in the competition. If I was just walking at my own rate for my own reasons, why did I speed up and try to stay with them when they occasionally poured on the coal? The answer was that we were fooling each other. Lou and Wick saw competition where it didn't always exist, and I, whether I admitted it to myself or not, was definitely competing when I matched my pace to that of the front-runners.

Leif was the only team member who was not the object of criticism by one team member or another. Lou told him privately that he was being considered for the summit, and Leif answered cautiously that it was a long way up K2 and things could change. That evening, Leif wrote this entry in his diary:

I am not surprised to hear that we are being "evaluated." If I had been the leader I, too, would have kept an eye on each man. But I hope deeply that no wedge will be driven among team members. I believe firmly that we are so small a group that we each need the other at some time. As of now, there is no doubt that Lou is by far the strongest, seemingly unaffected by altitude. Jim is also a physical power to be reckoned with. I could well imagine the twins crowning the summit. I believe Wick is a little affected by altitude lately, but in no way does this detract from his will power—and perhaps ability—to give *all* to make this mountain. Rob is in good shape; I think his ability to survive high altitude is not being appreciated. Galen has been full of "go" all along. I still believe he is a key man should we run into any technical problems. And he is strong. But there is a schism between Galen and the Whittakers (especially Lou), partly because of Galen's outspokenness. Galen can be both critical and argumentative—he has a good mind—but he would be wiser not to take up discussion with those who do not have his ability or patience to debate. Fred Stanley plays a modest role, but I have often found that when something or somebody is needed, Fred is there to help. Fred often brings up the rear; he seems slow on the move, but perhaps he just enjoys himself. But he is not in any way subdued and will give some pretty salty remarks, always loud and clear, and speaks up to the Whittakers if he sees fit. He shares with Fred Dunham what seems to be infinite disdain, if not hatred, for our useless Balti porters. There isn't one of us who hasn't cursed these primitive men for getting us into trouble with their unending strikes and breaking of commitments, but Fred Dunham is ready for violence, it seems, and stiff in his attitude that these people should think and act as we do in America. Otherwise, Fred D. is a good guy to have around. He is strong, too, if altitude will not fell him. He certainly is the professional wrapper-upper of everything that needs wrapping and boxing on this expedition. And Steve carries on his filming, cold or not, steadfastly day after day. He does not seem much affected by altitude yet. In his mind he must feel a bit bothered by his role on the expedition. He has a basically modest character. Gradually, patiently, we are no doubt discovering the various facets of each other—facets that are rather surprising and not always flattering.

I began the expedition feeling very close to both Wick and Manzoor, but our divergent behavior in stress situations began to drive us apart. Each had a radically different way of handling controversies. It would be hard to find three people in one small group who represented such a broad triangle of outlook.

Manzoor tended to use words more for emotional expression and sheer pragmatism than for true meaning. To his Asian mind, exaggeration was not necessarily a lie, but rather a normal means of advocating a point of view. The concept of objective truth seems to be far less precise in Asia than in Western culture, and is pursued less often for its own sake. If these sound like hasty generalizations, the specific misunderstandings that they have engendered over centuries between members of the two cultures are concrete enough. The relative lack of concern for factuality among Asians goes far toward explaining why democracy, the Renaissance, and the scientific method originated elsewhere, and why the Watergate crimes, for instance, were considered trifling by Eastern observers. Manzoor sought to represent things honestly far more often than most Pakistani officials, but nevertheless he had been raised in a world where saving face was more important than telling the truth. What counted was the emotion of the moment, rather than the accuracy of facts.

Wick, in contrast, was very concerned with factual accuracy. In a group he was a man of few words. He chose those words carefully and delivered them without much emotion. His legal training showed when he would drop verbal defense of his viewpoints the instant he discovered that they were clearly in the minority.

I was as concerned with facts as Wick, but I was far more outspoken. Rather than biding time when outnumbered, I continued to verbalize minority opinions on issues that I considered important. My father had been a professor of argumentative discourse, and from him I had learned to value advocacy of beliefs over saving face.

Manzoor, then, placed great value on self-image, Wick on the process, and I on the philosophy of the issues. Each of our modes was geared to special situations. In a book or a magazine, I could come off quite smartly. In a courtroom or an embassy, Wick would do likewise. But in real-life negotiations involving both Asian and American people, shaping the truth to meet the situation had its advantages.

Wick, too, wrote a new appraisal of his teammates on the approach march:

In the pre-expedition world of Seattle, Jim and I had comfortably concluded we had a highly compatible team. Yet, with the strains of the approach march not over, I'm not so sure. I haven't heard from Leif or Rob, but the Freds are definitely disgruntled with both Whittakers and most likely me, for the way things have been handled. They feel Manzoor is doing a terrible job and can't be trusted, yet at the same time admit no one else in Pakistan could do a better job. Both have considerable difficulty coping with the frustrations of things thus far.

Galen has taken a lot of verbal abuse from the Whittakers, particularly Lou. Everything he says somehow rubs Lou the wrong way. For instance,

Wick, Jim, Manzoor

yesterday he asked Lou what he should say in the book about Lou's climbing record. Angrily, Lou's response was to say, "I've been a mountaineer since I was sixteen. I'm a climber and that's that."

Lou says he knows who he is and doesn't need a list of climbs tacked on to tell him that. He is very much down on the publication of climbs by climbers. I don't know what lies beneath his thinking, but both Lou and Jim have never (almost, that is) shown any interest in doing a new route until K2. New routes were for the Fred Beckeys who would write them up in the journals and guidebooks. Yet, this attitude misses what for me has been the sheer joy of overcoming the challenge of an untrodden wall or ridge, dealing with the uncertainties of not having a pathfinder ahead of you. The articles in journals and descriptions in guidebooks are secondary. Self-satisfaction is foremost; respect of other climbers is secondarily important. I can't believe Jim and Lou have never yearned to do a new climb— the West Ridge of K2, for instance—but why have they not done them before? And if not, why should they look down on others who do?

Manzoor considered the Baltis to be ideologically part of the great nation of Pakistan that he revered. To us it seemed obvious that the Baltis did not think of themselves as subjects of Pakistan. We saw our situation as a triangle. At one corner was the government, which established regulations and sent a liaison officer along to make sure that we obeyed them; at the other were the Baltis, who neither believed in the authority of the government nor felt compelled to obey the regulations. In the third corner, bearing the brunt of the conflict, was our group.

May 24, at Ghoro campsite between Masherbrum and Concordia, was one of the expedition's lowest days. Dawn came in a snowy haze. Rob announced at breakfast that he had bronchitis, apparently contracted from one of his patients. Manzoor told us that regardless of past promises, the porters were striking again and that fewer than a hundred would continue on. This would mean that shuttling loads between camps would take four or five days, adding weeks to our travel time to base camp. The slowdown could result in our arrival at the mountain in midsummer after the weather had begun to shift. In that case making the climb would be out of the question.

The odds were high that we would not even make it to base camp. The day before, on May 23, Manzoor had made a most disturbing announcement: he told us we had only one day's food left for the porters. I had staunchly defended Manzoor's integrity in the past, but now I was no longer sure of it. After breakfast I played back a tape of a long conversation the group had had with Manzoor at Urdukas a week before. Manzoor had clearly told us not to worry about porter food:

Manzoor: From here to Concordia we are sufficient. We have got a bit more than what they require now.

Wickwire: If we are going to get them to go on past base camp [to the foot of Savoia Pass] they're going to have to have rations.

Manzoor: That's why I've got everything in. I don't want to run short of *atta*.

Nearing Concordia

Now, at Ghoro, Manzoor assured us that forty additional loads of *atta* (wheat) were on their way from Askole and would reach us within a day or two. We didn't know whether to believe him. After lunch, we began negotiations with the porters who, with a great show of righteous indignation, demanded immediate payment. Manzoor had promised, using wording quite different from ours and altering our meaning considerably, that some of the sick and old porters would be released at Ghoro camp. This resulted in a repeat of the Urdukas demands. Nearly all the porters wanted to qualify for going back. A day earlier we had increased the pay for future stages to forty rupees per day plus food. Now, with the expedition threatened more seriously than ever before, we offered sixty rupees if the majority of porters would continue. At first the offer excited them, but soon they were arguing and negotiating again.

At this point, the last of the Balti apologists in our party capitulated. With a look of Norse determination, Leif told us that if our expedition was left stranded on the glacier the Baltis should not go unpunished. He thought that the quitters should be stripped naked and marched home in shame. "They'll get out alive," he said with a prosecutor's glint in his eye. "They'll have a lesson. I don't want to kill them outright."

Late in the afternoon the expedition was on the verge of immediate collapse. Negotiations seemed useless. It seemed as if only a stroke of magic could save us. Then Lou had an ingenious idea: we could stage a counterstrike. If the Baltis walked out on us, we would walk out on them. Over Manzoor's strong objections we told the porters that if our expedition failed at Ghoro, we would burn all of our equipment and money on the spot and go home empty-handed without paying them. To underscore the threat, Lou suggested

Porter negotiations, near Concordia

burning a small amount of money. Jim pulled a ten-rupee note out of the payroll sack and Wick set his lighter to it. As it burned on the negotiating table in front of wide-eyed village headmen, the team members got up and walked back to their tents without a word.

Later we had great news. Virtually all the porters had agreed to carry to Concordia. But all was not well. Manzoor did not show up for dinner. Earlier in the afternoon, Lou had said some harsh words to Manzoor, blaming both him and Ghulam Rasul for hiring ill-equipped porters while knowing full well of the late winter and rugged terrain. Lou searched for Manzoor, found him with the porters, and apologized. Manzoor was lying down, totally devastated and in the depths of depression—not so much because of Lou's words as for the burning of the money.

Among the members of the expedition, three distinct interpretations of the Ghoro strike solution existed. Most of us believed that the shock of burning the money had been the major factor. Fred Stanley thought that walking out of the negotiating tent might have done more than the actual burning. And Manzoor claimed that the porters were infuriated by the burning and that they decided to continue solely out of respect for the Pakistani Army and himself. If Manzoor's claim was true, agreeing to continue was the only act we ever saw them perform out of respect for the government.

From Ghoro campsite we had occasional glimpses of Mustagh Tower through the clouds. This 23,860-foot peak had become world famous through the repeated publication of a single photograph. In 1909, Vittorio Sella shot an extreme telephoto view of the tower from the upper Baltoro Glacier; the picture showed an ice-plastered rock obelisk that was nearly vertical on all sides. The photograph became a symbol of the unclimbable mountain, even though the duke's text on the expedition clearly stated that Mustagh Tower had a very ordinary appearance from other directions. As late as 1954, Sella's photo appeared in a history of mountaineering captioned, "The Last Citadel . . . No man has dreamed of climbing it—yet." In 1956 two expeditions made separate attempts. Both were successful. British climbers Joe Brown and Ian McNaught-Davis made the first ascent by the northwest ridge; a few days later a French team reached the summit via the southeast ridge. Both ridges averaged about forty-five degrees and provided difficult but not unusual Himalayan mountaineering problems.

When we reached Ghoro, I waited expectantly for the clouds to break and Mustagh Tower to appear. Eagerly I cleaned and re-cleaned lenses, set up a tripod, and voiced concern lest I miss a good picture of such a famous peak. I was at the cook tent when the tower began to come out of the clouds. I dropped everything, rushed uphill fifty feet to my tent, and grabbed my cameras, already fitted with just the right lenses and filters for the scene. Leif lay reading in his sleeping bag, strangely unconcerned about my frantic rush. "Grab your camera, Leif," I said. "Mustagh Tower's coming out!"

Leif replied, "No, thank you. I have no interest in photographing that mountain."

"Why not?"

Camp under Mustagh Tower

"Because this is a false view. The mountain is not what it seems from here."

"But many mountains are like that."

"This one is different. The Sella photo has misrepresented it to the world, and I do not want to be a part of continuing that falsehood." As usual, Leif spoke totally without malice, never suggesting that I refrain from photographing the mountain because of his personal decision.

I disagreed with Leif on this matter. To me all good photography was an accentuation of strong and simple natural lines. I considered it human nature to exaggerate the things we cherish when we symbolize them in photos and other art forms. For me Sella's photography reflected this tendency in much the same way that a good anecdote distills a meaningful fragment from the complex horizon of life.

From a practical point of view, I knew that if I did photograph Mustagh Tower from its less spectacular sides, any editor or publisher would discard those images for the southeast view now before me. I also knew that this was precisely why Leif refused to add his own photograph to the myth.

As the tower came out from the cloud veil, I shot a dozen pictures. In a few minutes it disappeared again and I returned to the tent. Leif looked up pleasantly and asked, "Did you get some good shots?"

"Yes," I replied. "I think I did."

"I'm glad your chance came," Leif said. "You wanted that photograph pretty badly."

Section VII

The
Mountain

The man who, on such a dangerous enterprise, seeks the assurance of a safe retreat will not deserve to draw near to the Throne of the Gods.

—GÜNTHER DYHRENFURTH

1 The First Americans on K2

No human beings set foot on K2 for twenty-nine years after the Duke of Abruzzi's reconnaissance. Other Himalayan giants offered much greater hope of success, and several expeditions attempted Everest and Kanchenjunga, the highest and third highest peaks.

Until the thirties, high-altitude climbing in Asia was practiced almost exclusively by British and European expeditions. During that decade Americans began to pop up here and there on serious expeditions, usually as minority members of teams organized by other nations. In 1937, Fritz Wiessner, a German immigrant to the United States, planned a K2 attempt to be sponsored by the American Alpine Club. Wiessner had led the American contingent of Willi Merkl's 1932 German-American Nanga Parbat expedition and was a highly respected climber in both Europe and America. The club pursued the K2 idea and obtained permission for an expedition in 1938.

Wiessner was unable to go in 1938 and postponed his trip for a year. Permission to climb K2 had been obtained from the Indian government with difficulty, so the American Alpine Club decided to pass it on to another group of climbers led by Charles Houston, a young medical student. Houston had already led a successful expedition on 17,300-foot Mount Foraker in Alaska and in 1936 had reached over 24,000 feet with a British-American group on the successful first ascent of Nanda Devi, the highest summit climbed up to that time. Houston's primary purpose was to reconnoiter K2, but if he discovered a feasible route he planned to give it his best effort.

Charles Houston

Houston favored small, lightweight expeditions because they were more fun, easier to plan, and more challenging. Also, he did not believe that mountaineers should use a wide array of technical gadgets to subdue great peaks. He was convinced that climbs completed with the aid of large amounts of ironmongery were feats of engineering rather than exploration.

In making his plans for K2, Houston referred to the duke's experiences in 1909 as well as his own memories of the far lighter Nanda Devi expedition. While the duke had brought guides from the Alps, Houston planned to import six experienced Sherpas from Nepal, hand-picked for him by Bill Tilman, who was leading a 1938 Everest attempt. Houston was thrilled that Tilman was able to spare Pasang

Kikuli, one of the most experienced Sherpas. Pasang had been on four expeditions to Kanchenjunga, as well as to Everest and Nanga Parbat. Even more important, he had been Houston's personal Sherpa on Nanda Devi.

Besides Houston, only four other team members plus a liaison officer completed the group. Bob Bates was a veteran of several successful Alaskan expeditions which had been textbook examples of lightweight climbing, mobility, and efficiency. Dick Burdsall had been with a small expedition that climbed 24,891-foot Minya Konka in 1932. Bill House had made the first ascent of difficult and remote Mount Waddington in British Columbia with Fritz Wiessner. The last team member, Paul Petzoldt, was a Wyoming mountain guide who joined the group when the original fourth was unable to go. Petzoldt's endurance was legendary, and he had numerous first ascents in the Rockies to his credit, but no serious expedition experience. He would be a test case for the commonly stated proposition that first-time Himalayan climbers do not perform well.

Bob Bates

The expedition's liaison officer, Captain Norman R. Streatfield of the Bengal Mountain Artillery, was a British officer stationed in India. In 1936 he had accompanied a large French expedition to Hidden Peak, only ten miles from K2.

From Srinagar to Baltistan, the Americans followed in the footsteps of the duke with equal efficiency. In the lower parts of Kashmir porters were paid one-sixteenth of a rupee per mile, which allowed them to earn a month's normal wages in a few days. As the caravan passed by the Dras River, someone noticed a set of initials scratched onto a water-polished block of marble. They read, "H. H. G.-A. 1861-2-3"—the mark of Captain H. H. Godwin-Austen, on his way to discover the Baltoro approach to K2.

The Sherpas were lighthearted and gay except for a single instance in Baltistan when a group of porters struck for higher wages and advanced threateningly toward the climbers. At that moment the Sherpas instantly forsook their nonviolent ways, brandished ice axes in defense, and said, "Let us at them, sahibs. We do not like these men."

The strike was settled without violence and the expedition progressed to Askole, where porters from the Shigar area were dismissed and local men were hired. Only seventy-five porters were required to transport the entire expedition, even though the climbers themselves carried very light loads.

One day out of Askole the porters struck for higher wages. The uprising was quickly dispelled when the ringleaders were told that they were fired and could go home without pay, since the climbers had just decided to carry their own personal belongings to base camp. The ringleaders stayed on and no more strikes occurred.

On June 12 the expedition reached the base of K2 and began reconnoitering the three ridges that the duke had judged to be the only possible routes. The Americans split up and spent two weeks exploring the northeast ridge attempted by Crowley and Eckenstein, the northwest ridge that rose above Savoia Pass, and the Abruzzi Ridge on the southeast side of the peak. They found the

The First Americans on K2 179

northeast ridge to be highly questionable because of a long knife-edge of pinnacles that stretched from 22- to 25,000 feet. Like the duke before them, they were entranced by the northwest ridge, which rose in a bold, simple bulwark from 23,000 feet to the summit. The main problem was how to gain access to the ridgecrest.

Traveling up the Savoia Glacier, Bill House reported that it was impossible not to feel encouraged. He even regretted that the reconnaissance to the ridgecrest would be so short, "for it seemed as though there would be no question of gaining the pass and making fast progress on the ridge itself." Beyond the pass the summit appeared deceptively close through clear mountain air.

The duke and his guides had reached Savoia Pass in a single day from a camp on the Savoia Glacier. The 1938 climbers inferred from the duke's report of the ascent that they had encountered no great difficulties between their camp and the pass. For the duke's guides, reared in the Alps, cutting steps in hard ice was second nature. En route to Savoia Pass they had methodically alternated step-cutting for most of the daylight hours. But the 1938 climbers did not have that kind of ice-climbing background. They judged, probably rightly, that cutting steps and climbing to the pass would take them two days. After three abortive attempts to reach the pass, they concluded that conditions must have changed since the duke's time. Besides the laborious step-cutting, they were concerned about avalanche potential and the route's difficulty for the laden porters. Houston decided that the northwest ridge route was "out of the question for us that summer," and concluded, "we cannot say with any certainty how the northwest ridge can be climbed from the pass."

After a council of war the expedition decided to attempt the Abruzzi Ridge. As equipment was being moved from the Savoia Glacier, a slender pedestal of ice holding up a large rock collapsed, burying a quarter of the expedition's fuel supply. Captain Streatfield knew where the Hidden Peak expedition of two years before had cached extra fuel. With two Balti porters he set off across the glaciers, only to return empty-handed several days later. The men of Askole had returned to the base of Hidden Peak during the interim and had looted the cache.

The Abruzzi Ridge rose at an average angle of forty-five degrees, far steeper than any route yet climbed on a Himalayan peak. In the Alps a fast-moving party of climbers would not have found the lower part of the ridge very difficult, but the effects of 20,000 feet of altitude in reducing human efficiency drastically changed the situation. Not only was every motion slower and more tiring, but the need for campsites was far more frequent. The down-sloping strata offered no level areas suitable for camps. During one foray above base camp Houston spotted a few pieces of wood in a small saddle. This had been the duke's camp, cramped on a sloping platform directly below a couloir with a high avalanche potential. Houston decided against using the campsite but was deeply moved by finding traces of his predecessors in this remote spot.

All the lower camps that the group made on the ridge were in poor locations. Climbers in the lead continually loosened rock debris that rained down on men and tents below. Camp III, on top of an exposed shoulder, took direct hits that landed with the force of gunfire. Two tents were pierced by rocks before the decision was made to evacuate the camp while others were climbing directly above. Finally, the group decided that the route on the ridge was unsafe with so many people climbing. Burdsall and Streatfield descended with three Sherpas to busy themselves with mapping and photographing. Only four Americans and three Sherpas stayed on the ridge to continue the attempt.

By July 12, twenty days of food had been carried to Camp III and Petzoldt had made a brilliant lead up a steep rock tower to another exposed shoulder where Camp IV was placed at 21,500 feet. Above, House and Bates took over the lead and were confronted with the major obstacle of the entire Abruzzi Ridge, a vertical band of red rock, 150 feet high. House led up a wide crack that narrowed to a foot-and-a-half width near the top and became glazed with ice. The rock was rotten and did not lend itself to cracks for pitons. Luckily, House found an occasional resting place and was able to climb without resorting to a laborious series of direct-aid pitons. The slot became known as House's Chimney.

Petzoldt and Houston resumed the lead, placed Camp VI at 23,300 feet, and located a site for Camp VII at 24,700 feet. At that point they came to the end of the true Abruzzi Ridge. They were about 600 feet below the crest of a great shoulder that formed the largest low-angle area on any part of the mountain. This plateau rose gradually until it merged with the grand pyramid in a thrust toward the summit, a tantalizingly close 2,000 feet above.

When Petzoldt and Houston returned to Camp VI, another council of war was held. The group had experienced an unprecedented period of good weather, but they had no idea how long it would hold. For two weeks their climbing had been almost totally uninterrupted by storms. Previous expeditions to the Karakoram had reported no more than four consecutive storm-free days and a general average of more storms than clear weather. Now the team could see great cloud masses to the south, hiding the summit of Nanga Parbat. They had a policy of keeping a reserve of a week's food at all times, in case a long storm pinned them high on the mountain. In a raging blizzard they did not think they could descend the great difficulties of House's Chimney and Petzoldt's Gendarme. Since only ten days of food remained, the group had to make an agonizing decision. Should they go up and risk being stranded high on the mountain? Or should they go down and be happy that the route had been reconnoitered to high altitude without loss of life or limb?

Decisions were made by a majority vote. Each man was in prime physical condition and ready to push on toward the summit. Each man also felt responsible for both his own and his companions' safety. Finally they reached a compromise: no summit attempt would be made, but two men would go as high above Camp VII on the summit cone as they could manage in one day. The other two would help carry the equipment up to Camp VII and retreat to VI.

The First Americans on K2   181

When the high climbers returned to Camp VI, the expedition would begin its retreat.

Since both Petzoldt and Houston had the edge, knowing the route, and had spent more days at altitude, the team decided these two should make the final dash. The Sherpas would not go above Camp VI because of steep green ice just below the site of Camp VII. Expeditions often had trouble persuading their high-altitude porters to continue climbing, but Pasang Kikuli was as eager to go high as any of the team. All the climbers trusted Pasang's mountain sense, so they relented and asked him to join in the carry to Camp VII.

The morning of July 20 was crystal clear. Five men carried to 24,700 feet and three went down, leaving Petzoldt and Houston alone with two days of food and fuel. The pair dug a tent platform into the snow below the edge of the great plateau and prepared to spend the night. To their horror they discovered that the matches had been left behind. Without a stove they would not be able to melt water or cook food. Houston dug into his pockets and found nine scraggly matches. Petzoldt tried one. It fizzled briefly; then went out. Houston tried another. It broke off at the head. A third burst into flame and lit the waiting stove. Only six were left.

After dinner they melted water and placed the full pot, wrapped in clothes, under the feet of both sleeping bags, hoping to prevent the water from freezing. In the morning the water was not frozen. They used three more matches to light the stove and cook breakfast, and then they set off for the unknown, carrying no bivouac gear. The day was cool and windless. Nanga Parbat, 120 miles away, was etched sharply against a blue horizon. The going was not difficult but it was exceedingly tiring. In places they floundered in powder snow up to their hips. Houston felt the altitude more than Petzoldt and had difficulty keeping up. By one o'clock, they had reached the crest of the great shoulder, surveyed at 25,354 feet by the duke. The gentle incline was not the respite from exertion or danger that they had hoped for. Recent avalanche debris littered the scene, and deep snow slowed their progress to a snail's pace.

The two climbers crossed the dangerous final portion of the great shoulder as quickly as possible, eventually reaching safety at the base of the summit cone. At a slightly higher point, somewhat under 26,000 feet, Petzoldt found an excellent site for Camp VIII. It would have to wait for another expedition in another year. Houston was exhausted and decided not to continue. Petzoldt went on, scrambling a few hundred feet higher to see if the rock of the summit cone was really as climbable as it appeared to be. He reached a high point of about 25,600 feet.

Meanwhile, Houston retreated back across the great shoulder to the outer edge, where he could rest in the sun beyond the reach of avalanches. The psychological pressure to push upward for the top suddenly lifted, and he felt both regret and relief. For the first time he could enjoy the wild scene without trying to interpret in terms of his odds for success. He could see Concordia, 11,000 feet below him—a giant nerve center for the whole region. All the ice that hung from surrounding peaks would either evaporate or flow downward into glaciers that merged at Concordia. Multicolored stripes of rock debris also flowed with the ice, tearing down the great peaks.

Soon Petzoldt struggled down and sat next to Houston. He reported that the route looked good to the summit and that they had probably already conquered the greatest technical difficulties.

After a rest, the two men descended to Camp VII for the night. Stars dotted the dark sky even before the sun had set. They reached the tent in twilight, thirsty and cold from their ordeal; at that moment a hot drink seemed more important to them than anything else in the world. Carefully, they waxed one of the matches and struck it. It fizzled. They tried another. It broke at the head. The very last match burst into flame, and they enjoyed a blissful pot of hot tea, guaranteeing a cold breakfast the next morning.

The retreat was methodical and uneventful. A few weeks later the expedition returned to America, quite pleased with the result of the first solid attempt to climb a mountain that many had considered impregnable. From the comfort of civilization Houston described the feelings he had experienced that afternoon on the great shoulder: "I felt that all my previous life had reached a climax in these last hours of intense struggle against nature, and yet nature had been very indulgent. She had scarcely bothered to turn against us the full force of her elements . . . preferring to let our puny bodies exhaust themselves in the rarefied atmosphere. How small indeed we were to struggle so desperately to reach one point on the earth's surface. . . . I believe in those minutes at 26,000 feet on K2 I reached depths of feeling which I can never reach again."

The entire cost of the expedition, including personal travel, was $9434.03, of which expenses for Balti porters amounted to $567.47. No lives or friendships were lost. In a report for the *Himalayan Journal*, Houston summarized the results of the trip: "Ours was a united party in every sense; our shared experiences can never be forgotten. Our purpose, reconnaissance, was completely accomplished, and a way was found by which, with the smile of good fortune, a second party may reach the summit."

2   K2 at Last

On May 25, with 330 porters, we reached Concordia. The long-awaited view of K2 was suddenly before us. The base of the great peak lay hidden in roiling clouds while a white plume blew from its summit. The bulk and perfect symmetry of the mountain filled the valley of the Godwin-Austen Glacier as a diamond completes a fine setting. We had all expected that coming suddenly face to face with K2 at a distance of only seven miles would be a soul-stirring experience. To the contrary—the mountain was everything we expected it to be, and nothing more.

Staircase Peak   26,017   Broad Peak   Gasherbrum   24,019   Golden Throne   Bride Peak
                                                                                                Chogolisa Saddle

Godwin-Austen Glacier   +Station for Panorama D   Upper Baltoro and Vigne Glaciers

No pulses quickened; no tears flowed. Ecstasy, if anyone felt it, was well contained. Long days spent battling porters and each other had sapped our emotional energy. After six hard weeks of travel, we were just nearing the beginning of our task. The summit of K2 looked cold, remote, and distant. Our route was still hidden behind the left-hand skyline, and our base camp was fifteen miles away.

From a distance Concordia appeared to be as gentle as a mountain meadow. High peaks surrounded it on all sides. Countless glaciers, now totally white with fresh snow, flowed from every valley and mountain, linking once, twice, sometimes three times with other glaciers before merging at Concordia itself, where the Godwin-Austen and Baltoro ice joined forces in long, fluid arcs.

Our campsite was on the crest of a moraine that descended from the clouds at the base of K2 in a straight line until it began to curve at the edge of the Concordia amphitheater. Parallel to it were a dozen similar moraines resembling high-speed racetracks, complete with banked lanes and perfect-radius turns. These strips were several hundred feet wide, and they swung through Concordia en route to the Baltoro straightaway, where they converged in the distant haze. Between the moraines were deep furrows filled with frozen streams and strange ship-sized prows of ice, both features formed by decades of differential melting in the summer sun. The scene suggested motion and yet nothing moved. Surface waters flowed under a rigid crust of ice; the fleet of ice ships was at full sail on a frozen sea. The passage of the glacier was imperceptible.

The stillness at the Concordia sanctuary contrasted with the stronger impression we had of motion on the high peaks. Summits seemed to advance and retreat as clouds moved among foreground ridges, changing our sense of distance. Avalanches rustled as frequently as autumn leaves, descending in roaring clouds of white powder, crunching blocks of glacier ice, or wet snow slabs sliding

Mitre Peak   Masherbrum   Paiyu Peak

The main Baltoro valley   +Station for Panorama B

Panorama taken from the ridge forming the angle between the Baltoro and the Godwin-Austen Glaciers, 17,330 feet

with the slow power of a thousand bulldozers. The slides left once smooth slopes looking like cottage cheese.

The image of a mountain scene is often used to represent the immutable, the unchanging. Photographs of Concordia convey just these qualities but almost none of the sense of motion that a visitor experiences. A photograph records no more than a thirtieth of a second of eternity; human eyes have evolved to detect the fleeting motion of other animals. The mountain visitor's experiences are hours or days out of his lifetime, and he only begins to detect hints of motion. In order to truly appreciate the flowing feeling of Concordia, a person must alter his perspective of time away from the perception of moments, hours, or even human life spans into the timetable of the mountains themselves.

Teachers ask students to attempt a similar shift of perspective in an earth-sciences classroom, but the most to be hoped for in that context is a passive flashback, an imaginary concept that can be forgotten before the next hour's English class. At Concordia a person lives in the Pleistocene epoch, and ice rules his existence. He walks on it, lives on it, melts it for water, and climbs it toward the summits. He becomes a part of the ice age, and if he allows himself to think in its terms, he loses his impression of self and begins to feel a part of the forces surrounding him.

As I stood at Concordia, I felt the strong presence of those who had been there before me. The sight of each major peak brought Himalayan history to life. The perfect trapezoid of Gasherbrum IV evoked the figures of Walter Bonatti and Carlo Mauri as they stood on the summit in 1958 in a gathering storm, having just completed the most difficult ascent in the Karakoram Range. And Broad Peak, a mere hulk compared to the classic lines of Gasherbrum IV, reminded me of Buhl, Diemberger, Schmuck, and Wintersteller, who chose to forego the usual bevy of high-altitude porters and stocked

K2 at Last   185

their camps by themselves, all reaching the summit one summer evening in 1957. To the south lay Chogolisa, Herman Buhl's icy tomb, rising in a parabolic thrust toward a wedge-shaped crest. There on the southeast ridge was the point where Buhl walked off a cornice into the mist. At one end of Chogolisa's highest crest was the summit reached by the Japanese in 1958, using oxygen on a peak that the Duke of Abruzzi had come within 500 feet of climbing in 1909. But it was the wrong summit, and the highest point of Chogolisa was still untrodden.

Just behind foreground ridges were Hidden Peak and Masherbrum, first ascended by light, compatible American teams in 1958 and 1960, respectively.

Quite naturally, K2 was the strongest presence of all. Somewhere near the base of the grand pyramid was the spot where Crowley had pulled a pistol on Knowles in 1902. Nearby, Sella, in 1909, had developed his glass-plate negatives on the glacier while the duke's guides struggled on the ridge. Much higher was the 25,000-foot shoulder first reached by Houston and Petzoldt in 1938. And tantalizingly close to the summit was the point where Wiessner and Pasang had turned back in 1939, not realizing that their failure to reach the summit was just the beginning of their heartbreaks.

My eyes began to trace a descent of the peak. There, below the 25,000-foot shoulder, was the spot where, in 1953, five Americans had fallen; at the brink of death they were saved by one man's belay. Farther down, at the very base of the peak, was a simple memorial to the three Sherpas, two Americans, and one Italian who had perished on K2 in 1954, a bleak counterpart to the triumph of the Italians Lacedelli and Compagnoni, who stood on the summit in that year and whose feat has yet to be repeated.

I remembered pictures of the base camp below the Abruzzi Ridge, sunny dry places with bright colors like the American flag: blue for sky, white for snowy peaks, and red for the tents that dotted the glacier. In contrast, our own camp at Concordia was pitched in two feet of fresh snow under a gray sky. The climbers slept in small red mountain tents while the porters occupied what we had intended to be our base camp quarters: large canvas umbrella tents pitched a few hundred feet below us in order to preserve the purity of our water supply. Up to forty porters were crammed into each ten-foot-wide tent. For us camping that way would have been agony, but the Baltis preferred it. Previous expedition accounts had described how they pooled their blankets and clothes, making a single outer covering under which they slept in a warm, naked pile. We, in turn, slept in the same groups as always. Rob, Leif, and Steve shared a tent with me. Jim and Dianne shared another. Lou, Wick, and the two Freds were in the third.

Manzoor was in a two-man tent by himself. His spirits had been crushed by the porter problems and our methods of dealing with them. He told Rob that he was considering leaving the expedition, and that if he went back, all the HAPs wanted to go with him. It would have been unprecedented for a liaison officer to abandon an expedition high in the mountains, but Manzoor was beyond con-

The Northwest Ridge of K2

cern with protocol. His voice cracked as he talked, and Rob considered him depressed nearly to the point of suicide.

Meanwhile, the HAPs were unhappy because one of them, Akbar, had been issued high-altitude triple boots while the rest had single-weight boots. We had planned to wait until we reached base camp before issuing triple boots to the HAPs, but Akbar became an exception. He had been hired in Askole to take the place of Ibrahim, the HAP who acted like a dandy and refused to work. But in spite of repeated requests from us, Manzoor had yet to fire Ibrahim because of our tenuous relations with the main group of porters. Manzoor reasoned that the Askole men were the only ones who might stick with us to base camp. Since Ibrahim was a popular fellow in the Askole region, firing him could possibly create an incident.

An incident resulted anyway, however, though not the sort that Manzoor had predicted. Poor Akbar had become the outcast of the HAPs. Unlike the others, he had not been hand-picked by the sirdar and did not wear the "uniform" of climbing clothes identical to ours. Ibrahim continued to wear the clothes that we had intended to pass on to Akbar, who still wore cotton Pakistani trousers, an old military jacket, and cheap oxfords. All the HAPs knew through the grapevine that Akbar was replacing Ibrahim, but until the actual firing took place they regarded Akbar as a second-class HAP wearing second-class clothes. When Akbar complained of cold feet and we issued him triple boots, the other HAPs demanded equality.

We were very unhappy with the performance of the HAPs. Only Akbar did any work without being asked repeatedly. Before the expedition, Jim had told us how the Sherpas in Nepal awoke climbers each morning with a cup of tea and helped break camp. For us, the procedure was nearly reversed. Sometimes we had to light stoves for the HAPs and help them take down their tents. The man hired as a cook seemed unable to operate a kerosene stove. We wondered how these men would function high on K2.

At Concordia Steve and I both came down with Rob's bronchitis. We lay in the tent, kept prostrate by hacking coughs, and we stepped out only for meals or to take occasional photographs in unusual light.

Jim realized that the climbing team was now very fragmented. He hoped that we would regain our unity when we reached base camp, but as we continued to lose porters, our arrival date receded. More than 200 porters were paid off at Concordia, which left only 130 to carry over 400 loads. Base camp was only a long day's walk away, but at least ten more porter-days of shuttling loads separated us from that goal.

On May 27 Wick and Lou went ahead to find a route up the Savoia Glacier toward base camp. A route we had been hoping to take proved impassable, and Manzoor's proposal that we follow the right edge of the glacier was deemed by far the best way.

The next morning we moved to a site just short of the Abruzzi Ridge base camp. Leif and I used the two pairs of skis with touring bindings. One pair was equipped with standard bases and climbing skins, while the other, which I used, had narrow strips of mohair

Rob Schaller and
Manzoor Hussain

permanently affixed to the bases. The mohair skis were a lazy man's compromise, having less glide on the level and less climbing power than standard skis with skins. With my bronchitis still active, I suffered a painful coughing spasm every time I breathed too hard, so I quickly dropped out of the front of the procession and back to the rear with Fred Stanley. Fred and I stopped for an hour at a midway cache to make sure that loads were carried farther. Several porters loudly protested that the cache of loads was the day's destination, although it was only an hour's walk from Concordia. More than once Fred had to bodily lift a recalcitrant porter with his load and shove him on his way.

That evening it was apparent that neither our illnesses nor our battered personal relations were healing. Leif had developed signs of the same bronchial cough that plagued the rest of us in the tent. Wick, apparently unaware of the extent of the sickness, continued to record the day's march in a competitive fashion: "Lou and I smoked out in front of everyone. . . . It was a joy to run Galen into the ground."

Fred Stanley wrote about what should have been a trivial misunderstanding that had occurred in the morning. "Lou had Fred Dunham disgruntled by starting to take the tent down before he was out. I don't know what Fred said, but the more Lou thought about it, the more hot under the collar he became and he approached Fred, threatening to 'deck' him. I heard him say he'd only been untying the tent, but I saw him take the end poles off the top before Fred started hollering."

Dunham, nearly a foot shorter than Lou, recorded his responses to Lou's behavior in his own diary: "There is only one way to handle a guy like Lou who shoves his weight and size around. That is to say what you think to anyone and if he resorts to physical strength he should end up with an ice axe in the back of his head or a bullet between the eyes. There is no other way for a smaller person to get vengeance or justice."

We all were rankled to see Ibrahim the Dandy come waltzing into camp carrying only a five-pound folding table slung casually over his shoulder, while the other HAPs carried full loads. Several of us approached him and asked, using Ghulam as a translator, "Ibrahim, did you carry that table all by yourself?" The other HAPs laughed uproariously, but Manzoor later explained that he had sent Ibrahim off with just the table because it was the only item left after the other loads were counted out for the regular porters.

The following day we were even more irritated when we ended up four loads short at the Abruzzi camp, apparently as a result of Manzoor's miscalculation. We would have to send four men back to Concordia the next day. Rob, Steve, and I stayed in camp trying to recover while the others went on to find a base camp site somewhere over 17,000 feet and to reconnoiter a route for the porters.

I felt very guilty about not carrying a load toward base camp. At the beginning of the trek, when over six hundred porters were carrying every day, the weight that the climbers carried had no effect whatsoever on the expedition's rate of progress. Now the fourteen HAPs and ten team members represented a significant proportion of the work force shuttling loads between camps. I realized that the Whittakers' predictions about me were proving true: I was not doing my share of the work.

Rob handled our illness with a typical doctor's double standard. We were his patients, and since he was responsible for our well-being, he urged us to stay inactive. But Rob himself, with the same illness and in full knowledge of the risks involved, was far less cautious about his own health. To an outsider it appeared that those who obeyed the doctor's orders were slackers.

In camp that morning an old Balti came to the tent pleading, "Doctor sahib, doctor sahib," and pointing to his eyes. Not wanting to bother Rob, who was working in the cook tent, I looked at his eyelids. Reaching into my first-aid kit, I dug out some eye medication and motioned him closer. He raised his hands and said repeatedly, "No sahib, no sahib," gesturing toward the sunglasses next to my sleeping bag. I sympathized with him for having to walk in the blinding snow without sunglasses, and I imagined that he had not received plastic sunglasses at Urdukas. We had issued enough to go around, but many porters had hoarded two or three pairs while their companions marched on the glacier unprotected from the glare. Rob had felt so sorry for one chap that he lent him his own pair of glasses, which he had used on McKinley and other climbs. The porter absconded with them when he quit the expedition.

I had two pairs of new expedition glasses plus an old pair of my own. I was tempted to give a pair to the old Balti, but first I wanted to make sure that he did not have any plastic ones. When I tried to check inside his jacket, he quickly drew back, but not before I glimpsed something shiny. I grabbed him by the shirt and held him firmly while I extricated a pair of twenty-five dollar aviator's sunglasses from his pockets. He had purposely allowed his eyes to become burned in order to scam another pair from a sympathetic sahib.

Meanwhile, the rest of the team had climbed unroped through a relatively safe icefall and emerged onto a gently sloping roll of glacier covered with a thin blanket of snow. At this point, the two Freds roped up and explored a slightly different route while the others continued unroped closer to the edge of the moraine. Dianne described what happened next: "We were just approaching a place to stop for lunch—I was about fifty feet back from Lou and Jim—when I looked up just in time to see Jim disappear from sight with a 'whoop.' I began to run (very slowly was all I could manage) and saw Lou and Wick rush forward. By the time I reached the spot, they had pulled Jim from a gaping hole, five or six feet across and perhaps forty feet deep."

Jim had broken through the snow and stopped himself from going down only by bridging across the gap with his ski poles. He was in an awkward, helpless position when Lou and Wick rushed forward. "I dove for his foot," Lou reported, "and I believe I could have held him. If his poles had broken through he would have hung

Jim Whittaker carrying a double load through the Savoia Glacier icefall

upside down with his pack. Wick and Leif came running and then I grabbed Jim's belt while Wick grabbed his pack and we dragged him back off the crevasse."

After lunch all seven roped up and continued. At two o'clock on May 29, base camp was finally reached. The summit of the mountain lay hidden in cloud, but the lower section of the northwest ridge was plainly visible and looked encouraging. The campsite was at 17,500 feet on a very level portion of the glacier. A tent was erected, and a few items of equipment were cached before the group headed back down toward the Abruzzi camp.

While the others were establishing base camp, I was experiencing a wonderfully good omen below the Abruzzi Ridge. I made a most unusual addition to my collection of Karakoram precious stones, which already included topaz, tourmaline, sapphire, and aquamarine. While eating a smoked oyster out of a can, I bit into something hard—a pearl about three-sixteenths of an inch in diameter, a rare find at 16,000 feet.

But from this high point my emotions plunged to a new low. The porters were now completely out of *atta*, the main staple of their diet. They had only a few peas and some ghee, that grease in which they cooked everything. They refused to carry any further, arguing, with some justification, that they had fulfilled their contract by reaching K2 base camp. They had trouble comprehending that since we were taking a new route, our K2 base camp was higher and farther away.

We spent a good part of the next day negotiating with porters and waiting for rations that never arrived. During discussions the porters all spoke at once and the camp sounded like a human dog pound. Thirty men walked off without pay. Only a handful agreed to move on. Most of us thought the expedition was doomed to failure at that point. Leif mused, "It seems so unreal, like a journey that lasts forever." Stanley thought we should return all our gear to Skardu and come back next year. Lou suggested repeating the Abruzzi Ridge climb. Wickwire thought that if we could not get our gear to base camp, we should at least try to avoid possible lawsuits from expedition donors by making an almost certainly futile attempt on the ridge with what we and the HAPs could carry. The Whittakers formed a last-ditch plan: they would divide the trek to base camp into two stages and lure porters toward the intermediate camp without telling them about the second stage. Once the porters had carried to the intermediate camp, they would be dependent on our tents and stoves for their survival in the increasingly remote high-altitude region. Presumably then it would be easier to persuade them to carry one camp further.

By that evening the porter problems were unresolved. In the morning Ghulam told us that perhaps only fifty men would carry. We decided to adopt the Whittakers' plan. Jim asked that as many of us as possible carry full porter loads to the intermediate camp in order to set an example for the porters. I watched the group. We four sick ones stayed behind in our tent. Even Manzoor carried a load, although we later discovered that the full-sized box on his pack actually contained only twenty pounds of fragile oxygen regulators. Nevertheless, his presence on the trail was a shot in the arm, not only for the porters, but also for me. I didn't really feel well enough to carry, but I decided to try it at a slow pace. In the evening Lou commended me for carrying a load, but I felt much worse for the effort.

The next morning I stayed behind with Leif, whose cough had developed into serious bronchitis, while Rob and Steve carried loads. Rob was still not feeling up to par, and he returned from intermediate camp at noon while the others carried on to base camp itself.

In the afternoon Rob gave Ghulam Rasul a medical checkup and was not pleased with what he found. Ghulam had been sickly for the entire expedition. Although he had been on several courses of antibiotics, he suffered a middle ear blockage that had not cleared up and he still had a pleuritic rub in his chest. Rob did not believe it safe for Ghulam to continue on to higher altitudes, so he reluctantly decided that Ghulam should go down to the Skardu hospital for laboratory tests and treatment.

Porter counting rupees

Rob also participated in a face-saving melodrama designed to gracefully rid us of Ibrahim the Dandy. With Jim, Ghulam, and Manzoor in cahoots, Rob examined Ibrahim and pronounced him physically unfit to continue. In the ensuing discussion with Ibrahim himself, it became clear that he was not unhappy to leave with 1,850 rupees and enough clothing to get him safely to Askole with Ghulam.

As Ibrahim started to leave camp, I noticed that he had quite a bundle slung across his shoulder. I stopped him, looked inside his bag, and found expedition equipment that I was sure was meant for

K2 at Last 191

Akbar. Since I had not been part of the negotiations, I was unsure which items Ibrahim had been promised. He motioned convincingly that everything was his and acted peeved when I asked him to wait until I checked things out. I went from one tent to another to another. Wick told me to see Jim; Jim told me to see Manzoor; Manzoor told me to see Jim again. I returned to Jim's tent and told him that I could do nothing more unless I knew specifically what items Ibrahim was to have. A few minutes later Ibrahim left camp with his bag of plunder. So much for the greatly anticipated denuding of Ibrahim the Dandy. The man left with no clothes had an emperor's name: Akbar. Most of the team later blamed the incident on Manzoor.

Because crises had been befalling us in a continuing series, we had not had a full team meeting since Urdukas. Jim always polled the team informally before carrying out any important decision, but many of us felt far removed from the decision-making process. As Wick so aptly remarked during our first major strike, "The intensity of frustration seems to be inversely proportional to the amount of hard information one has."

At night in our tent Rob, Leif, Steve, and I constantly rehashed the expedition's problems, discussing how they could be solved both now and in the future. We never yelled or quarreled but shared our thoughts with each other as freely as we could. When we agreed on something, we each felt better just knowing we were not alone. When we disagreed, the expression of our viewpoints acted as a great catharsis. After analyzing them carefully together we found that many of our dreams were not as easy to realize as we had first imagined.

Each of us felt that what happened in our tent discussions should have been happening in group meetings. Leif expressed Rob's feelings too when he wrote in his diary, "I do not yet find it possible to argue with the Whittakers, who are very strongminded." I, in contrast, did find it possible to argue with the Whittakers, but all it had gained me was their wrath. I found them remarkably closed to my ideas—and even to my reports of events that I thought concerned them very directly, such as Ibrahim's full-laden departure. Leif, who never initiated a controversy, had had opposite experiences and considered Jim basically a good leader who listened to advice and suggestions, rarely bossed people around, and set a good example by doing hard chores himself. Leif regarded this leadership potential as quite distinct from Jim's capacity to make the wrong decisions. But he also believed that if Jim was guilty of relying too heavily on his favorable Nepal experience when deliberating on decisions to be made in Pakistan, the rest of us were equally guilty for going along with this way of thinking. I disagreed, stating that the reason the group went along with such decisions was not really because the majority believed in them, but because the majority felt intimidated about expressing themselves in front of the Big Four.

On the night of June 1, things came to a head. Wick wrote the following description:

For the past several days Jim has overheard the endless second-guessing that has gone on in the Rob-Leif-Galen-Steve tent concerning our present porter problems and the decisions or lack thereof that caused them. Finally, Jim couldn't take it any longer and yelled that if they had gripes they ought to lay them out on the table in a group meeting. "We haven't had any meetings," came the chorus from the tent. So we will have one this morning to hopefully clear the air. We cannot climb this mountain in the midst of behind-the-back carping.

The meeting was a dud. Jim asked everyone to air their views and no one responded. Finally I tried to open things up by bringing up a subject that a majority of the team had expressed concern about in private conversations: how would our delays affect our goal to stock camps on the mountain well enough so that all who were fit could have a shot at the summit? Jim answered that the original plan was unchanged. Wick remained silent but later wrote, "I have never believed that to be a realistic objective."

No one else raised a controversial issue. We sat like fidgety children in Sunday school until Jim finally left to handle some business with the porters. Then things began to open up. Manzoor was discussed and Fred Stanley commented, "I'll sure be glad when we start running the expedition instead of Manzoor." Wick retorted, "That's exactly the kind of remark you should have made when Jim was here." Soon afterwards, the meeting petered out.

Dianne, who had surprised all of us with her strength and load-carrying aility, wrote this entry in her diary:

I wonder if the bad things that are happening have anything to do with my being here? Am I, in some way that I don't understand, a disruptive influence? As much as I try to do my share of the work, to be friendly, to be open in my own feelings, I experience a horrible chill sometimes that makes me wonder if things wouldn't be quite different without my presence—perhaps "different" in a way that the men would call "better." I'll have to ask Wick—I think he'll be honest. If I ask Jim he'll just comfort and reassure me—which won't help a bit. I don't think I could ask anyone else. . . . There really is a barrier. Because I'm a woman there is a *real*, sometimes ugly, barrier. And I don't know if it is me or if it is just the fact that I'm a woman. If it's the former, perhaps I can do something about it—if the latter, it is quite hopeless.

③ An American Tragedy on K2

For most Americans the good life of the Roaring Twenties ended abruptly with the Great Depression. A young man named Dudley Wolfe was one of the exceptions. Coming from a family with independent means, Wolfe resembled a character in an F. Scott

Fitzgerald novel. He possessed both a Harvard education and a splendid physique, he married into an elite family that included a renowned conductor and a Pulitzer Prize winning playwright, and he spent his summers with similar gentry on Penobscot Bay in Maine.

Dudley Wolfe differed from most of his peers in one important way. While they sought self-satisfaction from social contacts with famous athletes and adventurers, he wanted to participate in the action himself. His greatest passion was the ocean. He watched it, lived next to it, and sailed upon it. In 1928 he sailed his small schooner to Spain, placing second in the trans-Atlantic race. Three years later he built a larger yacht and again raced in trans-Atlantic competition.

A lesser passion of Wolfe's was mountain climbing. He spent three seasons in Switzerland, making many ascents of Alpine summits; always, as befitting a gentleman of his position, in the company of excellent guides.

In the late thirties, Wolfe approached the well-known mountaineer Fritz Wiessner, who was seeking funds for an expedition to K2. Wiessner had come to America from Germany in 1929 in order to avoid the encroachment of fascism. In Europe he had become one of the top climbers of his generation, repeating many of the most difficult climbs in the Eastern Alps and making important first ascents of his own. In 1932 he had been a member of a German-American expedition to Nanga Parbat led by Willi Merkl, and now he sought to organize the first completely American attempt on an 8,000-meter peak.

Wolfe showed great interest in the project but refused to be merely a passive patron. Although he was over forty, he wanted to be a physical as well as a financial part of the venture. Wiessner advised Wolfe that his chances of reaching the summit were probably slim, but Wolfe saw the grand adventure as a welcome escape from the results of a failing marriage that had left him alone and adrift in high society. Realizing that Wolfe was a strong, tough man who kept physically fit, Wiessner consented to make him a full member of the expedition.

In the hard times of the late thirties, few American climbers could afford to leave their homes and families for months to attempt a Himalayan giant. Wiessner persuaded the American Alpine Club to secure permission for an expedition to K2 in 1938, but he was unable to put his personal or expedition affairs in order in time to go. The 1938 permission was given to Charles Houston's team, which reconnoitered the mountain to nearly 26,000 feet. Wiessner reapplied through the club for permission to climb K2 in 1939.

One of Wiessner's top choices for the climbing team was Bill House, with whom he had made important first ascents of Devil's Tower in Wyoming and Mount Waddington in Canada. Unfortunately, House had opted for K2 in 1938 and was unable to return. Wiessner also wanted Paul Petzoldt, who had reached the high point on K2 in 1938, but, for a rather bizarre reason, Petzoldt could not return to the region. While staying in India after the rest of the

Fritz Weissner

expedition had departed, he had become involved in a fist fight with a native, who died as a result. Only the political actions of Petzoldt's friends in America had saved him from years in an Indian jail.

The best climbers that Wiessner could muster for 1939 were Al Lindley, who had made the second ascent of Mount McKinley, and Bestor Robinson, who was one of the best technical rockclimbers in the western United States. Other members of the party included O. Eaton Cromwell, a forty-two-year-old gentleman mountaineer who had made hundreds of guided ascents in the Alps, plus many without guides in Canada, and two Dartmouth undergraduates, Chappel Cranmer and George Sheldon, who were very young for such an expedition, but nevertheless had had several seasons of climbing experience.

At the last minute Robinson and Lindley were unable to go. Undeterred, Wiessner left America with a weakened team. Two days out to sea, the expedition received the welcome radio message that Jack Durrance would join them. Durrance, a twenty-eight-year-old Dartmouth medical student, was a top rockclimber who had worked as a guide in the Tetons and had climbed for three seasons in the Western Alps, though he had no high-altitude or expedition experience.

To slow the usually frantic pace of the approach, Wiessner's team left weeks earlier than most expeditions and spent ten days skiing above the Vale of Kashmir. In Srinagar they met their nine Sherpas from Nepal, once again headed by the vastly experienced Pasang Kikuli. They also added a liaison officer, a Leftenant Trench, and two educated Kashmiris to their party—one as a cook and the other, who spoke English, Hindustani, Balti, and Sherpa, as an interpreter.

The approach march went well, and Wiessner wrote an optimistic report to a friend in the American Alpine Club: "They all are such a nice lot, taking everything from the easy side and hitting hard when necessary. It is fun to be a member of such a congenial group. . . . I feel quite certain that they will do well on the mountain, and that I will have no difficulties whatsoever in the running of a careful, efficient, and coordinated climb."

After the customary minor porter strikes above Askole, the expedition reached base camp on May 31, nearly two weeks ahead of the 1938 party's schedule. Benefiting from the previous year's reconnaissance, they quickly followed the now well-known series of camps, bypassing only old Camp III, which had been the repeated target of dangerous rockfall. By June 21 Camp IV was established at 21,500 feet. On July 6, after a period of bad weather, Wiessner and two Sherpas with loads reached the 24,700-foot site of Camp VII, the 1938 expedition's highest camp.

Wiessner promptly descended to Camp II at 18,300 to organize a summit attempt while Dudley Wolfe remained in Camp V, where expected loads had not yet arrived. Things on the lower mountain were not going well. Cranmer had not been able to go above base camp because of a sudden heart problem. Sheldon had developed frostbite in his feet while shuttling loads. Cromwell expressed no intention of carrying loads higher than 21,500 feet. And worst of all, Durrance, who had been considered Wiessner's most likely summit companion, was having great trouble adapting to the altitude. Durrance hoped that his condition was temporary, and he had relegated himself to carrying loads between lower camps, resolutely, day after day, while Wolfe had climbed on the lead rope with Wiessner.

As often happens on big expeditions, the morale of those high and in the lead was excellent, while the morale down below was poor. The expedition became divided into two groups: one believed that they were doing well and had a good chance to climb the mountain; the other thought that chances of reaching the summit were very poor. The pessimists agreed to give the expedition another two weeks to prove itself. Word was sent to Askole for porters to come to base camp on July 23. Cromwell, Trench, Sheldon, and Cranmer would go out on that date. If the mountain had not been climbed by then, Durrance, Wolfe, Wiessner, and the best of the Sherpas would stay on the mountain, since by that time all the camps would be amply stocked with provisions and reserve sleeping bags.

The scene was set for the most bizarre tragedy in the history of Himalayan mountaineering.

Wiessner believed that his expedition was still potentially stronger than the 1938 effort had been. During the first two weeks on the mountain, an average of seven Sherpas and five Americans had stocked the lower camps on all but severe storm days. Wiessner reached Camp VI on July 12 with three climbers and seven Sherpas, whereas in 1938 all work above Camp II had been done by four Americans and three Sherpas.

On the morning of July 13, Wiessner, Wolfe, Durrance, and seven Sherpas set out for Camp VII at 24,700 feet. Within a few hundred yards Durrance felt weak and decided to go back to VI. Wiessner talked to him, and they agreed that Durrance would rest for a day at VI and then try to continue if he was able. Meanwhile, the rest of the group would go to VII, keeping three Sherpas and sending four back down for additional loads.

That evening Wiessner, Wolfe, and three Sherpas spent the night at Camp VII, where eleven loads of supplies now rested. Even without further support from below, they were equipped well enough to push for the summit. They had been surprised when Pasang Kikuli, who had continually expressed a desire to go to the summit, opted to stay with the lower four Sherpas. Kikuli explained that his toes had been frostbitten on the first carry to VII and that if he returned home without his toes his wife would never look at him again. Kikuli was content to oversee more carries to VII from below so that the high climbers could wait out bad weather and make multiple attempts for the summit.

On July 14, Wiessner, Wolfe, and the three Sherpas established Camp VIII at 25,300 feet near the crest of K2's great shoulder. To Wiessner's delight Wolfe was actually doing better the higher they went. Wiessner sent back two of the Sherpas to shuttle additional loads between VII and VIII and kept only Pasang Dawa Lama, the strongest and most experienced. The climbers at Camp VIII had no knowledge of the events unfolding below them.

A person who feels weak at 24,000 feet is usually not in full possession of his judgment or memory. Durrance returned to Camp VI without a clear recollection of the understanding he had reached with Wiessner. The following morning he did not feel well enough to continue. Instead of allowing the four Sherpas to stock the upper camps as agreed, Durrance ordered Pasang Kikuli and Dawa Thondup to descend with him all the way to Camp II, at 18,300 feet. Thus the two strongest Sherpas, including their leader, were removed from the upper mountain. The two unsupervised Sherpas picked up loads at Camp IV, carried them to Camp VI, and stayed there for five straight days.

On the fifteenth and sixteenth it snowed steadily. Wiessner, Wolfe, and Pasang Dawa Lama waited out the storm, unaware that no American climbers remained on the mountain between Camps II and VIII. Had they known this, it is doubtful that they would have altered their plans, because whether or not other climbers remained in support, their retreat was well secured. Sleeping bags, food, and stoves were cached in Camps II, IV, VI, and VII. Although these camps were long hours apart on the up-climb, a descending party would pass a well-supplied camp every few hours where they could, if the need arose, remain for several days.

On the seventeenth the three men continued the ascent. Not far above Camp VIII they ran into a long section of bottomless snow. After a tremendous output of energy, both Wiessner and Pasang Dawa Lama reached an easier area on a steep slope beyond a bergschrund. Pasang and Wiessner were both small, lithe men; Wolfe was large and heavily muscled. Where they wallowed, he sank. With his greater weight he was completely unable to negotiate the soft, gentle slope. Finally he headed back for camp, only a few hundred feet away, hoping that the sun would firm up the tracks so that he could join the others the following morning. Meanwhile the exhausted Wiessner and Pasang stopped short of the intended site for Camp IX and set up a temporary camp. The next morning, the eighteenth, they established Camp IX at 26,000 feet. Wolfe waited in VIII for the arrival of the Sherpas who had been sent down to shuttle loads.

The two Sherpas never arrived in Camp VIII. After waiting out the storm of July 15–16 one of them decided that the three high climbers must have suffered the wrath of the gods and perished in one of the many avalanches they had witnessed. The sirdar, Pasang Kikuli, would not have put up with such superstitious banter, but he had been ordered down the mountain by Durrance and could not intervene. The Sherpas began to descend from the high camps and tried to persuade the other two Sherpas, who were loafing at Camp VI, that they should descend as well. The two at VI were not convinced and remained.

On the eighteenth, while Wiessner and Pasang prepared for a summit push, two pairs of Sherpas were moving toward a fateful meeting at Camp IV. Tendrup and Kitar were heading down with their unfounded story of the avalanche deaths. Pasang Kikuli and Dawa Thondup were going up on special instructions from Durrance. When the four met, Kikuli angrily chased Tendrup and Kitar back up the mountain to complete their assigned task as shuttle porters between Camps VII and VIII, but not before they found out what *he* had been assigned to do. Kikuli had grudgingly accepted Durrance's order to bring down all the sleeping bags from Camp IV.

On July 19, Durrance, Kikuli, and Dawa arrived at base camp with thirteen sleeping bags. Durrance had left a note at Camp II for Wiessner, congratulating him on reaching the summit and explaining that he had ordered the bags removed so that the expedition might be ready to leave when the porters arrived on the twenty-third.

This left no sleeping bags anywhere on the mountain between base camp and Camp VI.

While Wiessner and Pasang Lama were beginning their summit climb, Tendrup and Kitar were forming a plan of their own. They would climb above Camp VII and look for signs of life. If they found none, they would consider their avalanche theory proven and aid the expedition's retreat, as Kikuli had already been instructed to do in the lower camps, by bringing down all the sleeping bags from Camps VI and VII.

Wiessner and Pasang Lama awoke to clear skies on July 19. They had six days of supplies in IX and more in VIII with Wolfe, whom they expected to arrive at any time with the Sherpas from below. After a hot breakfast they set out for the summit with ropes, pitons, carabiners, ice axes, extra clothing, and food for the day. Their idealistic style of ascent was more clearly indicated by the items they did *not* have. Unlike many Everest climbers, they carried no extra ropes, no oxygen apparatus, and no emergency bivouac gear.

For hours Wiessner and Pasang moved very slowly up moderately difficult terrain. At just under 27,000 feet they reached a steep rock band and contemplated two possibilities. To the right, the route traversed under a dangerous-looking ice cliff. To the left, a couloir led to a short rock cliff that appeared to be more difficult than anything on the right-hand route. Wiessner, an exceptionally gifted rockclimber, opted for the safer left-hand way.

The day was so clear and windless that Wiessner was able to climb bare-handed up the ice-coated rocks, placing pitons for protection while Pasang belayed from below. Here and there, patches of snow alternated with the rock, providing a welcome respite.

By 6:00 P.M. Wiessner had reached a point only twenty-five feet from the crest of the rock band at 27,500 feet. Beyond him he could see much easier climbing leading to the summit, only 750 feet above. Pasang belayed from the top of a snowfield while Wiessner was in the middle of the last 50-foot rock slab. Suddenly, Pasang refused to pass out more rope. Wiessner realized that Pasang did not know that the difficult section was nearly over, but he could not convince him to continue. Pasang held the rope fast and said with a smile, "No sahib, tomorrow," and pointed across at the right-hand alternative, which now showed itself to be much less dangerous than it had seemed from below.

Wiessner was crestfallen. He had planned to reach the summit in the evening and descend by moonlight. Pasang now expressed fear of being near the summit after dark; he believed that evil spirits resided on mountain tops at night. For a moment Wiessner contemplated leaving Pasang below the ridgecrest while he climbed alone to the summit. But poor Pasang would have been even more terrified by himself at such a great height. (This point was about 27,500 feet, according to the accepted elevation of K2 at that time: 28,250 feet. If the 1974 Survey of Pakistan figure of 28,741 feet proves accurate, then 500 feet should be added to all upper elevations in this chapter.)

Wiessner felt great compassion for Pasang, who, except for this single instance, had been a splendid climbing companion, always ready to do his best. Since the weather looked as if it would hold for several days, Wiessner agreed to descend and try the right-hand side of the rock band on their next summit bid.

Top of K2, showing Weissner's 1939 high point

Darkness crept up on the climbers as they were still descending the difficult rocks. "We could not consider a bivouac," Wiessner wrote in his diary. "It was much too cold; only moving kept us reasonably warm." In one place a short rappel was necessary, and the rope became entangled with the crampons tied to the back of Pasang's pack. Wiessner began to climb up to help, but suddenly the tangle freed itself. All their crampons came loose from the pack and rattled down the mountain. Continuing without them, the two men reached their tent at 2:30 A.M. "I regretted many times on the way down that I had given in," Wiessner wrote. "It would have been much easier for us to go up to the summit and return over the difficult part of our route the next morning."

July 20 was a lovely day. Pasang and Wiessner rested in camp. It was so warm that Wiessner lay naked on top of his sleeping bag for several hours. By afternoon both men felt recovered from their ordeal of the previous night. They planned to go for the summit early in the morning.

While Wiessner sunbathed at 26,000 feet, Tendrup and two other Sherpas climbed a short distance above VII to about 24,900 feet and made a few cursory shouts. They received no answers. Considering this silence to be proof of Tendrup's avalanche theory, the three Sherpas returned to VII and broke camp. They left the tents open, threw supplies out in the snow, and took the sleeping bags. They also took the bags from Camp VI. The sahibs in base camp would surely praise them for rescuing such valuable items.

When the Sherpas did arrive in base camp, not everyone praised them. Three men tried to convince the sahibs that they should immediately have the sleeping bags returned to the high camps. They were the sirdar, Pasang Kikuli; the interpreter, Chandra Pandit; and the cook. But the sahibs, believing the story of the avalanche deaths, were very distraught and did not want to be disturbed. When Chandra Pandit tried to come into their tent, he was sent away and later forbidden to talk to the Sherpas lest he stir up trouble with his gossip.

On the twenty-first, Wiessner and Pasang made good progress to the point where the routes forked at the base of the rock band. The right-hand route was not as steep, but the slopes were covered with a hard ice crust. "If only we had not lost our crampons," Wiessner thought, "we could have walked right up this slope." Without crampons, the only method was laborious step-cutting, a full day's work for a few hundred feet at such an altitude. Realizing the futility of continuing, they turned around at 27,000 feet.

After another night at Camp IX, Wiessner and Pasang headed down for VIII on the twenty-second, hoping to return to IX with Wolfe, crampons, and more provisions. They left everything in the highest camp except for Pasang's sleeping bag, which he brought along in case there was another Sherpa at Camp VIII who could relieve him for the next summit attempt. At Camp VIII Wolfe greeted them with outstretched arms and said, "Those bastards haven't come yet." He had run out of matches two days earlier and had only obtained water by catching what melted during the day in the folds of the tent. The three cooked lunch, celebrated their re-union, and speculated on the failure of Durrance and the Sherpas to stock the camp.

They decided to descend to Camp VII, where they had personally cached many supplies, including crampons. They knew for certain that at least one sleeping bag was there, so Wiessner began the descent without one. Normally, the strongest climber goes last on a roped descent, but on the hard slope without crampons, Wiessner moved into the lead so that he could cut steps for the others.

Wolfe accidentally stepped on the rope and a loop wound around his ankle, jerking Wiessner off the slope. Suddenly, both men were sliding and their combined weight pulled Pasang out of his steps. Wiessner tried to self-arrest with his ice axe, but the others slid past him and he began to somersault with rapidly increasing speed. Righting himself, he forced his axe into the slope with the strength of desperation. For long moments nothing happened. Then he luck-ily crossed a small area of softer snow and stopped the fall. Below him, Wolfe and Pasang dangled from the rope against a hard sur-face. Only two hundred feet farther down, great ice cliffs dropped off 6,500 feet toward the Godwin-Austen Glacier. During the fall, all three men had given up hope of surviving.

The fall was only an overture for the entirely unanticipated tragedy to come. The events of the next two days proved irrevers-ible; excerpts from Wiessner's diary describe them best:

We reached Camp VII only at dark. Our calls from above had received no answer and we wondered what had gone wrong below. . . . A great shock awaited us. The tents had been completely cleared. One tent was broken down by snow, the poles broken and large holes in it—unusable. The second tent was covered with snow; it took us easily three-fourths of an hour before it was set up . . . it had no sleeping bags. . . . All we had as cover for the night were Pasang's bag and air mattress; Dud had lost his bag during the fall. What had been going on during the days when we were high—sabotage? We could not understand. . . .

It was miserable and cold—three men crowding on an air mattress partly covered by a narrow sleeping bag, awaiting the morning. I prepared breakfast at dawn; we were longing for Camp VI, some sleep in a warm bag, and an accounting for what had been done to us. Dudley wanted to stay at Camp VII, rest, and join me in the summit attack. I would come back in two or three days after having a rest and having made new preparations for the summit attack.

Pasang and I left camp around 10 A.M. . . . At Camp VI, not a soul! Two tents laid down, a duffle with food, no stove, no bags, no mattresses. We staggered on to Camps V and IV—the same terrific disappointment. With our last reserves, we continued to Camp II. Two Logan tents were up, but no living creature present . . . again no bags or mattresses. We just cannot go further and will have to stay a second night without bags.

To describe in words the horrible feelings and thoughts I had during the day would be futile indeed. Is there any possibility for an excuse for such a condition? Does one sacrifice a great goal and human beings in such a way?

We stagger to base camp. On the glacier we meet Tony [Cromwell] with three Sherpas. They had been behind the Abruzzi Ridge, searching for our bodies!

The mountain is far away. The weather is the best we had so far. Will it be possible for me to go up after a rest with some Sherpas and with Jack, if he is in shape, pick up Dudley, and then call on the summit? Seven days of good weather will be necessary. Maybe the gods will be with me and let me have what is due to me.

Everyone in base camp was greatly relieved that all were alive. Wiessner, however, was extremely angry. He tried his best to contain his rage, but his feelings were expressed by every motion of his body. He told the others that Wolfe was talking about legal action against whoever had destroyed the expedition and threatened lives unnecessarily.

The split that had divided the expedition before the summit attempts now grew even wider. Cranmer and Sheldon had already left base camp and Cromwell planned to leave the very next morning with Trench. Tendrup, who had become an instant outcast from the Sherpas when the truth of his avalanche story became known, would also go down. Cromwell offered to stay, but said he could not go to high altitudes. Wiessner looked at his face and felt it was better to let him go. Of all the Americans only Durrance stayed on with Wiessner.

On July 25, the morning after Wiessner's return, Cromwell and Trench headed home, while Durrance and three Sherpas started up for Camp VII, where they planned to join Wolfe, provision Camp VIII, and wait for Wiessner, who would rest for a day or two before meeting them for another summit bid.

Unfortunately, neither Wiessner nor Durrance was able to live up to their plans. Both Wiessner and Pasang Lama were physically broken men. Their toes were frostbitten, and their limbs were little more than skin and bones. Wiessner's throat was so sore that he could barely whisper. After a day's rest he felt no better and realized that he could not go on. Durrance, who had felt very fit at base camp, experienced the same old altitude problem and was unable to advance beyond Camp IV. He returned to base camp on July 27, and announced that the two Sherpas he had left on the mountain had flatly refused to go higher than Camp VI alone.

Wiessner, sick as he was, resolved to climb to Camp VII with Pasang Kikuli to bring down Wolfe. Then the expedition would go home. Kikuli was sure that Wiessner was not strong enough to make it and proposed to go with only one other Sherpa. Kikuli, a man with more high-altitude Himalayan experience than any human being of his generation, had a very bold plan. He and Tsering would climb to Camp VI in one day, meet the other two Sherpas there, go to Camp VII the next day, and then come down with Wolfe.

"Good luck for me to have a man like Pasang Kikuli left," Wiessner wrote in his diary. "He is dependable and always does what he plans. I could not do it better."

On July 28 Kikuli and Tsering lived up to their prediction and climbed from base camp to VI in a single day, a phenomenal altitude gain of 6,700 feet. The next day Kikuli and two Sherpas reached VII by noon and found Wolfe in his sleeping bag, very apathetic. The Sherpas had brought up mail and a note from Wiessner; Dudley read neither. The tent was strewn with bodily wastes, which had ruined much of his remaining food, and it appeared that he had not ventured outside for several days. He spoke rationally but refused to go down with the Sherpas, claiming that he was not ready yet. If they would come back tomorrow, he said, then he would be prepared to go down. When he stepped outside the tent, the Sherpas noticed that he staggered.

The Sherpas descended and waited out a day of bad weather at Camp VI. On the thirty-first, Kikuli, Pinsoo, and Kitar reascended toward Camp VII. Kikuli's plan was to either escort Wolfe down, or, if he still refused, to get a signed note stating his decision to take to base camp. But no one returned to VI that day. Tsering, still recovering from his 6,700-foot day, waited alone. Kikuli's men had left all their sleeping gear in Camp VI.

After two nights, a terrified Tsering returned to base camp. He knew that something terrible had happened. No man could survive many nights at 25,000 feet without food and sleeping gear. This time he knew his friends were really gone.

The grim-faced men in base camp felt powerless. Wiessner resolved to make a last-ditch effort to find out if anyone was still alive. "I am really not in shape to do it," Wiessner wrote. "My throat will certainly cause me trouble and I may lose my toes. . . . Pasang Lama says that it is absolutely impossible for him to accompany me no matter how much he feels he ought to go."

With great difficulty Wiessner reached Camp II but could go no further. He spent two nights there but did not recover. The weather had taken a turn for the worse. Feeling desperately low both in strength and spirit, he retreated to base camp for the final time, descending in a snowstorm.

On August 9, when the last glimmer of hope had faded, the expedition left for home. No one will ever know exactly what happened to Dudley Wolfe and the three brave Sherpas. They may have fallen while roped together. Or the Sherpas never reached Wolfe at all and he waned slowly by himself. A later expedition found the Sherpa's sleeping bags still intact at Camp VI, indicating that no one had returned since Tsering's lonely vigil. But Camp VII was never found. All traces of Wolfe's last days had vanished, probably erased by avalanches during the ensuing years.

After the expedition returned to the United States, Wiessner was hospitalized for several months with a severe back problem. During this time rumors spread throughout the American mountaineering community that Wiessner was to blame for the tragedy. Poor leadership on his part was cited as the direct cause of the four deaths. One man went so far as to approach a district attorney about filing a murder indictment against Wiessner. The action was not pursued.

Wiessner was a unique victim of circumstance. Not only was he hospitalized and unable to defend himself, but he was also the only English-speaking eyewitness to return from the scene of the alleged crime in the high camps. To make things worse, he was a man who had recently immigrated from his native Germany at a time when the motives of all German people were suspect in America. The media quoted him as saying, "In mountain expeditions, as in war, one must expect casualties," a statement that appeared to have fascist overtones in the isolationist United States of 1939.

When Wiessner came out of the hospital, many of his old climbing friends acted distant toward him. Only a few said, "We're sorry, Fritz. It could have happened to any of us." To those who believed the rumors, Wiessner became the grand villain of American mountaineering. The cause of the tragedy was directly attributed to his Teutonic lust for the summit, which had split a team down the middle and caused the porters to run all over the mountain without proper supervision.

In pre-World War II America, the cardinal rule of mountaineering was to turn back before taking risks. Few Americans died while climbing, but even fewer achieved successes that were comparable to those being made by European climbers. Wiessner's first ascent of Mount Waddington in Canada was an excellent case in point, since it followed on the heels of fourteen consecutive retreats from the peak by the top American climbers of the time.

In Switzerland, during 1939, Günther Dyhrenfurth wrote a critique of the 1938 American effort on K2, concluding, "The man who, on such a dangerous enterprise, seeks the assurance of a safe retreat will not deserve to draw near to the Throne of the Gods." Since all the 1938 climbers had returned from K2 healthy and happy, this criticism amounted to little more than a blow to their egos. Although Dyhrenfurth wrote sympathetically about Wiessner's 1939 expedition, many books, magazines, and journals described the tragedy in an entirely different vein. Kenneth Mason, professor of geography at Oxford and noted Himalayan authority, wrote the following for the prestigious *Himalayan Journal:*

The sooner climbers forget their little Alps and Rockies when they are climbing the great Himalayan summits the sooner they will meet with success. . . . Common sense and ordinary prudence demanded that the climb should be abandoned, because the party was too weak and because success could only be fluked by unwarrantable risks, the neglect of every rule, and the wanton sacrifice of porter's lives. . . . Such expeditions as that on K2 in 1939 can only be classed as inglorious failures, whatever peaks are climbed. "Eigerwand" tactics are criminal in the high Himalaya and Karakoram.

The sponsor of the expedition, the American Alpine Club, decided to conduct a sober investigation of the 1939 expedition. A committee was appointed "to enquire into the conduct of the expedition" and prepare a report for the membership. When a draft of the report was submitted to the AAC Council, it caused a bitter debate which was recorded in the minutes with a brilliant phrase that could have changed the course of history had it become a model for modern politics: "The report of the K2 committee was discussed for nearly an hour. So much was said that the secretary didn't attempt to record it."

The committee's final report did not condemn the expedition as harshly and directly as Kenneth Mason had. Instead, it established guilt by implication. The stripping of the camps occurred because "there was no clear understanding." The final tragedy was attributed to "indefinite understanding as to movements of summit and support parties and as to administration of camps; too much responsibility thrust on Sherpas; stormy weather at a critical time; weakened personnel . . . margin of safety was seriously undermined."

The committee also made a very professional-looking graph of the movements of climbers on the expedition, which was eventually printed and distributed to the entire AAC membership. The facts on

K2 from Concordia

the graph were undeniably accurate, but they were presented in a fashion that only proved how completely the sport of mountaineering defies statistical analysis. On the right side of the sheet was a bar graph that displayed the "approximate aggregate climbing done by climbers on K2." Wiessner and Durrance were nearly tied for first place, while Wolfe, Sheldon, and Cromwell were bunched together far behind. These figures appeared to refute Wiessner's charges that the men in support had not done their share of the work. Wolfe appeared to have climbed no more than the others. What had apparently been forgotten was the simple fact that lead climbers forging a path for the others at high elevation would quite normally amass far less aggregate altitude than those who shuttled loads on well-established routes between the widely spaced lower camps.

Before the AAC Council mailed the report, it was read by Robert L. M. Underhill, the dean of American technical climbers. Underhill did not think along the same lines as most American climbers of his day did, and his appraisal of the report was at odds with the majority. He had spent many years climbing in Europe during his youth, and a later generation would recognize that it was he, along with Wiessner, who had brought modern mountaineering ideas and techniques from Europe to the United States during the twenties and thirties, setting the stage for phenomenal postwar American achievements.

Underhill wrote a devastating letter to the AAC Council, stating that publication of the report would do Wiessner "a considerable injustice," and that the committee should "quash the whole report." He pointed out that the central cause of the tragedy was the stripping of the camps and Durrance's totally unexpected descent to base camp with Kikuli, the Sherpas' leader. "That the support should collapse so utterly," he wrote, "was not a contingency within reasonable anticipation." He concluded his long letter with praise for the expedition's leader:

What impresses me most is the fact that throughout all the bad weather, the killing labor, and the grievous disappointments, he still kept up his fighting spirit. Except Wolfe, the rest of the party were, excusably enough, finished and through, quite downed by the circumstances; toward the end they wanted only to go home. Wiessner, with Wolfe behind him, was the only one who still wanted to climb the mountain. Far be it from me to blame the others; I know that if I had been there myself I should have come to feel exactly the same way, and probably much sooner. But this leads me to appreciate Wiessner all the more. He had the guts! And there is no single thing finer in a climber, or in a man. This being the case it seems to me that we should be moved to deal with him in all generosity.

The report was never distributed to the AAC's general membership. The committee continued to vacillate and make small changes in their draft. Frustrated by his attempts to make them understand the truth, Wiessner resigned from the American Alpine Club. His resignation was unanimously and enthusiastically accepted as an end to the controversy.

But Wiessner's troubles were far from over. Many people had regarded the club's proceedings as a denunciation of his character. During World War II he was investigated by the FBI as a possible enemy agent on the basis of a tip from an AAC member. After the war, Kenneth Mason wrote a history of Himalayan climbing that would become a source book for most future writers dealing with the range. Though he dropped his earlier accusation that Wiessner used criminal Eigerwand tactics, he invented new ones. He stated, for instance, that Wolfe had been ill before the first summit attempt and had been left alone without sufficient food while Wiessner "roamed on the mountain above with Pasang Lama for five days."

In 1953 another American party returned from an attempt on K2. Members told stories of finding Camp IV fully stocked with tents, food, stoves, and sleeping bags. Here was direct evidence that at least one of the camps had not been stripped. Or was it?

Wiessner had never claimed that anything other than sleeping bags had been taken down, although at Camp VII equipment and provisions had been carelessly tossed out in the snow. The sleeping bags had not been in IV during Wiessner and Pasang's epic descent but had been placed there afterwards by one of the five men who visited the camp during attempts to rescue Wolfe.

In 1956 Wiessner published the first complete account in English of the high-altitude events on K2 in *Appalachia*, a journal edited by Miriam Underhill, wife of Robert Underhill, and one of America's top women climbers. Accompanying the article was an editor's note inviting any member of the expedition who disagreed with Wiessner's account to send in his own version for publication. No one responded.

Wiessner never again participated in a Himalayan expedition. He continued to be an active rockclimber, making ascents of 5.9 difficulty well into his sixties. Several major European alpine clubs made him an honorary member, but he remained an outcast from his own.

Meanwhile, Pasang Dawa Lama had become one of the most famous Sherpas of all time. He made the first ascent of 26,750-foot Cho Oyu with a tiny four-man expedition led by Herbert Tichy in 1954. Later he made the second ascent of Cho Oyu and climbed on dozens of other high Himalayan peaks. In the middle sixties, an American climber visiting Nepal met Pasang and asked him about the 1939 expedition. His eyes lit up as he talked about his friend "Fritz sahib," who had saved his life by not forcing him to continue to the summit. In every important way Pasang confirmed Wiessner's story. Wolfe had *not* been sick when they left Camp VII for the summit. Kikuli *had* been ordered to remove sleeping bags from the lower camps. "Give Fritz sahib my good wishes," said Pasang as the American left.

During the winter of 1965 several American climbers discussed just how to right the wrongs of what they saw as an alpine Dreyfus case. They decided to propose Wiessner as an honorary member of the American Alpine Club. Bill Putnam, later to become AAC president himself, organized a letter-writing campaign. The officers of

Aerial, from the west, of K2 rising over Mustagh Tower

Telephoto, from Camp I, of sunset on the summit rocks of K2

*Camp II at 20,500 feet,
on the Chinese border*

Savoia Pass, with Pakistan on the left and China on the right

Jim crosses a bergschrund below Savoia Pass on a fixed rope

Telephoto of climbers nearing the high point

Telephoto of Leif at the high point

Rob approaches Savoia Pass

Leif on the ridge above Camp II

The summit of K2 rises above the unclimbed Northwest Ridge

the AAC were deluged with letters from the top climbers in the country favoring honorary membership for Wiessner.

The new generation had answers for the veiled charges of the 1939 committee report. Leaders don't belong in the first summit team? *What about Maurice Herzog on Annapurna?* Sherpas must not move unsupervised over difficult terrain? *What about the repeated instances on many of the hallowed British attempts on Everest?* Mountain summits aren't worth risking lives for? *Only a rare windless night on May 22, 1963, kept four Americans from perishing in an open bivouac near the top of Mount Everest.* The team was not strong enough to continue? *This party set up nine camps and stocked them well enough to place many men on the summit.* Taking a climber of Wolfe's meager experience on a big mountain was unprecedented? *Andrew Irvine, Mallory's famous companion on Mount Everest in 1924, was even less experienced, but like Wolfe he outperformed those with better records.*

The final vote was unanimous, and Fritz Wiessner belatedly became an honorary member of the American Alpine Club in 1966. One man resigned from the club in protest. Another had struck the club from his will. The president told Bill Putnam, "If this had been a bullfight, I would award you the right ear." But the vote represented much more than the righting of an ancient wrong. It signified the end of an era. Americans were finally recognizing the duplicity of voluntarily participating in a high-risk activity while always looking for someone to blame in case of a serious accident. Lute Jerstad, who had been one of the four in that lucky, windless bivouac on Everest, wrote, "You, Fritz, have given encouragement and stimulation to us all. You will probably never know to whom, nor to how many, but that is the curse of all men who do things rather than talk about doing them."

4 Toward Savoia Pass

We arrived at base camp on June 5, with only 72 of our original 650 porters. It was a miracle that we got any of them to make the final portage. We offered them every possible enticement: tents floored with the foam plastic that had been used to wrap the oxygen bottles, kerosene stoves to keep them warm at night, and an all-time high of 85 rupees per day. They were unimpressed. Then Jim pulled out a reel of 7mm climbing rope and cut off a twenty-foot piece, indicating that every porter who carried would receive one. From a forest of dark Balti faces, eyes lit up like Christmas tree lights. Rope was the only item that they had consistently pilfered from us; apparently because making their own short strands took hours of laborious hand-weaving. We waited expectantly for the headmen to accept our offer. Nothing happened. The glowing eyes began to fade again. Just as all seemed lost, Akbar leapt up from the group of

Sunset on K2, seen from the Savoia Glacier

Jim Whittaker distributes ropes to the remaining porters below base camp

HAPs and began an impassioned speech accompanied by wild gesticulations. We didn't have to know the Balti language to understand the gist of his tirade. He berated his countrymen with every ounce of his energy. A few days earlier, Akbar would not have done such a thing, but he had acquired a new sense of dignity the instant he received his bona fide HAP clothing after Ibrahim had been sent home. From the few remnants that Ibrahim had left behind, and from our own personal boxes, Akbar had finally been fully outfitted. The man who confronted the mob was dressed proudly in shiny triple boots, wool climbing pants, and an American shirt with his own multicolored scarf jauntily tucked into the collar. Soon after he had his say, the porters agreed to carry.

Only fifty-seven porters carried on the following day. More than half the loads were still at intermediate camp, and if the porters quit then it would take the climbers and HAPs another ten days to bring up the loads.

Several things prevented us from holding the celebration we had planned for reaching base camp. Dianne and Jim arrived suffering from vomiting and diarrhea. Stanley decided to forego dinner because of a queasy stomach. And then the mail arrived by runner for the first time in weeks. Everyone in my tent was deluged with letters. I got ten from my family and began to chuckle at the insane contrasts between life in our frozen world and the everyday happenings in America. My eleven-year-old daughter wrote, "We have had three frogs from about fifty polliwogs. Two jumped out and died. We think the dog ate one." I found this hysterically funny. Then I opened a letter from my wife. It began, "Your mother just called. I don't know quite how to tell you. She said she was sitting with your dad, holding his hand, and he quietly passed away."

I closed my eyes for several minutes. My father had been ninety years old and had been in ill health for several years. One of my greatest fears had always been that something would happen to him while I was far off on a climbing trip. The letter was a month old. I tried to determine exactly where I had been and what I had been doing at the moment he died. It seemed odd not to know of something so intimately important to my life that had happened a month before. I felt guilty that I was not at home with my family and even more guilty when I realized that the time when I could have been of some help was already long past. I asked my tentmates not to tell the others about it. It was just too intimate to share with people from whom I felt so distant.

Base camp became the base of our planned pyramid of camps on the mountain. The glacier began to look like a Little America. In the middle of camp was the warehouse section, characterized by orderly rows of porter boxes and a stack of oxygen cylinders. Paths in the snow led to six private residence tents for us and the HAPs. We also set up two equipment tents, a cook tent, and even a recreation room complete with tape deck and a box of paperbacks. We dug a garbage pit for burnable trash, and a latrine covered by a tent made of bright nylon patchwork. Inside the latter, a real pink fuzzy toilet seat was attached to a converted folding stool that was poised over a hole in the ice. This ingenious arrangement was so comfortable and civilized that when I first used it I unconsciously reached back for a handle.

The climate wasn't as extreme as I had expected. Seventeen thousand feet in the Karakoram feels about like 10,000 feet in the Alaska Range in summer. The night we arrived the temperature dropped to 6 degrees Fahrenheit, but by nine in the morning it was so warm we could walk around in tee shirts. The air temperature was in the high twenties by afternoon, but the sun's heat reflecting off the snow made it feel like room temperature. Whenever a cloud blocked the sun, my body suddenly responded to the true air temperature rather than the radiated heat and I would dash for my down parka.

The summit was 11,000 feet above base camp, and I computed that nighttime temperatures there were usually lower than 30 degrees below zero. This corresponded closely with upper air temperatures broadcasted over the Pakistani government's special radio forecasts for mountaineering expeditions. We could hear them on our small portable receiver, but we had been unable to broadcast with our large transmitter. The outside world had no idea where we were. As Wick said, "We've been in the Bermuda Triangle for thirty days."

Every expedition complains at some time or other about their food. We had all had a chance to comment on the food list, but somehow we never realized just how boring and unpalatable our canned dinners of ravioli, spaghetti, beans, tamales, and macaroni would become. Even Leif, who usually took everything in his stride, began remarking that we were eating a lot of bulky junk food and almost no meat. In Seattle we had been thankful for the donations of canned goods we received, and no one had offered us meat. Now we all cast covetous glances at the high-altitude bags stuffed with freeze-dried beef, pork chops, and shrimp creole. Because of the strikes and high wages, it had cost us about twenty dollars to transport each large dinner can, money that we now would rather have spent on more freeze-dried meats. On the plus side, however, our canned juices and food saved us from having to cook with the seriously polluted water often found in the lower villages. Thus, we did not have a single case of serious dysentery, the prevention of which was our main reason for bringing the heavy food.

As soon as base camp was well established, we planned to travel up the glacier and find a site for Camp I at about 19,000 feet. Then the team and the HAPs could begin hauling over a hundred loads up the glacier. Fewer and fewer loads would go up the mountain into each succeeding camp until only 400 of the 17,000 pounds left in base camp would reach the apex of the pyramid—somewhere over 27,000 feet—from where we hoped the summit would be reachable in a day's outing. We expected it to take well over a month before we were in position for a summit attempt.

Base camp on the Savoia Glacier, K2 in background

Although Rob, Leif, and I were still coughing, we all planned to start carrying loads as soon as possible. The team maintained its original pairings. Jim and Dianne were in one tent, Lou and Wick in another, the two Freds in a third. Manzoor was by himself, and Rob, Leif, Steve, and I shared a large Eureka four-man tent.

On the night before we set off for Camp I, I lay in my sleeping bag thinking about the climb. For the first time it dawned on me that our informal pairs had become rigid, and that I was paired off with Steve, who was technically not a member of the climbing team. He had been quietly working on his movie and had remained aloof from the squabbling. He came along strictly to make the film, after promising his wife that he would not go high on the mountain. On the last days of the approach march I traveled with Leif because Rob had been sick, but I was sure that as soon as Rob was well the two would be paired off again. The only other person with a nonclimbing companion was Jim, with whom I did not get along well. I came to the inevitable conclusion that I would be little more than a porter with a camera.

On the next morning the thermometer registered exactly zero degrees. Ice crystals gleamed on the surface of the snow. The sky was perfectly clear. After breakfast Lou and Wick broke trail toward Camp I at a rapid pace. Leif and I followed on skis, dragging a sled with three porter loads. The snow was deep and the sled pulled hard. Leif had to stop quite often because of coughing fits. The three-mile trek up the gently sloping glacier took us about three hours. We stopped at a point about five hundred feet below where Lou and Wick were setting up a tent on top of an ice knoll. The last pitch steepened to 30 degrees and we knew we couldn't haul the sled up such a hill. Leif was tired, so we decided to leave the boxes and carry them up the final hill later.

We took the skins off the skis and aimed them downhill; then we floated down the glacier, taking care to follow our uphill tracks in order to avoid hidden crevasses. When we stopped to switch turns at pulling the empty sled, I saw that Leif's face was beaming with joy. Skiing underneath K2 was sheer pleasure. I looked up at the mountain and it suddenly seemed more friendly. The route to Savoia Pass looked easy, and the upper ridge did not appear nearly as steep as it had from the air. Independently, both of us scanned the slopes for lines of weakness, uptilted strata, snowfields, and possible campsites. The ridge looked elegant and climbable. We agreed that the hardest part might prove to be the nearly horizontal mile between the pass and the base of the true ridge, which now looked longer and more serrated than in any published view we had seen. Both of us had previously considered challenging the team's plan to move full scale onto the ridge without a reconnaissance, but this view removed our doubts. The route now seemed far and away the best possibility on the west side of the mountain. Avalanche trails scarred most of K2's facets, but here, on this defined ridge, we thought that we would be quite safe from them. For the first time in weeks, the mountaineer in me lusted for the summit.

I spent most of the week of June 7 above base camp working on

The Freds signing postcards at base camp

Dianne on skis, above base camp

the route. Meanwhile, Leif did not recover after pulling the sled with me toward Camp I. He caught pneumonia and remained in base camp under heavy medication. Most of the team had cheered him for carrying loads while recovering from a serious case of bronchitis, but Fred Stanley called Leif's participation "a typical case of enthusiasm and willingness to work for the expedition overcoming good sense." Steve moved into the equipment tent in order to get away from the sickness.

Through the rumor mill I learned that Jim had planned to team up with Leif on the mountain. When Leif did not seem to be recovering, Jim asked me to join him in establishing Camp II at Savoia Pass and exploring the route above. Neither of us looked forward to the other's company. Although our pairing marked the first real exchange of personnel between the Big Four and the rest of the team, fate, not choice, had thrown us together.

Meanwhile, Lou and Wick climbed to Savoia Pass on June 10. They fixed ropes over 600 feet of 45- to 50-degree ice, crested the pass, and peered into China. The snow ramp which they thought they had seen from the airplane was not there. A cornice overhung a 6,000-foot drop to the North K2 Glacier. They climbed a few hundred feet above the pass but were unable to discover a passable traverse on the north side of the ridge. Their altimeter readings, which throughout the approach had matched very closely the elevations shown on maps, now showed the pass to be at only 20,400 feet instead of 21,870 feet, the figure computed by the Duke of Abruzzi and used on all modern maps.

This discrepancy had a much deeper meaning than a mere pedantic correction of an old altitude measurement. Our logistics for climbing the ridge had been computed on the assumption that the pass was 6,380 feet from the summit. Before we left the United States, we had received word that the mountain had been resurveyed from 28,250 feet to 28,741 feet. This new figure added 491 feet to our climb. Now, with Savoia Pass at an altitude 1,470 feet lower than that shown on the map, our ridge turned out to be 1,961 feet longer than planned. This distance meant more camps, more carries, and more time.

The weather deteriorated while Wick and Lou were searching for a route above the pass, and they were forced to descend without having set up Camp II. On that same day Dunham, Stanley, and Marts carried loads up the fixed ropes and cached them at the pass. Jim and I were to make the next attempt to establish Camp II, and then explore the route to Camp III.

Everyone except Leif carried to Camp I the next day. The rest returned to base camp while Jim and I stayed on alone, planning to start up the pass the following morning. Both of us were surprised at how well we were getting along together. We were not crossing verbal swords as we had frequently done during group discussions, and each was finding the other more moderate and flexible than he had imagined. We openly discussed the unknowns of the route, and I admitted increasing optimism while Jim expressed a few doubts. Our attitudes toward the climb were much more similar than we

Lou and Wick, below Savoia Pass

Avalanche on the Savoia Glacier

had thought before. Both of us saw the unclimbed route as a real gamble.

During the night we both awoke to a tremendous roar coming out of the darkness from the west. It grew louder and louder. A giant avalanche was descending from a nearby peak into the opposite side of the basin below the pass. At first we felt totally safe. Our camp was on a knoll hundreds of feet above the main basin. But the noise continued to grow louder and closer. After a long minute it was still coming. Jim and I lay in our sleeping bags, absolutely powerless to do anything about the powerful forces outside the tent. We both felt anxiety but no panic. Long ago we had learned the absolute futility of panic in the face of uncontrollable danger. Then it came. First a rush of air rippled the walls of the tent. Snow struck with the sound of someone emptying a grain sack. Just as quickly, all was still. The avalanche had not reached us. Only its shock wave and a half-inch dusting of snow had touched the tent. The bulk of the debris was hundreds of feet away.

With a new feeling of comradeship, Jim and I set out the next morning for Savoia Pass. At first the going was easy walking up a steepening snowfield. Then, with Jim in the lead, we crossed a bergschrund, a crevasse which separated the snows of K2 from the moving ice of the Savoia Glacier. With crampons and ice axes we bridged the two-foot-wide gap and followed fixed ropes up the face. As we crested the pass, clouds moved in and the wind began to blow. Snow blew horizontally and visibility became less than ten feet. We had no view into China and often not even of each other. The rope connecting us simply disappeared into the moving gray murk.

Unable to locate a site for Camp II in the blizzard, we descended.

Toward Savoia Pass   221

Lou, Wick, and the two Freds arrived at Camp I soon after we did. Later in the day the storm partially cleared and Wick and Lou headed off to establish Camp II. I visited the two Freds in their tent and found them in a depressed mood. Stanley told me, "Wickwire seemed happy that you and Jim didn't reach his previous high point. Now they still have a chance to put in the whole route themselves." I was defensive. For the first time I was beginning to feel like a part of the Big Four. Their goals were my goals. Although I didn't approve of them hogging the lead, I had resigned myself to their holding onto it. If we were successful on the mountain, Stanley's criticism would seem exceedingly petty. Both Freds then told me that I had better open my eyes. According to their way of thinking, Wick and Lou's excessive enthusiasm and competitiveness were going to break the climb, not make it. "Just watch," Dunham told me. "Those guys took out of here like big heroes a few minutes ago. They'll never make it. It's too late in the day and the weather won't hold. Yet they're out there pissing into the wind."

Dunham also told me that he was upset over an incident concerning the radio transmitter. He said that he had personally borrowed it in the United States and had signed a note making himself responsible for its $6,000 value. Jim had allowed Manzoor to take the radio into his tent without supervision in order to try to make contact with Skardu. According to Dunham, the unit could blow up if someone attempted to broadcast on a different frequency without changing the corresponding aerial length. When he found Manzoor fiddling with the radio, he exploded with rage and demanded that Manzoor never touch the radio again. When the incident came to Jim's attention, he ordered Dunham to stay in camp and give Manzoor special instructions on how to use the radio. Dunham felt that he was being treated like an errant child. He was even more chagrined when Manzoor succeeded in making our first radio contact with the outside, something that Fred had been unable to do for the previous month.

I returned to my tent, which I was still sharing with Jim. My situation had changed greatly. Now when a controversy arose I felt free to talk man to man with the expedition leader in private, something that had never worked out before. Jim's explanation of the radio incident was perfectly understandable. He was not aware that the radio could be harmed by changing frequencies and he thought that Manzoor, who spoke all the possible broadcast languages, should have a try at making contact. When Dunham had blown up, Manzoor had become so depressed that he had threatened to quit the expedition. He had said that he wanted no further personal contact with either of the Freds. Jim thought that having Dunham instruct Manzoor in the use of the radio was the best solution. I agreed.

As we talked, Lou and Wick suddenly appeared in camp, having climbed only a short distance toward the pass before a snow squall turned them back. While they spoke to us in serious tones about the route, I overheard the Freds chuckling that their prediction had come true.

The next morning we set out for the pass again, this time with Lou and Wick in the lead, breaking trail through the fresh snow. The two Freds and Steve followed quite some distance behind. Cresting the pass, I stepped into Sinkiang Province of China and gazed at the countless ridges of snowy peaks fading into the distant haze. A barren valley lay surprisingly close to the north side of K2, and the climate appeared much drier east of the pass.

We decided to climb on in search of a route past the ridge of rock towers. Soon we were on a steep slope of soft snow overlying hard blue ice. After a storm or on a warm day such a slope could have considerable avalanche potential. Wick continued to lead out onto a corniced edge, where he was still unable to see if a route existed on the Chinese side of the ridge. At just over 21,000 feet, we turned around and descended to the pass, where we set up Camp II in a hollow just north of the ridge crest, about fifteen feet into China. Later in the day, Fred Stanley crested the pass with a sixty-five pound load which included a cast-iron winch for hauling equipment up the ice face. We all descended and reached base camp by evening.

We spent all of June 14 sorting equipment to take into the upper camps. Manzoor amused us with stories of his radio contacts. His first conversation had been received in the town of Gilgit. After he had introduced himself—"This is Major Manzoor Hussain, liaison officer for the American K2 Expedition, calling from base camp at 17,000 feet"—the Gilgit man had asked for his telephone number. Even more humorous was the reply we received from the Ministry of Tourism after telegramming them about the outrageous demands our porters were making when we were high on the Baltoro Glacier: "Next time, call the police!" I could imagine walking into the great silence of the glacier, one hundred miles from the nearest road, yelling, "Help! Police!"

By this time Manzoor was in much higher spirits. Both Rob and Leif were recovering quickly and were eager to go on to the mountain. But both the Freds were still very depressed. Steve and I had a long talk with Dunham. He felt that he was constantly being ridiculed, put down, and ignored. He therefore decided to continue working for the expedition as a peon only, refusing to humiliate himself by trying to contribute to strategy discussions. He told us that Stanley felt an even stronger sense of alienation from the group and had considered quitting the expedition. Stanley was especially unhappy over an exchange he had had with Jim the night before: when he returned from carrying by far the heaviest load to Savoia Pass, Jim chided him for always displaying a negative attitude. I was there, and I thought that both of them were trying to be humorous until Stanley suddenly took Jim's remark very seriously and Jim didn't back down.

I suggested to Dunham that it was nearly impossible to change people and that both he and Stanley should try to enjoy what they could of the expedition instead of fretting so much over the actions of others. I also said that I had recently been getting along quite well with the Whittakers and that by themselves they were good climbing companions. Only in group situations did I still feel a problem.

I told Fred that I thought Jim had, regrettably, become an aggressive general during our Thirty Day War with the porters en route to base camp, but that now he was settling into the role of a peacetime ruler. With a wary sideways glance, Fred replied, "The combat won't have ended until he's gotten Lou, Wick, and probably himself on top of K2. You don't think they'll let you go to the summit, do you?"

The question hit home. No matter how much I tried to convince myself that my situation with respect to the Big Four was changing, I had had a gnawing feeling inside ever since the two climbs up to Savoia Pass. I had been treated with utmost courtesy and respect by Jim, Lou, and Wick. But when I had asked Jim if I could lead for a while—and I had done so several times—my request had been either ignored or politely refused. Lou and Wick had always pushed ahead, never stopping to offer either of us a chance to be in the lead. In my heart I knew that I was not one of them, but I continued to believe that I was bridging the gap.

I remembered a story my mother likes to tell about me. On my third birthday she gushed, "What a big, big boy you are! Three years old! Three whole years! Do you know how long that is? My, you are really growing up!" Very calmly I replied, "Can I drive the car now, Mommy?" She ended the story there, but now I realized how deep my humiliation must have been when I saw by her face that I was not really a big boy and that I was not grown up. On this expedition we had been similarly deluded into high expectations and we were heading for a similar disappointment. On paper each of us had begun as an equal partner, and plans had been made to supply the high camps well enough so that anyone who was physically able would climb K2. As the journey progressed, most of us ignored telltale warnings and clung to verbal encouragements: "Yes, we are still a team; yes, everyone still has a chance for the summit; yes, the ridge will be climbed." For the Freds, the bubble had burst. They no longer believed in our goals or our leaders.

Most of us would have joined the expedition even if we had been clearly told that we had no chance for the summit. Just to be in the Karakoram and participate in a great enterprise would have been a reward in itself. But like on my third birthday, we had each been led to expect much more. We would not have felt humiliated or disappointed had it not been for our heightened expectations.

Leif thought that Jim should be informed of the potential revolt of the Freds. Jim was apparently unaware that they were anything more than temporarily miffed. If only tentmates had been rotated periodically, we might all have gotten to know each other better, as I finally did with Jim. In that way we could have avoided the stranglehold that the Big Four had on the rest and the resulting alienation of the two Freds. What grand irony it was that Alex Bertulis had been rejected because we feared a potential failure in communication.

Section VIII

The Struggle for K2

A climber has fallen. Let a hundred others arise for the morrow. Let other youths strew edelweiss and alpenrose upon the body of the fallen comrade; and lay it with trembling devotion face upturned under the soft turf. Then up, once more to the assault of the rocks and of the summit, to commemorate the fallen one in the highest and most difficult of victories!

—FROM AN OLD ITALIAN NEWSPAPER CLIPPING

1 Americans Return to K2

For fourteen years after the 1939 expedition, problems of access kept expeditions away from K2. First came World War II. Soon after the war ended, Americans approached Indian diplomats for permission to attempt K2 again. They were dissuaded because of the imminent partition of the subcontinent. Soon India and the new nation of Pakistan began fighting bitterly over Kashmir, which included the mountain kingdoms surrounding K2. When the smoke cleared, a semipermanent cease-fire line bisected Kashmir and blocked the southern half of the approach march through Srinagar. One minor result of the Kashmir conflict had a specific effect on future Karakoram expeditions. The quiet town of Skardu became a military outpost, and an airstrip was constructed on its outskirts.

On June 3, 1953, the Third American Karakoram Expedition landed at Skardu, having bypassed 220 miles of walking by taking the hour-and-a-half flight from Rawalpindi in a rickety DC–3. They were bound for K2. Nineteen fifty-three was already proving to be a year of grand destiny in Himalayan mountaineering. On the eve of the expedition's flight, which occurred coincidentally on Queen Elizabeth's coronation day, the Americans learned that a British expedition had reached the summit of Mount Everest. And during the flight one American climber thought he spotted a line of tracks on the flanks of Nanga Parbat, where Dr. Herligkoffer's expedition was setting the stage for Herman Buhl's remarkable solo first ascent.

The men of the K2 expedition were not entirely overjoyed at the success of the British team. On the surface, reaching the summit of Everest was a remarkable human achievement in which all mountaineers could take pride. But in practical terms it represented the ascendancy of one school of thought over another. Everest was the first of the earth's nine highest peaks to be climbed. Both the Everest expedition and the developing Nanga Parbat climb were extremely large ventures organized along military lines. Their success could usher in an era of large-expedition climbing on the world's high peaks. Small-party climbing might already have gained dominance had the scales of good fortune tipped in favor of the prewar climbs by Shipton and Wiessner, who reached over 27,500 feet on Everest and K2 without the aid of oxygen or the support of a large expedition.

Now, the fate of the K2 expedition could decide the direction that high-altitude climbing would take. If, in 1953, success was achieved on 8,000-meter peaks by two large expeditions and small teams failed in their attempts, the immediate future of Himalayan mountaineering would be decided. If, on the other hand, a small, mobile party was able to climb K2, which mountaineers universally regarded as more difficult than Everest or Nanga Parbat, then the way of the future might favor such expeditions. Already, a huge Italian expedition was seeking permission to attempt K2 the following year if the Americans failed.

The leader of the 1953 K2 effort was Dr. Charles Houston, the most experienced American Himalayan climber of his era. Besides climbing on Nanda Devi in 1936 and K2 in 1938, Houston had been the first to reconnoiter the southern approach to Everest in 1950. His companion on that venture, Bill Tilman, did not see much chance of Everest being climbed from the south. Both men agreed that the enormous Khumbu icefall appeared to be extremely dangerous, but Houston's greater optimism for the route led the British to explore what eventually became the path of success. Houston now approached K2 with a personal knowledge of the Abruzzi route to within 750 feet of the summit. His party consisted of eight climbers and only 125 porter loads of food and equipment. "It is too easy," he asserted, "to take everything and end up with a huge, unwieldy and expensive, slow-moving and easily disrupted caravan, carrying tons of equipment, much of which is left unused."

One major change in 1953 was the unavailability of Sherpas from Nepal because of the Kashmir conflict. Herligkoffer attempted to import a crew of Sherpas led by Pasang Dawa Lama, who had climbed with Wiessner in 1939, but all were turned back at the border. Both Houston and Herligkoffer decided to experiment with high-altitude porters from Hunza.

Houston's small team performed incredibly well. The expedition reached base camp only twenty-six days after leaving the United States—twice as fast as the trip and approach march during the thirties, and, ironically, during 1975. Once the party was on the mountain, the pace slowed because of the poor weather. Even so, the expedition was able to position itself for a summit bid forty days after reaching the mountain. On August 2, all eight members of the climbing team, along with ten days of food, were in Camp VIII at 25,000 feet. They hoped to put a pair on the summit in two days. On the first day they would establish two men and supplies in Camp IX near 27,000 feet; on the following day two would go for the top.

While waiting for the weather to clear, they chose their summit teams by a secret ballot. Bob Craig and George Bell were chosen as the first pair; Pete Schoening and Art Gilkey were the second. Amazingly, none of the chosen four had previous Himalayan experience, though three of the remaining four had such experience. Besides Charles Houston, they were Bob Bates, who had been to K2 in 1938, and Tony Streather, who had climbed 25,290-foot Tirich Mir. The eighth man, Dee Molenaar, had been a member of the first party to repeat the Duke of Abruzzi's ascent of Mount St. Elias in

Bob Craig

Dee Molenaar

Art Gilkey

Alaska. In their vote, the men had favored the youth and energy of four men in their twenties over the age and experience of the others. Interestingly, these criteria are the opposite of those used in selecting most advance teams at sea level.

While the men on K2 waited for a brief spell of good weather, the South Asian monsoon began to buffet the plains of India and Pakistan. Predictable annual winds from the southwest steadily pushed clouds inland from the Indian Ocean, guaranteeing weeks of torrential rains. Every year these storms hit the Himalaya, and mountaineers plan their expeditions to either precede or follow the monsoon season. The successful British on Everest had already returned when the monsoon hit. Herman Buhl reached the summit of Nanga Parbat just as the monsoon clouds approached in the distance. The Americans on K2 did not worry about the monsoon, for it was common knowledge that the weather system did not normally penetrate beyond the Himalayan barrier into the heart of the Karakoram.

Along the coast of India, most areas experienced average monsoon storms that year. Many towns recorded slightly less than normal winds and rainfall. But in one corridor of Pakistan the weather was exceedingly erratic. During July the coastal port of Karachi received only 2 percent of its normal rainfall for that month. Early in August Karachi was hit by the greatest storm in the history of the young nation of Pakistan. It continued at full force for many days, pushing the month's rainfall to 447 percent of normal, more than double the amount ever recorded for the same period. The prevailing winds from Karachi were aimed directly toward Kashmir. The storm front pushed farther inland than ever before, creeping up the foothills of the Himalaya and across the high crest. It then moved down into the gorge of the Indus River, up the arid valleys of the Karakoram, over the summits of the K2 region, and on into Sinkiang Province of China. On K2 it snowed and snowed and snowed.

At 25,000 feet on K2, eight men continued to wait for the weather to clear. Relentless west winds shook their tents with a sound like constant thunder while powdery spindrift sifted through every seam. The men had to wear all their clothing inside their sleeping bags in order to stay warm. But the worst danger of all was even more insidious than the cold. Because of the fierce winds, they could not keep the stoves lighted long enough to melt sufficient water or cook. That they could die of thirst on the frozen Karakoram desert was entirely possible. Sometimes they mixed snow, jam, and powdered milk, warming the concoction against their own bodies to make it edible.

One night Houston and Bell watched cracks appear spontaneously in their tent fabric. They were not sure that they could survive if the tent ripped apart in the darkness. How does an already shivering man put on his frozen boots in the dark at 25,000 feet while holding onto his sleeping bag and personal belongings? They agreed that if the tent burst, they would stay huddled inside the wreckage until morning.

Somehow, the damaged tent stood until shortly after dawn.

When it finally came apart, Houston and Bell wrapped up in the tatters until a brief lull in the wind allowed them to dash for other shelter. Three was a crowd in the tiny two-man tents. Streather and Bates were sharing a Swiss Everest tent with a profile so low that they could not sit up. When Houston joined them, they resembled three men trying to live under a cot. Yet their morale stayed high. They continued to plan for the eventual summit day. The storm would have to end soon.

Of those days, Houston wrote, "The deepest springs of character were tapped for our survival. The lack of oxygen at great altitudes may dull the mind and weaken the body, but there is an inner strength of spirit, a bigger power which emerges undiminished, even magnified, to bring a man through such an experience. We faced nature's wildest forces with our pitifully feeble tents and clothing as our only weapons, plus our inner determination. Perhaps it is this conquest, conquest of one's self through survival of such an ordeal, that brings a man back to frontiers again and again. It may be a frontier of the spirit or of the mind. By testing himself beyond endurance man learns to know himself. He endures and grows."

The ordeal was just beginning. On the sixth day of the storm, Art Gilkey stepped outside the tent and fainted in the snow. He quickly regained consciousness and insisted that he was all right, saying, "I've had this charley horse in my calf for a couple of days now. It's sure to clear up in another day, isn't it?" Dr. Houston examined him, and his heart sank. Gilkey had thrombophlebitis, an ominous condition in which blood clots form in the veins, blocking circulation. Normally seen only in the elderly or in surgical patients, the condition was almost unknown in young, healthy mountain climbers.

Ten years later another American almost died on Everest from thrombophlebitis, and it has since become recognized as a very real risk of high-altitude climbing. The odds of clotting are greatly increased by high altitude, dehydration, and long periods of inactivity. All of these conditions were present in the days before Gilkey's illness struck.

At sea level, Gilkey's condition would have been very serious and could have necessitated an amputation. Worse yet, the risk of a clot traveling to the lungs or heart was very high. In a hospital he would have been kept immobile for several weeks while he was treated with anticoagulants. On K2, Houston told the team that Gilkey's only hope was to be carried down. After considering several other alternatives, the climbers matter-of-factly discussed taking Gilkey down, resting for a few days at base camp, and then heading back up for the summit.

Only much later, as recorded in his unpublished notes, was Dr. Houston able to fully appreciate his team's decision: "These wearied men contemplated without dismay carrying a helpless body down cliffs which were hard and dangerous enough to tax a healthy, unladen party. So strong had become the bonds between them that none thought of leaving him and saving themselves—it was not to be dreamed of, even though he would probably die of his illness."

After Gilkey's illness was discovered, the team quickly broke camp and prepared to descend, taking only sleeping bags and personal effects. Houston believed in leaving the climb as unlittered as possible, so he began to throw all the surplus food over the edge and take down the tents. Time was short, and someone stopped Houston from completing his task, so that the rescue could begin. Within a few hundred yards, the group encountered two feet of fresh snow piled on steep, icy slabs. To continue in the face of such avalanche danger would have been suicidal. They spent the rest of the day wallowing uphill through the powder back to Camp VIII, thankful that Houston had not finished what would have been a fatal tidying of the campsite.

Once again they passively waited for the continual flurry of winds, storms, and snows to subside. Gilkey appeared to get better, and their hopes rose. Perhaps, if he recovered at Camp VIII, they could still continue toward the summit. In a gesture of defiance against the odds, Craig and Schoening headed up during a lull in the storm, seeing nothing in the dense clouds. Reaching an altitude of about 25,500 feet, they proved only that they still possessed the energy and the will to continue.

August 9 brought a serious turn for the worse. Gilkey developed at least two pulmonary embolisms as clots moved from his legs to his lungs. He coughed hard and his pulse rose to 140; his life was in immediate danger.

The team was low on food and the storm was in its ninth day. The normal descent was blocked by avalanche danger. Agreeing on a risky plan, the climbers decided to lower Gilkey down an unexplored rock rib that Schoening had noted during the ascent. This route formed a more direct line between Camps VIII and VII.

As they broke camp, their wizened faces were still able to grin. When asked how he felt, Gilkey would smile and answer, "Just fine." Talk was still of the summit. As soon as Gilkey was safely down, they would rest up for yet another attempt. The bad weather would have to end soon.

Gilkey, fully clothed, was placed inside his sleeping bag and wrapped in a tent. For several hours he was lowered, carried, and pulled along the steep descent. The storm continued and all the men lost feeling in their toes. Icicles dangled from their beards and eyebrows. As they came to a forty-foot cliff above an ice slope, an avalanche hit them; they were sure that the end had come. When the mist cleared, all eight men were still on the slope. Luckily, the slide had been small.

In order to lower Gilkey, Schoening set up an especially firm belay. He positioned himself in front of a boulder embedded in the ice and drove his ice axe above it in such a manner that it would not come loose unless the rock dislodged. He ran the rope around his hips, up around the shaft of the axe, and back down to Gilkey. In the event of a fall, the force would pull him inward and the pressure of his body would actually help to embed the axe and the boulder into the slope. He lowered Gilkey onto a small ledge and waited for the others to descend in ropes of two into positions where they

K2 from the Godwin-Austen Glacier

could start moving Gilkey horizontally to Camp VII, now only two hundred feet away.

Then it happened. George Bell, hands and feet numbed by the cold, slipped down the ice slope. His rope pulled taut on Tony Streather, who was whipped into the air like a fly. They felt a jerk as their rope snagged that of Bob Bates and Charles Houston, but it was only momentary, for that pair were also pulled from their stances. Another jerk came when both falling ropes crossed a third that connected Dee Molenaar to Art Gilkey. Minutes before, Molenaar had tied into Gilkey as an extra safety precaution when Bob Craig left him to begin setting up Camp VII. Now Molenaar was also flung into space.

Each man was sure that the end had come. Bates knew that he and Houston were falling together toward the distant Godwin-Austen Glacier. Bell helplessly felt himself plunge through the rest of the group. Craig, unroped near the Camp VII platform, was certain that he would be the sole survivor.

When the instant was over, Bates and Molenaar dangled next to each other at the brink of a rock crest; both had minor injuries. Streather lay in a tangle of ropes, while Bell, who had lost mittens, pack, and glasses, held his frozen hands in front of him like loose planks on a wooden fence. Close to his side lay Houston, curled up and unconscious.

Farther up the slope, Gilkey was unmoved. The rope connecting him to Schoening's belay was rigid. It had stopped the fall of five men. In a miracle, the ropes of three separate teams had fouled securely enough to save the lives of all. One by one the men came to their senses and gazed up the slope at a single strand of rope, taut as a bowstring, still connecting them to Schoening's ashen hands.

When the fall began, Schoening had anticipated the shock by letting a small amount of rope slide freely. Then he had forced his weight onto the axe to hold it into the slope. He had watched the rope stretch until it seemed only half its normal diameter. He couldn't tell what had happened below him and he hung on for long minutes until he was sure that everyone was able to move.

Houston was the most seriously injured. When Bates reached him, he was lying motionless on a small ledge. His eyes opened but did not focus. He did not respond to suggestions that he climb back up to the others. Hit on the head and suffering a concussion, Houston kept mumbling, "Where are we?" In a last-ditch effort, Bates said firmly, "Charlie, if you ever want to see Dorcas and Penny again [his wife and daughter], climb up there *right now*." Looking frightened and bewildered, Houston obeyed orders like a robot.

There was no time to muse over Schoening's amazing belay or Houston's injuries. The team moved to Camp VII, leaving Gilkey securely anchored to the slope by two ice axes until the tents were erected. They had originally planned to descend to Camp VI that day, where a haven of large tents with food and fuel awaited them. The entire platform where Dudley Wolfe had perished at Camp VII in 1939 had disappeared during the ensuing years, and now the campsite barely held one tent. But there was no chance of reaching Camp VI that day. They worked laboriously to chip out another platform in the ice for Schoening's tiny one-man bivouac tent.

When the tents were up, Bates, Craig, and Streather went back to bring Gilkey into camp. They found an empty slope. All traces of Art Gilkey—even the ice axes that had anchored him—were gone. The slope looked somehow different, and the three men theorized that an avalanche had ripped him from his moorings, although in the blinding storm it had gone unnoticed at the camp, two hundred feet away.

It is within the realm of possibility that Gilkey, appraising his hopeless condition and the risk that his companions were taking to save him, cut himself loose from the slope. Afterwards, one of the climbers said, "Yes, that is exactly the kind of thing Art would have done. He would have gladly sacrificed his life to keep the rest of us out of danger. But he didn't, because he couldn't have done it. Not only was he weak and sick, but he was also drugged and tied into a bundle. Nature performed a merciful act on all of us."

That night, four men huddled in one two-man tent while three others sat in the tiny bivouac tent. Houston was delirious. He kept asking how Art was and also complained that he was suffocating because the tent was tightly closed. Normally a modest, self-assured man, Houston talked with an arrogance that would have been humorous had the situation not been so serious. He was suffering from a chest injury which prevented him from breathing deeply. The rapid, short breaths he had to take caused him to repeatedly hyperventilate himself into unconsciousness. Each time he came to, he would breathe normally for a while and tell the others, "I know about these things. I've studied them. We'll all be dead in three minutes unless you let me cut a hole in the tent so we can breathe."

The next day, as they descended in a storm, the men found remnants of Gilkey's fall. Here and there were shreds of clothing, a broken ice axe, tangles of rope, and rocks splotched with blood, but Art Gilkey himself was never found. He had disappeared into the vastness of the mountain. The climbers moved down with a fatalistic attitude. They were doing their best to survive, and it might not be good enough.

In Camp VI they waited out a full day of storm. The next day they had to negotiate the most difficult part of the descent. When darkness arrived, not everyone had reached the safety of Camp IV. Bringing up the rear, Houston was alone at the top of House's Chimney. He was slowly recovering from his concussion and, as his memory returned, he became increasingly disheartened. The realizations of Gilkey's death, the expedition's defeat, and the months of wasted effort began to mingle with his outer sensations of darkness, cold, and wind-driven snow. Worse yet, Houston could feel three ropes in the darkness. Two, from 1938 and 1939, were rotten and untrustworthy; only one was new and safe. He could not tell them apart. For long minutes he considered jumping, ending it all without risking a fall down the chimney onto his companions below. But he could not do it, and he whispered the Lord's Prayer while kneeling in the snow. He was never able to remember what followed. Somehow he chose the right rope and climbed down under his own power to a point where Schoening helped him into camp.

The next morning the ordeal began anew. For ten hours the seven men down-climbed icy rocks and steep gullies. Bell's feet were so badly swollen from frostbite that he was forced to slit his boots. All had become shadows of their former selves. Every face was gaunt and bearded; every mind had adjusted its perspective to cope with an existence without enough food, water, living space, or level ground.

Just above Camp II things suddenly changed. All the Hunza high porters rushed out to greet the climbers. They took their packs and each Hunza embraced each climber, shedding tears of joy. The team was escorted into camp. Sleeping bags had been laid on rocks for them to sit on. Hot food and drinks were served to warm them, and the Hunzas massaged their tired muscles and frostbitten limbs. One climber summed up all their feelings when he said, "It was simply the warmest, deepest experience I've ever had with any human beings."

With the aid of the Hunzas the climbers descended to base camp and prepared to leave the mountain. On a point of rock at the junction of the Savoia and Godwin-Austen glaciers, they built a large cairn and held a memorial service for Art Gilkey. Each of them realized how lucky he was to be alive after their appalling descent. At least half the team had frostbite and George Bell's feet were so badly affected that he could not walk out. Much of the path leading back to civilization was too narrow and rugged for men carrying a litter, and Bell wondered how he would ever get home. When the party reached the first rough terrain, a young Balti knelt beside the litter and motioned for the 6 foot 5 inch Bell to climb onto his shoulders. For miles the stalwart Balti strode barefoot from rock to rock, across streams and narrow ledges. Although the porter's name was Mohammed Hussain, Bell called him John Ridd after the Herculean hero of the novel *Lorna Doone*. Because Bell did not have to walk on his damaged feet, he lost only one small toe and part of another.

In later years both George Bell and Pete Schoening returned to the Karakoram and they reached the summits of the two highest peaks ever first ascended by Americans. In 1958, Schoening and Andy Kauffman climbed Hidden Peak, and in 1960 Bell and Willi Unsoeld reached the top of Masherbrum. Tony Streather came back to another part of the Himalaya in 1955 and was on the second summit team of the first ascent of 28,207-foot Kanchenjunga.

Although the 1953 K2 expedition was a failure in terms of reaching the summit, exploring new ground, and especially in the unfortunate death of Art Gilkey, its members plucked a laurel that escaped Herman Buhl on Nanga Parbat: they formed lasting bonds of friendship. Tony Streather, the only British member of the group, believed that it was not just luck that seven men returned alive from the eye of an ultimate storm. "Had we not been such a closely knit team," he wrote, " it is doubtful that we would have survived." Charles Houston had expressed the same sentiments on the day the team descended to base camp when he said, "We entered the mountains as strangers, but we are leaving as brothers."

2 The Revolt

On June 16, I climbed to Camp II with Lou, Wick, Rob, and Steve. Jim and Dianne stayed below to help with the lower end of the winching system up to Savoia Pass. The two Freds were in base camp with Leif, both very subdued after a wild confrontation with the rest of the team. I sympathized fully with their emotions about the expedition, but not with their threats to go home. During the approach, both Freds had been more upset than anyone about the porters' failure to honor their contract when the going got rough. Now, to my way of thinking, they were doing exactly the same thing. We owed it to each other, even if we were no longer friends, to stick together long enough to make a serious attempt on the mountain. Otherwise, many man-years of effort and hope would have been spent in vain.

The Freds believed that the Whittakers and Wickwire formed a conspiracy in Seattle to place themselves on the summit to the exclusion of others. I didn't believe it. The kinds of partnerships that are often called conspiracies are usually nothing more than expressions of mutual self-interest. Wick and Lou *seemed* as if they were involved in a conspiracy because each was individually motivated toward the same goal: being first on the summit. Jim recognized them as the winners of a self-styled competition. But if an agreement on the summit team existed beforehand, why had Wick and Lou pushed so hard to prove themselves? If a conspiracy had really existed, why didn't they just take it easy, waiting for Jim to pull them out of a hat after we prepared the lower camps?

Each of us had a slightly different interpretation of the Freds' revolt. Unfortunately, Fred Dunham did not keep a diary, but what follows are the descriptions that the other team members recorded at the time.

Lou Whittaker:

Big crisis today! Last night the Freds talked til midnight and today Stanley says he has *quit* the expedition. Feels he has no say in anything and that Jim and Wick and myself are running the expedition without letting anyone else have a vote. They were both very quiet yesterday after a ribbing that they got when they laughed because Wick and I were turned back from Camp II because of snow. Jim said usually when someone tries to do what we all want, like try to climb the mountain, failure would not be something to delight in. . . . The Freds have been so negative on everything—the country, the coolies, the HAPs, Manzoor, and now the rest of the team. I think a fear of the mountain may have them both stymied.

Dunham said he would carry tomorrow but Stanley may not. . . . He is really in a pout right now like a five-year-old—hard to sympathize with. . . . I didn't think I was being too strong with the Freds, but Wick said we (Jim and I) can tend to bulldoze through problems and can come on very strong.

Rob Schaller:

Two days ago we had a real crisis with the two Freds, both suddenly admitting to being alienated by the Big Three and not feeling a part of the expedition. Stanley believes there is a conspiracy to get the Big Three on the top and we are only coolies to accomplish that purpose. He seems to have transferred his hostilities toward the Baltis to the rest of us. . . . Stanley talks seriously of leaving and I talk with him for hours but to little avail.

Dianne Roberts:

I haven't been able to sort out the thing with the Freds in my own mind. A few days ago they began being deliberately uncommunicative after going to Camp II with Lou and Wick. Then in an odd series of conversations they revealed, first to Galen and Steve, then to Wick and Jim, that they were totally pissed off with the way things were going, that they felt cut off and ignored by the others, that their opinions were being laughed at and a lot of other paranoid bullshit including the accusation that Jim, Wick, and Lou were involved in a conspiracy (hatched in Seattle) to get the three of them to the summit of K2 by employing the forced labor of the rest of the team. Whew. It came as a shock to everyone—both in its content and in its intensity, but it did serve as a catalyst to bring out feelings that have been brewing for weeks. The rest of us (except Leif) sat at Camp I talking about it for most of one afternoon and the next morning. Galen got into it a lot, trying to justify, or at least explain the Freds' outburst in terms of the

Jim and Lou Whittaker, below Gasherbrum IV

"autocratic/dictatorial" running of the expedition all along the way. Hell—all kinds of accusations were flung about with rare abandon. But not too much of it made any sense—except the clear revelation that our group has been divided in half all along, with neither half understanding the other since the beginning.

Jim Whittaker:

Stanley is really running off at the mouth. Claims he is going to quit the expedition—that Lou, Wick, and I have a pact, made in Seattle, that the three of us are going to reach the summit of K2 and he is just going to carry for us. Claims no one else will get a chance. He says that I am a dictator, Wick is ignoring everyone else but Lou and I and to hell with everyone.

Manzoor Hussain [in a letter written after the expedition]:

Fighting and quarrels had started between Freds and Lou and Wick. . . . In fact the team had started breaking itself into four sections right from the beginning. Fred Dunham and Fred Stanley formed one section (the extremist left). Lou Whittaker and Jim Wickwire, another (whom everybody called the most ambitious for the peak). Steve Marts, Rob Schaller, Galen Rowell and Leif Patterson formed the third section (the moderate ones). . . . Jim Whittaker and Dianne Roberts formed the fourth section, isolated from whatever was happening in the expedition. Fred Stanley had a bitter quarrel with Jim Whittaker and thought he was amongst foes rather than friends.

Leif Patterson:

The fifteenth opens with a tremendous crisis. Dunham is disgusted with the way things have been going. Stanley wants to quit. They have some poignant reasons. Feel pretty bad, as if expedition is falling apart. . . . Last night Galen had a long talk with the Freds. Very late in the morning some of the party sets off without resolution of the dispute. . . . My line with all I talk to in the team is that we need each other, that we must be honest toward each other. Imagine then, that same evening, just before Rob arrives in Camp I, a radio conversation with Wick in the same camp. Wick instructs Manzoor to send a telegram to Wick's wife, censuring Joanne [Rob's fiancée] for giving personal information about Rob to newspapers—and threatening Joanne with later court action. Why isn't Rob notified? Why isn't telegram sent directly to Joanne? Where does this information about releases come from up here? This is intrigue behind each others' backs, a real shock to me.

On morning of June 16th, Fred Stanley cuts in on the radio to have it out with Jim Whittaker. He inquires about the telegram, which cannot now be hidden from Rob. Whittaker refuses any discussion. Fred is bitter. But the net result is that the telegram is called off—a good thing.

[After a carry to Camp I] Fred Stanley and I . . . had a talk . . . got along fine. Fred is very strong and very conscientious. Why won't the upper echelons in our team recognize his fine qualities? Fred is deeply disappointed. He came to climb with Wick and Dunham as much as to scale K2—and what has he got from Wick?

Fred loves to needle Whittaker. It is not the right approach. I have a plan: if Camp III gets established, I want the two Freds and myself to take the lead in putting in Camp IV, provided only our health will hold.

My lungs are not clear. . . . This is such a messed-up trip: my own sickness would mean little in a good team of first-rate friends. But the team is an unhappy one. It is nearly split apart from inner tensions. It is my lot to help pull together, unify, and without sufficient health I cannot succeed in that. I believe that you do not remedy a disastrous confidence crisis merely by talking it over. That is a first step. But the crisis was precipitated by cumulative *actions* in the first place, and actions cannot be eradicated by words, only by other actions. I believe we can still overcome difficulties and unify our team by actions which will allow each individual recognition for his efforts, and by honesty. The Wick-Lou summit consideration should be dissolved. Wick should do his job as deputy leader, which would first and foremost be to mend his relations with his close friends: the two Freds and Rob. The summit must be there to tempt all of us, not only a couple of gung-hos. The illness afflicting us as a team is already dangerously far advanced.

Leif, Lou, Wick, and Jim at base camp

Jim Wickwire:

A major new crisis has hit the expedition: the possible defection of the two Freds. The problem has been brooding for some time. Both have felt they have had little involvement in expedition decision-making, that any ideas or comments they have about what should be done are not listened to or are rejected out of hand. Fred Dunham has been in deep gloom since the Manzoor radio incident of the tenth. Last night after dinner Fred D. unloaded to Galen and Steve how unhappy he was that "his friend Jim Wickwire had been distant," and that he was fed up with constantly being put down by Jim. Last night, I could hear both of them talking in subdued voices far into the night. Something serious was up and was confirmed by Galen's relation of his discussion the previous evening with Dunham. Apparently, Stanley felt the same way and there was talk of their leaving the expedition.

I could not accept the assertion that the entire problem was one of a clash of personalities. Granted, Jim has come on a trifle strong at times; Lou, too, but I believe . . . that both of them are intimidated by the mountain and by the time and distance from persons they care a great deal for.

After breakfast, Jim and I went to their tent to talk with them. Jim led off, saying that his principal objective was to get up the mountain and that everything he had done had been directed toward that end. That to reach the summit every person on the team was important and if he stepped on their toes he was sorry. Fred S. remarkably responded: "Nice pep talk, but I don't believe a word you said." I angrily interjected, "That's completely unfair." And so it went, in a very unsatisfactory way, for a few minutes with Jim there and then for another half hour with them alone. . . . Finally I walked away. Just before leaving for Camp I, talked briefly to Fred Dunham, who said he would continue to work for the expedition because of what he felt was an obligation to those persons who had made contributions at his behest. During the discussion with both Freds, I conceded I wanted to get to the top of K2, that was why I was here, and if I didn't make it to the top, I wanted to leave here with no regrets and knowing that I had given everything to the effort of getting there. Curiously, Fred Stanley said that the reason he came on the expedition was because of Fred's and my presence. That's nice, but not a sufficient reason for coming all the way to Pakistan and K2. . . .

Spent the entire afternoon in our tent discussing pros and cons of what to do. Galen, Jim, Dianne, Lou, and Steve. Nothing conclusive, except maybe to offer them the route-finding to Camp III. To me this is an admission we have been wrong. I don't think we have. At least to the extent they think. . . .

Rob . . . spent nearly four hours with the Freds in their tent that afternoon. No startling new allegations. They feel the expedition is divided into two camps: Jim, Lou, and I in one; everyone else in the other. They thought it would be poetic justice if Steve Marts and a Balti got to the summit and none of us did. Or, better yet, and here is a real twist, both Whittakers get to the summit and I don't. These are my friends? . . .

Motivation on any Himalayan expedition is the name of the game. If you don't have a lot of it, you won't put up with what you have to go through to reach the high summit you are striving for. I admit to having very strong motivation for climbing K2. I make no apologies for it. The Whittakers have it. They should not have to make apologies for it. Rob and Leif—and I think Galen—also have it. But the Freds don't. That's why I resent and refute the notion this is all some giant putdown of them by us. Of course there have been and will continue to be personality clashes, but to hang it all on that is utter bullshit.

But in the last analysis, I am spending four months in Pakistan because I want to reach the summit of my dream mountain. For various reasons the Freds (particularly Stanley) are opting out. Lou has the same dream I do, and—if the route goes, and if we stay strong—we will go to the summit together. And if we don't, it will not be because we haven't given the effort of our lives.

(Next morning) Things have really gone to hell vis-à-vis Stanley. At 8:00 A.M. he came on the radio and wanted to know the basis for the telegram to Mary Lou. Rob and Steve were in the tent for breakfast, and I hadn't yet told Rob about the telegram, mainly because I was reluctant to compromise Steve as the source. Stanley was insistent, so in Rob's presence, I explained the genesis of the telegram. Rob nodded in understanding. Stanley charged that I had stabbed Rob in the back. There followed one of the most irrational, hate-filled diatribes I have ever heard, directed at Jim and me. He yelled that there was a conspiracy among Jim, Lou, and me to put the three of us on the summit to the exclusion of all the others. . . . There had been discussions about who was strongest in the team . . .—Lou, Jim, and me—but absolutely no pact to put all three of us on the summit. We had simply looked around and concluded that we had greater motivation than the others, except perhaps for Leif and Rob. . . .

A few minutes ago Galen said that on the approach march the other five felt alienated from Jim, Lou, and me, as though we had formed a group with its own ambitions for the summit—that we had not been warm and compatible on the approach. Compatibility is a two-way street, and he would place the entire burden on us to walk the full length of the street. To me, the whole thing is a commentary on the insecurity of the others, an indication of their need to be wet-nursed. I was happy on the approach just to be here in this great country. Why should I have sought out those who did not share my feelings as opposed to one who did—Lou? Friendship is mutuality, not sitting back waiting for your "friend" to come minister to you.

Fred Stanley:

Last evening when I got to camp with Steve, the porters and Manzoor welcomed us, untying our rope and carrying our packs to our tents. A kind of warm glow came over me. I got into my sweater and down vest and wind shirt, got my cup out, and headed for the cook tent. . . . Dinner was ready. I was feeling pretty good and somewhere into the conversation I mentioned that Fred and I could hardly contain ourselves at the irony of Wick and Lou starting out for Camp II the previous *afternoon* and then returning fifteen minutes later (in a snowstorm) after all their noise and valorous talk. That is, I started to mention it and Jim jumped on me, shouting me out, saying how the two Freds were happy about their failures . . . how we're always happy when something goes wrong, how we were happy when he didn't make Camp I from base camp in 45 minutes as he had bragged he would (this I knew nothing of), etc. I just shut up and slowly finished my dinner. . . .

I am really at a low ebb. I have lost all enthusiasm for the expedition, wishing there was some way out without leaving the rest in the lurch. Each person in this small group counts a lot. The talk this morning is to have Wick and Lou return to the lead with Rob and Galen going to II to set up the winch system. I left earlier when the talk turned to the virtues of the first two fixing the route or not, to finish my cocoa and pancakes in peace away from the sound of the Whittakers' voices drowning out Galen's and even Fred's, I think. . . . Lou and Jim can always shout a little more than the other guy is willing to, knowing it's no use to argue with them, or they can attack him personally, saying his knowledge of fixed lines in Yosemite is of no use here, etc. Jim asked Fred—it sounded like a challenge to me—if he had any objections to Wick and Lou going into the lead again. I really don't give a shit. I was even hoping I would wake up good and sick this morning so I could just have an excuse to lie about—maybe even go down. If I had Alex Bertulis's address I would send him a letter telling him how lucky he was to get off this thing when he did even as he did. A blackballing by Whittaker raises him a notch in my eyes. And I know damn well no one besides Wick, Lou, and perhaps Jim have a chance for the summit. . . .

Wick is sitting on the fence, I think, wanting to stay in good with Jim and Lou, certain that Lou as the leader's brother and he as deputy leader will be the ones for the summit. . . . I hope it's a picket fence and he gets one up the ass. . . .

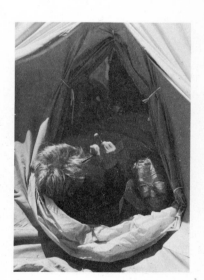

The Freds at base camp

Jim sent a couple of telegrams . . . saying how we were gouged on the approach but how nice things are going now. . . .

Fred just came in from what he called a psychotherapy session with Galen and Steve. He said they talked over some of the same feelings we've all had. Galen says he's just going to enjoy the company of others and work toward the success of the expedition. I tell Fred that's what I find depressing. The success of the expedition means putting a Whittaker on the summit. . . .

I've never had any great Nazi fervor about climbing K2 as perhaps Wick has. I came on the expedition for enjoyment and have had little. I can still remember Jim saying things will get better when we reach the mountain, the morning Lou threatened Fred at Concordia. They've gotten worse. Galen has struck up a psychoanalysis session with the rest of the group this morning, discussing Fred and me and himself, also. I believe he's found it an opportunity to bring out his problems with the Whittakers and air them—a good catharsis for him. Lou, Wick, and everyone are getting into the act now, psychoanalyzing us. I can't hear it all, actually only a phrase or two, but I sure have to chuckle. It sounds to me like Galen's good intentions of trying to get us treated better, listened to, respected for our positions, not put down every time we open our mouths, are being shouted down.

Wick is talking vehemently. I hear noises about fragile egos, losing a few on Himalayan expeditions, crying in the tent. . . . Fred came back saying the Jims wanted to talk to us. I finally got them to understand I didn't really care to talk about it other than to say I was unhappy with personal relationships and was ready to bail out. Fred said he was ready to stay and do as he was told. . . . Jim made a pep talk and plea that he was doing things as he thought they ought to be done and was only interested in getting the expedition to the summit, and unless I was willing to talk about it there wasn't much he could do. What it boiled down to was he was begging for bodies to stay on; otherwise the expedition had had it. He finally left and Fred talked a little more with Wick, who tried to explain his position and actions, talking about safety, our supposed preoccupation with safety, technique, technical competence. . . . All I could think of was what does this have to do with the Whittakers treating people like shit?

I remembered just a minute ago that when I was a kid we used to talk about digging a hole deep enough to come out in China. What reminded me was that I just pissed a hole in the snow. . . . I'd like to jump down it and come out in Washington.

Rob came by earlier and said he tried to keep out of the morning's psychoanalysis and we talked about the situation. He said he's felt out of it—left out by the Big Three ever since Rawalpindi. . . . He seems to think as Galen, that things will get better if we five stick together, that there are or will be changes in the Whittakers. . . . Wick's aloofness to him since getting to Pakistan has hurt him. . . .

I think Wick was pretty shook this morning and I don't blame him, but I haven't laid awake the past two nights for no reason, either. When I replied "you and Fred" to his question of why did I come along on the expedition, he said that was a pretty poor reason. It was enough for me and half that reason is gone now. I don't think I've anything to prove or find out on K2. I was along for an adventure with friends.

A radio call (from Camp I) at 6:00 P.M. while we (Fred, Leif, Manzoor, and I) were finishing dinner: Wick wanted to send out a telegram to Mary Lou (his wife).

WE HAVE REPORTS JOANNE [Rob's fiancée] IS ACTING AS OFFICIAL OR UNOFFI-
CIAL LIAISON WITH NEWS MEDIA REGARDING EXPEDITION MATTERS. SHE IS NOT
AUTHORIZED TO DO SO. OUR CONTRACTUAL OBLIGATIONS TO NATIONAL GEO-
GRAPHIC SOCIETY AND SIERRA CLUB REQUIRE CAREFUL REVIEW BY US OF ALL
INFORMATION RELEASED TO NEWS MEDIA. ALTHOUGH WE CANNOT PREVENT
JOANNE FROM TALKING TO MEDIA, PLEASE ADVISE SHE FACES LEGAL ACTION IF
SHE CONTINUES TO RELEASE FIRST-PERSON DIARY ACCOUNTS OR PHOTO-
GRAPHS TO MEDIA. OTHERWISE, EVERYTHING FINE. LOVE YOU AND MISS YOU
SO.

The threat of legal action caught us by surprise and really floored us. Jim came on to Manzoor and said, "Yes, I think that's something that should be sent." I had looked out the tent door just a few minutes before to see Rob moving (in the distance) up the last slope to Camp I. Fred got on the radio and asked to speak to Jim. Jim Whittaker came on and asked, "Which Jim?" (Wick or Whittaker) and Fred said it didn't matter, he just wanted to find out the source of the rumor. Jim said he thought he'd let Fred talk to Wick, Rob was coming into camp. Wick came on, and without answering the question, said a few words and said the next radio contact would be at eight in the morning and signed off. We sat back shocked. What a stab in the back to Rob. . . . Leif said he just couldn't believe the deceit, the behind-the-back things going on in this expedition. We agreed to make sure in the morning that Rob knew of the telegram. We thought of sending another saying to Joanne this was not an expression of the whole expedi-tion.

We talked on; Fred finally left. . . . Leif kept remarking that the five of us had the power to get the expedition running the way we wanted it. I realized that we could, on our own, stock the camps as high as we wished for as many as we wished. It's his opinion that the summit team will be chosen by expedition vote. . . . During the conversation he managed to impart to me some of his fantastic strength. Enough that I decided to stick around for awhile and start being the person I'd like to be in situations like this. . . .

After talking with all the climbers other than the Big Three, I realize they all have many of the same feelings I do, that if there come any corporate votes, it'll be 5 to 4 (corporate votes affecting me brought up by our legal eagle, Wick). . . .

I woke at seven this morning, my mind immediately in high gear—one of those situations when everything is spread before one with perfect clar-ity. . . . Everything I would have liked to have said to Wick and Jim the previous morning is completely sorted out in my mind now. I am looking forward to the radio contact and tell the others I would like to make it. I also prepared to do a thing I was less than proud of—recording a conversa-tion with others when they didn't know it. Something I wanted as a per-sonal reference . . . something I can present to Wick or Whittakers if things are said which there is going to be a question about. At eight Jim is on. I ask for Wick. He is on. I ask him if he is ready to supply the source of his rumor. In his careful lawyer's voice and words, he replies that it has only just now come to his attention that possibly first-person diary ac-counts of the expedition have been printed in the Seattle papers. I think he hemmed and hawed before this, saying he wanted to speak to Rob first. At some point he said that before he went further he wanted to know if I was still a member of the expedition in light of the previous day's happenings. I replied that I was still a member of the expedition until I was run out by them the way Alex was. Jim burst in on the conversation somewhere and I told him that he, Wick, and Lou were going to have to quit treating the rest

The Revolt 241

of us as piles of shit into which they could pick their crampons to get a little higher on K2. I also said they should forget about any plans made in Seattle to put them on the summit first; Jim said I was bordering on insanity. Wick finally came back on the radio to speak to Manzoor and told him to cancel the telegram. Fred, Leif, and I spent a while discussing things afterwards, at least relieved by Wick's cancellation of the telegram, but not otherwise very happy.

③ Victory on K2

After the Americans left K2 in August, 1953, two Italians walked up the Braldu gorge in September. Village paths were carpeted in golden leaves and each morning the trekkers awoke to find frost on their sleeping bags and the air as pure as crystal. The season for climbing the high peaks was long past, but these men had come, not to climb, but rather to scout the path for an expedition in 1954.

Although both were mountaineers, the backgrounds of the two were as different from each other as night and day. Riccardo Cassin was often considered the greatest Italian climber of his generation. During the thirties he had made extreme climbs similar to the Eigerwand—first ascents of two of the fabled six great north faces of the Alps—the Piz Badile and the Walker Spur of the Grandes Jorasses. As a youth he had financed his climbs by working as a mechanic. Now, at age forty-four, he owned his own climbing equipment factory. Ardito Desio, on the other hand, was a professor of geology who had written over three hundred scientific papers and had organized ten expeditions abroad. A tiny, frail-appearing man of fifty-six, Desio had only moderate climbing experience but was known as an organizer par excellence. None of Italy's top climbers had climbed in the Himalaya, but Desio had been a member of a 1929 expedition to the Baltoro region led by the Duke of Spoleto, a nephew of the Duke of Abruzzi. Desio had walked to the base of K2 and had vowed that he would someday lead an expedition to conquer it. Before the war he had made several unsuccessful attempts to organize a K2 climb, and he had been very disappointed to discover from Pakistani officials that Americans were trying the mountain in 1953.

Now the coast was clear. As the two men walked up the Baltoro Glacier, they discussed how the trip would be managed. Desio had already secured the backing of the Italian National Olympic Committee and several scientific organizations. He planned to follow in the footsteps of the two dukes, trying not only to reach mountaintops, but also to pursue a broad range of scientific objectives. He would bring a geographer, an anthropologist, a meteorologist, a topographer, and a geologist. By stringent tests he would select the top climbers in Italy and train them to work together as a group. His dictum was, "Everything must be subordinated to the attainment of the final goal, which is the conquest of K2."

Desio and Cassin climbed to Camp I on the Abruzzi Ridge. Desio took notes and photographs with the careful precision of an expert military theoretician. He talked of using planes or helicopters to airdrop supplies at Camp I. He also advocated bringing a gasoline engine to power a winch for hauling equipment up House's Chimney. Cassin grew increasingly disenchanted with the enterprise. He favored the small-party strategy of Shipton and Houston, whereas Desio, with history to back him, pointed to the 1953 ascents of Everest and Nanga Parbat as working models of how to reach high summits.

When they returned to Italy, Cassin bowed out of the venture completely. But Italy's top climbers were extremely interested. Walter Bonatti, who was eventually chosen for the expedition, reported, "There was real competition in human daring among Italian climbers, who set out on the most reckless ice climbs in the Alps . . . each hoping secretly that he would therefore be chosen." Desio made a preliminary choice of more than double the number of men he would need. Assembling them at the university where he taught, he put them through a series of rigorous medical and physiological tests and immediately eliminated the bottom six. The remaining men participated in two ten-day trial camps in the mountains. Each of the candidates acted as leader for a day, and his ability to make decisions was rated by an observer from an Alpine military school. At the final camp a committee from the Italian Alpine Club assessed each climber's ability to form mutual bonds of friendship and trust with the others. Eleven climbers passed muster, and although the original plans called for only ten on the team, the committee unanimously recommended to accept them all. Not one of the climbers had had Himalayan expedition experience, because Italy had not staged such an expedition since before the war. The majority were professional Alpine guides who were very experienced at climbing in cold weather on snow and ice. The oldest was Gino Soldà, a forty-seven-year-old guide; the youngest was Walter Bonatti, a twenty-four-year-old hut keeper.

The expedition arrived in Pakistan in mid-April. It was divided into a scientific and a mountaineering contingent. The two groups intended to operate quite distinctly from one another until the mountain had been climbed. Only then would Desio devote his full energy to science. The mountaineering group had three liaison officers and ten Hunza porters, including one man, Mahdi, who had carried the exhausted and frostbitten Herman Buhl down from Nanga Parbat on his shoulders the year before. They planned to move in three separate groups, rather than one large one, so that base camp could be established and climbing could begin before all the equipment arrived.

In 1953 Houston had experienced more porter strikes than he had expected, but he was able to resolve them because his party was so small. Desio's sprawled group required up to seven hundred porters and, because it was traveling a month earlier than Houston's had, it also had the added problem of traveling a month earlier in unusually deep snows. Only four hundred porters continued past Urdukas and the entire group quit at Concordia. Desio reached base camp with six porter loads on May 15, but the remainder of the expedition's baggage did not arrive for another two weeks.

Meanwhile, much of the climbing party bided time at Urdukas until other men could be hired and brought up the glacier to complete the portage. One morning Lino Lacedelli jokingly picked up a snoozing Walter Bonatti, sleeping bag and all. Bonatti woke suddenly, fell out of his bag, and rolled down the steep icy hillside stark naked. Lacedelli watched in horror as Bonatti slid helplessly into a pile of rocks and lay unconscious. Luckily Bonatti's injuries were minor, but he was not able to hike or climb for many days. Fearing the strict disciplinarian Desio's wrath, both men agreed to report that Bonatti was indisposed from a stomach ailment.

When Sadiq, the expedition's sirdar, finally arrived at base camp with more Balti porters, he was able to persuade sixty-two of them to carry on to Camp I, thus saving the expedition a week's back-breaking labor to move a ton and a half of gear. After the porters left, the quiet at base camp was shattered by a gasoline engine used to power a generator for the radio transmitter. It sounded like a small motorcycle and most of the climbers found the loud noise quite odd amidst the silent, frozen wilds of the Baltoro peaks.

For several weeks climbing went according to schedule. The first four camps were stocked and House's Chimney was reconnoitered. On June 21, the expedition suffered an unexpected shock. Mario Puchoz, a thirty-six-year-old guide from Courmayeur, suddenly died in the night at Camp II. For two days he had been suffering from a sore throat and some minor difficulty in breathing, but neither he nor the doctor thought him sick enough to warrant his descent to base camp. A few hours before he died, his symptoms began to resemble pneumonia, and he was treated with oxygen and antibiotics to no avail. Most probably he had contracted high-altitude pulmonary edema, which still was not well known at the time and does not respond to antibiotics.

In pre-expedition tests, Puchoz had been among the healthiest and the strongest of the climbers. His companions were greatly shocked at his death and everyone evacuated the mountain. Six days later, Puchoz was buried next to the monument that the Americans had built for Art Gilkey only ten months earlier. No climber could hope for a finer burial place. Nature had provided the Concordia amphitheater, a dome of blue sky, and the grand design of the peaks. The climbers brought mountain flowers from Urdukas, incense, a statuette of the Madonna to the gravesite. They vowed to climb the mountain in Puchoz's memory and to inscribe the date on a plaque above his grave when they next returned.

A month later, though plagued by poor weather, the expedition was nearly in position for a summit attempt. As with the Americans a year before, eight men were high on the mountain. Six were Italians—Compagnoni, Abram, Bonatti, Gallotti, Lacedelli, and Rey. Two were Hunza high-altitude porters—Isakhan and Mahdi.

Plaques at Gilkey Memorial, below K2

On the night of July 29, four men occupied Camp VIII at 25,400 feet. Lacedelli and Compagnoni had been chosen to go to the summit, and they had already explored a few hundred feet above the camp. Bonatti and Gallotti had brought up loads from below. A few days earlier, Bonatti had not been a candidate for the summit assault because he had eaten something that did not agree with him and was temporarily down with a real stomach ailment. Now he had recovered while others had become so exhausted that they felt compelled to descend. Bonatti saw that Compagnoni looked beaten, and he was tempted to volunteer to take his place. Sensing Bonatti's thoughts, Compagnoni, who was in charge of the summit maneuvers, told him, "If you are still in good shape tomorrow up there at Camp IX, it might well be that you will have to change places with one of us."

The situation was far from simple. Diminishing food and fuel supplies meant that the summit attempt could not be delayed any longer. The oxygen and other items of equipment were still below. The plan was for Lacedelli and Compagnoni to establish Camp IX on the following day while Bonatti and Gallotti descended to Camp VII and reascended to Camp IX carrying heavy loads. If Bonatti now traded places with a tired member of the summit pair, that climber might not be able to bring up the equipment in support, a task that could prove more physically taxing than the summit climb itself.

The next morning Bonatti and Gallotti descended. When they reached the cache of equipment, Gallotti felt too exhausted to climb back. They met Abram, Mahdi, and Isakhan, who were carrying loads to Camp VIII, and Bonatti persuaded Mahdi to trade places with Gallotti. In the middle of the afternoon the two headed up for

Camp IX, soon discovering that the tracks of the lead climbers were very hard to follow across the hard crust. They climbed up and up and up, shouting and hearing no answer. When night fell they were below a steep icy section that they could not climb in the dark. They were at 26,000 feet with no bivouac gear, and for one of the few times in his life Walter Bonatti was really afraid. He quietly dug a small platform while Mahdi cursed and screamed into the gathering blackness, brandishing his ice axe toward the heights. Bonatti realized that Mahdi was nearly out of his senses, and he was glad that darkness prevented him from seeing the terror on Mahdi's face. Finally, Mahdi calmed down and resigned himself to Allah's will.

Suddenly a light appeared hundreds of feet above them, and during a lull in the wind they were able to talk briefly with the men at Camp IX. The conversation was confusing, since neither side was able to fully understand the other. The high climbers crawled back into their tents, thinking that Bonatti and Mahdi were leaving the gear in the snow and descending in the darkness. Bonatti believed that he and Mahdi had a far better chance of surviving if they waited out the night rather than trying to descend the icy terrain at 26,000 feet without oxygen on a moonless night. He looked seven thousand feet below him to the lower camps and realized that he and Mahdi could instantly restore themselves to that level by merely turning on the valves of the oxygen apparatus. But if they did that the summit climbers would have no oxygen, and all their efforts would have been in vain. The two men prepared to spend a night in the open. Only one man had survived a similar ordeal at that altitude—Herman Buhl on his solo climb of Nanga Parbat.

The night began calm. Although there was no moon, the stars were so bright that they lit the surrounding peaks and that light reflected off the surrounding snow. Billowing clouds filled the valleys and crept slowly upward toward the summits; the peaks themselves were blue-white islands in a milky sea. The men were at about level with the 26,000-foot tops of Broad Peak, Hidden Peak, and Gasherbrums II, III, and IV. As Bonatti and Mahdi huddled together the white ocean of clouds gradually overwhelmed the summits, and wind and snow started to beat against their bodies. Bonatti described those hours: "Like shipwrecked men in a stormy sea, we hung on to life with every fiber of our being so as not to be overwhelmed. The struggle became more and more desperate and unequal and we no longer knew if we were fighting for our lives or if we continued to live at all."

Gasherbrum IV

The men wore identical high-altitude climbing gear and boots. Near dawn, Mahdi could take it no longer, and he took off down the slope by himself, bent and hunched by the cold so that he looked like a very old man. Bonatti waited for the sun and soon followed in Mahdi's footsteps. They had survived an impossible night without oxygen, tent, or sleeping bags at 26,000 feet. It had not been a windless night, either, but a harsh night of storm. Bonatti, who had proved time and again in the mountains that he possessed an abnormal ability to withstand cold, emerged totally unscathed. Poor

Leif celebrates the sight of green grass at Urdukas

Wild primrose at Urdukas

Snowy peaks encircle the sandy floor of the Skardu Valley

Meadow detail, Urdukas

Mahdi, like Herman Buhl, the frostbitten man he had carried only a year before, had to be carried in a stretcher to the Skardu hospital. There he underwent amputations of various fingers and half of both feet.

That morning Lacedelli and Compagnoni climbed down to pick up the oxygen just as Bonatti was disappearing down the slope. They did not understand that he and Mahdi had bivouacked there, but they were thankful for the equipment. Although the weather looked questionable, they decided to give the summit a try.

For hours they climbed up the slope until they reached the rock cliff that Wiessner had climbed fifteen years before. Conditions had changed; where Wiessner had climbed bare-handed on exposed rock, the Italians were confronted with a hanging mass of snow. Compagnoni tried a parallel rock pitch and fell off into the snow, luckily not hurting himself. For almost two hours they searched for an alternate route. Finally Lacedelli forced a passage up the rock band and emerged in the mist below a steep wall of ice. It looked so fragile and dangerous that they were afraid even to speak for fear that the noise might bring down an avalanche. Roped together, they carefully traversed far to the left of the ice wall "with no less caution than we should have used to walk on nitroglycerine."

Hours went by and the men continued to climb. They watched the mist disappear into a dark violet sky. Sun and stars shone together as each labored step brought them closer to their goal. Suddenly Compagnoni staggered. "A steel hand gripped me by the temples, my head pounded and thudded and hammered a wave of heat through my body. Then I shuddered, transfixed by a searing cold." The oxygen had run out, and a few minutes later Lacedelli's unit followed suit. They stopped in their tracks, terrified, but gradually the feeling of constriction passed. Because they were on steep terrain and the movements to detach the oxygen apparatus were complex, they continued to wear the forty-two useless pounds like leaden cloaks. At about six in the evening they found themselves on firmer snow and the terrain leveled out. The sun broke through a hole in the clouds just as the minds of the oxygen-starved men were beginning to realize that their task was completed. There was no more mountain above them. They dropped their heavy loads, embraced each other, and set up three tiny flags—of Italy, Pakistan, and the Italian Alpine Club. They were the first humans ever to set foot on the summit of K2.

After spending only half an hour on the summit of their dreams, they began descending into the twilight. In one place Compagnoni, whose hands had become stiff as boards, slipped on icy rocks and plunged downward fifty feet into soft snow. At eleven o'clock that night, the two men reached Camp VIII and stumbled into the arms of Abram, Bonatti, and Gallotti, who had known of the success for hours, ever since the sharp-eyed Isakhan had pointed to two tiny dots on the crest of the distant skyline and announced in perfect English, "A sahib is about to climb K2!"

The next day Compagnoni took an unroped 650-foot fall. Only a

Horseman on a Skardu road

patch of soft snow stopped him from plunging all the way to the Godwin-Austen Glacier. Luckily he was only bruised and he continued the descent under his own power.

At base camp, word of victory was sent out by radio. The team had agreed to keep secret the identity of those who had reached the summit. Eventually, of course, the names of Lacedelli and Compagnoni would become well known from books, newspapers, and magazines, but for the time being credit for the climb went to the team as a whole rather than just to those who had reached the top.

Desio congratulated his team, then told them, "Now I must leave you without delay in order to turn my attention to the scientific program. . . . I have made all the necessary arrangements for your return. Goodbye, then, until we meet again in Italy in a few months time."

Later, in Italy, both Compagnoni and Lacedelli were treated for mental problems that some experts believe resulted from oxygen starvation high on the mountain. For months they were not themselves, but who would be after such an intense experience? It is impossible to separate the effects of slight physical brain damage from those of an extended experience in a deprived environment. Whatever the cause of their problems, both men recovered fully after a few months and lived normal lives. The question of how high men can climb without oxygen was not resolved. Could they have made the summit if they had not used oxygen during the early hours of their summit day? No one knows. Did their brains suffer any significant permanent damage? Probably not.

Only one member of the team, Walter Bonatti, returned to the Karakoram to do significant climbing. Five years later he reached the summit of 26,000-foot Gasherbrum IV by a route that was more difficult than the Abruzzi Ridge of K2.

Ardito Desio's task was finished. He believed that the expedition had succeeded where others had failed because "it was undertaken with the specific objective of *conquering* K2, and not merely of *making an attempt* on it." Yet regardless of Desio's meticulous plans and the expedition's giant scope, the ultimate attainment was a fragile thread, totally dependent on the selfless actions of a few men in the high camps. The true roots of triumph came from deep within the human spirit.

4   The Enduring Ridge

June 21, 1975, was the solstice. But there was no summer at base camp. Nothing was green. No birds chirped, no insects buzzed. It had been snowing steadily for three days, and the camp took on the appearance of a deserted outpost in the Arctic.

My life seemed as empty and as barren as the landscape. My

Camp II after a storm

bronchitis had developed into pneumonia, and I was trying to bide the time until I was well again. I realized that this dark day was the twenty-first anniversary of Mario Puchoz's death on K2, officially from pneumonia. That scared me, but I tried cheering myself by remembering that Puchoz had probably died of pulmonary edema, misdiagnosed as pneumonia. My only contact with the doctor was by radio. Rob, Steve, Wick, and Lou were waiting out the storm in Camp II, unable to descend because of blizzard conditions and avalanche danger. Rob prescribed Keflex, a strong antibiotic, and kept trying to boost my morale by suggesting that I probably just had the flu. But I was only too aware that my symptoms were the same as Leif's when he had pneumonia. I had come down with bronchitis, and then suddenly succumbed to great weakness and fever. I tried to sleep sitting up because I couldn't breathe well lying down. Every night I sat half awake under the strange delusion that I had two heads attached to the same body. At the height of his illness, Leif had a somewhat similar vision of being in two bodies.

The two Freds were also in base camp. Stanley had some sort of stomach ailment and Dunham had a very bad cough. Their behavior resembled that of unskilled laborers who believe they have no chance of advancement in their jobs. When they were healthy they were willing to work, but not too hard and not too long. If they felt sick, as they did that day, they simply took sick leave.

The Enduring Ridge 257

Those in the high camps were constantly insinuating that the Freds were fudging, and that they could have gone up on the mountain if only they had had the desire. The Freds overheard many of these thinly veiled sarcasms and were reinforced in the belief that the Big Four's only concern for their welfare had to do with their ability to shuttle loads. The attitude of those up high was, "If I had a cough or a stomachache it wouldn't stop me from going on the mountain," and it was sincere. Feeling under the weather might not have prevented *them* from climbing to higher altitudes. But the Freds valued their health and safety far more than the glory of reaching the summit. Maybe, as some had suggested, they really did not belong on K2. But this attitude implied that we had cornered the market on the one right way to climb a mountain, and I didn't buy that notion at all. Moral considerations aside, the Freds had definitely lost interest in the climb by this time, and this might not have happened if they had been treated differently. Dunham no longer took the expedition seriously and called it "the highest Boy Scout Jamboree in history."

The week before, I had been in agreement with the Whittakers and Wickwire. I thought the Freds were letting the expedition down by threatening to quit. After all, I had taken more abuse from the Big Four than anyone else had, yet I was sticking with it. I was prepared to work hard at high altitude day after day in order to establish the route for whomever would go to the summit. I had geared myself to suffer all manner of discomfort and discontent. I was ready to be away from base camp for a month or more, ready to sleep in camps that grew increasingly colder and smaller, ready to feel my breathing change from an automatic reflex to a consciously controlled effort, ready to temporarily deprive myself of tiny luxuries of human existence that even the poorest street dweller of Calcutta might take for granted.

I was ready to climb the mountain, but I was not prepared for what would soon happen to me. Because of the Freds' illness, Lou had developed an eagle eye for malingerers. I became an unfortunate victim of circumstances.

Still recovering from bronchitis, I had arrived at Savoia Pass on the afternoon of June 16 with Lou, Wick, Rob, and Steve. This was the same day that Fred Stanley had challenged Jim over the radio. The five of us were on our way to Camp II, and most of our camp gear was on a sled below the ice face, where Jim and Dianne were waiting for us to set up the winch that Stanley had hauled up to the pass. The winch was designed to be mounted on an absolutely flat surface, and positioning it on an angular rock so that the base was tight and flush while the long handle could be cranked with considerable force was very difficult. After an hour's work I was able to temporarily jury-rig the winch with nylon hold-down straps going all over the place. We hauled up a single load of gear shortly before dark.

For five people we had five sleeping bags and several days of food, but only two tents and one stove. The small two-man tents were designed with a low and narrow profile for stability in high winds. Inside, two were too many and three were crammed like sardines in a can. Lou and Wick, the two broadest men, took one tent while Rob, Steve, and I squeezed into the other. Since Lou and Wick had the most room, they offered to cook for all of us. Melting enough snow for five men over one tiny stove took hours. In pitch darkness at 9:30 P.M. Lou passed us enough water to rehydrate our freeze-dried dinners. After eating I asked if we could melt more for drinking and filling our bottles. The stove had been turned off and they did not intend to relight it. I resigned myself to passing the night with no water—no great hardship at sea level. At high elevation, however, a person loses considerable water just by normal breathing, since hot, humid, exhaled air contains far more moisture than cold, dry, inhaled air.

By midnight I had not slept a wink. My mouth felt as if I were trying to swallow a ball of cotton. Finally I could stand it no longer, and I crawled over my companions to the tent door. I opened it and plunged my lips into the soft powder snow. It was strange to be consumed by thirst and yet, like an ocean sailor, surrounded by a form of water that I could not drink. At a temperature near zero, the light powder snow provided only a few teaspoons of moisture before my mouth grew so cold that snow stuck to my lips. I returned to my bag and lay awake. Water was so near and yet so far. Like a drug addict deprived of a fix, my every thought was directed toward one substance, and I longed for the dawn as I never had before.

June 17 broke clear, and after what seemed an eternity the stove was lit and my body and mind were renewed by water. But it was not enough. I felt very weak and told the others that I could not join them on the route to Camp III. Rob and Steve opted to stay behind with me. Together we would try to remount the winch and haul up more tents, stoves, and food.

Lou and Wick set off on the ridge above Camp II. When they neared their old high point, Wick led up a fifty-five-degree snow gully to a perch where he could see most of the corniced north side of the pass. The snow ramp that Wick and Lou had seen from the plane was nowhere to be found. Unless a narrow, hidden traverse existed higher up, the route to Camp III would have to go directly along the crest of the pinnacled ridge itself. Sadly disappointed, the two men returned to Camp II and helped us with the winching. By evening we had hauled several hundred pounds of new supplies into camp.

Rob talked over the radio to Fred Dunham in base camp, who complained about a severe cough. Rob prescribed the usual Empirin with codeine. After the radio transmission we discussed the irony of the Freds having slight ailments and feeling depressed because they did not want to be on the mountain, while Leif had a major illness and felt depressed because he wanted to be working on the mountain with us.

Each of us realized that the next day would be a critical one. We would have to find a route over which thousands of pounds of supplies could be moved to the higher camps, even though we knew that the ridge was composed of steep rock gendarmes coated

Lou Whittaker climbing at 21,500 feet on the Northwest Ridge

with unstable snow and ice. Going over the top would be something like traversing a mile of the Manhattan skyline *after* it had been relocated to a spot at 20,000 feet elevation where storms raged more than half the time. When we got past the ridge, there would still be a vertical mile of unclimbed, unexplored ridge between us and the summit.

On the morning of the eighteenth I dragged myself into the roomy three-man tent where breakfast was being prepared. As soon as I sat down I announced, "I can't go with you today."

"Why not this time?" Lou asked with a tone of suspicion.

"Because I feel very sick. I've got a headache, muscular pains and chills, I feel extremely weak, and my eyes are sensitive to light."

"I've got the same symptoms," Lou answered, "and I'm going to climb this mountain. If you wanted to climb K2 as much as we do, you wouldn't stay back for every little thing. I thought you were shaping up, but now I see you're no better than the Freds. I think you're just scared of the mountain."

Lou's diatribe seemed unreal to me. As if in a dream, I felt too sick and sluggish to argue. I repeated that I felt very weak and feverish and I could not go on. While the others ate breakfast and packed equipment, I curled up in a corner of the tent and lay silent. Finally, I returned to the small tent and crawled back into my sleeping bag.

Lou had implied that anyone who stayed behind was scared of the mountain. It was a challenge I could not meet. I knew that I should descend to base camp, but I felt too weak to go by myself. All four of my companions were packing up for an attempt on the ridge. Soon I would be alone.

Rob poked his head into the tent, turned around to make sure that he wasn't overheard, and told me, "I think you made the right decision. If you still feel sick tonight you should go down. I'll go down with you if necessary. Today is a perfect day that we don't want to miss." I knew this was true. The team had been trying for more than a week to push the route past the gendarmes.

"I'll be okay here," I replied. "I hope you guys make it. Lou is wrong about me. I'd like to be up there with you today and I want to climb this mountain."

"I know," Rob said as he backed out of the tent. Behind him the others were profiled against the skyline, walking out of camp on snow that squeaked with the cold. Rob shouldered his pack and stepped briskly to catch them. In a minute they were gone.

Throughout the morning my illness increased. I tried to write in my diary, but felt too weak to put down anything more than the date and temperature. When I stepped outside to urinate, I fell dizzily to my knees.

Just before noon I heard footsteps coming into camp. Peering through the tent door, I caught a glimpse of Lou and rolled back onto my stomach. I did not think Lou would believe that I was really sick, and I planned to wait for Rob. His credibility as a doctor might convince the others that I should be taken down. But the figure that walked into camp was not Lou. I had seen Jim, who had decided to carry a load alone from Camp I. Haltingly, I told Jim about some of my symptoms, expecting another lecture about chickening out. Instead, even before I finished describing my sickness Jim said, "You should go down and I'll help you."

I descended the ice face under my own power, but I was so weak by the time we reached the easy slopes below that I had to support myself on two ski poles and slowly lurch along one step at a time. I rested for a long time at Camp I before donning skis for the three downhill miles to base camp.

Meanwhile, the others were fixing ropes up the ridge. Wick led up several hundred feet of steep, hard ice to a point just below the first gendarme where the upper Northwest Ridge came into view. The climbing up high looked fine, but the area directly in front of Wick on the lower ridge looked more difficult than ever. The route going directly up was very tough, but beyond the top of the first gendarme the horizontal traversing would be even more difficult, especially for those with heavy loads trying to follow on fixed ropes.

That evening a five-day storm moved in. No one moved from Camp II because of the obvious avalanche danger and white-out conditions. For the first time, Wick voiced aloud the possibility that our attempt on the mountain might fail. Still, he adamantly insisted that he would not leave until the expedition had "given everything we have to put forth."

In base camp my temperature was over 101° for three straight days. It was hard for me to imagine what those days would have been like stormbound in a tiny tent at 20,500 feet. Jim may very well have saved my life.

On the night of June 20 I wrote this entry in my diary:

Perhaps one of the biggest flaws in expedition mountaineering is that it can sometimes promote a ruthless brand of militant enthusiasm that runs roughshod over friendships, health, safety, and reason. For a time, in the face of storms, avalanches, and extreme altitudes, climbers in the militant rut must consider themselves immortal. Perhaps they never consciously think about immortality, but with their minds and bodies they act out a role as if they were immune from death. They seek that one memory of standing for a few moments above everyone else, and in order to get there they constantly try to elevate themselves and lower others. It doesn't have to be so.

Base camp was a somber place inhabited by the sick and the dispirited. The Freds' spirits sunk to a new low after they discussed avalanche hazards over the radio with Wick and Lou and received only skeptical replies. Lou and Wick believed that Stanley had an abnormal fear of avalanches as a result of being buried by a big one in 1974 in the Soviet Pamir Range, where he climbed with Pete Schoening's expedition. Stanley saw his caution as intelligent, not neurotic, and claimed that Lou and Wick wouldn't listen to reason. "What it boils down to is that campsites they have picked as safe I would place a short distance away in what I consider a safer place because of my experience. Both Lou and Wick said the slope to Savoia Pass was a good one even after the wind caused sloughs. Now it's avalanched several times. Lou said the slope above the pass was a safe one. Later it slid over the anchor points, and we lost some items we had cached there."

Leif had proved to be very different from the somewhat meek and submissive man we judged him to be during the early stages of the expedition. We all knew that he had a tremendous drive to climb mountains, but we had seen him absorb direct insults without reacting in his own defense. At that time Stanley thought that Leif might be a little naive. I believed Leif to be too modest and gentle for his own good. But after all our weeks of discord and conflict, Leif emerged as the man with the greatest strength of character among us. When humility was a virtue, he had it. When a backbone was needed, his became unbendable. He was the only member of the climbing team to be fully accepted by both of the opposing factions.

On June 21 Leif visited Jim in Camp I to discuss what he termed the "fanaticism" of the lead climbers. The statements on this subject in his diary had been growing increasingly strong, until they culminated in, "Are they willing to go over dead bodies?" Instead of holding his emotions inside until they burst, as the Freds did, Leif brought them into the open as tactfully as possible. Jim agreed that a problem existed and that changes should be made, although he held a far more benevolent view of the men who had so far forged every step of new ground on the ridge. Jim was definitely becoming more mellow and he showed a new awareness of how critical his own decisions were in healing the breach in our social order.

When Leif returned he and I had long pleasant discussions about the arts, science, and life for two evenings running. I had sorely missed this sort of unobstructed conversation on the trip; it had always developed during the normal course of other expeditions I had been on. When our conversation touched on our own expedition, however, we held back, afraid to reveal too much of ourselves to each other. We hid many of our true feelings and weighed each other's words for emotional content on a delicately balanced scale. On this subject we reserved our deepest feelings for our inanimate diaries. One night, for instance, Leif wrote, "What is this adventure about? Where is the beauty when I can't share it? Life is love and love is sharing. For sharing is the detection of universal unity. . . . The thought haunts me that not the ridge of K2, but our own disunity will defeat us."

Another week passed, one day blending into another while I passively waited out my illness. The first storm had lasted for five days. After Jim, Lou, Wick, Leif, and Steve made another attempt on the ridge, a new storm began, forcing them once again to sit it out in Camp II. Their second try on the ridge had not been encouraging. They had left late, at 9:30 A.M., climbed to the old high point, and covered only a hundred vertical feet of new terrain before the worsening weather forced them to descend. Wick led all that day, and he judged the last part to be the most difficult climbing encountered on the expedition to date.

That evening, Wick, Jim, and Lou discussed the odds of climbing the mountain. Wick's diary entry reflected the doubts that were beginning to surface:

It was the first time I've heard Jim openly talk about failure. So many things have gone against us . . . I still think we have a chance, but we need some big breaks—absence of poor weather, sickness, and continued route problems low on the mountain. If we don't climb K2, which now is surely a possibility, if not a probability, I will say it again: I want to walk away from this mountain with no regrets, knowing I have given the effort to reach its high summit all that I had to give. Even now, with nothing more, the expedition, despite all the problems and frustrations, has been a richly rewarding experience: the new friendship with Lou (at the cost of hurting old friendships); the challenge of climbing on steep rock, ice, and snow at 21,000 feet—these are enormously satisfying. K2 is one hell of a mountain and just to have been on its flanks is a rare privilege.

Meanwhile, in Camp I, Dianne was having long talks with the two Freds, who had moved up from base camp. They told her that they felt little motivation for the mountain because they had not been treated like equal partners in the venture and because their boyhood friend, Jim Wickwire, had turned his back on them. Dianne tried to convince them that they were misreading Wick. She said that he was on a continuing high about the climb and it was only natural for him to seek out people such as Jim and Lou, who shared his feelings rather than spend time with pessimists like themselves. Fred Dunham turned to her and replied in a tranquil voice, "It's just a mountain, Dianne."

Dunham, however, had been working hard. One day he climbed up to Camp II to help with the winch, reached camp before the others left for an attempt on the ridge, and descended to Camp I for the night. The next day he went up to Camp II again. The climbers

Lou on the Northwest Ridge, above Camp II

reported by radio that one of the two HAPs in Camp II, Akbar, appeared to be suffering from the altitude and was unable to work. He had spent the night moaning and complaining. Dunham took up Hussain as a replacement and brought Akbar down.

The HAPs were a great disappointment. Only a few were able to make it to Savoia Pass at all, although almost all of them had claimed previous high-altitude experience with other expeditions. Without their load-carrying in the lower camps, we were seriously crippled logistically. Our original plans called for a total of 414 load movements between camps (one load to Camp V counting as five load movements). With the full crew of eight climbers and twelve HAPs carrying every other day, it would have taken forty days to move supplies into position for the summit. But with only two or three HAPs and a fraction of the team, even if all route problems were resolved, supplying the camps seemed impossible.

The priorities of various expedition members were clearly shifting. Jim radioed down from Camp II asking Manzoor to calculate the date by which we had to send for a runner for the porters so that we could fly back home by August 11, the date on which our 120-day excursion fare ran out. Missing the August date would cost the expedition an additional ten thousand dollars in air fare. After much discussion and negotiation with Manzoor it was determined that we would have to give word to the Askole porters by July 6—in less than a week—if we were to make it out in time.

The group became split along quite different lines than before. The Big Four wanted to make one last all-out try on the lower ridge, and then go home if they could not push the route. The Freds, of course, were all for this. The two holdouts were Rob and Manzoor. They considered ten thousand dollars to be too small a part of the total expedition budget to be the deciding factor. They wanted us to stay on and explore both the ridge we were on and the Southwest Ridge, which rose steeply above base camp. Leif and I were somewhere in the middle. Leif very much wanted the personal satisfaction of pushing the route onto the main Northwest Ridge, but he did not argue to stay on because he believed the odds for success were very remote. I was recovering rapidly from pneumonia. On the day after Rob pronounced my chest clear of fluid, I moved up to Camp I. There I wrote the following diary entry:

One part of me wants to give up and go home to family and loved ones. This side sees the futility of dealing with the powerful forces on this expedition. The other part of me is mountaineer. It wants to get together a few people who will get up early and give the ridge a full-scale try.

Our time was running out. Eighteen days had passed since we had made our first attempt on the ridge—eighteen days of back-to-back storms. There was no hope for the climb unless the route suddenly opened up. The next week would tell the story.

Camp at Savoia Pass

Section IX

End of
Many Roads

*The matters of common knowledge in moun-
taineering are the emotions which form its very
flesh and blood.*

—C. DONALD ROBERTSON

1 Akbar's Plight

On the way to Camp II, Akbar Ali felt very proud of himself. His winter dreams had all come true. He had joined the American expedition, worked to become a high-altitude porter, and now he had been chosen to go to the sahibs' highest camp. Perhaps he would even go to the summit! Then he would be a great man, and the world would be at his feet. On the ice slope below the camp he had moved as quickly as the fastest sahib. Deep inside he believed that he was a stronger walker than any of the sahibs. If they would only teach him about their ropes and metal spikes, he could climb with them to the top of the great peak. None of the other high porters cared much. They didn't want to climb the mountain. They only wanted to bide the time until they could go home with great riches.

Only one thing bothered Akbar. A tingling that he had felt in his stomach for months had now become much stronger and more painful. He did not want to tell the sahibs how badly he felt for fear they would send him back down. If he prayed to Allah, it might go away.

After one night at Camp II the pain became worse. Akbar complained to the sahibs, and they told him that the height of the mountain was making him sick. He wondered. All of them were on the same high mountain, yet only he was sick. Why had Allah chosen him?

For a long day Akbar curled up in his tent while the mountain was in storm. No one could climb up or down in the blizzard. In the evening the pain grew worse. He moaned and called on Allah for most of the long night. The next morning there was a lull in the storm but he felt no better. Now he pleaded with the sahibs to take him down. In the back of his mind he thought that Allah might take his life if he stayed much longer. Maybe the power of the doctor sahib could change Allah's will, but the doctor sahib was in base camp and that was where he must go.

Akbar refused the sahibs' offer to lower him down the steep ice face tied into the sled. He would walk until he could no longer stand rather than be bound helplessly into such an infernal contraption. An hour later, Fred Sahib came up from below with Hussain. Akbar tied into the rope and began the descent. Very near base camp he met the doctor sahib, who was on his way to Camp II to join the lead climbers.

Akbar lay in the snow and moaned while Rob examined him, finding nothing unusual. Rob could hear no fluid in the lungs through the stethoscope. Akbar was not feverish and did not have abdominal tenderness near his stomach pain. Hearing that Akbar had not been eating or drinking for several days, Rob surmised that he was badly dehydrated and suffering from mild but not serious altitude sickness. He recommended that Akbar rest in base camp and be given lots of liquids. Akbar continued on toward base camp and Rob climbed up to Camp I.

The next morning Rob talked to base camp over the radio. Manzoor reported that Akbar had vomited many times and had passed about twenty-five worms, each up to ten inches long. Rob decided to go back to base camp rather than join the climbing team. He identified the worms as *Ascaris lumbricoides,* a common roundworm that infests a high percentage of the people in Baltistan. Many natives support such parasites all their lives without obvious ill effects. At 17,500 feet, Akbar was not so lucky. From his constant vomiting he was dangerously dehydrated and undernourished. In order to restore the water and food balance, Rob placed him on intravenous fluids.

For most of the day Akbar rested peacefully. Toward evening his condition suddenly worsened. First Rob detected signs of intestinal obstruction; then of generalized peritonitis, a widespread infection inside the abdominal cavity. Using a needle, he withdrew a sample of fluid from Akbar's abdomen that looked like intestinal leakage. The situation became desperately clear. The roundworms had caused an obstruction of the small intestine, and the intestine itself had now perforated. Akbar's wastes were leaking back into his body.

In a hospital, Rob would have performed major abdominal surgery to close the intestinal perforation and wash out the peritoneal cavity. At base camp such a procedure would almost certainly prove fatal. Few places on earth were so poorly matched to the task. The air at 17,500 feet was dangerously thin. Outside the tent a blizzard raged. Wind and snow blew in through the seams. Ice crystals began to form in the intravenous lines, and Rob started a kerosene stove in an attempt to raise the inside temperature. Akbar lay in his sleeping bag, motionless except for his eyes, which darted back and forth from the plastic I.V. bottle hanging from the ceiling down to his arm where the tube carrying life-sustaining fluids entered his veins. Had it not been for that bottle and tube, the scene inside the smoke-blackened HAP tent could have been transposed from the distant past.

Just as Rob thought he might have the situation temporarily under control, Akbar's condition changed abruptly. After an episode of profuse vomiting, Akbar became delirious and quickly lapsed into deep shock. His temperature rose from 99° to over 105° in fifteen minutes. His blood pressure became almost undetectable. Rob was nearly certain that Akbar would not last the night.

A sudden release of bacteria somewhere in Akbar's system had caused septic shock. Rob treated him with intravenous antibiotics,

Akbar on intravenous fluids at base camp

steroids, vasopressors, and plasma. The sick man's blood pressure slowly rose, but the septicemia appeared to be a type that did not respond well to normal drugs. Even in a modern sea-level hospital, Akbar's odds of survival would not have been good. On the mountain, Rob waited out the long night dealing with each minor crisis as it came, but he expected every hour to bring the worst. Several times that night Rob was on the brink of attempting major surgery. A surgeon by profession, he had a full set of instruments and the equipment to give a spinal anaesthetic. His education and training informed his urge to operate, but the desperate conditions in the tent forced him to reconsider. Akbar's chances of surviving such an operation were very small.

In the morning Akbar was still alive. He had rallied from the episode of septic shock, but his condition remained very critical. Just as Rob was gaining confidence, Akbar lapsed into another episode of septicemia. Once again his temperature rose to over 105°. Rob made every possible use of the contents of a few cardboard boxes of medical gear. He sorely needed a laboratory, a pharmacy, nurses, and consulting physicians. The situation was exceedingly desperate.

As Akbar continued to survive against appalling odds, Rob had the impression that it was not he who was doing the healing. "I am an instrument of God (or fate, if you are an agnostic)," he wrote in his diary during a few spare moments. "The patient does the healing. It is a truly humbling, remarkable experience to see a person pass so close to the threshold of death and somehow gather the strength and endurance to struggle away alive and whole. Every time I live through this experience with a patient I am awed and impressed by the capacity and strength of the human body and soul to somehow find a way to survive against 'impossible' odds (but then our humble computer brains calculated those odds of survival). Man seems always capable of more than expected."

Throughout the course of the expedition, Rob had felt his native patients to be quite distant from him. Something far more complex than a mere language barrier kept them from accepting him. When he was with them as an individual—on the trail or around their campfires—he was readily welcomed, but when he dealt with them as a doctor, they did not seem to consider him a member of the human race. The Baltis used charms and sacks of herbs to ward off evil spirits, so one might logically have expected them to reject the practice of modern medicine. Such was not the case. To a man (but unfortunately, for religious reasons, not to a woman), the Baltis accepted Rob's medical talents with open arms. Why, then, did they behave so distantly with him?

The answer was most probably a synthesis of several factors. The Baltis believed that death is Allah's will. Rob's antibiotic medicines were far more effective against native germs than they were against those in America, which have developed resistant strains. In several instances, men who visited him with fevers over 105°, shaking chills, disorientation, and bilateral pneumonia were back to full activity in just a few days. Normally they would have died or remained incapacitated for weeks. After seeing these dramatic recoveries, the Baltis considered Rob a powerful force, and not necessarily a human one, that could influence Allah's will. Once his power was recognized he could do little wrong. If he brought about a miraculous cure, he had changed Allah's will. If the patient worsened, that too was Allah's will. And so the doctor sahib, when he practiced his Power, was a force that commanded awe and respect. One did not make jokes or carefree gestures in such a presence. Allah might be offended.

It is all too easy for us to pass off the Baltis' response to Rob as resulting from a lack of scientific knowledge. If they only understood, we argue, the relationships of hygiene to health or germs to disease, then they might cease to believe that life and death are *Inshallah*. But we ourselves place so much emphasis on the mechanics of disease that we lose our sense of the mysteries that govern them. We take pride in isolating and naming the specific bacteria that cause various diseases, yet we usually ignore the fact that in a world full of such germs only some of the people become sick some of the time. We concentrate on the direct causes of illness in the sick, and we ignore the more subtle problems of why the majority stay healthy. In the rare event that more than a small percentage of the population becomes sick from exposure to a prevalent germ, we grow upset and call the phenomenon an epidemic.

But in the case of Akbar's miraculous survival, where explanations were beyond the power of logical comprehension, Dr. Robert T. Schaller unknowingly cast himself in precisely the role that the Baltis had ascribed to him: "I am an instrument of God. . . ."

The miracle continued. Akbar clung to life in the stormbound tent. For three days his temperature hovered between 104.5° and 106°. For some reason the HAPs who shared his tent seemed incapable of refilling the kerosene stove every few hours. Several times Rob returned to the tent to find the stove empty, the I.V. lines frozen, and the HAPs lying about casually. He maintained a strict vigil, sleeping only at odd minutes of the day.

At the beginning of July Akbar began very slowly to recover. The ruptured wall of his intestine started to seal itself. The peritonitis began to localize in the upper middle section of his abdomen. Delirium gave way to awareness. The now frail Akbar began to smile and demand cigarettes.

When it was obvious that Akbar's condition was improving, a new problem arose. How would he return to his village? Not only was he too weak to walk, but also too sick to be jostled day after day across the rock-strewn glacier. Worse yet, Rob had only a limited supply of I.V. bottles. Already he had used more than most expedition doctors would ever think of bringing to the mountains. As soon as Akbar was able to take liquid orally, Rob removed the intravenous lines.

During the crisis at base camp the team on the mountain was finding the route impassable. The high climbers decided to abandon the attempt and return to base camp for the final time. Over the radio they asked Rob to descend through the ice fall to the

Godwin-Austen Glacier in order to fix any ropes that might be necessary for upcoming porters and to find a site for caching the valuable unused oxygen bottles. On the fourth of July Rob and another climber skied down the glacier, walked through the ice fall, and climbed up to the Gilkey Memorial on a rock spur above the old K2 base camp. Plaques commemorating the six men who had lost their lives on K2 were attached to the rock with pitons. A cross marked the grave of Mario Puchoz. Rob was glad that Akbar's name was not yet a candidate for a plaque. He found the memorial a bewilderingly happy place. For the first time there were signs that it was summer somewhere. A fly landed on his shirt and a finch flew not far behind. Sedums and saxifrage sprouted out of barren cracks in the rocks. The snowfield we had crossed six weeks earlier was now a multifaceted moraine dotted with lakelets, ice ships, and sinuous ridges of rock debris. A stream burbled across the middle of the scene and Concordia seemed a stone's throw away through the clear air.

During the next three days, Akbar's temperature dropped to normal and his peritonitis seemed greatly improved. On the evening of the third day he stepped outside the tent for the first time and sat in the sun for an hour. That evening the high climbers returned to base camp and visited him in his tent. He was touched by their concern, which seemed far greater than that of the other HAPs, his countrymen.

But on the morning of July 8, Akbar suffered another setback. He vomited several times, and Rob detected new signs of partial intestinal obstruction. The man's condition was again critical. The team decided that Akbar's only chance was to be flown out by helicopter. At the start of our trip the Ministry of Tourism had indicated that the army maintained for rescue use an Alouette III helicopter with the capability to land at over 18,000 feet. We radioed the deputy commissioner (the ranking government official) in Skardu to say that the necessity for an air evacuation was imminent.

On July 9, Akbar was no better. Rob told us that he was unlikely to survive a tedious ground evacuation. Only four days' worth of I.V. fluids remained. A telegram was sent to the commissioner in Skardu requesting immediate helicopter transport from base camp, Abruzzi base camp, or Concordia. Plans were made for Wick to go out with Akbar so that he could coordinate the retreat march from the other end. But at the time of evening radio contact, we received no confirmation of the flight. Manzoor learned that the commissioner had not used his specially established mountain-rescue authority to order the helicopter directly from the army. Instead he had gone through his own superior, who in turn had to contact the Ministry of Tourism in Rawalpindi. The ministry was then responsible for contacting the army. Rob sent a strong telegram to the United States Embassy requesting their aid. Manzoor sent another to the army and the Ministry of Tourism. A rare clear day wasted.

Early on the morning of July 10 word was received that a helicopter was on its way to K2 base camp! Wick packed furiously and the rest of us stomped a helipad into the snow. For a windsock they used a tent stuff sack tied to a ski pole. Long hours passed. Finally Manzoor radioed Skardu and discovered that the pilot had just returned from another mountain rescue, the first of the year. He had flown to Paiyu camp where he had picked up a man with a broken leg from a French expedition. Manzoor talked directly to the pilot by radio; the man refused to fly above 11,000 feet. "Call me when you have your patient at that level," the pilot said abruptly. Base camp was fifty miles and a week's walking on glaciers from the 11,000-foot level. Manzoor had seen the same helicopter land Prime Minister Bhutto at 15,500 feet for the opening of a highway pass. With increasing frustration, more telegrams were drafted. That evening word was received that the Ministry of Tourism had convinced the Ministry of Defense to issue an order for a helicopter. Since there was no indication of where it would land, the team planned to carry Akbar down to Concordia at 14,900 feet. At 4:45 A.M. on yet another clear morning, Akbar was bound into a sled and hauled down the glacier by twelve HAPs. Half the team accompanied them. The others remained in camp to wait for the porters, expected to arrive on July 15. In the steep part of the ice fall Akbar walked supported by a HAP on either side. On the loose rock moraine below, the largest of the HAPs, Mohammed Hussain, carried Akbar on his shoulders. Mohammed, now nearly fifty years old, was the same Balti strong-man who had carried George Bell, suffering from frostbite, the many long miles down the Baltoro in 1953. By noon our group had reached Concordia. The trek from Concordia to base camp had taken eleven days on the approach march; we had covered the distance in a little more than seven hours. No helicopter came. Yet another clear day was lost.

Transporting Akbar

On the morning of July 12 Akbar felt worse. His stomach pains were back and he was badly dehydrated. Rob placed him on I.V. fluids again. Akbar spun his finger in the air, made a whirring noise like a helicopter, looked at Rob quizzically, and said, "No, sahib?" Rob tried valiantly to translate the concept of "maybe" into Balti. Before noon a string of eighty porters arrived, led by Ghulam Rasul and bound for base camp. Akbar broke down and cried when he saw them, and tears were in their eyes when they greeted him. Soon they were gone and the camp seemed empty. The longest spell of clear weather was still continuing.

Akbar being carried by Mohmud Hussain

That afternoon Jim sent out the following telegram from base camp:

WE HAVE BEEN WAITING FIVE DAYS. MUST EVACUATE HIGH ALTITUDE PORTER IMMEDIATELY. LIFE OR DEATH MATTER. SEND HELICOPTER TO CONCORDIA 15000 FEET FOR LIFT OFF. URGENT.

One copy was sent to the U.S. Embassy, another went to the Ministry of Tourism, and a third went to Jim's personal friend, Senator Edward Kennedy. Toward evening a reply came from the army repeating that evacuation must take place at 11,000 feet or below. Some of the team thought that it had been a mistake to identify the victim as a porter in the telegram. How else could we explain the

Akbar's Plight 271

government's refusal to evacuate a desperately ill man from a broad, flat area at an elevation lower than that at which they landed their own prime minister?

While we exchanged radio contacts with the group at base camp and talked angrily of how human failings in the government could cost a man's life, Akbar himself was remarkably calm. The events of the past days had presumably shown him that Allah's will was more likely to be expressed through the doctor sahib than the government's noisy flying machine. He seemed to accept his fate with equanimity: the helicopter would not come for him. It was just another facet of the inevitability of existence. He had lived on the ground, he would die on the ground, but now he was ready to try walking home.

2 Concordia Again

I was one of the five team members who descended with Akbar to wait for the helicopter. On the morning of July 12, when the eighty porters passed through on their way to pick up our equipment at base camp, they delivered a large batch of mail. I was deeply moved by one bulky envelope from my mother. It contained my ninety-year-old father's ashes and a note asking me to spread them below K2.

My father had been one of those rare people who never complained about old age. For him, the sun was always rising, and he had busied himself with many projects until he was well into his eighties. My mother's letter described the expression on his face after death as th fullest look of peace and serenity she had ever seen. "There was not a sign of a wrinkle—it was smooth like marble—absolutely *beautiful.*"

For several hours I gazed about Concordia. The chaotic jumble of ice and rock, far removed from human habitation, seemed most remote from my father's life. Although he had greatly enjoyed hiking in the mountains, the rugged world above timberline had never attracted him.

K2 from Concordia, on return trip

From a distance dark moraines alternated with white snow like the patterns on a zebra's back. Close at hand, each moraine was composed of strikingly different colored rocks which had been torn by the ice from widely separated mountainsides. Our camp was perched on a rather drab crest of grayish granitoid gneiss, but as I wandered eastward I crossed yellowish sandstones, reddish conglomerates, flat-black hornfels, and velvety black slates. Finally, I came to a moraine that was nearly pure white marble. Here I released my father's ashes to the winds. The old face that had been lineless and marble-like in death met the virgin marble that flowed from the high peaks through the world's greatest mountain sanctuary.

Concordia was vast and wild. Its tranquility was broken only by the rare passage of an expedition crawling like an army of ants across the floor of a palace. During our months in the mountains we had not heard a single aircraft pass overhead. Although now we all yearned for the arrival of a helicopter to save Akbar's life, each of us valued the silence of this wild place.

I spent an hour by myself on the highest rock of the moraine thinking about my father, my life, and the conclusion of the expedition. Although my father had spent most of his life teaching speech at the University of California, his training had been in philosophy and theology. I tried to remember a sermon he had given on a Sunday morning to more than a hundred people on a Sierra Club pack trip when I was young. Titled "Mountains and the Human Spirit," his theme had been the powerful beneficial effect that the mountains have always had on human endeavors. He mentioned how mountains had provided security from attack for ancient peoples and how the Latin saying *montani semper liberi*, "mountaineers are always free," had survived from those times. The ancients considered mountains to be the thrones of their gods, and the words of an old Hebrew poet, "I will lift up mine eyes unto the hills," reflected this belief into modern times. My father talked of how mountains had also represented a sense of mastery that was cherished as a symbol of achievement, but he did not consider this their most important value. He saw that from time immemorial human beings had gained something special from mountain solitude. People had gone to mountain retreats to clarify and purify their motives, make firm their resolves, and build up their courage. Even in the modern age—then the 1950s—he saw that people returned from mountain sojourns with a new wholeness of personality that was nearly impossible to realize in the complex bustle of civilization.

I felt quite empty. We had neither achieved mastery nor improvement of our personalities on our expedition to K2. Now that all chances for climbing the mountain were gone, I vowed to work to bring the team together, to make it possible for us to return home as friends. I knew that since the Freds' revolt, Jim Whittaker had managed the expedition in an increasingly benevolent manner, but he alone could not close rifts that had been growing for months. Renewal of the team feeling could only be achieved by the conscious effort of each one of us.

Our failure on K2 had become official on July 3. A few days earlier, Jim had obtained the consensus of all the team (with the exception of Rob, who was treating Akbar in base camp) that the summons to the porters should be sent out on July 6 if a route to Camp III had not been established by then. In the event that the route did open up so that we could climb and carry loads onto the upper ridge, we would stay on for several more weeks. Having been free of pneumonia for only a few days when this agreement was reached, I chose to descend from Camp I to base camp and take the necessary photos of products that had been donated to the expedition. Lou, Wick, Leif, and Steve waited for the weather to clear in Camp II.

The morning of the third had been the finest of the expedition; the sky was absolutely clear and there was not a breath of wind. Through my 500mm lens I had watched four dots move up the ridge from four miles away. Wick later described that final day of climbing in his diary:

Got away at 8:00 A.M. and headed up the moderate slopes above camp; snow very soft and deep. . . . The only way to make any upward progress was to clear away about eight to ten inches with a mitten and then step upward. Only about one out of every five steps hit anything solid. Laboriously slow. . . . About two hundred feet from the base of the steep wall, Leif took over—one of the only times in the expedition that someone else has kicked steps with us (except Jim between Camps I and II). But Leif is so light that I kept plunging through behind him. And where I didn't, Lou did.

Lou stayed in the lead through the lower section of fixed rope. . . . I went past him . . . feeling very strong . . . making the entire climb from Camp II (to the old high point) in two hours and ten minutes. Lou and Leif came up; Steve was somewhere below.

I continued up. . . . It got very steep, approaching the vertical. An easy stretch at lower elevations, it was quite hard up there nearing 22,000 feet. It was a matter of carefully picking your way upward and not relying on the loose rocks. . . . I finally got a piton into a good crack and felt much better. I was on the verge of sewing-machine leg a couple of times but managed to suppress it. The hardest move was getting up around a big rock. I had to jam my arm into a four-inch crack to move up. A good-sized rock alongside the big one was loose; I nearly pulled it off on top of myself. . . . I went a little higher and saw for the first time the rest of the pinnacled ridge. Our further progress along the ridge, except for reaching the top of the first pinnacle, seemed out of the question. Extremely steep on both sides (75 to 80 feet), the ridge was a knife-edge between the pinnacles, and the two pinnacles I could see, including the highest, looked possible only if one were to spend a hell of a long time in getting over them—clearly out of the question for load-carrying and maybe not even climbable. The quest for height on K2 was over. . . .

The three of us proceeded to take turns climbing the last twenty-five feet to the top of the first pinnacle. Lou went first, but because the top was so small, only stood up and looked over it at armpit height. Leif, following Lou, went up a bit higher by throwing his left leg over the narrow top so that he straddled it like a sawhorse. When my turn came, I did the same thing. The exposure was terrible. I have never been on such a small summit with awesome views in all directions. To the east, K2 blotted out the sky with the remaining pinnacles in the foreground. The drop to China was as unbelievable as it was steep. Over seven thousand feet of sheer nothingness. . . . It was beautiful up there and a fine way to end the serious climbing of the expedition.

Leif concurred with Wick's impression of the route, saying that "it is absolutely clear this route truly ends here!" Leif did not, however, feel like an equal partner on that final day's climbing, and he de-

Lou and Leif nearing the 22,000 foot high point

Jim Whittaker at 21,000 feet, looking into China

274　END OF MANY ROADS

scribed his brief stint at leading by writing, "Even I am allowed to break trail."

The next day both Dianne and Manzoor climbed up to Camp II to have a look into China. They were the final members of the team to reach Savoia Pass at 20,400 feet. After another, shorter storm the evacuation of the mountain began.

When Leif returned to base camp, he was eager to try climbing the Angelus, a beautiful 22,490-foot snow pyramid directly above camp. He wanted to make the climb sometime during the nine days before the porters came. He estimated that the climb would take two or three days, but his biggest question was, "Will they let me?" Rob, Manzoor, and I also wanted to climb the peak, but Jim, Lou, Dianne, and the Freds had no interest in it. Wick was not sure whether he wanted to go.

Can't blame them [he wrote in his diary]. I would be looking for an Angelus, too, if I hadn't had the climbing with Lou that I've had. . . . One can also see Rowell making that climb the big event of the expedition. With one of the biggest reputations among us, Galen simply did not perform well on the main objective: finding a route up K2's West Ridge. Admittedly his sickness played a major role in his nonperformance, but it doesn't account for everything. He could have, for instance, come up here for the final effort, instead of bolting for base camp with the Freds when the decision was made for the porters to come in. And if he had not recovered enough to come up here, how in hell does he think he is fit for a serious attempt on the Angelus? If they go, maybe Lou and I should go too—following behind, of course, so that they can kick steps up through deep snow for a change.

The Angelus

Jim told us that we could not climb the Angelus until base camp was packed up for the incoming porters. We worked like beavers for two days, and then it was decided that the matter should be voted on by the whole group. For the first time in weeks, the weather had remained excellent for several days. At the meeting Jim said that we could endanger the whole team's departure if anything happened to us. Lou said that everyone should forget about climbing while a human life was at stake—Akbar's. The Freds, who were all for our climb but did not wish to take part in it, remained silent. So did Leif, who didn't want to make waves. Rob said that whatever the decision, he would have to stay down with Akbar until he was evacuated. Wick later recorded the decision: "It was the consensus of the team that they should not go."

In his usually restrained manner, Leif later wrote in his diary, "It is decided 'formally' that Galen and I *not* climb the Angelus because every hand may be needed in the evacuation of Akbar. Lou is particularly vehement. Can it make that much difference, with twenty men available anyway? Both Galen and I are deeply disappointed, for the weather is excellent. . . . It is sad not to have freedom in such a marvelous place. At night the sky is filled with more stars than I have ever seen."

I, on the other hand, was far less temperate. In my diary I wrote, "Mistakenly, I thought I was coming on a mountaineering expedi-

Concordia Again   275

tion, but it is more like a high-altitude chain gang where order is maintained from without, rather than from pursuit of a common goal. . . . What a pity to have to beg to climb!"

For a while I even considered soloing the Angelus. The route looked straightforward and I thought I could make it with one bivouac. I sorted the necessary gear and kept it in a sack next to my sleeping bag. But over the next two days, I came around to Leif's way of thinking. The Angelus was a nice climb, but it was not worth doing if it would cause a major incident with the rest of the team. With the weight of the K2 climb off our heads, Leif said, "These last days in the high mountains could be filled with relaxed joy. They are not, but they will become worse for everyone if people leave camp against orders." I decided to bury the hatchet and try not to mention the Angelus again in front of those who did not favor the climb.

Now, the five of us at Concordia—Wick, Lou, Rob, Steve, and myself—were getting along fine. We were no longer divided by varying degrees of optimism or conflicting tactics for reaching the summit of K2. I hoped we would stay united while we evacuated Akbar and completed a trouble-free retreat march.

Akbar was so thin that his cheeks seemed to touch each other. He stayed in the tent during most of his first two days at Concordia, but on the third he fetched water from a nearby lakelet and gave one of the HAPs a haircut. When I pointed to my hair, the longest on the expedition, he laughed and motioned for me to sit on the rock next to him. During my haircut, he looked off in the distance and excitedly said that he saw another expedition. I peered through binoculars, but could see nothing. An hour later, we all watched a large expedition moving single file on the crest of a moraine about a mile from us, bound for the upper Baltoro. It passed on without a halt.

After my haircut Akbar pointed in the opposite direction—toward K2—and said, "Bara sahib and memsahib," which meant leader and lady. After several minutes of looking through ten-power binoculars, I spotted two tiny dots moving down the moraine at least two miles away. Only half an hour later, and then through the binoculars, was I able to recognize Jim and Dianne. I now understood why George Schaller, the zoologist, always hired natives from nearby villages to help him spot wildlife.

The Polish Broad Peak expedition had its base camp on the Godwin-Austen Glacier between K2 and Concordia. Individually or in small groups, all of us had dropped in to say hello en route to Concordia. The Polish were very cordial and served us tea in a large diningtent that had American *Playboy* centerfolds taped to its walls. Only six of their 150 Balti porters had reached the base camp, delaying them considerably. Nevertheless, they were making good progress on the mountain during the long clear spell and we could see the tiny figures of their high climbers moving at about 22,000 feet between Camps II and III.

When our entire team plus the porters finally gathered again at Concordia, we learned that Manzoor had received yet another telegram from the army, stating, "Landing at 15,000 feet impossible."

Realizing that it was futile to wait any longer for the helicopter, we began walking down the Baltoro. A heavy rain was falling as we began our descent.

That evening we reached Ghoro, the camp where the burning of the money had occurred on the approach. We found that the porters' attitude was entirely different on the return. They were cheerfully prepared to double each day's march the entire way home without a day of rest. The difference was that they were aiming toward their homes rather than away from them.

On the way to Ghoro we had passed a widely spread out expedition of Austrian college students bound for unclimbed 24,750-foot Skyang Kangri near K2. After we had stopped for the night, the expedition's young leader, Ferdinand Deutschman, straggled into our camp with two porters. He was completely soaked by the rain and had no tent. Since he was almost sure that he would not be able to catch up with his group by nightfall, I invited him to stay for dinner. I did not realize that some of the team did not share my hospitable inclinations. Deutschman watched a large can of chicken and noodles heat over the stove, and then saw eleven portions being served to our team. I didn't realize what was happening until

Mitre Peak, from Concordia

the can was empty and someone thrust a package of freeze-dried casserole in his hand, saying, "We don't have enough dinner for an extra portion, but here, we'll have some boiling water to mix this in a few minutes." Deutschman accepted the package with a calm "thank you," and turned toward me with a look of shock and disgust. I offered him some of my dinner, but he quickly refused, saying, "Your friends do not wish me to have it."

Deutschman spoke fluent English and poured forth a great flow of information about events in the Karakoram that were unknown to us. The expedition that we had seen pass Concordia was Hans Schell's Austrian group, bound for the American route on Hidden Peak. A few days behind them, Reinhold Messner and Peter Habeler were also on their way to Hidden Peak to attempt the unclimbed north face alpine style. We had previously heard over the radio that the French had failed on Gasherbrum II because of great porter problems. Deutschman now told me that they had climbed the peak, but had somehow lost one man in the process. We also learned that the British had failed on the Trango Towers and that the quiet village of Askole had become a traffic jam of expeditions.

I suggested that Deutschman stay with us for the night in whichever tent had the most room. Favorable answers were not forthcoming from the team powers, and Deutschman was just about ready to walk on into the night when Manzoor intervened and said, "You will stay with me. I have plenty of room in my tent." Before breakfast the next morning, I heard Deutschman's footsteps as he left camp. I realized that our team had a long way to go toward achieving any unity.

That day we walked two stages to Urdukas. Through the veil of falling rain, I became aware of the most intense color I had ever seen. It shocked my vision more than the brightest sunset or the bluest sky would have done. It was simply the color of life, green, emanating from the hanging meadows next to the ice. For months I had lived without seeing it; now it rushed back into my mind with incredible force. I took several pictures of my vivid green; when I saw them later I realized that the hillside had actually been quite drab, muted by the falling rain. But to my green-starved brain the sight of those hillsides brought forth images of green vegetables, meadows and forests, oceans and emeralds, and home.

Urdukas

When we had left Urdukas in May the campsite was buried under a foot of snow. Now we found a green paradise of steep meadows and wildflowers resembling the lower slopes of Alaskan mountains in summer. The two regions even shared, as a gift from the ice age, many of the same species of flowers: fireweed, cinquefoil, aster, forget-me-not, gentian, and heather.

I found something else that reminded me of home. Camped at Urdukas was a group of trekkers from Mountain Travel, an adventure travel agency with offices only two blocks from my house in California. I was extremely surprised to meet more than half a dozen people I knew from the States, including a man who had climbed in Yosemite with John Salathé, the father of modern big-wall climbing, and a grandmother whom I had once guided up a difficult Grade IV climb. Their leader, Allen Steck, was an old friend of mine and editor of *Ascent* magazine, to which I have been a frequent contributor. I spent several pleasant hours in their tent, waiting for the rest of our expedition to arrive.

The first of our group to arrive at Urdukas had been a pleasant surprise. Moving through the twelve miles of wet, loose boulders with the grace of a cat, Akbar had led Wick, Lou, and Fred into camp before anyone else! He, of course, carried no pack, but that he had so quickly regained the strength to walk through rugged terrain was miraculous.

Urdukas resembled a somewhat random version of Stonehenge, with its giant boulders lying haphazardly on the smooth grass. We never gave a moment's thought to how those boulders happened to arrive there until we saw an incredible natural spectacle. Rocks as big as boxcars, loosened by torrential rains, began spewing from a chute a thousand feet above us and several hundred yards to the side. "Never have I seen anything so big, falling so fast with a roar to match its size," Wick wrote in his diary about the first big one. They continued to fall throughout the night, and we feared for the safety of the campsite.

Our cardboard porter boxes were so wet that we decided to stay in Urdukas for an extra day to let them dry. When the sun came out the next morning I began to see the large boulders around camp in a new light. As I looked at a long crack in the largest boulder, one of the porters saw me and said, "Bonatti climb!" Several of our porters had been with the Italians on both K2 and Gasherbrum IV, so the porter's remark that Bonatti had climbed the crack was probably true. Many of them talked of Bonatti as if he were a god; their awe of him was probably due to the oft-repeated tale of his emergence unscathed from the bivouac in the open at 26,000 feet on K2 while his native companion suffered severe frostbite.

To the delight of the watching Baltis, I climbed the crack unroped. I knew it wasn't very difficult, because I had climbed it on the way in. The Baltis cheered their approval, then led me uphill to a shorter, steeper crack. "Bonatti climb," they repeated with great enthusiasm. Fifteen feet up the crack, hanging from an overhang by my wedged forearm above a bed of pointed rocks, I gave up. The Baltis led me still higher on the hill to a giant rock with an absolutely flawless overhanging side; it was capped with a ceiling fifty feet above the ground. "Bonatti climb," they repeated with precisely the same expression. I had been had.

Later in the day I borrowed a rope from Lou in order to climb on the biggest rocks. A large group of Baltis assembled to watch. Leif and I belayed each other with the safety rope while Steve shot film. I was very close to my limit of ability, but I struggled up one steep face that had an overhanging start. Neither Leif nor Steve could make more than one move off the ground. One of the Baltis asked to try and promptly fell off, to the jeers of his companions. Several other Baltis also tried and failed. Just as the fans were losing interest, one Balti approached and asked if I would give the rope to the man who could climb the face. The rope was one hundred feet of

Balti climbing a difficult rockface barefoot, Urdukas

thin 7mm; we originally brought it with us to fix for the porters on the steep parts of the icefall just below base camp. Smugly confident that none of the Baltis could make the climb, I agreed. The game was great fun. One by one the Baltis were tied into the safety rope and one by one they fell. They showed an amazing ability to cling to the overhang by their fingers for long minutes, but none could make the delicate step onto a small edge with their bare feet. We were all surprised when a man with a bouquet of flowers in his hat hoisted himself up the overhang on pure arm strength; he then curled a big toe around a small knob at a point higher than anyone else had reached. After making the single most difficult move of the climb, he grabbed the rope and hauled himself up for a few feet. I tried to explain that he had broken the rules by holding onto the rope, but he vehemently insisted that he had made the climb. Sensing the mood of the crowd and remembering our need to keep on good terms with the Baltis, I made a compromise that was accepted by all. I cut off thirty feet of the rope and gave it to the climber. Everyone cheered and we descended to camp for dinner.

When I told Lou that I had given away a third of the rope, he exploded. For a moment I thought he was going to hit me, but instead he loudly berated my dishonesty for giving away a piece of his personal property. He said that he had carried the rope from base camp and had a special use for it which was now not possible. I told him that I had not realized the rope was so valuable to him, that it was the same rope which we had used for tying porter boxes, that we had already given away seventy-two segments to the Baltis the day before we reached base camp, and that I would pay for or replace the rope if he wished.

"I don't want to hear an explanation," Lou told me. "Just admit you were wrong." Begrudgingly, I did.

That night I went to sleep discouraged. Leif wrote in his diary, "Whenever we have a good time on this trip, some unfortunate aftermath occurs." The only positive note was that no one had fanned the brief argument by taking sides. Even Jim remained aloof from his twin's dispute and it died a fast, natural death.

In the morning Fred Dunham and I left before anyone else and reached Paiyu camp by noon, enjoying a quiet walk together. Near the toe of the glacier we met a French woman, Simone Badier, who was walking up to Urdukas for a look around. She was part of the Paiyu Peak expedition, and she told us that the leader's wife had suffered a broken ankle before the helicopter had come to pick up their man with the badly broken leg. When the injured woman hobbled to the helicopter, the pilot had refused to take her out, saying that he had orders to pick up only one person, and that she didn't look injured enough to require evacuation anyway. She was still waiting, and the expedition's effort to climb the mountain had been abandoned.

Porter near death with perforated ulcer

At Paiyu Fred and I met Captain Liaquat Ali Shah, liaison officer for the Italian Grand Cathedral Expedition. He told me that they had had a wonderfully successful expedition and had climbed the great granite bastion of the Baltoro by two different routes. The Italians had taught him how to climb, and he himself had made the summit by the hardest route—the 6,000-foot Baltoro rock face.

We were unaware of the drama unfolding in our own party behind us. A porter named Jaffar had collapsed on the trail not far from Urdukas. Rob examined him and discovered his condition to be similar to Akbar's at its worst: deep coma, no detectable blood pressure, shallow respiration, rigid abdomen, and profuse sweating. The main difference in the situation was that Rob did not have his medical gear. It was far ahead on the backs of porters bound for Paiyu.

Rob strongly suspected a perforated ulcer and sent runners ahead to bring back his gear. Two hours later his small traveling case was brought back, but his larger boxes containing such things as intravenous fluids did not appear. Three Baltis were recruited to carry Jaffar on their backs, but one stocky man, appropriately named "Mustagh," did 80 percent of the work. By the time they reached Liliwa camp, the midpoint of the day's trek, the Baltis prepared to stop for the night. With a swish of his hand across his neck, Rob convinced them that Jaffar would be dead by morning unless they carried on into the night.

Rob was tortured by the thought that Jaffar's condition was basically treatable. To prevent his immediate death Rob only had to replace the huge fluid losses with intravenous fluids. Instead, he watched Jaffar slowly die as he was carried along; his blood pressure gradually fell and his pulse rate rose. More than once Rob thought that he himself could not continue the pace carrying his seventy-pound pack in the dark; every step was on loose rock and only a thin crescent moon lit the way. But he renewed his strength by watching

Concordia Again 281

Mustagh carrying the seemingly lifeless 140-pound bundle without complaint, mile after endless mile through the night. Rob was nearly certain that the march was futile and that Mustagh was already bearing a corpse. At 10:00 P.M., as they neared camp, a HAP arrived carrying the box of medical gear. Rob discovered that Jaffar was still alive, administered a few drugs on the spot, and then rushed the final distance into camp at Paiyu.

Inside a hastily erected tent, Rob gave Jaffar vasopressors and intravenous fluids. As if by a miracle, the sick man's vital signs reappeared, and he regained consciousness. An abdominal tap confirmed a perforated ulcer, and Rob's job was now to keep Jaffar alive until he could be evacuated to a hospital for surgery. Once again, a life was dependent on the arrival of a helicopter, but this time there were only enough I.V. fluids for one day.

Meanwhile, Rob could hear the sounds of joking and laughter. The Italian expedition was having a party, complete with imported wines, and several of our team had joined them. But Rob spent another all-night vigil with death. He thought of how much the scene resembled a big city, where tragedy existed alongside celebration with the participants in each unaware of the other.

The Italians had invited all of us to join in their festivities but only Wick, Fred Stanley, and I attended. It was a joyous affair and even with the language barrier we got along famously. Wick later wrote in his diary, "Perhaps the finest evening of the expedition."

One of the Italians, Giacomo Stefani, had once been an American Field Service exchange student in Minnesota. He motioned me off to the side and said in perfect English, "There is something I should tell you. Our captain did not make the summit. He tried to climb but he gave up at a very low camp. He said that unless we took pictures of him on a point of rock and said that he reached the top, he would confiscate all our film and make it very difficult to get out of Pakistan with our equipment. Please don't tell any Pakistanis until we are safely out of the country."

The next morning we set up our radio transmitter, and Manzoor once again asked for a helicopter. At the request of the captain, he also radioed a message to the government and the media that a Pakistani had climbed the face of the Grand Cathedral.

Nearly certain that no helicopter would arrive that day, we planned to move on, leaving Rob and Manzoor with the sick man. They would catch up after the situation was resolved by either evacuation, surgery, slow cure, or death. Only hours of intravenous fluids remained, and Rob contemplated mixing his own when they ran out. Several porters stayed back to carry out Jaffar, the tent, and the medical gear.

The river was in flood, and I was walking above it near Bardomal when I thought I heard the crashing of a rock avalanche. Fearing that I would be swept into the waters, I ducked under an overhang just as the source of the noise passed over me: a helicopter.

Our bitter telegrams about Akbar had been brought to the attention of the prime minister, who had ordered the army to do everything humanly possible to complete the evacuation. Although pre-

Porters fording a stream

sumably this did not include flying above 11,000 feet, the army had kept its helicopter on standby in Skardu, waiting for us to radio when Akbar had been brought down. Paiyu was precisely at the 11,000-foot level, and the pilot assumed that the porter he was evacuating had been carried from base camp. He congratulated Rob on keeping the man alive for twelve days, then helped load Jaffar onto his ship. Neither Rob nor Manzoor said anything to contradict the pilot's impression, especially since they had yet another delicate request to make: would the pilot please fly about a mile downstream and pick up a French woman in serious condition?

Act Two of the evacuation drama was a masterful scene: four Italians carried a woman, screaming in feigned pain, to the door of the helicopter. Halfway around the world her performance might have won an Oscar; here the beautiful Frenchwoman's prize was a hospital bed, nine days late. But she wasn't the only winner that day. Jaffar was brought into the Skardu hospital with the I.V. bottle still flowing life into his veins. He was operated on for a perforated ulcer and recovered quickly.

One reason for the ridiculously low 11,000-foot ceiling now became obvious. The army weighted down the small helicopter with a pilot, a co-pilot, and a flight engineer.

During the day of the evacuation I met an expedition of older men from Switzerland. One spoke English quite well and began asking me pointed questions.

"Are you with the Americans on K2?"

"Yes."

"Are you the first in your group?"

"No."

He stopped for a moment with a distant, sad look on his face before asking, "Where is your leader, Jim Whittaker?"

"About a mile behind me."

"Are you sure?"

"Yes. Why do you ask?"

Once again the man paused and thought for a minute, obviously feeling very uncomfortable. Finally he queried, "Who is in front of you on the trail today?"

"Lou Whittaker and a high-altitude porter."

"*Lou* Whittaker?"

"Yes. Jim Whittaker's twin brother."

A smile of tremendous relief crossed the man's face. He introduced himself as Dolf Reist. I instantly recognized the name of the man who had made the second ascent of Mount Everest, in 1956. He knew Jim quite well and had been horrified to see his friend walk down the trail past him in the remote Karakoram without even stopping to say hello. Lou, who did not like to fraternize with people from other expeditions, had decided that it slowed him down too much to acknowledge everyone he passed, especially as he found himself wending his way through an increasingly crowded logjam of expeditions and their porters. Later that afternoon, Dolf and the real Jim had a warm reunion on the trail.

On the walk in, the side stream from the Panmah Glacier had

been knee-deep and easily wadeable. Now, as the summer heat melted the ice, it roared along at perhaps 100 times its old volume. We had to walk five miles out of our way up a side canyon to where a rope bridge, built of twisted vines, crossed a narrow point in the gorge. By evening, five expeditions were camped at the bridge: ourselves, the American trekkers, the Itàlians, a small Japanese group, and the smallest team of all—Reinhold Messner and Peter Habeler.

Ever since the Austrian leader had told us of Messner and Habeler's bold plan for Hidden Peak, we had privately speculated on their odds of returning alive. Most of us tried to imagine ourselves attempting a three-day ascent of an 8,000-meter peak without oxygen, and we concluded that the pair's chances were not good.

Meeting them changed my mind. These were no swaggering superclimbers who believed in their own immortality as they blustered their way toward an early end. They seemed to have an intense inner calm, derived from a full understanding of their own limits. Messner had the modesty and quiet confidence of a successful scientist. Habeler, outwardly more intense, projected a sense of precision and absolute control. He was the kind of man I would like to see wearing the pilot's cap each time I board a commercial flight. I ended up talking more to Habeler because his English was far better than Messner's.

During the fifties, when giant expeditions were trying to find the easiest routes up each of the world's 8,000-meter peaks, Himalayan experts had dismissed the north face of Hidden Peak as too difficult for the contemporary standards. Now, Habeler told me, the pair planned to climb the route unroped. They would establish an advance base camp at Gasherbrum La, 19,356 feet; then they planned

Wick, Jim, and Messner meet on the trail, above Askole

to rush up 7,000 feet to the summit and come back down, all in three days. When Habeler described their tactics, they no longer sounded rash. In 1939 Pasang Kikuli had climbed up 6,700 feet to 23,000 feet on K2 in a single day. This modern pair proposed to climb 3- or 4,000 feet on the first day above Gasherbrum La, bivouac, and then climb and descend the remaining 3- or 4,000 feet on the following day. Unlike Pasang Kikuli, they would be covering new ground rather than following fixed ropes toward an established camp.

Habeler and Messner found that each traditional expedition item became unnecessary only when others were discarded at the same time. No high-altitude porters meant no need for fixed ropes on steep sections; this in turn meant no need for ropes or hardware and no need for extra food for the extra time required to carry the extra gear. Oxygen was not even considered, partly because they planned to spend only one day above 23,000 feet. They had brought only two hundred pounds of gear from Europe; with that and the food purchased in Pakistan they required only twelve porters.

On the other side of the ledger, they had no back-up systems whatever. Their plans were dependent on their own perfect health and a three-day spell of good weather as well as a phenomenal physical performance by both and a climbable route. A sprained ankle or a lost crampon could mean death high on the mountain, but these were risks they accepted. They planned to climb not at their limits, but a cut below. They hoped they would always remain in control of the situation, and if they did not reach the top by 4:00 P.M. on their summit day, they would descend rather than chance a bivouac in the open near the summit without the support of others below.

Peter Habeler had visited the United States and worked as a ski instructor in Jackson, Wyoming, during the 1968–69 winter. The following summer he met George Lowe, one of America's top alpine climbers, who was working as a backcountry ranger in the Grand Tetons. Lowe was well known for his endurance and a few years later made an amazing one-day winter ascent of the Grand Teton from the floor of Jackson Hole.

Lowe invited Habeler to join him on a new route he had been eyeing up the direct north face of nearby Mount Moran. Hiking at high altitude in the backcountry almost every day, Lowe thought he was in excellent condition—until he tried to keep up with Habeler, who consistently outdistanced him on the steep approach to the climb. When they reached the cliff, Habeler began climbing unroped with a rucksack. Lowe, breathing heavily, tried to keep up. At one point he came to an overhang and saw Habeler waiting for him above. Lowe tried it, backed down, and asked Habeler for a rope from above. "Are you sure? It's not that hard." Lowe said that he was sure, and without further discussion Habeler passed down the rope. Lowe tried it again and fell off—held, of course, by Habeler's belay. By noon they reached the summit, having completed an unclimbed route that Lowe had guessed might take up to two days.

On the descent Lowe could not keep up. When he came to the top of a steep fifty-five-degree snow couloir, he saw two parallel tracks going straight down until they disappeared from sight 1,500 feet below. The couloir was normally climbed with ropes, ice axes, and crampons. Habeler had done a standing glissade on his heels in perfect control. Lowe descended far more slowly, kicking steps and facing into the slope. He found Habeler to be a complete gentleman, but not a well-matched climbing companion.

Coincidentally, both Lowe and Habeler visited the Karakoram for the first time in 1975, Lowe as a member of the American Lobsang Expedition that had first been bound for the Trango Towers.

In 1969 Habeler had also made the first non-American ascent of the Salathé Wall of El Capitan in Yosemite, one of the world's most highly regarded rock climbs. His companion, a young Englishman named Doug Scott, was also in the Karakoram in 1975; he was leading an expedition to a huge rock wall on 21,040-foot Sosbun Brakk up the nearby Biafo Glacier. Due to porter problems and flight delays, Scott's expedition had failed to reach even the base of its objective. He had rushed his retreat in order to join Chris Bonington's postmonsoon attempt on the southwest face of Everest.

On the El Capitan climb, Scott had not always enjoyed climbing with Habeler and later remarked, "He was a smart little bugger, always plastering his blond hair down with the palms of his hands. Unknown to him, however, he was rubbing aluminum dye [from handling carabiners] all over his face. In the end he looked as though he'd spent the day in a coal mine. If he'd been anyone other than a bloody kraut, I'd have gone down." Habeler had quite the opposite experience when he began climbing with Messner. The two were nearly perfectly matched in skill, judgment, and endurance. Hidden Peak would test that harmony to the fullest.

Wishing the duo luck, we headed down the trail toward Askole the next morning.

3   At the Heels of Happiness

Askole was so pleasantly uncivilized, in the modern sense of the word, that I was not sure if we had really reached civilization at all. On other expeditions the return to human habitation had always meant a clash of values. I would walk down a trail, then quite suddenly reach pavement, and step into a chaos of motor vehicles, powerlines, and Coca-Cola signs.

Askole, however, represented that beautiful in-between point at which the human race had hovered for most of its development up until the past two centuries. Like an ideal garden, the village was dominated by vegetation yet ordered by the discerning labor of the

Nightfall at Concordia, with Chogolisa reflected in a glacial lake

K2, seen from Concordia camp, on a rare clear night

A crescent moon passes behind an unnamed peak above base camp

Overleaf: Moonlight on Concordia camp, looking down the Baltoro Glacier at Paiyu Peak

A full moon over Mitre Peak

Gasherbrum IV at night

The ever-changing spectacle of sunset on Broad Peak

Askole

human hand. There were no machines. No wire fences or power lines. No telephones or tractors. No asphalt or concrete. No loud noises or square corners. Yet it was not paradise.

We entered Askole by a long shady lane lined with willows and sycamores. The village had a storybook setting, fronted by a river and backdropped by fields that abutted sheer cliffs. Water flowed in irrigation ditches and flowers dotted the edge of the path. Vast wheatfields were turned into smooth carpets of glowing green by the backlighting of the afternoon sun. Once again we set up camp in a courtyard fringed with ancient fences built from natural stone.

The residents of Askole were surprisingly physically fit. There were no fat people, but neither were there cases of serious malnutrition. The only visible and prevalent symptoms of illness were goiters from lack of iodine in the water. Excesses of any kind were few. The food and space in the village appeared to have been divided evenly until there was no more to go around. Life was balanced slightly on the minus side of abundance.

In the natural order of Askole, there were prices to be paid for such simple living. The women, like the flowers in the fields they worked, bloomed early in their youth, then faded and wilted rapidly from the long hours of labor. A girl of eighteen might look forty, and a woman of forty was rarely seen. If the population seemed younger on the average than one would expect, this was because death usually came before its time.

After only a few hours in the village, I came to the conclusion that Askole itself was dying. Outwardly it appeared beautiful and stable, but the fragile culture here had undergone changes during the two and a half months since our last visit, changes that could and probably would prove fatal.

At the Heels of Happiness 295

Crossing a rope bridge above Askole

The presence of many expeditions had caused the prices of some high-demand commodities to go much higher. Each succeeding expedition had contributed its share to this trend, the greatest impact coming from a *National Geographic* movie crew that lived in the village for quite some time. Wheat, eggs, meat, and poultry had doubled in price since May. Embroidery now cost up to four times more. Begging had previously been very rare, but now more than half the populace openly asked for candy and cigarettes.

The fine balance of Askole life had been disturbed by the huge influx of climbers into the area. The village didn't produce enough goods for the villagers and the hundreds of expeditioners. And the climbers did not help to replenish stocks as the residents did. In trade for Askole goods they paid money which could only be used many miles away. Askole had no marketplace because it normally had no surpluses. To the residents, folding money was nearly as useless as it had been to us on the flanks of K2. It could buy nothing if there was nothing to buy.

Askole was changing rapidly from a cashless, self-sufficient society which had no throw-away items into a competitive scramble for visitors' goods and dollars. The government believed that increasing the amount of money flowing into the villages could only help. Officials must have wondered why, since the reopening of the Karakoram, they have had to subsidize Askole with wheat in the winter. Subsidies had not normally been required to keep the people alive before, when everyone was considered very poor because they had no money.

The worst change was yet to come. Manzoor, an engineer who worked on roads for the army, told us that the government planned to build a road to Askole within the next five years. Our first reaction was doubt. If we had ever seen a gorge in which road-building would be impossible, this was it. Huge areas slid every few weeks and sheer cliffs hung out over the river. But high on the slopes, sometimes 1,500 feet above the water, such a road might be feasible. Leif wrote his impressions of what he felt was to be Askole's future:

Instead of that pleasant shady path through the greenery, jeeps will be able to hurl dust over the neighborhood. The wood plows and animals will give way to metals and noisy tractors. New houses—square, rectangular, tall—will rise and dominate over the modest, irregular stone cells now woven harmoniously into the landscape. The economy of wheat, barley, and apricots will change to money. The Askole mukluks, almost the exclusive footwear of the porters who took us to base at 17,600 fet, will give way to plastic and rubber shoes of inferior quality, produced far away. The independence of the community will be exchanged for communication and outside control. The health facilities of the region will improve—and the population will rise.

And yet, who were we to deny the villagers progress? Could we in good conscience deny them the very comforts of civilization to which we ourselves so eagerly returned? We realized that if Askole was to preserve the balance it had maintained for centuries, some agonizing decisions would have to be made. The easiest of these would be to reduce the number of expeditions allowed in and to control the artificially inflated rates of porter payment. An outside source of easy money was affecting the economy of the village as would the distribution of new currency which had nothing to back it up.

Social and economic concerns were only part of the picture. The land itself was suffering. At each place where our six hundred porters had stopped for the night and gathered firewood, the hillsides looked as if a swarm of giant locusts had passed through. By government regulation every expedition camped at exactly the same sites. On our approach, a three-day porter strike meant eighteen hundred turds. On our return march we smelled both Liliwa and Paiyu before we reached them. The Baltis had no understanding of hygiene. Acres surrounding Paiyu were scattered with feces. Once we even watched a man empty his bowels into the river while another man drank a few feet downstream. Without proper control, the Baltoro region could turn into the cesspool for the world's high mountains.

Turd field, Paiyu

I discussed some of these fears with Fred Dunham in Askole. He replied that "the only way to straighten out Pakistan is to totally destroy the culture and start all over again." I didn't agree. Fred, however, felt most bitter about the treatment our expedition had received at the hands of the Pakistanis. As we talked, Captain Shah,

Captain Shah

the Italian expedition's liaison officer, interrupted Fred to defend Pakistan. Fred was especially frustrated because he knew of the captain's false claim on the Grand Cathedral, but could not confront him about it without risking trouble for the Italians. When he finally uttered a four-letter word in reference to Pakistan, the captain turned livid and said, "You have challenged the honor of my country. I can arrest you for that. Our joint dinner tonight is off. I forbid my men to mix with your expedition!"

Fred stood his ground, and the captain threatened to hire "twenty-five coolies and beat you into submission."

After an hour of intense negotiation, Wick, Manzoor, and I managed to close the rift. That evening we joined the Italians in a wonderful feast of food and wine. The chicken, unfortunately, was so tough that more calories were lost in chewing than were gained in eating.

The atmosphere of the party was wonderful. Moonlight shone through an orderly row of poplars into our courtyard while an older Italian climber named Columbari played his accordian. The others sang, laughed, and poured wine. The evening ended with a beautiful Italian song of the mountains.

When we tried to leave Askole, we had new trouble. Many of the porters who had deserted us at Urdukas on the approach appeared. They demanded payment; we refused. Then they put pressure on our eighty porters, trying to convince them not to carry until all were paid. In an effort to get the porters moving, Jim promised the deserters half-wages; the offer was refused. When further discussion seemed fruitless, Wick, Lou, and Jim decided to use the same tactics that had worked before. If the porters refused to go on, we would burn everything we could not carry and leave nothing in the village. At first Manzoor refused to translate this threat for fear of angering the village Lambardar. Finally, under Wick's firm order, he did so. Soon thereafter the porters began to shoulder their loads. But, again, this was not the last we would see of the deserters.

When Lou and Wick reached the hot springs below Askole, Fred Dunham was already soaking in one of the pools. As Wick climbed into an adjoining pool, Fred said in a barely audible voice, "I'm sorry for what I've said and done."

Wick wasn't sure that he heard properly and asked Fred to repeat what he had said. Once again Fred said, "I'm sorry for what I've said and done."

"What's happening, Fred?" Wick replied. "Are you undergoing some kind of religious conversion in these holy waters?"

Fred didn't answer, and Wick wondered if the apology had been serious. Later that same day, Wick wrote, "Everyone seems to be in good spirits this close to the end, almost as though a conscious effort were being made to bury the friction of the past three months."

Two days later we reached the end of the trail and traveled the last fifty miles into Skardu by jeep. The rest house in which we had stayed before was now filled with expeditions waiting for the daily scheduled flight to Rawalpindi. One small room was available in the town's only other rest house. Jim and Dianne took it while the remainder of the team accepted an invitation from the British Trango Expedition to share their large room.

In one corner of the dark room, a British foursome sat at a table playing bridge. I recognized a small, graying man with a cigarette dangling from the corner of his mouth as Joe Brown, who had climbed Mustagh Tower with Ian McNaught-Davis in 1956 and had made the first ascent of Kanchenjunga, the third highest peak in the world. Brown was best known, not as a Himalayan climber, but as the top rockclimber of his generation. The Trango Tower required a blend of his two disciplines, since its sheer rock walls rose to over 20,000 feet.

Joe Brown and Ian McNaught-Davis

The small six-man expedition had failed only six hundred feet from the summit of the tower, for Martin Boysen had a climber's worst nightmare come true. While climbing a vertical crack about four inches wide, his knee became stuck and he could not free it. For two hours he hung from the crack at nearly 20,000 feet while his companions considered bringing him bivouac gear so that he could survive the night. With great difficulty, Boysen cut the leg off his thick pants with a piton. The bruised knee then slid out of the crack.

The Trango expedition had lost so much time from flight and porter problems that they retreated rather than continue the attempt. They were quite sure that the Trango Tower could be climbed, given reasonable luck with the weather, the following year. Boysen was anxious to return home in time to join Bonington's Everest team. He had already been waiting five days in Skardu for a flight out—five days during which the Trango Tower might have been climbed had they stayed on.

The British had suffered many of our same problems on a smaller scale. Not only had they failed on their climb and experienced flight and porter delays, but also a split had occurred in their team. Half the party had climbed actively while the other half had stayed relatively low.

Whatever their differences on the mountain, the British took it in stride and kept their group united by a constant sharing of humor. They turned their frustrating wait in Skardu into a continual situation comedy, with Ian McNaught-Davis in the leading role. When someone complained about the crowded, unsanitary conditions in the rest house, McNaught-Davis outlined his itinerary for a reciprocal visit of Pakistani climbers to the British Isles; they included two weeks camped in the center of an Irish pig farm. When others began talking of the constant demands for more money in every transaction, Martin Boysen said, "I went fishing yesterday and didn't catch anything. Maybe if I'd used rupee notes for bait these Pakistani fish would bite."

Even the British expedition's liaison officer had become infected by their easy-going style. He caught himself giving a report on the expedition to a superior officer in a strong British accent mixed liberally with four-letter words. The team treated him as one of the guys, and he laughed as hard as anyone else when he was the butt of a joke. One morning, in Skardu's only restaurant, he was caught slurping his soup. Mo Anthoine addressed him in mock indignation, "Stop that at once. You sound like a horse climbing out of a swamp!"

A United Nations group which had come to observe the cease-fire line occupied the only wing of the rest house that had a bathroom. All the expeditioners used a cliff that dropped toward the banks of the Indus River. On the day after we arrived, a Skardu flight was aborted by mechanical difficulties. We roared with laughter when Ian McNaught-Davis returned from the cliff, buttoning his pants, and saying, "The bloody Pakistanis can't even maintain an outhouse, let alone an airplane!"

It would have been wonderful if our team could have shared the carefree mood of the British, but we were not able to do so. Their small expedition had fulfilled its obligations. Their only worry was the length of the wait for a plane home. Our large expedition had a great deal of unfinished business to attend to. On the approach march our porters had cost us more than $50,000—far above the budgeted amount. We had completely run out of funds and had been forced to wire for a bank loan from the United States in order to pay our HAPs, our mail runners, our return porters, and a loan from the Askole Lambardar.

Manzoor was ntractable with regard to our financial dealings. He insisted that we pay the HAPs considerably more than we had once agreed because they deserved to get more than our regular porters had received on the final stages of the approach. We disagreed. That our regular porters had succeeded in extorting extra pay from us did not mean that we owed corresponding plunder to those who had not held a gun to our heads. Manzoor also said that we must pay Ghulam Rasul his full wage of $720. He claimed that not to do so would be a slap in the face to the best sirdar in Baltistan. While we did not doubt Ghulam's capabilities, he had not performed for us because of an illness that he had contracted before the expedition began. He had left the expedition before base camp and returned only after our attempt was over. Reluctantly, we agreed to pay him 70 percent of his wage.

HAPs in Askole homes

Manzoor insisted that we pay the deserters half-wages, as Jim had promised in Askole. The deserters, however, had not accepted that offer, which had at any event been made only when they waylaid our expedition and threatened to keep us from reaching Skardu. We wanted to use our remaining money to pay the eighty-one porters who had carried so well for us on the retreat.

Our primary reason for not paying deserters was breach of contract. I had taped what Manzoor said at Urdukas when they first deserted: "I have made it very clear that you are not going to get any payment. You can go back. Sue us in the court or whatever you do. But 'til I let you go, you are not going to get the payment."

Reluctantly, Manzoor finally agreed to our terms. We prepared individual envelopes with 590 rupees for each return porter. Although this amount was more than that required by the government, it was slightly less than the 620 rupees each porter expected as the result of demands for fringe benefits. We simply did not have the extra money, so we distributed what we had as evenly as possible.

Jim thought that Manzoor should go alone by jeep to Dasso, where the porters were waiting to be paid. Manzoor refused. He said it was not his job to pay off the porters, and, besides, he was worried that the deserters who had gathered there would cause a riot. Leif broke the ice by volunteering to go with Manzoor on the fifty-mile drive. Early next morning they left, in the company of a Skardu police sergeant.

The distribution of the pay envelopes went quite smoothly. Afterwards, Manzoor and Leif headed back to the jeep to give a large bundle containing 27,000 rupees to the Askole Lambardar, who had walked thirty-five miles to personally receive the payment. The driver started the engine and the crowd of Urdukas deserters suddenly realized that Leif and Manzoor were planning to leave without paying them. The furious mob surrounded the vehicle and threatened to upset it. Leif described the incident in his diary:

The HAPs in Skardu (Akbar second from left, standing)

Now I must admit to being scared. The angry faces leave no doubt they are serious. . . . One old fellow, #504, whom I remember from his visits to the sick tent, is worked up into a rage, his eyes staring wildly, his large teeth sprawling out of his mouth, the muscles in his goiter-enlarged neck tensing and flexing in spasms. He is right in front and looks like he could lift the jeep alone—certainly he believes that himself.

The police sergeant from Skardu, however, keeps his cool after the initial rush and tries to talk to the excited Baltis. Manzoor gets into the act and pretty soon everybody negotiates in the usual Balti way: by shouting at each other, handwaving, and pushing. A few appeal to me directly, holding out their hands, begging, as if for pity. I feel rather sorry for these poor wretches. It is all too easy to see their point: they carried to Urdukas, they had no decent footgear, the snow on the glacier was cold—and besides, they're afraid of it. How could they go on? Shouldn't they be paid for what they've done so far? Contract, what is that?

After a long three hours and much arguing the Baltis agree to send five men with us to Skardu as representatives, receiving the promise that they will be negotiated with. Manzoor puts this in writing. The row of hostility finally opens up. We are free almost unexpectedly.

In Skardu the jeep driver had another surprise for us. He had charged us 600 rupees ($60) for previous trips to Dasso when the jeep was fully loaded with a ton of expedition boxes. Now he demanded 1,200 rupees because he had performed a service for us in both directions. We tried to explain that no matter what he did on a trip to Dasso he would have had to drive both ways. We refused to pay double. He, in turn, told us that all the jeeps in town would strike us until we paid. No one would haul our three thousand pounds of gear the eight miles to the airport when the plane arrived. We paid.

After a relatively short wait of three days in Skardu, a C-130 cargo plane arrived on July 26. When it lifted off the runway carrying us along with four other expeditions, a giant cheer resounded through the plane and drowned out the noise of the engines. There were exclamations of joy in five languages. In earlier years, mountaineers from all nations had written of their sadness upon leaving such a beautiful country.

Soon we all flew home and merged back into our normal lives. We found a unity with families, friends, and co-workers that had escaped us in the Karakoram. On one of our final days in Pakistan, Wick had written, "Let's face it. There is still—and will continue to be—a split among the members of this expedition."

The expedition seemed to end far more abruptly than it had begun. Our hopes and dreams lay shattered. Now it was time to forget and live normal lives again. For a long time, team members did not socialize with each other. To do so was too painful; it reminded us of all that had gone wrong. No one even remotely entertained the idea that future events might bring the group together again.

4 1975 in Retrospect

When our team returned to the United States, we all took comfort in the fact that we had not been alone in our misfortunes. The 1975 season in the Karakoram seemed to have set an all-time record for low percentage of achievements. Out of nineteen expeditions, we knew of only one besides the Grand Cathedral rock climb that had succeeded on a major peak. The French climbers Yannick Seigneur and Marc Batard had made the second ascent of 26,360-foot Gasherbrum II by a new route up the south spur. Because of porter troubles, fifty-six of their loads never reached base camp. With limited equipment they had pushed for the top from Camp II at only 22,000 feet. They bivouacked without food at 25,000 feet, climbed to the summit, and descended the next day, June 18. Meanwhile, the second summit pair, Audobert and Villaret, moved into the 25,000-foot bivouac and were forced back from a summit bid by the same storm that had pinned the K2 climbers at Savoia Pass for five days. After two days above 25,000 feet they began to descend.

For a reason now never to be known, Villaret turned around and went back to the bivouac. Audobert, the friendly abbot who had dedicated his life to helping people, continued down through the storm, completely unaware that Villaret was no longer behind him. When he discovered Villaret's absence, he was nearing the limit of his own endurance and could not go up again. After he reached camp the storm raged with only two short interruptions for eighteen days. No one was able to climb back for Villaret. A remarkable ascent of an 8,000-meter peak without oxygen or high-altitude porters had become a Pyrrhic victory.

A combination of supply problems and great avalanches had defeated two Japanese expeditions with a total of twenty-one climbers bound for Latok I and Latok II above the Biafo Glacier. The smaller of the two groups turned their trip into a glacier-exploring trek, while the larger headed home immediately.

In the same area a British expedition led by Don Morrison had hoped to make the first ascent of the highest peak above the Biafo Glacier—the Ogre, a 23,950-foot granite fortress frosted with ice. They never reached base camp because their Askole porters struck just *after* the expedition issued boots and goggles at the snowline. The porters departed with the new equipment while the British tried to carry loads by themselves. After a day they realized that they could never get their gear to the Ogre in time for a serious attempt. They split into three groups and turned their expedition into a partial success by making alpine-style first ascents of two neighboring peaks—"Pamshe" and "Pajo," about 21,000 and 19,000 feet, respectively.

The American Trango Tower Expedition, of which I had been a member before joining the K2 party, had done even worse. They had lost their objective even before they started their trek! The alternatives offered by the Ministry of Tourism—Mitre and Lobsang peaks—were hardly worthy goals for a group of America's top alpine climbers who had traveled halfway around the world. In order to procure expedition funding, they had made a deal with a movie crew, which in turn had a contract with the National Geographic Society to make a film for television.

The Ogre

The expedition eventually split into two opposing sides: those who wanted to make a movie and those who wanted to do a good alpine climb. The two goals were mutually incompatible because of the film crew's large size, orientation toward heavy equipment, slowness, and lack of hard-core mountaineering experience. On paper in the United States the idea had sounded great. In Pakistan, after two weeks of waiting for the film crew to arrive, more waiting for a flight to Skardu, and even more delays arising from problems with the porters, several of the climbers felt that they had to actively choose between filmmaking and climbing. Historically, many good movies have been made of minor climbs and many poor movies have been made of great climbs. The rare instance of a good movie made on a good climb usually resulted only when expeditionary tactics, including fixed ropes and camps for the cameramen, were employed.

As in our K2 expedition, discord within the group grew until one member threatened to leave. Mike Covington, a fine mountaineer from Colorado, did not go straight home, however. He, Don Lauria, and Dennis Hennek made an alpine-style ascent of 20,423-foot Lobsang Peak without including the film crew. Four of the other climbers—Yvon Chouinard, Doug Tompkins, George Lowe, and Joel Matta—took the film crew up 19,560-foot Karphogang, an easy snow dome above Mustagh Pass. Covington then left the expedition, and Lowe, Lauria, and Hennek made three attempts on a sheer granite spire that jutted from a spur of Mount Biange. A storm forced them to retreat when they were only seven hundred feet from the top. The expedition returned to America without resolving

*Peter Habeler on the summit
of Hidden Peak*

their differences and entered into a legal tangle with the film crew over who owed whom for what. When the dust settled, several of the climbers vowed never again to become involved with filmmaking on a serious climb.

On K2 we had an opposite experience with filming. Steve Marts was a quiet, sensitive person who never interfered with our progress. He had carefully chosen to take the lightest equipment, including a tiny two-pound tape recorder with broadcast quality. We had not, of course, reached the altitude where film considerations and cameraman could conflict with summit climbing logistics. But in alpine-style climbing, such a conflict begins right at the base of the route.

Our next news from the Karakoram was of the Polish Broad Peak expedition we had passed near Concordia. At 7:30 P.M. on July 28, Kazimierz Glazek, Marek Kesicki, Janusz Kulis, Bohdan Nowaczyk, and Andrzej Sikorski stood on Broad Peak's 26,300-foot central summit in a snowstorm that had overtaken them just as they neared the top. Darkness caught them descending in hurricane winds and snow. Even with headlamps they could see only an arm's length during the height of the gusts. Snow crystals hit their faces like a thousand tiny darts. Only a hundred feet above a col that meant safety, Nowaczyk, the last man, slipped off the icy rocks down the steep Chinese side of the mountain. His companions could not locate him either by yelling into the storm or shining their lights over the brink of the cliff. Nowaczyk was lost along with all of the ropes. In order to save their own lives, the rest of the high climbers had to continue down, bivouacking in the open without sleeping bags or tents.

In the morning the weather cleared and the group returned to the place where Nowaczyk had fallen. After hours of searching they

*Reinhold Messner climbing on
the northwest face of Hidden Peak*

found no trace of their companion. Late in the day they headed down, unroped. Just as they were about to bivouac again, three of the four men fell. Kulis stopped himself after two hundred feet, but Sikorski and Kesicki were killed.

Only two of the five summit climbers returned, and one later lost all his toes. Success on Broad Peak had cost even more than the victory on neighboring Gasherbrum II.

By the time we had been home for a month, all the reports from other expeditions had confirmed my belief that we had been fighting insurmountable odds in the Karakoram that season. Porter problems, flight delays, and unusually bad weather in May and June had either stopped climbers in their tracks or caused grief to teams that pushed on for summits with weakened logistics. Every expedition to a major peak had experienced either failure or deaths.

I was soon to eat my words. Early in September I received a postcard carrying a brief message that by itself turned 1975 into a year to be remembered for success. It read:

Galen,
We reached top of Hidden Peak after a very difficult climb (3 bivy) August 10th, 12:30 P.M. Hope to see you sometime again.

Yours,
Peter Habeler
Reinhold Messner

The details came later. On the approach Habeler went ahead to locate a base camp site while Messner followed with the porters. In an attempt to cross a stream next to the Baltoro Glacier, Habeler was swept off his feet and carried down by the rapids. He was totally out of control in the raging waters, and only by sheer luck was he

1975 in Retrospect   305

washed up onto a rock. Bruised and wet, he crawled into his soaked-through sleeping bag for a miserable night.

On July 26, only twelve days after leaving Skardu, they established a base camp at 16,750 feet. The porters departed for their villages, leaving the pair completely alone. Habeler, fully recovered from his fall into the stream, felt that he was in the best physical condition of his life.

For the next thirteen days they prepared for their summit attempt. First they reconnoitered a route through two icefalls to a supply depot at 19,356 feet on Gasherbrum La, a pass between Gasherbrums I and II. After a second trip carrying loads, they retreated to base camp to wait for a spell of optitum weather. The lower part of the face looked steeper and more continuous than they had expected. An unbroken ice wall rose for 4,000 feet into a belt of ice-covered rock. They hoped to reach a bivouac above the rocks in one day of unroped climbing without oxygen. They estimated that the climb would take at least a week if they used ropes and pitons.

At base camp they watched the weather carefully and determined that a rhythm existed: three or four days of storm followed by three or four days of good weather. Near the end of a bad-weather cycle they headed up for Gasherbrum La. At 6:30 A.M. on the morning of August 9 they began climbing the ice wall in clearing weather. The weather turned fair. Their packs contained only the barest necessities, with one exception. Reinhold had brought along a small movie camera.

For eight hours they climbed steep bare ice that often rose at an angle of sixty degrees. Messner compared this section to the north face of the Matterhorn. Habeler later wrote, "Only the confidence I had in my friend Reinhold, only the limitless trust we felt for one another, gave me the feeling of certain success. Yet each was alone. Slowly we climbed higher, thrusting the tips of our crampons into hard ice. I know of no other climber with whom I would have dared something like this."

At two in the afternoon they reached 23,300 feet at the top of the ice face. Dead tired, they brewed some tea and erected a small bivouac tent. By five o'clock they were in their sleeping bags, resting for the hardest day of all. A dreamlike sunset promised more good weather.

The next morning dawned cold and clear. All systems were go. They left everything in their tent except for a little food, their cameras, and a first-aid kit. For the first hour they walked up easy snowslopes. Then the terrain steepened. Even though both of them were gasping for air, Messner continued to film wherever possible. Every fifty feet they rested on their ice axes, then started anew.

By noon they were resting after every five steps. A traverse to the left placed them on a gentle ridge. Half an hour later the ridge leveled off, and they stood together on the summit, hugging each other with childlike joy. For a moment they forgot their incredible remoteness from the rest of the world. In every direction giant mountains stretched for hundreds of miles under a cloudless sky. Only the nearby pyramid of K2 rose above their 26,470-foot perch.

They spent forty minutes on the summit, and then retraced their steps back to the tent, where they spent another night. A storm moved in and completely shredded the fabric of their light tent. At first light they continued their unroped descent down the ice face. They had no reserves for another bivouac and were forced to keep going, bad weather or not. Habeler had to wiggle his toes continually to keep them from freezing. The steep ice seemed endless and even more difficult than on the ascent. When they finally reached the base of the ice face they were too tired to continue to base camp. For two days they rested and waited at Gasherbrum La for the weather to clear. On the morning of August 13, exactly a month after leaving Skardu, they hiked leisurely down to base camp, their ordeal completed.

Never had an 8,000-meter peak been climbed so quickly, so lightly, so cheaply, or by such a small expedition. For such an ascent to take place on an unclimbed 7,000-foot face was a major step in mountaineering history. When the pair returned home, Habeler was invited to lecture on the climb in England under the title "The Edge of the Possible." He refused the title, saying that Hidden Peak was nowhere near the edge of possibility. It was merely an early example of a new style of climbing Himalayan giants. He and Messner were already planning a 1978 alpine-style ascent of Mount Everest.

Messner was asked if the climb had not set a dangerous example that might lure others into trouble. He answered that after each epoch-making climb in mountaineering history similar climbs were soon made by others. He cited the Eigerwand as an example of a climb once considered ultimately dangerous but now "not too unusual an undertaking." He guessed that the Hidden Peak climb would be viewed similarly by a future generation. He tried to make clear that the goals of a true mountaineer are not always to do something higher or steeper. "I am not after success by any means. I am fascinated by difficulties and sporting considerations. I would like to climb for another twenty-five years, even if I will no longer be setting new standards. And I would like to finish where it all started twenty-five years ago, namely alpine rambles."

While Messner and Habeler were climbing on the north side of Hidden Peak, the Austrian expedition that Akbar had spotted passing Concordia was attempting to repeat the easier 1958 American route on the other side of the mountain. On August 4 they took a side trip from their Camp III at 22,300 feet to make the first ascent of Hidden Peak's neighbor, 23,950-foot Urdok I. On the eleventh, only one day after Messner and Habeler's climb, Robert Schauer, Herbert Zefferer, and Hans Schell also stood on top of Hidden Peak. Seventeen years after the first ascent, the second and third ascents had been made by separate expeditions on successive days.

At the same time, unknown to us on the Baltoro, still another Austrian expedition was attempting Chogolisa from the opposite side. The beautiful trapezoidal crest of this 25,110-foot peak had been ascended by a Japanese expedition in 1958; they had climbed the northeast summit and claimed the first ascent. G. O. Dyhrenfurth's measurements showed that the southwest summit, at the other end of a half-mile-long ridge, was forty-five feet higher. The Austrians, led by Eduard Koblmuller, gambled on approaching Chogolisa from its nearly unknown south side. Their small expedition was composed of seven climbers, no HAPs, and only sixty-two porters. They were forced to place base camp at only 13,775 feet when the porters refused to walk through fresh snow. This caused an acute supply problem to the foot of the face, twelve miles up the glacier. They spent several weeks carrying loads to the mountain and finding a route through a large icefall. Then they went up a 3,000-foot 50-degree ice face to a saddle at 22,000 feet. As Koblmuller tried to bypass the icefall on a corniced ridge, the same thing happened to him that had happened to Herman Buhl on Chogolisa eighteen years before: a cornice broke and he fell through the hole. Unlike Buhl, however, Koblmuller was roped and his companion stopped the fall after a hundred feet. Unhurt, Koblmuller resumed climbing. On August 2, Fred Pressl and Gustav Ammerer spent twelve hours climbing the final 2,000 feet of the west ridge. At 3 P.M. they stood on the true summit on a perfect, clear day. Two days later Alois Furtner and Hilmar Sturm also reached the summit. Chogolisa, which the Duke of Abruzzi had come within five hundred feet of climbing in 1909, had finally succumbed after sixty-six long years.

Later in September, I received news of yet another enormously successful Karakoram expedition. The "Polish Ladies Expedition" had made four separate ascents of three different routes on two different mountains, putting ten climbers on top of peaks exceeding 26,000 feet. A party of two women and two men—the leader, Wanda Rutkiewicz, plus Kzysztof Zdzitowiecki and Janusz and Ali-

The summit of Chogolisa (first ascent Aug. 2, 1975): climber, Gustav Ammerer

son Onyszkiewicz—had reached the top of Gasherbrum III, which had been the highest unclimbed peak in the world for more than a decade. The expedition also accomplished the first all-female ascent of an 8,000-meter peak—on Gasherbrum II, where Halina Kruger and Anna Okopinska climbed the original 1956 Austrian route. Two men's teams also climbed Gasherbrum II, one by a new route on the northwest face, which was technically a short distance into China.

A venture sponsored by International Women's Year which included men made for a potentially explosive situation. The expedition could have easily degenerated into a battle between the sexes, but because the trip was organized in a fashion that minimized individual competition, no such conflict arose.

The pace of the expedition was never rushed unless it was absolutely necessary, with the first members leaving Poland in April and not returning until September. The expedition had the money and supplies to stay in the mountains a very long time. Once on the mountain, they averaged between five and fourteen hours for the carries between each of the lower three camps. On K2 we had normally rushed between camps in two hours or less, but since we had rarely moved more than one camp in a day, no net time had been saved.

Alison Chadwick Onyszkiewicz, the British-born climber who had married a Pole, described later in a letter how the men and women shared tasks:

The summit of Chogolisa from the Austrians' Camp IV

The work of load carrying, establishing camps, etc., was usually done in mixed groups of five or six people, the girls carrying about 22 pounds and the boys about 33 pounds of so-called "expedition load," in addition to personal gear. If there were ropes to be fixed, two or three would go ahead and do the job with the "porters" following an hour or so behind. Several times we had to make dumps between camps when the weather broke and as a rule we descended to base to wait for better weather. This policy caused us to take longer than we might otherwise have done but probably led to better acclimatization and meant that everyone did a fair share of load carrying—avoiding the situation where two or three climbers hog the lead and the rest are relegated to portering for them!

The leader had planned all along to save the unclimbed summit of Gasherbrum III for "ladies only," but when two men and two women were in position for an attempt, she decided that all of them should go together.

A day after the foursome reached the top of Gasherbrum III, another mixed group set off for Gasherbrum II. This team was composed of three women plus Captain Saeed Malik, the expedition's unusually tall and stalwart Pakistani liaison officer. "Saeed soon began to feel the effects of altitude," Alison wrote, "and declared that he couldn't go on. Krystyna volunteered to go back with him. So even the vaunted 'purely female' ascent of GII was an accident!"

Their expedition proved, once again, that great physical strength and ability to carry heavy loads are not prerequisites for the climbing of Himalayan giants. A greater number of lesser loads over a longer time period can still establish the camps needed for a conventional large expedition. The occupants of a high camp on a mountain, like those of a new high-rise building, are more concerned with the basic architecture of the structure than the speed with which it was erected. In the case of Messner and Habeler, who chose to forego fixed camps on the mountain, their very success was dependent on plans that made carrying heavy loads at altitude unnecessary. Messner later said, "This was my first eight-thousander attempt where there was climbing only and no hard work."

The successful Karakoram expeditions of 1975 proved to be either highly flexible or very patient. Small groups had a definite edge over the more conventional large expeditions, which were overly dependent on vast quantities of porters and supplies. There is little doubt that large expeditions will continue to visit the Karakoram in the future, especially from countries that have yet to prove themselves on the high peaks. However, the significance of large-expedition climbs is declining. Elevation, steepness, and distance have all been conquered. What remains is style.

On September 24 word came from Nepal that the British had succeeded in climbing the great southwest face of Mount Everest. Although Everest was a thousand miles away, the ascent had great relevance to the 1975 Karakoram season. Two of the climbers who reached the highest camp had just failed in the Karakoram!

Martin Boysen, of the Trango Tower attempt, would have reached the summit had he not lost a crampon at 28,000 feet. Doug Scott, who had led one of the year's most unsuccessful expeditions—it had failed to even reach its base camp—had become the first Englishman to reach the top of Everest. (In 1953, a British expedition placed a Sherpa, Tenzing Norgay, and a New Zealander, Ed Hillary, on the summit.)

In a period of two months, Scott had gone from a dismal Karakoram failure to one of the grandest successes in mountaineering history. I wrote to him asking for details of his Karakoram trip, thinking it especially important to get his perspective on the failure because his ego had been so totally salved by success so soon after the defeat. Notes in magazines and journals clearly stated that his Karakoram effort had succumbed to delays and porter problems, but in his reply to me these factors were mentioned only incidentally. He wrote that after his team realized that they could not reach and climb their original objective, they had turned toward a smaller but closer unclimbed 20,000-foot peak. Eight hundred feet from the top the climbers had had a "heated exchange" over whether to continue. "I had always thought that men were more important than the mountain," Scott wrote. "There it stretched the principles to the limit. . . . I will never again go the mountains without proven friends."

The last news of the Karakoram season was, for me, the saddest of all. The expedition of Austrian college students had failed to climb 24,750-foot Skyang Kangri. During the attempt their leader, Ferdinand Deutschman, had disappeared without a trace. The sound of his footsteps leaving our camp before breakfast will haunt me forever.

Epilogue

Unexpected Aftermath

The causes of events are more interesting than the events themselves.

—CICERO

The story of the 1975 K2 expedition might have ended with our return to the United States, or even sooner. Several of the team members stopped writing in their expedition diaries on the day that we found the ridge to be impassable. Future histories of mountaineering would record that five American expeditions had failed on K2. Besides the expeditions of 1938, 1939, and 1953, a lesser-known German-American team had failed at 23,500 feet in an attempt to repeat the Abruzzi Ridge in 1960. A graph of heights reached by Americans on the mountain would peak before World War II and reach a new low in 1975. But, as it turned out, the story was not quite over.

Immediately after we returned, we considered the trip to have been simply a miserable failure. The majority of us were sure that we would never want to return to Pakistan for climbing of any kind. Slowly, though, our memories of the experience began to change imperceptibly. These were the kinds of changes that make one always remember a trail as shorter, a beach as whiter, or a home as larger than it really was. The golden sieve of memory gradually softened the harshness of our experiences. We remembered the view of K2 on a clear morning and all but forgot the constant grayness of a five-day storm. In our mind's eye, the light from a single Balti smile blinded us to the hundreds of frowns with which we were confronted during the long days of the strikes.

We were experiencing a most remarkable facet of human existence: the ability to locate a kernel of joy in a field of sorrow. Those who always find the kernel are able to live happy lives no matter what they experience. Those who cannot are doomed to misery, no matter what other benefits they reap from the material world. Both this ability and our highly touted human intellects are not so much dependent on our capacity to remember as upon our capacity to selectively forget.

A less praiseworthy turn of our memories was the tendency to exaggerate the importance of events that placed the blame for our failure on others. The Big Four overstressed the others' sickness and lack of commitment, while the Minority Five overstressed their inability to influence decisions. We all recognized that we had been stopped cold by the ridge itself, but we hunted for other reasons to satisfy our bruised egos.

In late September I attended a board of directors meeting of the American Alpine Club in Washington, D.C., along with fellow directors Jim and Wick. Another member of the board, Bob Craig, who had been on K2 in 1953, invited Wick and me to join him for a night on the town. Wick and I divulged our deepest feelings about the expedition to each other in a way that we had somehow never been able to do on the trip. Perhaps Craig, the old sage, had planned it that way. Both of us returned home feeling much better for having shared our common experiences.

Strange things began to happen in October. A veteran Himalayan climber approached me in private to ask about the government involvement with our expedition.

"What government involvement?" I asked.

"You know, the CIA."

"You're joking, aren't you?"

"No. The word's out that you guys never intended to climb the mountain, but that you succeeded in your mission to place a listening device on that pass on the Chinese border."

"Nothing like that happened. Who told you about that?"

"A friend. The AAC is investigating it, you know."

Later that day I talked on the phone to another director who confirmed that the club really was checking into the matter. His answers to my questions were vague, but when I mentioned that I was sure our trip had no such purpose, he said, "I believe you, but you probably don't know what went on. They kept you in the dark."

"About what? I saw all the opened boxes at base camp. I saw everything that was sent above. Besides, the idea of a listening

Uli Biaho Tower

device on a mountain became instantly obsolete years ago when the first satellites were launched."

"I don't know much about that, but that's not all the club is concerned about. An important Pakistani official has complained about the trouble your expedition caused in the country."

"What do you mean! The native people caused *us* trouble. We were *their* victims!"

"That's not the way I heard it."

"Who is saying these things? Where can I see the documents? Who in the club is doing the investigating?"

He gave me no hard information, only vague reassurances that I would be informed when the investigation was complete. I repeated that both the charges were false and that he should pass on my response to whomever was spreading the rumors. "I almost wish that what you are saying were true," I said as a parting shot. "With the CIA picking up the tab we wouldn't have come back $50,000 in debt. I'll be working for another year to pay off my share."

I wrote to both Jim and Wick about the rumors, but none of us could get any more specific information. When we heard nothing more, we assumed that someone had found out the truth and the matter had been dropped.

Meanwhile, another arm of the AAC asked me to give the featured program at the club's annual meeting to be held near Seattle in December. I was somewhat bewildered when they asked me to play down K2 as much as possible, to leave the name of the mountain out of the title, and emphasize other parts of the region. Two days before the meeting I received a long-distance call from Bill Putnam, the club's president, telling me not to show aerials of K2 in my lecture—or anywhere else if I had a conscience. When I asked for an explanation, I was told that Manzoor would get in trouble if we showed any aerials.

I asked, "Who told you that?"

"I have it on good authority."

"Whose authority?"

"I can't say, but just don't show them."

"How come we haven't been notified through other channels? Those pictures were cleared through the embassy and *National Geographic.* George Schaller, the zoologist, was on the same flight with us along with a Pakistani companion who was an official armed forces photographer. George was just sent original transparencies of K2 from that flight by his friend in Pakistan with absolutely no restriction on their use. What gives?"

"Just do everyone a big favor and don't show them."

"Okay, I'll do that. Say, this doesn't have anything to do with that rumor that we were working for the CIA, does it?"

"Not directly."

"You do know about the rumor, then?"

"Yes. Some serious charges have been made against your expedition, and we're investigating them."

"What are the charges and who's investigating them?"

"I can't tell you that right now until we know a little more."

Aerial of K2 from the west

"Look, Bill, this involves me directly and I have a right to know. I was on the expedition and I'm a director of the club."

"Galen, I don't think you were involved. You probably didn't know what the others were doing."

"That's bullshit. I was with them for three months. I know which way they brush their teeth. Exactly what has been said and by whom?"

"I'm sorry. I can't talk about it now. Maybe things will be cleared up in Seattle."

After Putnam hung up, things began to click in my head. I remembered that when I had been editor of the club's newsletter we had once discussed CIA involvement with climbing. At that time not many people knew that the agency had placed a surveillance device on a mountain in India before the advent of satellites. The effort was made with India's cooperation and was kept secret so that the Chinese would not become aware of the device. Many of America's top climbers had been recruited to do that one job and hardly a major expedition in the last decade has been without a veteran of that outing. When recent books and news articles published descriptions of the agency's past activities, the planting of the device became public knowledge. The danger, as both Putnam and I had then seen it, was that someone would do a sensationalized exposé that would cast American climbers in the role of agents involved in illegal espionage. In reality the climbers had participated, on a one-time basis, in the setting-up of an outsized border lookout. If an inaccurate story were ever published, American climbers could be barred from some areas of the Himalaya.

Knowing that Putnam was aware of the truth of the old CIA matter, I couldn't understand why he refused to discuss the present one. Things just didn't add up. How did the CIA, our alleged offensive behavior in Pakistan, and aerial photographs tie in together?

When I arrived at the meeting, I was given a note to call a number. It was a radio commentator who had been given a hot tip that I would have a story for him about government espionage on our expedition. I told him that I had heard such a rumor but determined that it was false. He thanked me.

Before the board of directors met, I greeted Jim and Wick in the hall. We shook hands warmly and talked about the rumors. Each of us had been confronted in the building by other climbers who asked for the real story about the CIA and our behavior in Pakistan. Some had seen photocopies of letters about the matter but had promised not to reveal who wrote them. Not one of the other directors admitted to being directly involved in the investigation.

The three of us decided to confront the issue head on. We asked Putnam to talk with us privately about the allegations before the meeting. He declined. We said that we would then bring them up for open discussion in the board meeting, which was already gathering a moderate audience. He reluctantly agreed to talk to us briefly.

A minute later we were walking on the snow-covered lawn of the convention center, firing questions at Putnam and still receiving vague answers. I realized that for the first time since the expedition began, Jim, Wick, and I were seeing completely eye-to-eye. The events of the expedition were our common bond, and we each knew that we had nothing to hide.

While the club's other directors peered out through the window, five of us paced back and forth on the lawn. The fifth man, seventy-five years old and with a spring in his step, was none other than Fritz Wiessner.

The irony of his presence was overwhelming. Thirty-six years earlier, Fritz's K2 expedition had suffered greatly at the hands of the American Alpine Club. Twenty-seven years after that Bill Putnam had led the fight to reinstate Fritz as an honorary member. Now Putnam had stepped into the president's shoes and seemed to be faced with the same sort of innuendo that had originally hurt Fritz. In 1939 Fritz had been swept out of the club on an apparent wave of anti-German sentiment. In 1975 we were at the crest of a wave of distrust of the CIA.

Our situation differed from Fritz's original plight in two important ways. First, three of us were directors of the club and could fight the process from within. Second, we had Fritz and his experiences to guide us. He remained silent while we quizzed Putnam at length.

Gradually, Putnam acknowledged that we might be telling the truth. He still refused to divulge his sources and told us that if we ignored everything the affair would die a natural death.

Wick pointed to the window, where dozens of people were watching us. "How many people know about this?"

Putnam answered, "Only two or three."

I replied, "Between the three of us we've talked to at least a dozen people who've heard the rumors directly from you."

Once again Putnam said, "If you call attention to them, they'll just get worse. Just ignore them and they'll go away."

Fritz grabbed Putnam's arm and said, "No, Bill. You must stop them right now. I know."

Putnam did not argue with his old friend. He agreed, most reluctantly, to show us his evidence later in the day and help put an end to the rumors. We walked back inside and the meeting began.

That evening, a Friday, a story appeared in the Tacoma *News Tribune* under the title "Alpine Club Leader Claims K2 Climbers Left an Abyss of Ill Will." It read, in part, "The American team of climbers that unsuccessfully attempted to climb K2 last summer left ill will behind them in Pakistan, the president of the American Alpine Club said here Thursday. 'People who could influence the government have given us real indications of serious unhappiness with the group headed by Seattle's Jim Whittaker,' William L. Putnam of Springfield, Mass., said in an interview." The article discussed porter and access problems and concluded with a quote from Putnam to the effect that climbers must learn "to conduct ourselves as members of the human race."

On Saturday the entire K2 team, with the exception of Leif, who was in British Columbia, gathered together for the first time since our return to the States. With spontaneous zeal we listened to each other's remarks and suggestions about the current crisis. We unanimously confirmed each other's personal feelings. Despite our harsh internal bickerings we all believed that our expedition had been courteous and respectful to the Pakistani government. None of us had been contacted afterwards about a ban on aerial photos nor had the CIA been involved with our expedition. Dunham looked around the room, chuckled, and said, "We're together on this thing in a way that never happened on the mountain. Why couldn't it have been like this before?"

It was a moment of truth. We had been stripped of all pretensions. Now that there were no laurels to share we realized that we had far more in common than we had presumed. No matter how badly our team had failed on the mountain or in personal relationships, a core of dignity remained. That dignity was not rooted in what we had done, but in what we understood about ourselves. When the cloak of potential achievement was removed, one thing remained: a desire to climb the mountain. It had been for this that each of us had gone to K2.

The suggestion that we had gone to the mountain at the request of the government made us see that we had shared precisely the opposite experience: we had been a private group motivated solely by the sheer whimsy of climbing a great mountain. Our personal differences in motivation were suddenly of minimal importance. The old team cliques seemed even less meaningful. What counted was that we were the only ones who knew from personal experience that the rumors were untrue. What we were thought to be mattered not so much as what in our souls we knew we were. Experiences that had often been bitter to endure were becoming sweet to remember.

When Putnam came into the room, he was still unwilling to show us his data. With the entire K2 team in obvious harmony on the issue, Jim confronted Putnam face-to-face with a demand for the facts. Finally, Putnam showed us the "evidence." It was little wonder that he had been reluctant to produce it. There were two personal letters and nothing more. One was from Manzoor and the other from Alex Bertulis. Manzoor had not written to the American Alpine Club, but a photocopy of a personal letter describing the expedition to a friend in the United States had been passed on to Putnam without that friend's permission. It stated only Manzoor's side of the issues and was quite understandable. He saw the burning of the money as a deed against Pakistan. Our press conference in Pakistan, during which our problems had been described in the most polite terms, was cited as another indignity to the country. He also mentioned that publication of the aerial photographs could put him in an awkward position, but with no explanation of why other photos taken on the same flight had no such restrictions. Nothing was said of the possibility of CIA activities.

Manzoor, by himself, had been Putnam's "people who could influence the government."

The Bertulis letter was far more difficult to comprehend. It was a letter written by an understandably unhappy man who had helped choose the leaders of two major expeditions only to be rejected by both. Bertulis' letter charged that he had been dropped from the K2 team so that the expedition could be staffed with CIA agents. The letter presented only wild speculation that this had occurred.

The letter had been written not just to expose the K2 expedition but also to discredit Jim Wickwire in order to force his resignation from the AAC board. According to the letter, Bertulis had promised Putnam information about CIA involvement on K2 and Wick's misconduct. Putnam had been most unhappy with Wick's performance as secretary of the board ever since Wick had worked behind the scenes in opposition to one of Putnam's pet projects. I had also worked hard against the same project; I had written several magazine articles criticizing it.

At first I could not believe that the motive for all the damaging intrigue involved petty power struggles within the club. But as with circulation of the letters, there seemed to be no other explanation. Perhaps the most revealing single fact was the date on the Bertulis letter: November 22, 1975, *after* the CIA rumors had already been spread. This supported Bertulis' later assertion that he had written the letter at Putnam's request after telling him verbally of his CIA suspicions.

Obviously, those seeking to discredit the expedition by linking it to the CIA had not expected to be caught bluffing with such a poor hand in a game where the stakes were people's reputations. They had been defeated by something totally unexpected: the unity of our team. The team members themselves were perhaps the most surprised of all. If we had arrived at the base of the mountain with such unity of purpose, and if we had quickly found the Northwest Ridge to be a blind alley, we might have stayed on and made the summit by another route on the western side. But this was idle thought. The chance had been lost.

Now we had become the third of the eight K2 expeditions in history to suffer at the hands of their own national alpine club. We felt lucky not to have been arrested, as Eckenstein had been in 1902, or maligned for years, as Wiessner was after 1939. But our actions at the meeting had shown us that no one would be able to pit us against each other. If the rumors continued to circulate, we would fight them as a team.

After the meeting, Putnam wrote several long letters detaching himself from the fiasco. Copies were sent to the entire board of directors, including those who had no previous knowledge of the rumors.

To Alex Bertulis, Putnam wrote: "The points you raise are not deserving of serious attention, nor do they, in fact, appear credible. . . . I find no evidence of clandestine operations, predictably improper behavior or any activity on the part of the K2 participants that would merit concern on my part. . . . I strongly urge you to make apology."

And to Jim Whittaker, he wrote: "Insofar as you may feel that some sort of whispering campaign has been conducted including members or officials of the club to the detriment of your good name, I have no knowledge that this has been done."

In a letter to me without extra copies Putnam explained his rationale for the story that had appeared in the *News Tribune*: "When confronted by a news reporter who was obviously going to publish some sort of story and had heard all kinds of speculations in the Northwest, I thought I did everyone a favor by diverting his attention to the porter problem. If it makes anyone feel good to beat up on me for that, please go right ahead, but I don't think I owe anyone an apology for having done you that favor."

I, in turn, wrote a letter resigning from both the board of directors and the club. As is my custom with serious letters, I let it cool on my desk for a few days before sending it. I never mailed it. I began to realize that quitting in a pique would benefit no one. The great majority of the club's actions were good. With a change in leadership the club could once again become a force for the cooperation, not the regulation, of American mountaineering. Ironically, the very issue that had originally raised Putnam's ire against Wick and myself was our opposition to his plan for the club to certify and regulate mountain guides. I believed that the ethos of mountaineering was basically incompatible with firm regulations. As an example, had

Messner and Habeler's climb taken place in certain American national parks during the sixties, they would have been cited for being unroped on the mountain. Such things had actually happened to top American climbers. I decided that I could best work for a greater degree of individual responsibility in climbing if I remained on the AAC Board.

Meanwhile, Jim Whittaker wrote a long letter to the Pakistani government explaining our problems and making suggestions to help future expeditions. He received a perceptive and broadminded reply from the Minister of State. It stated that Jim's constructive suggestions about the porter situation, which he had previously given verbally to the Ministry of Tourism, were already being incorporated into plans for 1976. The minister also extended an invitation to us to bring another expedition to Pakistan.

Through other channels we learned that Manzoor's bitterness, like our own, had cooled off. Nick Clinch, the dean of American climbing in Pakistan, was planning an attempt on unclimbed Paiyu Peak with a Pakistani climbing team of which Manzoor would be a member.

One morning I received a phone call that brought the 1975 K2 expedition full circle. It was Jim inviting me to go to K2 in 1978. The Polish had the mountain for 1976 and the Japanese for 1977. Most of the team was returning, including three of the old Big Four and three of the old Minority Five. The plan was to attempt one of the other unclimbed ridges on the west side of the mountain from our same base camp. With a far deeper understanding of both the men and the mountain than I had possessed the first time I made such a decision, I answered, "Yes. Count me in."

Rock tower near Dasso

LIST OF ILLUSTRATIONS

321

SELECTED KARAKORAM BIBLIOGRAPHY

Bates, Robert, Houston, Charles et al. *Five Miles High.* New York: Dodd, Mead and Company, 1939.
    A superb book about the 1938 American K2 expedition.

Bonatti, Walter. *On the Heights.* Translated by Lovett F. Edwards. London: Rupert Hart-Davis, 1964.
    An autobiography with chapters on the first ascents of K2 and Gasherbrum IV.

Brown, Joe. *The Hard Years: An Autobiography.* London: Victor Gollancz Limited, 1967.
    Includes a chapter on the first ascent of Mustagh Tower.

Buhl, Hermann. *Lonely Challenge.* Translated by Hugh Merrick. New York: E. P. Dutton & Company, Inc., 1956.
    An autobiography that includes Buhl's account of his solo first ascent of Nanga Parbat.

Conway, W. M. *Climbing in the Himalaya.* London: T. Fisher Unwin, 1894.
    An account of the first mountaineering expedition to visit the K2 region.

Crowley, Aleister. *The Confessions of Aleister Crowley: An Autobiography*. Edited by John Symonds and Kenneth Grant. New York: Bantam Books, 1971.
1,058 pages of Crowley's biting wit and bizarre occult activities, interspersed with accounts of the first expeditions to K2 and Kanchenjunga.

Di Filippi, Filippo. *Karakoram and Western Himalaya 1909: An Account of the Expedition of H.R.H. Prince Luigi Amedeo of Savoy, Duke of the Abruzzi*. Translated by Caroline De Filippi and H. T. Porter. New York: E. P. Dutton & Company, 1912.
Remains the classic work on the Baltoro region, unsurpassed both for accuracy of text and the quality of Vittorio Sella's photography.

Diemburger, Kurt. *Summits and Secrets*. Translated by Hugh Merrick. London: George Allen & Unwin Limited, 1971.
An impressionistic autobiography with a long section devoted to Broad Peak and Chogolisa.

Drew, F. *The Jummoo and Kashmir Territories*. Delhi: Oriental Publishers, 1875.
Contains information on culture and trade routes in the Karakoram during the nineteenth century.

Dyhrenfurth, G. O. *To the Third Pole: The History of the High Himalaya*. Translated by Hugh Merrick. London: T. Werner Laurie Limited, 1955.
The most complete and accurate portrayal of Karakoram climbing and exploration up to 1954.

Eckenstein, Oscar. The Karakorams and Kashmir. (1896).
About the 1892 Conway expedition; a slow read.

Foreign Area Studies. The American University. *Area Handbook of Pakistan*. Washington, D.C.: U.S. Government Printing Office, 1971.
A highly detailed compendium of facts about Pakistan.

Guillarmod, J. Jacot. *Six Mois dans l'Himalaya*. Neuchatel. (1903).
An account of the first K2 expedition in 1902 with Oscar Eckenstein and Aleister Crowley.

Houston, Charles S., M.D., Bates, Robert H. et al. *K2—The Savage Mountain*. New York, Toronto and London: McGraw-Hill Book Company, Inc., 1954.
A beautifully written depiction of the 1953 American attempt on K2.

Maraini, Fosco. *Karakoram: The Ascent of Gasherbrum IV*. Translated by James Cadell. New York: The Viking Press, Inc., 1961.
The best general work on the Baltoro region.

Maraini, Fosco. *Where Four Worlds Meet: Hindu Kush, 1959*. Translated by Peter Green. New York: Harcourt, Brace & World, Inc., 1964.
A sensitive and authoritative work on the native people of the Hindu Kush and Karakoram.

Robbins, Leonard H. *Mountains and Men*. New York: Dodd, Mead & Company, 1931.
Romantic accounts of famous mountaineers and explorers. Several chapters on the Duke of the Abruzzi. A good read.

Shipton, Eric. *Blank on the Map*. London: Hodder and Stoughton, 1938.
A small expedition explores and maps remote areas of the Karakoram.

Shipton, Eric. *That Untravelled World*. London: Hodder & Stoughton, 1969.
An autobiography; contains a chapter on how Shipton and two companions fielded a Karakoram expedition at a total cost of about $2,500.

Shipton, Eric. *Upon that Mountain*. London: Hodder & Stoughton, 1943.
The father of the small Himalayan expedition describes myriad mountain adventures in Europe, Africa and Asia. Concluding chapters deal with his explorations on the Chinese side of K2 and in the Ogre region at the head of the Biafo Glacier.

Vigne, G. T. *Travels in Kashmir, Ladak, Iskardo, the Countries adjoining the Mountain Course of the Indus, and the Himalaya North of the Punjab*. London. 1842.
The pioneer journeys of one of the first Europeans to explore the Karakoram near K2.

Williams, L. F. Rushbrook. *Pakistan Under Challenge*. London: Stacey International, 1975.
A sympathetic history of the young nation and its current problems.

Workman, Fanny Bullock, and Workman, William Hunter. *In the Ice World of Himalaya*. New York: Cassell, 1900.
A Boston woman explores the Himalaya with her husband. Several colorful chapters on a trip through Askole to the Biafo Glacier.

Workman, W. H., and Workman, F. B. *Ice-bound Heights of the Mustagh*. London: Constable, 1908.
An account of two seasons in the Karakoram range of Baltistan.

Younghusband, Sir Francis. *Kashmir*. Delhi: Sagar Publications, 1970.
A reprint of a work on Kashmiri history and culture by an important explorer.

SELECTED INDEX OF PEOPLE AND PLACES